U0143887

高考凯旋门

全新高考英语

词汇必备手册

高考英语命题研究组

李宗骥 / 主编

文匯出版社

编 写 说 明

词汇是语言的基础。要想学好一门语言，必须掌握足够的词汇。对于即将参加高考的同学来说，同样要过好词汇这一关。因为不熟悉词汇而做错选择、或误解了句子的意思、或苦苦琢磨而耽误了大量时间的教训不胜枚举。正因为如此，高中毕业生才需人手一册高考英语词汇手册。

然而，仅仅认识或是牢记词汇是远远不够的。更重要的是掌握词汇的用法，以及相关词汇之间的异同。如果只是简单地记住单词的词义，而没有很好掌握它们各自的用法，就难免会出差错。而高考的目的显然不是考查学生究竟"认识"了几个单词，而是考查他们对所学词汇的运用能力。

正是出于这种考虑，我们编写了这本《高考英语词汇手册》。这本词汇手册的特点是：

1. 重点介绍词语的常用词组、句型及其用法。例句基本上都是从历届高考试卷中选用，以便让同学们体会到，这些词汇曾真真切切地出现在我们的高考试卷里。另外，单从说明词汇的用法上来看，有些例句似乎偏难。但这正是我们的目的：让同学们提前接触考卷，适应考卷的难度，以免到考试的时候措手不及。

2. 在介绍一个词汇的同时，对其同义、近义的单词或短语进行辨析，通过归类、比较、举例的方法，使同学们对所学词汇的用法有清楚的了解。对使用中应该注意的问题，也特别加以说明。

3. 掌握更多的表达方式，从而扩大考生能够驾驭的"有效词汇"量，提高翻译及作文的水平。

我们相信本书的这些特色一定能对参加高考的同学有较大的帮助。

A

a /eɪ, ə/ *art*. 一(个、只、件、…)

（注意：a 和其它词汇组成的短语在其它词条中列举。）

abandon /əˈbændən/ *vt*. 放弃；抛弃

abandon sth.

（考题）... the structure had been abandoned years earlier and the roof of the main building had fallen down.

（考题）... fashion magazines have almost abandoned the practice of putting models on the cover.

ability /əˈbɪlɪtɪ/ *n*. 能力

（考题）Malaria has five thousand genes，and its ability to change rapidly to defend itself and resist new drugs has made it nearly impossible to control.

have the ability to do sth. 有能力做某事

（考题）At the root of volunteering is the idea that one person may have the ability to offer services that can help other people.

do sth. to the best of one's ability 尽力做好某事

able /ˈeɪbl/ *adj*. 有能力的、能干的

be able to do sth. 有能力做某事

（考题）They are able to use their own rich imagination and inventions without fear of blame.

（注意：在表示"过去做成了某事"时，可使用 was/were able to do sth.，而避免使用 could。）

abnormal /əbˈnɔːməl/ *adj*. 反常的、异常的

（考题）I was astonished by what appeared to me to be his completely abnormal mental state.

aboard /əˈbɔːd/ *adv*. 在船(飞机、汽车)上；登机、上船等

（考题）Just as he jumped aboard，half a dozen red spots showed on his arm

prep. 在船(飞机、汽车)上

（考题）It's time to get aboard the plane.

about /əˈbaʊt/ *prep*. 关于；在…周围

What/How about (doing) sth.? 做…如何？

（考题）What about having a drink？

adv. 附近；大约

be up and about（尤指病后）起来走动

be about to do sth. 正要做某事

（考题）A device that stops drivers from falling asleep at the wheel is about to undergo testing at Department of Transport laboratories and could go on sale within 12 months.

above all 首先、最重要的是

（考题）I'd like to buy a house —— modern，comfortable，and above all，in a quiet neighborhood.

adj. 上面的；上述的

（考题）There is still a long way to go before the above questions could be answered.

adv. 在上面；上方

the above-mentioned 上述的

abroad /əˈbrɔːd/ *adv*. 国外

（考题）Sometimes the Chinese abroad reach out their hands too often to be polite.

go abroad 出国

（考题）... many young people have gone abroad，leaving their parents behind with no clear idea of when they will return home.

at home and abroad 国内外

absence /ˈæbsəns/ *n*. 缺席、不在；不存在

（考题）... can work in the absence of electricity.

（考题）I can hardly recognize the place after a long absence.

absent /ˈæbsənt/ *adj*. 缺席；不存在

be absent from 缺席

（考题）The number of people invited was fifty，but a number of them were absent for different reasons.

absent-minded 心不在焉的

（考题）Professor Reason recently persuaded 35 people to keep a diary of all their absent-minded actions for two weeks.

absolute /ˈæbsəljuːt/ *adj*. 绝对的、肯定的、完全的

absorb /əbˈsɔːb/ *vt*. 吸收、接受；吸引

  absorb sth. 吸收…

  （考题）Water can absorb and give off a lot of heat without big changes in temperature, thus creating a stable environment.

  be absorbed in … 被吸引；着迷于

  （考题）But new figures show birdwatching is fast becoming a popular pastime, with almost three million of us absorbed in our fluttering feathered friends.

abstract /ˈæbstrækt/ *adj*. 抽象的 *n*. 摘要、梗概

academic /ˌækəˈdemɪk/ *adj*. 学校的；学术的

  （考题）Children need risk if they are to grow up self-sufficient and confident. They need homework, too, if they are to fulfill their academic potential.

accept /əkˈsept/ *vt*. 接受；认同

  accept sth. 接受…

  （考题）It makes us tend to accept what we are told even when it is little more than hearsay and rumor.

  （比较：accept 表示"同意接收下来"，而 receive 只表示"收到"，而不一定非接受不可，如：I've received his invitation, but I can't accept it, I'm afraid.）

acceptable /əkˈseptəbl/ *adj*. 可以接受的

  （考题）The action group has also found acceptable paper made from materials other than wood, such as agricultural waste.

access /ˈækses/ *n*. 接近、进入；

  （考题）Easy access to a wide range of everyday goods leads to a sense of powerlessness in many people, …

  have access to sth. 可以得到、使用

  （考题）Across the world, 1.1 billion people have no access to clean drinking water.

accessible /əkˈsesɪbl/ *adj*. 可以接近、进入的

  be accessible to sb. 某人可以接近、使用、得到的

accident /ˈæksɪdənt/ *n*. 事故；偶然发生的事

  by accident 碰巧、偶然

  （考题）He discovered that by pure accident.

accidental /ˌæksɪˈdentl/ *adj*. 意外的

accommodation /əˌkɒməˈdeɪʃən/ *n*. 住处；设施

（考题）A reference directory includes easy-to-use comparative data on everything from accommodation to courses and fees.

accompany /əˈkʌmpənɪ/ *vt*. 陪伴；伴随；伴奏、伴唱

accompany sb. /sth. 陪伴…

（考题）It's so dark. I'd like someone to accompany me home.

accomplish /əˈkɒmplɪʃ/ *vt*. 实现；完成

accomplish sth. 完成、实现…

（考题）It's not something easily accomplished by parents these days.

（辨析：accomplish 强调成功，达到了目标；finish、complete 则表示完成，结束。）

according /əˈkɔːdɪŋ/ *adv*. 根据

according to sth. /sb.... 根据…

（考题）Certain men were very clever at measuring the time of day according to the beating of their own hearts.

according as ... 根据（后接从句）

（考题）We will win or lose according as you can finish the job on time or not.

account /əˈkaʊnt/ *n*. 账户；说明、陈述

give/offer an account of ... 对…加以说明

（考题）This book offers a pathbreaking new account of language acquisition, variation and change

on account of ... 由于

（考题）On account of his poor health, he is never left alone.

on no account 决不（见 case）

take sth. into account 对某事加以考虑

（考题）... they often failed to take into account that those people most at risk for skin cancer — people with fair skin and freckles — are more likely to use sunscreen.

（同义词：**take sth. into consideration**）

vt. 认为…是　*vi*. 说明

account for sth. 对某事加以说明、解释

（考题）According to Holowka, buildings account for 65 percent

of total U. S. electricity use.

accountant /əˈkaʊntənt/ *n*. 会计

accuracy /ˈækjʊrəsɪ/ *n*. 准确性

accuse /əˈkjuːz/ *vt*. 指责

accuse sb. (of sth.)（因某事）指责某人

（考题）The man was accused of murder and was sentenced to death.

（辨析：accuse、criticize、blame、charge 都有指责、责怪的意思。用法是：criticize sb. for sth. 、blame sb. for sth. 、sb. is to blame for sth. charge sb. with sth.)

accustomed /əˈkʌstəmd/ *adj*. 适应的、习惯的

be/get accustomed to (doing, do) sth. 习惯于做某事

（考题）They are accustomed to not talking at meals.

（辨析：be used to (doing) sth. 和 be adapted to (doing) sth. 也可表达同样的意思，但后面只能使用动名词或名词、代词；而 be accustomed to 后面也可使用动词不定式。）

ache /eɪk/ *n*. 疼痛

aches and pains 疼痛

（注意：ache 常指某种持续的疼痛。在复合词 stomachache, toothache, earache 等词中，冠词可有可无，但在 headache 前总有不定冠词 a）。

vi. 疼痛；伤心；渴望

ache for/to do sth. 渴望得到/渴望做某事

（考题）Having been away for months, he is now aching for home.

achieve /əˈtʃiːv/ *vt*. 完成、实现；获得、达到

achieve sth. (one's goal, purpose, aim . . .)

（考题）We can achieve knowledge either actively or passively.

（考题）It taught me discipline, friendship and the pride related to setting a task every day and working hard to achieve it.

achievement /əˈtʃiːvmənt/ *n*. 成就、成绩

（考题）One's achievement is determined by his particular skills

（注意：在表示"成就"时，可以有复数形式。）

acid /ˈæsɪd/ *adj*. 酸的 *n*. (化学)酸

acknowledge /əkˈnɒlɪdʒ/ *vt*. 承认；确认(收到信件等)；

acknowledge sth. (…) 承认…

(考题)He refused to acknowledge his error.

(考题)We acknowledged the receipt of his letter by calling him immediately.

It is acknowledged that …

(考题)It is acknowledged that the preparations you have made are quite to our satisfaction.

acquire /əˈkwaɪə/ *vt.* 取得、获得

acquire sth. 获得、得到…

(考题)These internal states are acquired throughout life from situations one is faced with in the home, in the streets, and in the school.

(注意：acquire 主要指通过技术、能力, 或努力而获得。)

across /əˈkrɒs/ *prep. adv.* 穿过

(辨析：across 指的是"横穿", 如穿马路或到河的对岸, 也可用于湖泊、广场等；而 through 则表示纵向的穿过, 如 go through the corridor。)

act /ækt/ *vi.* 行动；表演 *vt.* 扮演角色

(考题)Animals' ability to act reasonably is believed to come partly from what we may call "genetic learning".

act as … 扮演…的角色、充当

(考题)Stage schools often act as agencies to supply children for stage and television work.

act for sb. 代理某人办事

act on/upon sth. 对某物起作用

(考题)Many acids act on metals.

n. 行为、动作；法令、条例

(考题)It is also an act of generosity that's never forgotten.

(辨析：act 往往表示独立的、简单的、较为具体的动作, 而 action 表示持续的、复杂的、较为抽象的动作。有时可互换, 如 It was an act/action he was to regret。但在某些固定短语中用 act, 如 an act of kindness, in the act of doing sth.。)

action /ˈækʃən/ *n.* 行动；作用

take action 采取行动

(考题)… to help ensure that the American public has the

information they need to take action to protect themselves and their families before, and during, disasters and other emergencies.

put ... into action 使…开始行动、运行

（考题）Marty Dettling is a project manager for a building that put these ideas into action.

（注意：在上述短语中，action 不能使用复数形式）

active /ˈæktɪv/ *adj*. 积极地、活跃的、主动的

（考题）Unlike watching TV, reading is a highly active process.

be active in (doing) sth. 在…中很积极

（考题）My only concern is that you are not active enough in putting forward your suggestions.

take an active part in ... 积极参加…

（同义词：**energetic, lively, vigorous**）

activity /ækˈtɪvɪtɪ/ *n*. 活动

actor /ˈæktə/ *n*. 男演员

actress /ˈæktrɪs/ *n*. 女演员

actual /ˈæktjuəl/ *adj*. 真实的、实际的

（考题）Photojournalists make an actual record of what they see.

（辨析：true, real 也可表示"真实的"。但 true 可以作表语，actual 和 real 不作表语；true 和 real 强调"真的、不是仿造的"；actual 和 true 可表示"符合实际情况的"。）

adapt /əˈdæpt/ *vt*. *vi*. (使)适应、(使)适合；改编

adapt (sb.) to sth.

（考题）It can only be hoped that other animal species will adapt as extraordinarily well to changes as the desert elephant.

（考题）Many children's books have been adapted from films.

be/get adapted to (doing) sth. 适应(做)某事

（见 accustom）

add /æd/ *vt*. *vi*. 加、添加

add sth. (to sth.) 增加…(到…中)

（考题）It would add several hundred dollars to the cost of their cars.

add up to 总数达到；意味着

（考题）However, the quantity of serious writing which I

produced all through my childhood would not add up to half a dozen pages.

（考题）What he said and did added up to this — he is a fool.

add to 增加、加强、加剧

（考题）The engine of the ship was out of order and the bad weather added to the helplessness of the crew at sea.

added to that 除此之外，还有

（考题）He's very clever. Added to that, he works very hard. No wonder he always does best in the exams.

（见 besides）

addition /əˈdɪʃən/ *n*. 加、增加

in addition 此外、还有

（考题）In addition, promising drugs hold out hope of better health and longer life.

（同义词：**besides, additionally, what's more, furthermore, moreover**）

in addition to . . . 除…之外，还有

（考题）In addition to Koreans, some Asian husbands and wives do not share the same family names.

additional /əˈdɪʃənəl/ *adj*. 附加的、另外的

address /əˈdres/ *n*. 地址；演讲

（考题）"The woods" was our part-time address, destination, purpose, and excuse.

vt. **address sb.** 对某人发表演讲；对某人说话

（考题）To address a married woman properly, you'd better ask her which name she likes.

（辨析：address 和 speak 都可以表示"演说"。但前者是及物动词，后面直接跟 sb.，而 speak 是不及物动词，后面要使用介词 to。）

adequate /ˈædɪkwɪt/ *adj*. 足够的、适当的

be adequate to . . .

adjust /əˈdʒʌst/ *v*. 调整、校准

administration /ədˌmɪnɪˈstreɪʃən/ *n*. 管理、经营；行政机关

admire /ədˈmaɪə/ *vt*. 羡慕、赞赏

admire sth. 羡慕…

（考题）People will admire his courage in overpowering dangerous animals.

admire sb.（for sth.） 因…而羡慕某人

（考题）All girls admire her for her cleverness and beauty.

admission /əd'mɪʃən/ *n*. 进入；入场费；承认

admit /əd'mɪt/ *vt*. 允许进入；承认

admit sb.（into ...） 允许某人进入（加入）…

（考题）Only ticket holders are admitted.

admit（doing）sth. 承认做某事

The boy admitted having learned the news from someone else before he came here.

admit that ... 承认…

（考题）He had to admit at last that he knew nothing about it and only won by chance.

admit of ... 容许、有…的余地

This decision admits of no other explanation.

（同义词：**allow of** 和 **permit of** 也可表示相同的意思）

adopt /ə'dɒpt/ *vt*. 采纳；通过；收养

（考题）You should adopt a more active attitude toward the matter.

（考题）For example，one show had an adopted child try to guess the identity of her real father.

adult /'ædʌlt/ *n*. 成年人

advance /əd'vɑːns/ *n*. 前进、进步

（考题）Technology — the application of science — has made big advances that have benefited us in nearly every part of life.

in advance（of ...） 提前

（考题）At proper horse races everyone has already studied the form of the horse in advance.

（同义词：**ahead（of），beforehand**）

v. 前进；发展、进步

（考题）They were going to advance thirty-five miles a day to their destination.

advanced /əd'vɑːnst/ *adj*. 先进的；进步的

advancement /əd'vɑːnsmənt/ *n*. 前进、进步；提升

advantage /əd'vɑːntɪdʒ/ *n*. 优势、优越之处；利益

（考题）Sometimes, something that is considered to be negative turns out to be an advantage on the job.

take advantage of 利用

（考题）Many experts complain that media too often take advantage of the science fiction aspects of nanotech.

（辨析：make use of 也可表示"利用"。但如果表示利用别人的弱点来达到某种目的，则只能使用 take advantage of。）

have an advantage over . . . 在某方面优于某人

（考题）The researchers say they have some advantages over live dogs, especially for old people.

to sb.'s advantage 对某人有利

（考题）It is only when the tipper is a stranger and likely to remain so that the system does not work to his or her advantage.

adventure /əd'ventʃə/ n. 冒险；冒险的经历、活动

advertise /'ædvətaɪz/ vi. vt. 登广告

advertise sth. 为某物登广告

（考题）We would also demonstrate that we cannot lie trusted, since we advertise our dishonor by telling our family and friends.

advertise for sth. 登广告等征求某物

（考题）If you haven't found a satisfying house, advertise for one.

advertisement /əd'vɜːtɪsmənt/ n. 广告

（考题）People still relied on advertisements to get most information about products.

（注意：一则的广告是可数名词；而做广告这种行为是不可数名词。）

advice /əd'vaɪs/ n. 劝告、忠告；建议

accept/adopt/follow/take sb.'s advice 采纳某人的建议

（考题）If customers had followed all the advice given, they would have been £1,263.60 worse off.

（注意：advice 是不可数名词。对某事的建议常用介词 on。）

do sth. on, /by sb.'s advice 按某人的建议做某事

advise /əd'vaɪz/ v. 建议、劝告

advise sb. (to do sth.) 建议某人做某事

（考题）As a university student，you can get first-class research facilities with trained teachers to help, support and advise you in your study.

advise (doing) sth. 建议（做）某事

He advised waiting till proper time.

（注意：advise 后面一般不直接使用动词不定式，但可以使用动词不定式担任宾语补足语）

（辨析：见 suggest）

aeroplane /ˈeərəpleɪn/ *n.* 飞机（airplane /eəpleɪn/）

affair /əˈfeə/ *n.* 事情；事务；事件

Mind your own affairs. 管好你自己的事。

international/foreign affairs 国际（外交）事务

（考题）For them, playing well and winning are often life-and-death affairs.

（辨析：affair, event, matter, business 都可表示"事情，事务"。affair 可指个人小事，也可指重要事情；even 指重大事件；matter 表示情况、要紧事、麻烦事，在表示事态时常用复数；business 常指商业、生意，也可指某人的事务。）

affect /əˈfekt/ *v.* 影响；打动；感染（疾病）

affect sth. /sb. 影响某事/某人

（考题）Lack of sleep can affect learning and memory.

affection /əˈfekʃən/ *n.* 感情；慈爱

afford /əˈfɔːd/ *vt.* 能承担、经得起、承受得起

afford (to do) sth. 承受得起做某事

（考题）They feel that they are not wealthy enough to afford 'quality food'.

（考题）They got two free tickets to Canada, otherwise they'd never have been able to afford to go.

afraid /əˈfreɪd/ *adj.* 害怕；担心

be afraid of sth. /sb. 害怕某物/某人

be afraid of doing sth. /be afraid that… 担心会发生某事

（考题）He was afraid of having a heart attack.

be afraid to do sth. 不敢、不愿、讨厌做某事

（考题）Everyone was too afraid to go in because the fire was out of control.

after /'ɑːftə/ *prep*. 在…之后　*adv*. 随后、之后

after all 毕竟、终究

（考题）Why are you so anxious? It isn't your problem after all.

after class/school 课后

（注意：after school 也可表示"毕业以后"）

one after another 一个接一个

be (go) after sth. 追求、追逐

（考题）What he is after is nothing but fame and money.

（注意：after 在表示"过了多久"时，只用于过去时，如 He came last Monday and left after two days. 此处也可用 two days after 或 two days later 来表示。但如果表示将来时，则使用介词 in，如 in two days 表示（从现在起）两天以后。）

afternoon /ɑːftə'nuːn/ *n*. 下午

afterwards /'ɑːftəwədz/ *adv*. 随后、其后；后来

soon afterwards 不久以后

immediately afterwards 很快、立即

two days afterwards 两天后

（注意：有时也有 afterward 的形式。）

（同义词：later, after）

again /ə'ɡeɪn/ *adv*. 再一次

again and again 一遍一遍地、反复地

over and over again 一遍一遍地

time and again 一遍一遍地

now and again 不时地、时常

（同义词：now and then, from time to time, at times）

all over again 重新、再次

once again 再次

（同义词：once more）

against /ə'ɡeɪnst/ *prep*. 反对；对抗

be against sth. /sb. 反对某事/某人

（考题）It's against the law to make false statements so they try to mislead you with the truth.

（反义词：be for sth. /sb. 、be in favor of sth. /sb. ）

against one's will/wishes 违背自己的意愿

age /eɪdʒ/ *n*. 年龄；时代　*v*. 变老

at one's age 在某人这个岁数时

at the age of 在…岁时

be over age 超龄

be under age 年龄不到、未成年

of（about）sb.'s age 与某人同年（年龄相仿）

Children like to play with children about their age.

aged /ˈeɪdʒɪd/ *adj.* 年老的

the aged 老年人

agency /ˈeɪdʒənsɪ/ *n.* 代理处、代办机构；作用、力量

a news agency 通讯社

through/by the agency of 通过、借助于…的力量

agent /ˈeɪdʒənt/ *n.* 代理人

aggressive /əˈgresɪv/ *adj.* 侵犯的；有进取心的

ago /əˈgəʊ/ *adv.*（一段时间）以前

（注意：ago 前面需有表示一段时间的词或词组，如 many years/ some time/a long time/a minute ago，和过去时连用。）

（辨析：before 作介词时也表示"在…之前"。但 before 的宾语是某一点时间，而不是一段时间，如：before breakfast，before the meeting。）

agree /əˈgriː/ *vi. vt.* 同意、赞成；符合、一致

agree to do sth. 答应做某事

（考题）They can be personalized and the company will offer reductions on the expense if people agree to sell exterior advertising space.

agree with sth. /sb. 赞成某事/同意某人的观点

（考题）Broadly speaking, I would agree with Shirley, though not entirely.

agree that ... 答应、赞同…

（考题）She and I agree that, at certain times, we seem to be parts of the same mind.

agree to sth. 答应某事

（考题）Make sure each group member understands and agrees to the task given to him or her.

agree on sth. （多方）就某事达成一致意见

（考题）Most of the scientists agreed on several points.

（注意：agree with 表示"赞成，具有相同的看法"；agree to sth. 表示"答应某件事"，如某个要求、某项条件等，有时，人们也可能不得不 agree to 一件他并不 agree with 的事；而 agree on 则是两方或两方以上对某一问题达成一致看法。）

agreeable /ə'griːəbl/ *adj.* 令人愉快的；同意的

（考题）You are definitely growing in social maturity when you try to be an agreeable table companion.

be agreeable to (doing) sth. 赞成（做）某事

agreement /ə'griːmənt/ *n.* 同意、一致；协议、协定；

（考题）It's very difficult for the scientists to reach an agreement because different results can be got from the same fossils.

（注意：表示"达成协议"常用的词组有 reach/come to/arrive at an agreement。这些词组也常和 decision，conclusion 等名词连用。）

agriculture /'ægrikʌltʃə/ *n.* 农业；农艺

ahead /ə'hed/ *adv.* 在前面

（考题）Keep looking ahead so that you can give the driver lots of warning before having to make a turn，or you'll have to move to the back seat.

ahead of ... 在…的前面

（考题）If they fly in the wrong direction，they may be flying ahead of a storm.

ahead of time 提前

（考题）I thought we'd be late for the concert，but we ended up getting there ahead of time.

（同义词：**ahead of schedule, earlier, before time**）

go ahead (with sth.) 继续做某事

（同义词：**go on with sth. , continue**）

aid /eid/ *v.* 帮助、援助

（考题）It is thought that strong blues will stimulate clear thought and lighter，soft colours will calm the mind and aid concentration.

aid sb. in (doing) sth. 帮助某人做某事

n. 援助、帮助；辅助用品、助手

come/go to sb.'s aid 来（去）帮助某人

（考题）She believes the story might have had a different ending if those good people had not come to her aid.

（注意：类似的短语有 **come to sb. 's assistance**,帮助某人,**come to sb. 's rescue** 救助某人。）

give/lend aid to sb. 帮助某人

first aid 急救

with the aid of ... 在…的帮助下

（辨析：aid, help, assist 都表示"帮助"。aid 较为正式,主要指危险和困难情况下的援助。help 是普通用语,可指各种类型的帮助。assist 则强调"协助"。）

AIDS /eɪdz/ *n*. 艾滋病,获得性免疫功能丧失综合症

（Acquired Immurne Deficiency Syndrome）

aim /eɪm/ *n*. 目标;目的

（考题）Our aim is to help students produce more ideas and use language in a new way.

achieve one's aim 实现了目标

miss one's aim 未打中目标;未实现目标

take aim at ... 瞄准…

v. 瞄准

aim at ... 瞄准…、以…为目标

aim at doing sth. 目的是做某事

aim for ... 争取某种结果

aim sth. at ... 用某物瞄准…

（考题）The hunter aimed his gun at the lion and fired, but missed it.

aim to do sth. 打算、希望做某事

（考题）The programs at Shadow Ridge mainly aim to help people have fun above other things.

be aimed at ... 目标是…;针对…

（考题）Celebrity clothing lines aren't a completely new phenomenon, but in the past they were typically aimed at the ordinary consumers, and limited to a few TV actresses.

air /eə/ *n*. 空气;天空

air attack 空袭

air force 空军

be on the air (广播节目)正在播送

by air 乘飞机

(考题)There are three ways to experience the Grand Canyon: on foot，on mules or by air.

in the open air 露天地，公开地

(考题)Most performances at British festivals are given in the open air.

vt. 通风；表达

air one's view 表达自己的观点

(考题)Everyone can take the occasion to air his view.

air-conditioned /ˈeəkənˌdɪʃ(ə)nd/ *adj.* 有空调设备的

aircraft /ˈeəkrɑːft/ *n.* 飞机

airline /ˈeəlaɪn/ *n.* 航空公司

airmail /ˈeəmeɪl/ *n.* 航空邮件

airport /ˈeəpɔːt/ *n.* 机场

alarm /əˈlɑːm/ *n.* 警报；警报器；惊慌

(考题)If the driver's response continues to slow down，the sounds become more frequent until a nonstop alarm warns that the driver must stop as soon as possible.

alarm clock 闹钟

sound the alarm 发出警报

in alarm 惊恐地

album /ˈælbəm/ *n.* 照相簿、影集；集邮簿

alcohol /ˈælkəhɒl/ *n.* 酒精、乙醇；烈酒

(考题)Life is tough in the city. In order to lose their pressure，some people drink alcohol.

alcoholic /ælkəˈhɒlik/ *adj.* 含酒精的

alert /əˈlɜːt/ *n.* 警报；

(考题)The first would be a national alert from the president，likely involving a terrorist attack or natural disaster.

adj. 警觉的，警惕的

be alert to sth. 对某事保持警觉

vt. **alert sb.** (**to sth.**) 提醒、警告某人注意某事

(考题)An alarm alerts officers if a prisoner's breathing stops and carries on ringing until the door is opened.

（辨析：表示类似意思的还有 remind，warn 等词。注意用法的区别：remind sb. of sth.，warn sb. of sth.）

alike /əˈlaɪk/ *adj*．相像的、同样的

（考题）Business people，foreigners and families alike are making good use of the growing industry.

（注意：这是一个表语形容词，用在联系动词后面，或是在名词后面担任后置定语。）

alive /əˈlaɪv/ *adj*．活着的、活跃的

（考题）The boy's mind seemed to come alive.

be alive with … 由于…而充满生机

（考题）Humans could create copies of anything alive with high technology.

（注意：这是一个表语形容词，用在联系动词后面，或是在名词后面担任后置定语。）

（辨析：alive，living，live 都可表示类似的意思。alive 是表语形容词；living 可担任表语，也可在名词前修饰名词；live 用于名词前，但很少用来修饰人，如：a live mouse 一只活老鼠，a live wire 一根带电的电线。）

all /ɔːl/ *n*．所有、一切

above all 首先、最重要的是（见 above）

first of all 首先

（考题）First of all，jogging is very hard on the body. Your legs and feet a real pounding ruining down a road for two or three miles.

after all 毕竟

（考题）The author learned from his experience that human beings are kind after all.

all together 总计、全部

in all 总计

(not) at all 全然、究竟；既然…就（条件句）

（考题）If you prefer some other selection，or none at all，just mail the answer card always provided by the date specified. And you'll always have 14 days to decide.

（注意：这一短语只用于否定句、疑问句或条件句中）

adj．所有的、全部的

all one's life 一生

all the way 一路上

all the same 仍然、依旧

（考题）— When shall we meet again? — Make it any day you like; it's all the same to me.

all the time 始终、一直

（考题）So he is screaming all the time, whether he can see an outsider or not.

adv. 完全、全部

all but 几乎、差一点

（考题）To our great surprise, he all but lost the game.

all at once 突然

all over 到处、全身

（考题）Listening to Pops just makes you feel good all over.

allow /əˈlaʊ/ *vt.* 允许；答应给与；承认

    allow (doing) sth. 允许（做）某事

（考题）Though doctors may advise taking naps, employers do not allow it.

    allow sb. to do sth. 允许某人做某事

（考题）Riding horses allowed people to travel far greater distance in much less time.

    allow sb. sth. 答应给某人某物

（考题）Sweden decided to allow new fathers two months' paid leave, with a warning: use it or lose it.

    vi. **allow of sth.** 容许、有余地

（注意：这一短语常用于否定句中，表示"容不得"。同义词词组有 **admit of**、**permit of**。见 admit）

almost /ˈɔːlməʊst/ *adv.* 几乎、差不多

（考题）There's almost no time to just hang out.

（注意：almost 后面不使用 not。）

alone /əˈləʊn/ *adj.* 单独的；仅仅 *adv.* 独自地、单独地

（考题）It is roughly calculated that in 1997 alone, about 2 to 3 million people died of it.

（注意：在做形容词时，alone 是表语形容词）

    leave (let) sb. alone 别打扰某人

（考题）He had gone out of the study for some reason，leaving me alone.

let alone ... 更不用说…了

（辨析：alone 表示"独处"，但并没有"孤单"的含义；而 lonely 则表示"孤单、寂寞之感"。Someone alone does not have to be lonely.）

along /əˈlɒŋ/ *prep.* 沿着；顺着

（同义词：by 也可表示"沿着"的意思，如：have a walk along/by the river）

alongside /əˈlɒŋsaɪd/ *adv.* 在旁边、靠边

aloud /əˈlaʊd/ *adv.* 出声地、大声地

（考题）Reading aloud will help to improve your speaking ability.

（辨析：aloud 强调"出声地"，而非"默默地"；loud 表示"大声地、声音响亮地"；loudly 也可表示"大声地"，与 loud 替换使用。但有时有"喧闹"的含义。）

alphabet /ˈælfəbɪt/ *n.* 字母表

already /ɔːlˈredɪ/ *adv.* 已经

（考题）Having already achieved great wealth and public recognition，many celebrities see fashion as the next frontier to be conquered.

（注意：already 一般用在肯定句中，常和动词完成时连用。在疑问句或否定句中，则多使用 yet）

also /ˈɔːlsəʊ/ *adv.* 也

alter /ˈɔːltə/ *vt.* 使改变

alter sth. 改变…

（考题）Eugene's never willing to alter any of his opinions. It's no use arguing with him.

vi. ... **alter** ... 改变

He has altered a great deal in the past few years.

（辨析：在表示"改变"时，**change** 使用更加普遍。Alter 主要指对局部、部分进行的改变。）

alternative /ɔːlˈtɜːnətɪv/ *adj.* 可选择的、可替代的

（考题）The alternative treatment is not easily available to most people.

n. 选择；替代物

（考题）Successful alternatives that help prevent resistance are already available，but they have been in short supply and are very expensive.

have an/no alternative to sth. 有/无某物的替代品

have no alternative but to do sth. 只能做某事

（见 choice）

although /ɔːlˈðəʊ/ *conj.* 尽管

altogether /ˌɔːltəˈɡeðə/ *adv.* 全部、总共；总的说来

always /ˈɔːlweɪz/ *adv.* 总是

（辨析：always，usually，often 中，always 的语气最强，表示"总是、一向"，可与完成时连用；often 强调"经常性"，有比较级和最高级；usually 指"习惯、惯常"，语气较 often 重。常见频度副词的强弱依次为 always，usually，often，sometimes，occasionally，seldom，hardly，never）

a.m. /ˌeɪem/ *adv.* 上午（ante meridiem）

amateur /ˈæmətə/ *n.* 业余爱好者 *adj.* 业余的

amaze /əˈmeɪz/ *vt.* 使惊异、使大惑不解

be amazed at sth. 对…大为惊讶

（辨析：amaze，surprise 均表示使人惊奇的感觉，如困窘、迷惑、惊奇等。surprise 是普通用词，侧重未曾料到、意外；amaze 则强调迷惑及由此而产生的惊异。）

ambition /æmˈbɪʃən/ *n.* 雄心、志向；野心

（考题）I think from the very start my literary ambitions were mixed up with the feeling of being isolated and undervalued.

ambulance /ˈæmbjʊləns/ *n.* 救护车

America /əˈmærɪkə/ *n.* 美洲；美国

American /əˈmærɪkən/ *n.* 美国人 *adj.* 美洲的、美国的

among /əˈmʌŋ/ *prep.* 在…之中

（考题）Surprise is the most contagious among emotions.

（辨析：among，between 都表示"在…中"。among 用于三者或三者以上之间，而 between 用于两者之间，多者之间如强调两两之间时，也用 between，如：Agreements have been separately reached between all countries in the area.）

amount /əˈmaʊnt/ *n.* 数量

a large amount of 大量的

large/huge/great amounts of 大量的

（辨析：amount 常用来修饰不可数名词。修饰可数名词应使用 a large number of；另外，a large quantity of 既可用于可数名词，也可用于不可数名词。）

amuse /əˈmjuːz/ *vt.* 使…快乐

amuse sb. /oneself 使某人快乐/自娱

（考题）She makes great efforts to amuse students' interest in literature.

be amused at/by sth. 因…感到开心、好笑

amusement /əˈmjuːzmənt/ *n.* 娱乐；乐趣

analysis /əˈnæləsɪs/（*pl.* analyses /əˈnæləsiːz/）*n.* 分析

（考题）And through the study of philosophy, one develops sound methods of research and analysis that can be applied to any field.

analyze /ˈænəlaɪz/（analyse）*vt.* 分析；解析

analyze sth. 分析…

（考题）It now takes years for scientists to collect all the data they need to describes and analyze species.

ancestor /ˈænˈsɪstə/ *n.* 祖先

ancient /ˈeɪʃənt/ *adj.* 古代的　*n.* 古人

and /ænd, ənd/ *conj.* 和

and so on, and so forth 等等

（注意：and 连接的两个单数名词担任主语时，谓语动词用复数的形式；但如果两个名词表示的是同一个人或同一件事物，则动词用单数的形式。如：A poet statesman will attend the gathering 一位诗人政治家将出席这次聚会。）

anger /ˈæŋgə/ *n.* 愤怒、气愤

（考题）When I met him, I had a lot of anger inside me.

in anger 愤怒的、怒气冲冲的

with anger 愤怒地

（考题）The parents blamed their son with anger.

angry /ˈæŋgrɪ/ *adj.* 愤怒的、生气的

（考题）To walk around their small home, and imagine the angry storm outside beating against the walls, is to take a step towards understanding the lives they had.

be angry at/about sth. 因某事生气

（考题）I was angry about my parents' quarrel.

be angry with sb.（for sth.） （因某事）与某人生气

（考题）I do get angry with people who leave their offices like a place for raising pigs.

animal /ˈæmɪməl/ n. 动物

ankle /ˈæŋkl/ n. 脚踝

anniversary /ˌænɪˈvɜːsərɪ/ n. 周年纪念日 adj. 周年的

announce /əˈnaʊns/ vt. 宣布、宣告

announce sth.（to sb.） （向某人）宣布某事

（考题）Today，we at Amazon are excited to announce Mindle，a wireless，portable reading device with instant access to more than 90,000 books，magazines，and newspapers.

（辨析：announce, declare 都表示"宣布"。Announce 侧重"让别人了解、知道"；declare 则强调"公开发布、宣告"。）

announcement /əˈnaʊnsmənt/ n. 宣布、通告

announcer /əˈnaʊnsə/ n. 通知人、发言人；播音员

annoy /əˈnɔɪ/ vt. 打扰、使烦恼

be annoyed at sth. 对某事感到恼火

（考题）I'm really annoyed at my frequent mistakes.

be annoyed with sb. 对某人感到恼火

be annoyed that ... 因…而感到烦恼

annual /ˈænjuəl/ adj. 每年的、年度的 n. 周刊

another /əˈnʌðə/ adj. 另一个，别的

one another 相互（用于三者或三者以上）

（考题）That encouraged populations living in different areas to interact with one another.

(in) one way or another 以某种方式、想方设法

one after another 一个接一个

another ... （数词）另外…个、再加…个

（注意：这个短语表示的是在原先基础上再增加两个。如：We've talked about quite a few questions. We'll talk about another two today。同样的意思也可用 two more 来表示。Another 用在数词的前面，而 more 用在数词的后面。）

answer /ˈɑːnsə/ v. 回答；回应

（考题）"Do you remember what I was doing?" was a question frequently asked，but rarely answered.

answer the door (letter, phone) 开门(写回信,接电话)

（考题）When I called you this morning，nobody answered the phone. Where were you?

answer for sth. 对…负责、承担责任

n. 回答、答复;答案

an answer to sth. 对…的答案、答复

（考题）I won't tell the student the answer to the math problem until he has been working on it for more than an hour.

ant /ænt/ *n.* 蚂蚁

anti-pollution /ˈæntɪpəˈluːʃən/ *n.* 反污染

anxious /ˈæŋkʃəs/ *adj.* 迫切的;焦虑的

（考题）My mother always gets a bit anxious if we don't arrive when we say we will.

be anxious for sth. 迫切、渴望获得某物

（考题）Marc and Rachel's reactions to the move were similar in the way that both were anxious for more details.

be anxious to do sth. 迫切想做某事

（考题）The local and visiting Italian dogs are anxious to run after hares.

（见 be eager to do sth. ）

be anxious about sth. /sb. 为某事/某人担心

（考题）... the author is anxious about the huge number of nuclear weapons on the earth.

any /ˈenɪ/ *pron.* 任何一个 *adj.* 任何

anybody /ˈenɪbɒdɪ/ *pron.* 任何人

anyhow /ˈenɪhaʊ/ *adv.* 不管怎样、反正

anyone /ˈenɪwʌn/ *pron.* 任何人

anything /ˈenɪθɪŋ/ *pron.* 任何东西、任何事

　anything but ... 除…之外

（考题）Life on the ship is anything but cruising.

anyway /ˈenɪweɪ/ *adv.* 不管怎样、无论如何

anywhere /ˈenɪweə/ *adv.* 在任何地方

apart /əˈpɑːt/ *adv.* 相隔;分离

apart from 除…之外

（考题）Apart from them, I know nobody here to talk to.

（注意：apart from 有时相当于 besides 的意思，表示"除…之外，还有"，如：Apart from the cost, the job will take a lot of time；有时又具有 except for 的含义，表示"除…之外，别无…"或"要不是"的含义，如：We had a pleasant time, apart from the weather。）

take sth. apart 把某物拆开

tell sth. apart 区分开

They are so alike that very few can tell the twins apart.

apartment /əˈpɑːtmənt/ n. 一套公寓房间

apologize /əˈpɒlədʒaɪz/ vi. 道歉

apologize to sb. for (doing) sth. 因（做了）某事向某人道歉

（考题）I apologize for not being able to join you for dinner.

apology /əˈpɒlədʒi/ n. 道歉

make an apology to sb. for (doing) sth. 因（做了）某事向某人道歉

（考题）Someone had come to make an apology.

apparent /əˈpeərənt/ adj. 显然的、显而易见的；表面的

（考题）It became apparent that she'd written it.

appeal /əˈpiːl/ vi. 呼吁、请求；有吸引力

appeal to sb. for sth. /to do sth. 向某人呼吁某事/做某事

appeal to sb. 对某人有吸引力

（考题）Certainly, reality TV seems to appeal much more to the younger audience.

n. 呼吁；吸引力

The famous charity's appeal to aid postwar Greece had been so successful that it had been flooded with donations.

appear /əˈpɪə/ vi. 出现；看起来

（考题）Cinderella, or the central idea of a good child protected by her goodness, appears in various forms in almost every culture of the world.

It appears (to sb.) that ... （在某人）看来…

（考题）（考题）It appears that the ability to let go thoughts that come into mind frees the brain to attend to more rapidly changing things and events in the outside world.

appear + *adj.* 看起来…

(考题)Why does France appear less foreign than Germany to Americans on their first visit to Europe?

(辨析：appear，seem 都表示"看起来"。appear 着重外表、表象；seem 则有根据事实得出的判断之意。)

appearance /əˈpɪərəns/ *n.* 出现；外表、外观

(考题)The environmentalists and wild goats' appearance on the vast grasslands was a good indication of the better environment.

judge by/from one's appearance 根据外表判断

have a good/bad appearance 外表好/坏

appetite /ˈæpɪtaɪt/ *n.* 食欲、胃口

have an/no appetite for sth. 对…有/无兴趣

applaud /əˈplɔːd/ *vt.* *vi.* 鼓掌、喝彩；欢呼

applaud sb./sth. （向某人、为某事）鼓掌

(考题)The audience will applaud anything that pleases them.

applaud sth. 赞成、欢迎某事

(考题)We applauded your timely decision.

applause /əˈplɔːz/ *n.* 鼓掌、欢呼

burst/break into applause 爆发出欢呼、鼓掌

apple /ˈæpl/ *n.* 苹果

appliance /əˈplaɪəns/ *n.* 器具、器械

applicant /ˈæplɪkənt/ *n.* 申请人

application /æplɪˈkeɪʃən/ *n.* 运用；申请

(考题)Technology — the application of science — has made big advances that have benefited us in nearly every part of life.

(考题)I don't' think your application will be accepted.

apply /əˈplaɪ/ *vt.* 运用

apply sth.（to sth.） 运用某物（到某处）

(考题)Let me apply some ointment to your wound.

apply oneself to sth. 专心于某事

(考题)You can't do the job well without applying yourself to it.

vi. 申请

apply to sb. for sth. 向某人申请某物

(考题)... the television viewers are asked to telephone the program to vote or to apply to take part in the show.

appoint /əˈpɔɪnt/ *vt*. 任命；指定

　　appoint sb. to a post/position 被任命为

　　appoint the time/place 指定时间/地点

appointment /əˈpɔɪntmənt/ *n*. 约会；预约；任命

　　have an appointment with sb. 与某人有约

　　by appointment 依约，经预先约定

　　make an appointment with sb. 与某人预约

　　（考题）So Roberta had made an appointment with the head of the Drama Club.

　　take/accept an appointment 接受任命、上任

appreciate /əˈpriːʃieɪt/ *vt*. 欣赏；表示感激

　　appreciate (doing) sth. 欣赏（做）某事

　　（考题）I appreciate the human story that can make me laugh and cry.

　　（辨析：appreciate，enjoy 都表示"欣赏"。appreciate 表示有一定的理解力和鉴赏水平；而 enjoy 则强调能从中得到乐趣享受。）

appreciation /əˌpriːʃiˈeɪʃən/ *n*. 欣赏

　　（考题）Chinese arts have won the appreciation of a lot of people outside China.

　　have an appreciation of sth. 欣赏某物

　　（考题）— What is Chris Daniels' purpose of writing this letter?

　　— To express his appreciation of the programme.

approach /əˈprəʊtʃ/ *n*. 道路；方法；接近

　　The writer of this passage aims to recommend an approach to correcting children's bad behavior.

　　v. 接近、来临

　　（考题）But you can approach it yourself, show them there is nothing to be afraid of, stroke it, and talk about the dog being friendly.

appropriate /əˈprəʊpriət/ *adj*. 合适的、适当的

approve /əˈpruːv/ *vi*. 赞成、赞同

　　approve of (doing) sth. 赞成（做）某事

　　（考题）I do not approve at all of his proposal.

April /ˈeɪprəl/ *n*. 四月

Arab /ˈærəb/ *n*. 阿拉伯

Arabian /əˈreɪbjɪən/ *adj*. 阿拉伯的

Arabic /ˈærəbɪk/ *n*. 阿拉伯语 *adj*. 阿拉伯语的,阿拉伯人的

architect /ˈɑːkɪtekt/ *n*. 建筑师

architecture /ˈɑːkɪtektʃə/ *n*. 建筑学

area /ˈeəriə/ *n*. 地区;面积;领域、方面

argue /ˈɑːgjuː/ *v*. 争论、争吵;坚持、争辩

　argue with sb. about/over sth. 与某人争论某事

　(考题)Eugene's never willing to alter any of his opinions. It's no use arguing with him.

　argue that . . . 主张……

　(辨析:argue,discuss,quarrel 都有"争论、争辩"的意思。discuss 指根据各自的观点进行商讨,以解决问题;argue 气氛较 discuss 更为激烈,着重坚持己见,与人争论;quarrel 则有争辩、争吵,发生口角的意思。)

argument /ˈɑːgjuːmənt/ *n*. 争论、争辩

arise /əˈraɪz/ *vi*. 出现、发生、呈现;起身、起立

　sth. arise 出现了…

　(考题)Serious disagreement arose between them.

　arise from 由…而引起

　(辨析:arise,rise rise 表示"向上",位置从低处移向高处;arise 则表示"导致、引起、产生"。)

arithmetic /əˈrɪθmetɪk/ *n*. 计算;算数

arm /ɑːm/ *n*. 手臂;武器(复数)

　take up arms 拿起武器

　with open arms 张开双臂

army /ˈɑːmɪ/ *n*. 军队;陆军

　(辨析:army 可统指军队,但有时指陆军;navy 是海军;air force 是空军。the armed forces 是一国陆海空军的总称。)

around /əˈraund/ *prep*. 环绕、在…周围 *adv*. 在周围;大约

　look around 四下张望

　show sb. around(a place) 带某人参观游览(某处)

arouse /əˈrauz/ *vt*. 唤醒;激起

arrange /əˈreɪndʒ/ *vt*. *vi*. 安排;整理

　arrange sth. 安排某事

　(考题)Weekly film and concert schedules, which are being

arranged，will be posted each Wednesday outside of the student club.

arrange to do sth. 准备做某事

arrange for sb. to do sth. 安排某人做某事

（考题）You see, I had arranged for us to have dinner with a friend tonight.

arrangement /əˈreɪndʒmənt/ *n*. 安排

make arrangements for sth. /to do sth. 为…做安排

（注意：在这个短语中，arrangements 用复数形式。）

arrest /əˈrest/ *vt*. 拘捕、逮捕；吸引（注意力等）

arrival /əˈraɪvl/ *n*. 抵达、到达；到的人或物品

on arrival 一到、刚到

arrive /əˈraɪv/ *vi*. 到达、抵达；来到

arrive at 到达（某一具体地点）

arrive in（某个国家、城市等）

arrive at a decision/conclusion/agreement 做出决定/得出结论/达成一致

（辨析：arrive，get to 和 reach 都可表示"到达"。get 和 arrive 是不及物动词，后面分别跟介词；reach 是及物动词，直接跟地名，也可跟某人，表示"某人收到了某物"。如：Your letter reached me last week。）

arrow /ˈærəʊ/ *n*. 箭；箭形符号

art /ɑːt/ *n*. 艺术、美术；工艺、技艺

a work of art 艺术品

art for art's sake 为艺术而艺术

fine arts 美术；美术作品

an art gallery 美术馆

article /ˈɑːtɪkl/ *n*. 文章；物品；冠词

（辨析：article 指纪事、描写、论述等各类文章；composition 指著作物，尤指练习写作的作文；essay 侧重指阐述某种观点的论文。）

artificial /ˌɑːtɪˈfɪʃəl/ *adj*. 人工的、仿真的

an artificial smile 假笑

artificial fabrics 人造纤维织品

artificial flower 假花

artificial rain 人工降雨

artist /ˈɑːtist/ *n.* 艺术家

as /æs，əs/ *conj.* 当…的时候；像…一样；因为、由于…；*prep.* 作为…；*adv.* 一样地

（见 when）

（见 because）

as a matter of fact 实际上

（考题）As a matter of fact, I'm merely an employee — the lowest kind of employee.

as a result (of) 结果

（考题）As a result, it may appear that sunscreen users get cancer more often.

as ... as possible/one can 尽可能…地

（考题）The auctioneer therefore has a direct interest in pushing up the bidding as high as possible.

as far as I know 据我所知

（考题）As far as I know, there just is nobody else for whom there is this sort of broadcast records

as for 说到、至于

（考题）As for those Asian countries that import labour, as in Europe, falling birth rates mean they are going to need more foreign workers.

as if/though 似乎、仿佛

（考题）The countries that lie in their path are naturally worried because it looks as if nothing can be done to stop them.

（注意：在 as if 或 as though 引导的从句中，常使用动词的虚拟语气。但现在，人们也常常使用陈述语气，尤其是在 look，seem，taste，smell 等动词之后。）

as/so long as 只要

（考题）As long as you try, you can make it.

as many as ... 多达…

（考题）Malaria, the world's most widespread parasitic disease, kills as many as three million people every year

as soon as 一…，就…

as to 说到、至于

（考题）As to whether dinosaurs cared for their young, dinosaur

scientists have turned to the closest living relatives of dinosaurs — birds and crocodiles — for possible models.

as well（as . . .） 也、还有

（考题）During his career Harrison has been responsible for approving large quantities of the sweet ice cream — as well as for developing over 75 flavors.

（辨析：表示"像 A 一样,不仅 A,还有 B"时,注意不同短语用法上的区别: not only A, but also B; A . . ., and B, too; A . . ., and also B. ;但是: B as well as A。）

the same/such as 如…一样

（考题）Clearly, this belief is the same as that of true competitors who try to prove themselves.

（注意: the same（. . .）as . . . 和 the same（. . .）that . . . 表示不同的含义。前者表示"与…相同的",后者则表示"同一个"。）

（辨析: as 和 like 有时都翻译成"像…一样"。但 like 是介词;而 as 只是在担任连词时才表示这个意思;作为介词,as 表示"作为",如: As the mother, she takes good care of the child,译成"作为母亲,她悉心照顾这个孩子";如果换成 like,She takes good care of the child like a mother,意思就成了"她像个母亲那样照顾这个孩子",言下之意,她并不是孩子的母亲。）

ash /æʃ/ *n .* 灰;（*pl .*）灰烬;废墟

ashamed /əˈʃeɪmd/ *adj .* 羞愧的、惭愧

（考题）Personally she feels ashamed and embarrassed for her shoplifting actions

be ashamed of . . . 为…感到羞愧

（考题）Thompson was ashamed of herself.

be ashamed to do sth. /that . . . 为做某事感到羞愧

Asia /ˈeɪʃə/ *n .* 亚洲

Asian /ˈeɪʃən/ *adj .* 亚洲的 *n .* 亚洲人

aside /əˈsaɪd/ *adv .* 到旁边、到一边

set sth. aside 把…放到一边、不予理会;存储

（考题）Einstein liked Bose's paper so much that he set aside his own work and translated it into German.

（同义词: set sth. aside, save）

ask /ɑːsk/ *vt .* 问

ask sb. /sth. 问某人/某事

ask sb. sth. 问某人某事

（考题）— Could I ask you a rather personal question? — Sure, go ahead.

ask sb. (not) to do sth. 叫某人（别）做某事

ask sb. for sth. /ask sth. of sb. /ask for sth. from sb. 向某人要求某物

（考题）Faced with a difficult situation，Arnold decided to ask his boss for advice.

ask after/about sth. /sb. 打听、询问某事/某人

（考题）Every time I meet him，he asks about you.

ask for leave 请假

asleep /əˈsliːp/ *adj.* 睡着的

be fast/sound asleep 睡得很熟

fall asleep 入睡、睡着

（同义词：go to sleep）

（注意：asleep 是个表语形容词，用于联系动词之后或担任名词的后置定语。）

aspect /ˈæspekt/ *n.* 方面

in this aspect 在这方面

in every aspect/in all aspects 各方面

We consider the plan practicable in every aspect.

aspirin /ˈæspərm/ *n.* 阿司匹林（药片）

assemble /əˈsembl/ *v.* 集合、召集；组装、装配

assess /əˈses/ *vt.* 评估、估价；评论

assign /əˈsaɪn/ *vt.* 分配、布置；指派

assign sb. sth. /assign sth. to sb. 布置某人做某事

（考题）Whatever the task your group is assigned, a few rules need to be followed to ensure a productive and successful experience.

assign sb. to do sth. 分派某人做某事

assist /əˈsɪst/ *vt. vt.* 帮助；协助

assist (sb.) in (doing) sth. 帮助某人做某事

（考题）He had even been allowed to assist a surgeon during an emergency operation.

assist sb. with sth. 在某方面(件事上)帮助某人

assistant /əˈsɪstənt/ *n.* 助手 *adj.* 辅助的

associate /əˈsəʊʃɪeɪt/ *vi.* *vt.* 交往；联系；使结合

associate with sb. 与某人交往

associate sth. with sth. 把…与…联系起来

(考题)If they associate you with this emotion of fear, they will become less functional around you.

be associated with ... 与…相互联系、关系密切

association /əˌsəʊʃɪˈeɪʃən/ *n.* 联盟、协会；联系、关联

(考题)Researchers from the University of Lows based their findings on a review of 18 earlier studies that looked at the association between sunscreen use and melanoma.

assume /əˈsjuːm/ *vt.* 假定、假设

assume that ... 假设…

(考题)If you're viewed positively within the critical first four minutes, the person you've met will probably assume everything you do is positive.

assure /əˈʃʊə/ *vt.* 使相信

assure sb. of sth. 向某人保证某事

(考题)If you come, I can assure you a warm welcome.

assure sb. that ... 向某人保证…；使某人确信

(考题)They assured me that everything would be all right and I could rest assured.

rest assured 放心

astonish /əˈstɒnɪʃ/ *vt.* 使惊讶

be astonished at sth. 对某事感到惊讶

astronaut /ˈæstrənɔːt/ *n.* 宇航员

at /æt, ət/ *prep.* 在…(某处)；在某时；某方面；因某种原因

at a time (每)一次

(考题)The dogs were placed in a large wooden box with an opening at the front to allow for them to view various stimuli. They were tested one at a time.

at any cost/at all costs 不惜代价

(考题)The order is the job be finished on time at any cost.

at any rate 不管怎样、无论如何

at first 最初、开始

at first sight 第一眼、一见

at hand 不远、近在手头

（考题）European countries, realizing crisis is at hand, are providing great encouragement for parents to create more babies in the 21st century.

at last 最后、终于

at least 至少

（考题）The house still needed a lot of work, but at least the kitchen was finished.

at (the) most 至多、最多

at once 立刻、马上

be good (poor) at sth. 某方面很好/差

（考题）People poor at one thing can be good at another.

Athens /ˈæθɪnz/ *n.* 雅典（希腊首都）

athlete /ˈæθliːt/ *n.* 运动员

athletic /æθˈletɪk/ *adj.* 运动的；运动员的

Atlantic /ətˈlæntik/ *n.* 大西洋；*adj.* 大西洋的

atmosphere /ˈætməsfɪə/ *n.* 大气；气氛

atom /ˈætəm/ *n.* 原子

atomic /əˈtɒmɪk/ *adj.* 原子（能）的

　atomic energy 原子能

　atomic bomb 原子弹

attach /əˈtætʃ/ *vi.* 归属于　*vt.* 连接；联系；使附属

　attach to sb. 归属于，归结于

　attach sth. to ... 把…联系于、连接于…

（考题）Fans used to be crazy about a specific film, but now the public tends to base its consumption on the interest of celebrity attached to any given product.

　attach importance to sth. 重视某事

　be attached to 附属于

attack /əˈtæk/ *vi. vt.* 攻击、袭击、侵害

（考题）Cougar like to attack running people.

　n. 攻击

　be under attack 收到袭击

（考题）When an animal is under attack, it can run away or fight back.

a heart attack 心脏病发作

attempt /əˈtempt/ *n*. 企图、试图

in a attempt to do sth. 企图做某事

（考题）A small town in southwest Britain is banning plastic bags in an attempt to help the environment and cut waste — a step that environmentalists believe is a first for Europe.

make an attempt at (doing,)/to do sth. 试图做某事

（考题）He made no attempt to turn off the loud TV he was watching ...

vt. 企图、试图

attempt (to do) sth. 试图做某事

（考题）That accident cost the driver of the Firebird plenty — a thousand dollars for the new engine — not to mention the charges for driving without a license, attempting to run away, and dangerous driving.

attend /əˈtend/ *vi*. *vt*. 出席；照顾；关注

attend school/a lecture/a meeting/church 上学（听讲座、出席会议、做礼拜）

（考题）In my mind, attending my dream university would be the only way to realize my dream of becoming a world-class writer.

attend (to) sb. 照顾、看护某人

attend to sth. 关心、关注、处理某事

（考题）As they breathe in and out, they attend to their feelings.

（同义词：表示"关心、关注、处理"的其它短语还有 **take care of, see to, deal with, cope with** 等。）

attend on/upon sb. 照顾、伺候某人

attention /əˈtenʃən/ *n*. 注意；注意力；关注

pay attention to sth. 注意某事

give (one's) attention to sth. 注意某事

attract/bring/call/catch/draw sb.'s attention 吸引某人注意

（考题）We are embarrassed to draw attention to something that is happening, while in a football match, people get involved, and a fight would easily follow.

attitude /ˈætɪtjuːd/ *n*. 态度；看法

（考题）Critical thinking is an attitude as much as an activity.

attitude towards/toward/to sth. 对某事的态度

（考题）Donald Louria's attitude towards long living is that it is possible for humans to live longer in the future.

attract /əˈtrækt/ *vt*. 吸引

（考题）The popularity of the igloo is beyond doubt：it is now attracting tourists from all over the world.

attraction /əˈtrækʃən/ *n*. 吸引；有吸引力的事物

attractive /əˈtræktɪv/ *adj*. 有吸引力的

audience /ˈɔːdɪəns/ *n*. 听众、观众

a large/small audience 观众很多/少

（注意：audience 后面的动词用单、复数形式均可；但 audience 是集合名词，本身没有复数形式，也不可以用 many，much，more 等修饰。）

audio-visual /ˈɔːdɪəuˈvɪʒuəl/ *adj*. 视听的

August /ˈɔːɡəst/ *n*. 八月

aunt /ɑːnt/ *n*. 姨妈；姑妈；婶母；舅母

Australia /ɒˈstreɪlɪə/ *n*. 澳大利亚

Austria /ˈɒstrɪə/ *n*. 奥地利

author /ˈɔːθə/ *n*. 作者

authority /ɔːˈθɒrɪtɪ/ *n*. 权威；权力；权威人士；(*pl*)当局

（考题）There's still a lot of strictness and authority on the part of parents out there，but there is a change happening.

have authority to do sth. 有权做某事

an authority on sth. 某方面的权威

auto /ˈɔːtəu/ *n*. 汽车

automatic /ˌɔːtəˈmætɪk/ *adj*. 自动的

autumn /ˈɔːtəm/ *n*. 秋天

available /əˈveɪləbl/ *adj*. 可以得到的；可以利用的；

sth. is available to sb. 某人可以得到/使用某物

（考题）... the alternative treatment is not easily available to most people.

avenue /ˈævənjuː/ *n*. 林荫大道

average /ˈævərɪdʒ/ *adj*. 中等的；平常的；平均的

（考题）The traveler can also estimate the journey time, average speed and fuel consumption.

of average intelligence/height 智力平平/中等身高

above/below average 平均以上/以下

on (the) average 平均说来、一般说来

（考题）Researchers find that, on average, wealthier people are happier.

avoid /əˈvɔid/ *vt.* 避免

avoid (doing) sth. 避免做某事

（考题）... and in doing so, we are not just protecting ourselves but are avoiding overloading other people as well.

（注意：avoid 后面的动词只能用动名词的形式。）

await /əˈweit/ *vt.* 等

await sb. /sth. 等某人/某物

（辨析：await 是及物动词。而 wait 后面要使用介词 for。）

awake /əˈweik/ *adj.* 醒着的；意识到、明白的

（考题）Smoking before bedtime keeps you awake.

be awake to sth. （开始）意识到某事

vi. 醒过来；意识到 *vt.* 叫醒、唤醒某人

awake to sth. 意识到某事

awake sb. 叫醒某人

（见 wake）

awaken /əˈweikn/ *vt.* 唤醒；引起 *vi.* 醒来

awaken sb. to sth. 使某人意识到某事

（见 wake）

award /əˈwɔːd/ *n.* 颁发（奖品等）；奖品、奖金

（考题）The book won an award in 1985 and has been used in classes from high school through graduate school level.

an award for sth. 因某事而颁发的奖品

（考题）In 1993, she was given a Caring Award for her efforts by the Caring Institute.

vt. 发奖

award sb. sth. /award sth. to sb. (for sth.) 因某事向某人颁发奖品

（考题）She was awarded a prize in Brazil.

aware /əˈweə/ *adj.* 意识到的、明白的

be aware of sth. /be aware that . . . 意识到…

（考题）Now that we are aware of the effects that diet products have on us，it is time to seriously think about buying them.

（考题）You are aware that people often judge you by your table manners.

away /əˈweɪ/ *adv*. 离开、不在

　　be away from . . . 离开…

awful /ˈɔːfʊl/ *adj*. 可怕的、糟糕的

awkward /ˈɔːkwəd/ *adj*. 笨拙的；尴尬的

B

baby /'beɪbɪ/ *n*. 婴儿

back /bæk/ *adv*. 后面；向后；回来　*adj*. 后面的；过去的　*n*. 背部；反面

　be/come/go back 回来/去

　back and forth 来来回回

　（考题）... their long, dark, shiny hair is thrown back and forth in the wind to the rhythm of their dance.

background /'bækgraʊnd/ *n*. 背景

　the background music 背景音乐

backward /'bækwəd/（backwards）*adj*. 向后的；落后的　*adv*. 向后；倒退

　（考题）"Why don't you photograph a sunrise?" she suggested. "And then play it backwards? Then it'll look like a sunset."

bacteria（复数）/bæk'tɪərɪə/ *n*. 细菌（单数 bacterium）

bad /bæd/ *adj*. 坏的

　be bad for ... 对…有害、不利

　DON'T SMOKE. Smoking is always bad for the body.

　go from bad to worse 每况愈下

badly /'bædlɪ/ *adv*. 坏的、恶劣地；非常地；极大地

　Although badly hurt in the accident, the driver was still able to make a phone call.

bag /bæg/ *n*. 包、袋

baggage /'bægɪdʒ/ *n*. 行李

bake /beɪk/ *v*. 烘烤

bakery /'beɪkərɪ/ *n*. 面包店

balance /'bæləns/ *n*. 平衡

　keep balance 保持平衡

　lose one's balance 失去平衡

　（考题）It has been discovered that a shark senses pressure using hair cells in its balance system.

vt. 使平衡

The ROM balances blood sugar, and repairs bad backs and shoulders.

ball /bɔːl/ *n.* 球;舞会

give a ball 举办舞会

ballet /ˈbæleɪ/ *n.* 芭蕾舞

balloon /bəˈluːn/ *n.* 气球

bamboo /bænˈbuː/ *n.* 竹

ban /bæn/ *n.* 禁止、禁令

(考题)In a way, calling for bans on research into molecular manufacturing is like calling for a delay on faster-than-light travel because no one is doing it.

vt. **ban sth.** 禁止…

(考题)Smoking is strictly banned in this building.

ban sb. from doing sth. 禁止某人做某事

banana /bəˈnɑːnə/ *n.* 香蕉

band /bænd/ *n.* 乐队;带状物

bandage /ˈbændɪdʒ/ *n.* 绷带

band-aid /ˈbændeɪd/ *n.* 护创胶布

bank /bæŋk/ *n.* 银行;河岸

bar /bɑː/ *n.* 酒吧;出售酒类、饮料等的柜台

a snack bar 快餐店

barber /ˈbɑːbə/ *n.* 理发师

bare /beə/ *adj.* 赤裸的

barely /ˈbeəlɪ/ *adv.* 勉强;几乎不

(考题)He was lucky. He barely passed the test.

(考题)I have barely met him in the past two weeks.

(辨析:barely 有时可以和 hardly、rarely 等表示否定意义的副词替换使用,如:It's so dark outside that I can barely/hardly see anything;I rarely/barely meet him these days。但 barely 不属于具有否定意义的副词一类。)

bargain /ˈbɑːɡɪn/ *n.* 讨价还价、协议;便宜货

(考题)I bought a dress for only 10 dollars in a sale; it was a real bargain.

make a bargain with sth. 与某人成交

v. 讨价还价

bargain about/over/for sth. with sb. 与某人就某物讨价还价

bark /bɑːk/ *n.* 树皮

bark /bɑːk/ *n.* (狗、狐)吠声 *vi.* 吠、叫;咆哮 *vt.* 大声叫出

barrier /ˈbærɪə/ *n.* 障碍(物);栅栏

base /beɪs/ *n.* 根基、基础;基地

on the base of ... 在…的基础上

(考题)The surface of the road lies on the base of concrete and steel.

(辨析:base 常指有形的、物质的基础,而 basis 可指非物质的基础,如:on the basis of the mutual understanding)

vt. **base sth. on sth.** 以…为基础,根据…

(考题)Such a diet is based primarily on grain products, fruits, and vegetables, with moderate amounts of meat and dairy products and with small amounts of snacks and desserts.

baseball /ˈbeɪsbɔːl/ *n.* 棒球

basement /ˈbeɪsmənt/ *n.* 地下室

basic /beɪsɪk/ *adj.* 基本的、基础的

(考题)Mankind could often not be content just to put up a basic structure, but felt the need, even in such an isolated place, to build with an artistic touch.

basic concept 基本概念

basic principle 基本原理

basin /beɪsn/ *n.* 盆;盆地

basis /ˈbeɪsɪs/ *n.* 基础、根据;主要成分

on the basis of 以…为基础

(考题)In Hong Kong, men and women mix socially on a day-to-day basis.

(见 base)

basket /ˈbɑːskɪt/ *n.* 篮子

basketball /ˈbɑːskɪtbɔːl/ *n.* 篮球

bat /bæt/ *n.* 球拍、球棒;蝙蝠

bath /bɑːθ/ *n.* 洗澡;浴盆

have/take a bath 洗澡

bathroom 浴室

bathtub 浴缸

bathrobe 浴衣

bathe /beɪð/ *vi*. 洗澡 *vt*. 给某人洗澡

　　bathing cap 泳帽

　　bathing suit 游泳衣

bathroom /ˈbɑːθruːm/ *n*. 浴室

battery /ˈbætərɪ/ *n*. 电池

battle /ˈbætl/ *n*. 战斗、战役、战争

　　join battle 参战

　　an air battle 空战

　　a close battle 近战、肉搏

　　a street battle 巷战

　　（考题）Nevertheless，there are fresh reasons for optimism in the battle against AIDS.

　　（辨析：battle 和 fight 指具体的战斗，fight 还有打架的含义；campaign 指大的战役；struggle 有奋斗的含义，可表示其它意义上的努力；war 则指广义的战争，如世界大战。）

bay /beɪ/ *n*. 海湾

　　（辨析：gulf 也表示海湾，通常比 bay 大。）

　　B. C.（before Christ）公元前

beach /biːtʃ/ *n*. 海滩、湖滨、河滩

　　on the beach 在海滩上

bean /biːn/ *n*. 豆；豆类

bear /beə/（bore，born/borne）*n*. 熊

vt. 忍受；承受；生育；标有

　　be born 出生

　　bear sth. 忍受、承受…

　　（考题）Who will bear the losses caused by the permit issue?

　　（考题）I couldn't bear the pain of the bites.

　　(can't) bear to do (doing) sth.（不）能忍受做某事

　　(can't) bear sb. to do sth. 不能容忍某人做某事

　　bear sth. in mind 牢记某事

　　（考题）That's what I will always bear in mind.

　　（同义词：keep sth. in mind, learn sth. by heart）

beard /bɪəd/ *n*. 胡须

beast /biːst/ *n*. 野兽

beat /biːt/（beat，beaten）*vt*. 打；打败　*vi*.（心脏等）跳动

（考题）Within days，however，his heart was not beating properly.

beat sb. at/in sth. 在某方面击败某人

（考题）The final score of the basketball match was 93-94. We were only narrowly beaten.

beat time 打拍子

n. 跳动；节拍

（考题）He could even hear the beat of his own heart.

beautiful /ˈbjuːtəfʊl/ *adj*. 美丽的、漂亮的

beauty /ˈbjuːtɪ/ *n*. 美丽；美人

because /bɪˈkɒz/ *conj*. 因为

（注意：可以引导原因状语从句的连词有 because，as，since 等，但如果是回答 why 的提问，只能使用 because。）

because of 因为、由于

（考题）They were late because of the heavy rain.

（注意：because 是连词，引导原因状语从句，尤其用来回答 why 提出的问题；because of 是介词，后面使用短语。）

become /bɪˈkʌm/（became，become）*vi*. 变成；变得

（考题）As I've grown old，life has become smaller. Tastes have bulled. Surprises have turned into shocks. Days go by unnoticed. How can I regain childhood when it was an illusion?

（考题）Last month，San Francisco became the first U. S. city to ban plastic grocery bags.

（注意：become 在表示上述意思时，不论后面跟形容词还是名词，它都是联系动词。表示相同意思的联系动词还有 get，turn，grow，go，come，fall 等。）

become of sb. 某人发生了某种情况、遭遇

（考题）What will become of those poor children who lost their parents in the disaster.

（同义词：... **happen to sb.**）

bed /bed/ *n*. 床

go to bed 睡觉，就寝

in bed 卧床

（考题）Having been ill in bed for nearly a month，he had a hard

time passing the exam.

bedroom /ˈbedrʊm/ *n*. 卧室

bee /biː/ n，蜜蜂

beef /biːf/ *n*. 牛肉

beer /bɪə/ *n*. 啤酒

Beethoven /ˈbeɪtəʊvən/ 贝多芬

before /bɪˈfɔː/ *prep*. 在…之前   *adv*. 以前、从前   *conj*. 在…之前

before long 不久

（考题）Before long，many diners stayed open around the clock.

long before 很久以前

（考题）I remember meeting him once long before.

before time 提前

It is … before … 过…才会…

（考题）Now they hope it won't be too long before they are able to prove its existence.

（辨析：在表示位置关系"在…之前"时，in front of 和 before 意思相同。但通常表示在建筑物之前时，用 in front of。）

beg /beg/ *vt*. *vi*. 乞求；恳求

beg (for) sth. 请求、乞求某物

（考题）When a rather dirty，poorly dressed person kneels at your feet and puts out his hands to beg for a few coins，do you hurry on，not knowing what to do，or do you feel sad and hurriedly hand over some money?

beg sth. of sb. 向某人乞求某物

beg a favor of sb. 请求某人帮助

beg sb. to do sth. 乞求、恳求某人做某事

（考题）The poor man begged us to have pity on him.

begin /bɪˈgɪn/（began，begun）*vi*. *vt*. 开始

begin (to do，doing) sth. 开始（做）某事

begin with sth. 以…作为开始

（辨析：begin 和 start 意思相同。但 start 还可表示发动机器。另外，当主语是物而不是人，或用于进行时态，或后面的动词表示心理和意识时，begin 和 start 后面使用不定式，而不使用动名词，如：begin to realize …、beginning to see …。）

beginning /bɪˈɡɪnɪŋ/ *n*. 开始、开端

at the beginning 起初、开始时

（考题）It seems that most shows do well at the beginning but then the viewing figures begin to fall.

from beginning to end 从头到尾

from the beginning 从一开始

behave /bɪˈheɪv/ *vi*. *vt*. 举止、表现；行为

behave oneself 表现得规矩

（考题）It is based on the general idea that people have the ability to change the way they think and behave.

baheviour /bɪˈheɪvɪə/ *n*. 行为、举止、表现

behind /bɪˈhaɪnd/ *prep*. 在…后面 *adv*. 在后面、向后面

behind time 晚点、误点

（考题）The flight from Tokyo is behind time again.

behind the times 过时、落后

（考题）Those old ideas in your mind are long behind the times. Get rid of them.

be/fall/lag behind (sb.) in ... 在某方面落在(某人)后面

being /ˈbiːɪŋ/ *n*. 人；生物

a human being 一个人

come into being 出现、产生

（考题）In this pioneering study, David Lightfoot explains how languages come into being, arguing that children are the driving force.

（同义词：**come into existence**）

for the time being 暂时、眼下

（考题）I have nothing to tell for the time being.

belief /bɪˈliːf/ *n*. 相信；信念、信仰

believe /bɪˈliːv/ *vi*. *vt*. 相信；认为

believe sb./sth. 相信某人/某事

believe sb./sth. to be ... 相信某人/某事…

（考题）The flu is believed to be caused by viruses that like to reproduce in the cells inside the human nose and throat.

believe that ... 相信、认为…

（考题）People believed nothing could stop the brain slowing

down.

believe it or not 信不信由你

(考题)Fred is second to none in maths in our class，but believe it or not，he hardly passed the last exam.

believe in sb. /sth. 信任、信仰某人/某事

(考题)If you believe in yourself and work hard，you can achieve great results.

It is believed that . . . 据信…

(考题)It is believed that they have made a breakthrough.

sb. /sth. is believed to be/do sth. 相信某人…

(考题)Animals' ability to act reasonably is believed to come partly from what we may call "genetic learning."

bell /bel/ *n*. 铃、钟声

There goes the bell. 铃响了。

belong /bɪˈlɒŋ/ *vi*. 属于

belong to 属于

(考题)I saw their bodies，but I couldn't feel their souls because their souls belonged to the net.

below /bɪˈləʊ/ *prep*. 在…下面、下方　*adv*. 在下面、下方

below sea level 海平面以下

below the standard/expectation . . . 不符合标准/低于预期…

(考题)If the heat is reduced by cooling the material below a certain temperature，the fire goes out.

(考题). . . their income is below their expectation.

(辨析：在表示位置关系时，below 强调在水平位置的下方；under 则表示在正下方、垂直位置的下方；而 beneath 则表示在某一物体的下面，有更接近的位置关系。)

belt /belt/ *n*. 皮带、腰带；长形地带

hit below the belt 犯规(尤指拳击比赛中)

bench /bentʃ/ *n*. 长凳

bend /bend/ *n*. 弯曲、弯角　*v*. (使)弯曲

beneath /bɪˈniːθ/ *prep*. 在…下面　*adv*. 在下面

beneficial /ˌbenɪˈfɪʃəl/ *adj*. 有益的、有利的

be beneficial to sb. /sth. 对某人/物有利

benefit /ˈbenɪfɪt/ *vi*. *vt*. 受益；有益于

benefit sb. 使某人获益

（考题）Technology — the application of science — has made big advances that have benefited us in nearly every part of life.

benefit from ... 从…中受益

（考题）She said that she had benefited from lessons on personal finance，but admitted that she still had a lot to learn about money.

n. 利益

for the benefit of ... 为了…的利益

beside /bɪ'saɪd/ *prep.* 在旁边

beside oneself 忘乎所以

beside the point 不切题、走题

besides /bɪ'saɪdz/ *prep.* 除…之外还有；*adv.* 除此之外、不仅

（同义词：见 **addition**）

（辨析：beside 表示"除此之外，还有"，提到的人或事物也包括在内；而 except"除了这个，其它的…"，提到的人或物不包括在内。）

best /best/ *adj.* 最好的　*adv.* 最好的

do/try one's best 尽力

make the best of ... 充分利用

（考题）Creative people can make the best of what they have.

bet /bet/（betted 或 bet，bet）*v.* 打赌　*n.* 打赌

make a bet on sth. with sb. 就某事与某人打赌

better /'betə/ *adj. adv.* 更好、较好

had better do sth. 最好做某事

It's better to do sth. 最好做某事

no/little better than 不比…强，一样

（考题）Baker found that the subjects were no better at telling when they were stared at and when they weren't.

so much the better 当然更好

the ... the better 越…越好

（考题）The better you are at managing the time you devote to your studies，the more time you'll have to spend on your outside interests

between /bɪ'twiːn/ *prep.* 在…（两者）之间　*adj.* 在之间…

beyond /bɪ'jɒnd/ *prep.* 在…那边、超过、越过　*adv.* 在更远处

beyond cure 无法治愈的

beyond comparison 无法比拟的

beyond control 无法控制的

（考题）The growing speed of a plant is influenced by a number of factors, most of which are beyond our control.

beyond description (words) 难以描述的

beyond doubt 毫无疑问

beyond expectation 没有料到的

（考题）Merlin succeeded beyond expectation.

beyond hope 没有希望的

beyond imagination/understanding 无法想象/理解的

（考题）Art museum exhibits, on the other hand, would most probably fill visitors with a feeling that there is something beyond their understanding.

beyond sb. (sb.'s ability, reach, power, means) 某人力不能及的、无能为力的

（考题）He wanted to construct a calculating machine to work out the solutions to maths problems not only with correctness but also with a speed beyond the power of any human mind.

beyond sb.'s knowledge 某人不知道的

Bible /ˈbaɪbl/ *n.* 圣经

bicycle /ˈbaɪsɪkl/ *n.* 自行车

big /bɪg/ *adj.* 大的

bike /baɪk/ *n.* 自行车

bill /bɪl/ *n.* 账单；钞票、纸币

foot the bill 付账、承担费用

billion /ˈbɪliən/ *num.* 十亿

bin /bɪn/ *n.* 储藏盒、储藏箱

dust bin 垃圾桶

bind /baɪnd/（bound, bound）*vi.* 粘合 *vt.* 使粘合；捆绑；束缚

bind ... 绑起、扎起…

（考题）He bound these boxes together with a rope.

be bound to do sth. 感到有义务做某事

（考题）We are bound to do what we have promised to.

be bound up with 与…密切相关

biology /baɪˈɒlədʒɪ/ *n*. 生物学

bird /bɜːd/ *n*. 鸟

birds of a feather 情趣相投的人，臭味相投的人

A bird in the hand is worth two in the bush. 二鸟在林不如一鸟在手

kill two birds with one stone 一石二鸟、一箭双雕

birth /bɜːθ/ *n*. 出生、诞生

by birth 一出生就、天生就

from birth 从一出生

（考题）Scientists believe that everybody possesses a sense of direction from birth.

give birth to 生产、生出

birthday /ˈbɜːθdɪ/ *n*. 生日

biscuit /ˈbɪskɪt/ *n*. 饼干

bit /bɪt/ *n*. 少许、一点儿

a bit of ... 一点、少许…（注意：a bit of 修饰不可数名词。）

a bit ＋*adj*. 或 *adv*. 稍许有些…

（辨析：在肯定句中，a bit，a little 和 a little bit 修饰形容词和副词时，意思相同，表示"稍稍、有些"。但在否定形式时，not a bit 表示"一点也不"，而 not a little 则表示"非常，不是一点点"，意思截然相反。）

bit by bit 一点一点地

（考题）Bit by bit, the dunes grow over the years, always moving with the winds and changing the shape.

do one's bit 尽力、尽自己的本分

not a bit 一点也不

（考题）I didn't eat anything, but I'm not a bit hungry now.

quite a bit 许多、相当

bite /baɪt/ *n*. 咬一口　　*v*.（bit，bitten/bit）咬

have/take a bit of sth. 咬了一口…

bitter /ˈbɪtə/ *adj*. 苦的；难以忍受的；强烈的

bitter to the taste 苦味

a bitter lesson 沉痛的教训

a bitter blow 沉重的打击

black /blæk/ *adj*. 黑色的　　*n*. 黑色

black tea 红茶

black coffee 清咖啡

be in a black mood 情绪低落

blackboard /ˈblækbɔːd/ *n.* 黑板

blacksmith /ˈblæksmiθ/ *n.* 铁匠

blame /bleɪm/ *vi. vt.* 责备、责怪、指责

sb. is to blame 某人应受到指责

（考题）I feel it is your husband who is to blame for the spoiled child.

blame sb. for (doing) sth. 因某事指责某人

（考题）Blamed for the breakdown of the school computer network，Alice was in low spirits.

blame sth. on sb. 将某事归咎于某人

n. 责怪、责备

lay blame on sb. 责怪某人

blank /blæŋk/ *adj.* 空白的；空虚的　　*n.* 空白处、空格

fill in the blanks 填空

a blank cheque 空白支票

blanket /ˈblæŋkɪt/ *n.* 毯子；覆盖物

bleed /bliːd/ (bled, bled) *vi.* 流血　　*vt.* 使流血

bleed to death 流血致死

bless /bles/ *vt.* 祝福

bless sb. 为某人祝福

be blessed with sth. 幸运地拥有…

God bless me! 我的天啊！

blind /blaɪnd/ *adj.* 失明的、瞎的　　*vt.* 使失明；使看不清

（考题）The newspaper reported that round bowls don't give enough oxygen for fish and may make them go blind.

be blind in one eye 一只眼瞎了

blind sb. in the ... eye 把某人的…眼弄瞎了

block /blɒk/ *n.* 大块（木头、石头等）；街区

a block of ... 一大块…

vt. block sth. 堵塞、阻挡

（考题）The building also has windows with a coating that blocks heat while letting in light.

be blocked with 被…堵塞

blood /blʌd/ *n*. 血，血液

　　blood type/group 血型

　　blood test 验血

　　blood transfusion 输血

　　blood vessel 血管

　　in cold blood 冷酷地、残忍地

　　Blood is thicker than water. 血浓于水

bloom /bluːm/ *v*. 开花

　　bloom with ... 洋溢、体现…

　　n. 开花、(花)开放

　　be in full bloom 盛开

blouse /blaʊs/ *n*. 短外衣

blow /bləʊ/ (blew, blown) *vi*. *vt*. 吹；刮风；断、炸毁

　　(考题)Most waves are created when winds blow across the ocean.

　　blow sth. down 把…吹倒

　　(考题)The trees blown down in the storm have been moved off the road.

　　blow sth. open 把某物吹开

　　blow off 吹走

　　blow sth. out 吹灭

　　blow (sth.) up 把某物吹起；爆炸

　　(考题)I don't think it's my fault that the TV blew up. I just turned it on, that's all.

　　n. 打击

　　with one blow 一下子

blue /bluː/ *adj*. 蓝色的；沮丧的　*n*. 蓝色

　　feel blue 感到沮丧

　　out of the blue 出其不意地

board /bɔːd/ *n*. 板、木板；委员会；搭伙

　　go (get) on board (the ship ...) 登船等

　　on board (the ship) 在船上

　　board of directors 董事会

　　v. 搭伙；登车、船等

　　(考题)Unfortunately, there were so many people waiting to

board the subway that I could not even get down the stairs to the platform.

board sb. 为某人提供伙食

boast /bəust/ *n*. 自吹自擂 *v*. 自吹自擂、夸口

boat /bəut/ *n*. 小船 *vi*. 划船

go boating 划船

body /'bɒdɪ/ *n*. 身体、躯体；机体

boil /bɔɪl/ *vi*. 沸腾 *vt*. 煮沸

boil down to ... 压缩、浓缩到…

（考题）The argument boiled down to the question of whether the government should take measures to stabilize the prices.

boiling point 沸点

bomb /bɒm/ *n*. 炸弹 *vt*. 轰炸

bone /bəun/ *n*. 骨头、鱼刺

book /buk/ *n*. 书 *vt*. 预定（票、房间等）

booking office 售票处

booklet /'buklɪt/ *n*. 小册子

bookshop /'bukʃɒp/ *n*. 书店

boot /buːt/ *n*. 靴子 *v*. 引导（计算机启动程序）

border /'bɔːdə/ *n*. 边界、边境

bore /bɔː/ *vt*. 使厌烦 *n*. 令人厌烦的人或物

（考题）Well, my thoughts began to bore me, and most of them were on how much my legs hurt.

be bored with sth. 对…感到厌烦

（考题）Holidaymakers who are bored with baking beaches and overheated hotel rooms head for a big igloo.

borrow /'bɒrəu/ *v*. 借；借用、引进

borrow sth. from sb. 向某人借某物

（考题）Mostly borrowed from English and Chinese, these terms are often changed into forms no longer understood by native speakers.

（辨析：borrow 是指向别人借入某物；lend 则是将某物借给别人，用法是 lend sb. sth. 或 lend sth. to sb. ）

boss /bɒs/ *n*. 老板；上司

botanist /'bɒtənɪst/ *n*. 植物学家

botany /ˈbɒtənɪ/ *n*. 植物学

both /bəʊθ/ *adj*. *adv*. 两者都　*pron*. *n*. 两者

　　both A and B A 和 B 都…

　　（辨析：both 强调"两者都"。两者中的任意一个使用 either，一个也没有则使用 neither。如果是三者以上，则分别使用 all，any 以及 none。）

bother /ˈbɒðə/ *vt*. *vi*. 打扰、麻烦；费心

　　bother sb. 打扰某人

　　（考题）Stop bothering him! Can't you see he's only trying to get home?

　　bother（oneself）with（about）sth. 为某事操心、烦神

　　bother to do sth. 费心做某事

　　（考题）So why bother even to try imagining life far in the future?

　　n. 麻烦；费心

　　have bother doing sth. 做某事有困难

bottle /ˈbɒtl/ *n*. 瓶子

bottom /ˈbɒtm/ *n*. 底、底部

　　at bottom 实际上，内里

　　Bottoms up! 干杯！

　　from top to bottom 从上到下

bow /baʊ/ *vi*. *vt*. *n*. 鞠躬

　　bow one's head 低头

　　bow to sb. /sth. 向某人/事低头、接受

bowl /bəʊl/ *n*. 碗

bowling /ˈbəʊlɪŋ/ *n*. 保龄球

box /bɒks/ *n*. 箱子、盒子

boy /bɔɪ/ *n*. 男孩

brain /breɪn/ *n*. 脑、头脑

　　have a fine brain 有头脑、聪明

　　have/have no/little brains 有/没有头脑、智慧

　　（考题）Boris has brains. In fact，I doubt whether anyone in the class has a higher IQ.

　　use one's brains 动脑筋

brake /breɪk/ *n*. 刹车、制动器

branch /brɑːntʃ/ *n*. 树枝;分店、分支机构

brand /brænd/ *n*. 商标、牌子;印记

　brand-new 崭新的

　(考题)When I got back out into the street, the world seemed brand-new to me.

　vt. 打上印记

　brand sth. with ... 在…打上印记

brass /brɑːs/ *n*. 黄铜

brave /breɪv/ *adj*. 勇敢的

bread /bred/ *n*. 面包

　bread and butter 黄油面包、日常生计

break /breɪk/ (broke, broken) *vt. vi*. 打破、损坏;破裂;违背

　(考题)Only the sound of the big freezer broke the quiet.

　break away (from) 摆脱、脱离

　break down 抛锚;恶化;停止

　(考题)Then his health broke down, and he had to take a long holiday abroad.

　break sb. of sth. 使某人摆脱某事

　(考题)What can I do to break him of this bad habit?

　break in (into ...) 闯入

　(考题)The museum was broken into last night and a lot of valuable things taken away.

　break out (战争、疾病等)暴发

　break the ice 打破僵局

　break through 突破、穿透

　break up 停止;散开

　(考题)He told of different men and of strange civilizations, broken up by long 'dark ages' in between.

　n. 破裂;间歇、休息

　(考题)... where standards-based learning was the focus and music just provided a break for students and teachers.

　have a break 休息一会儿

breakfast /ˈbrekfəst/ *n*. 早饭

breast /brest/ *n*. 胸部;乳房

breath /breθ/ *n*. 呼吸

catch one's breath 屏住呼吸

（考题）What I saw really made me catch my breath.

hold one's breath 屏住呼吸

out of breath 气喘吁吁

（考题）We were all out of breath when we got to the top of the mountain.

get back/recover one's breath 缓过气来

The old man had to stop half way upstairs to recover his breath.

take（a deep）breath（深深）喘口气,（深）呼吸

（考题）I collected my thoughts, took a deep breath, and rang the number.

breathe /briːð/ *vt. vi.* 呼吸;轻声说出

（考题）The sandhills still breathed heat from yesterday's sun, though the top of the sand was cool.

breed /briːd/ *n.* 品种、种类　*v.*（bred, bred）繁殖、培育

breeze /briːz/ *n.* 微风

bribe /braɪb/ *v.　n.* 行贿

brick /brɪk/ *n.* 砖头

bride /braɪd/ *n.* 新娘

bridegroom /ˈbraɪdɡrʊm/ *n.* 新郎

bridge /brɪdʒ/ *n.* 桥;桥牌　*v.* 架桥;弥合

play bridge 打桥牌

burn one's bridge 不留退路

（考题）"Martha, I hope you didn't burn your bridges," Maria said. "I think I would have handled it differently."

brief /briːf/ *adj.* 简要的　*n.* 摘要

（考题）The impressionists saw reality in brief emotional effects, the realists in everyday subjects and in forest scenes, and the Cro-Magnon cave people in their naturalistic drawings of the animals in the ancient forests.

in brief 总而言之

（考题）This, in brief, is my view on the problem.

v. 做简要介绍

brief sb. on sth. 向某人简单介绍某事

brigade /brɪˈɡeɪd/ *n.*（军队）旅;（执行某种任务的）队

a fire brigade 消防队

bright /braɪt/ *adj.* 明亮的；鲜艳的；聪明的

brilliant /ˈbrɪlɪənt/ *adj.* 明亮的、光彩夺目的；极聪明的

bring /brɪŋ/ (brought，brought) *vt. vi.* 带来

bring sth. to sb. /bring sb. sth. 给某人带来某物

（考题）It has brought us a better understanding of the nature of life and of its continuous development.

bring sth. about 带来、引起

（考题）Hine's pictures helped bring about laws to protect such children.

（同义词：**cause，lead to，result in，produce**）

bring sb. over/around to sth. 说服某人接受某事

（同义词：**talk sb. over、win sb. over**）

bring ... back to life 使复生

（考题）I thought the program was wonderful. They helped to bring to life the stories the people were telling.

bring sth. back (to one's mind) 回想起

（考题）However hard I tried, I couldn't bring his name back to my mind.

bring sth. forth/forward 造成、提出、引发

（考题）No matter what objects they select，artists are to bring forth new forces and forms that cause change.

bring sth. to an end 结束某事

bring sth. to sb.'s attention 使某人注意某事

（考题）He couldn't have noticed it himself. There must have been someone who brought the matter to his attention.

bring sb. to safety 使某人脱离危险

bring sb. up 抚养某人

（考题）Brought up in the city，he found it hard for him to get used to the country life.

bring sth. under control 控制住某事

（考题）First and foremost，we should try to bring the situation under control.

bring sb. to do sth. 使某人做某事

（考题）... that Computertowns bring people to learn to use

computers.

（辨析：只有表示这一意义时，bring 后面才用动词不定式担任宾补。有类似用法的还有 lead sb. to do sth.）

bring sb. over（to sth.）使某人改变看法，同意…

（考题）No matter what I said，I couldn't bring him over to our view.

（同义词：**talk sb. over to . . .**、**win sb. over to . . .**都可表示同样的意思。短语中 to 是介词，后面不能使用动词不定式。）

Britain /ˈbrɪtən/ *n*. 不列颠（英格兰、威尔士和苏格兰的总称，也常用来指英国）

　　Great Britain 大不列颠

British /ˈbrɪtɪʃ/ *adj*. 英国的、英联邦的

broad /brɔːd/ *adj*. 宽广的；广泛的

broadcast /ˈbrɔːdkɑːst/ *n*. 广播　*v*. 播送、广播

　　broadcast program 广播节目

brother /ˈbrʌðə/ *n*. 兄弟

brow /braʊ/ *n*. 眉毛

brown /braʊn/ *adj*. 棕色的　*n*. 棕色

browse /braʊz/ *vi*. 随意翻阅

　　browse through/over . . . 随意翻阅…　浏览…

brush /brʌʃ/ *n*. 刷子；画笔　*v*. 用刷子刷

B. S.（Bachelor of Science）理学士

bubble /ˈbʌbl/ *n*. 泡

bucket /ˈbʌkɪt/ *n*. 水桶；一桶的量

budget /ˈbʌdʒɪt/ *n*. 预算；收支计划

build /bɪld/（built，built）*vt*. 建设、建造

　　build up 增强；积累

（考题）Mastery of those skills will be good for the students to build up their creativity in every way.

　　built-in 内装的、事先装好的

building /ˈbɪldɪŋ/ *n*. 大楼

bulb /bʌlb/ *n*. 灯泡；（植物的）球茎

bull /bʊl/ *n*. 公牛

bullet /ˈbʊlɪt/ *n*. 子弹

bump /bʌmp/ *vi*. 碰、撞　*n*. 碰撞

bump against . . . 撞上…

bump into . . . 撞上；巧遇…

bunch /bʌntʃ/ *n*. 束、捆、串

a bunch of flowers 一束花

bundle /ˈbʌndl/ *n*. 捆、包

burden /ˈbɜːdən/ *n*. 负担、负荷；*vt*. 给添负担

burden sb. with sth. 给某人添…麻烦

（考题）. . . as this generation of young people is likely to be burdened with greater debts than any before.

burn /bɜːn/（burnt, burnt）*n*. 燃烧；烧毁；晒黑

（考题）. . . which not only reduces the weight of a car, but also makes the motor burn less oil and work better.

burn sth. down 烧毁某物

burn (sth.) out 烧光；消耗完

（考题）They were just burned-out with all the pressure they felt from the coach or their parents.

burn with sth. 有强烈的情绪或要求

（考题）She was burning with a desire for success.

burn the midnight oil 开夜车

burst /bɜːst/（burst, burst）*n*. 爆裂 *vi*. 爆裂；突然发出

burst into laughter/tears/flames/applause 突然大笑（哭，燃烧，鼓掌欢呼）

（考题）Hospital staff burst into cheers after doctors completed a 20-hour operation to have separated one-year-old twins at the head.

burst out doing sth. 突然做某事

（考题）He burst out laughing at the good news.

burst sth. open 突然打开某物

（考题）I was really scared when someone burst the door open.

bury /ˈberɪ/ *vt*. 埋葬；埋藏；专心致志于

（考题）No matter what feelings are present, facing them honestly will serve one better than burying them.

bury oneself in sth. 专心致志于某事

bus /bʌs/ *n*. 公共汽车

bush /buʃ/ *n*. 灌木丛

business /ˈbɪznɪs/ *n.* 生意、商业;事务、事情

（考题）The concern for a safer and cleaner environment is making companies rethink how they do business.

business hours 营业时间

business letter 商业信函

Business is business. 公事公办。

It's none of your business. 与你无关。

（考题）In a word，Rip was ready to attend to everybody's business but his own.

busy /ˈbɪzɪ/ *adj.* 忙碌的;热闹的

be busy with sth. 忙于某事

be busy doing sth. 忙着做某事

but /bʌt/ *conj.* 但是;*prep.* 除了

have no choice/alternative but to do sth. 只能做某事

（考题）Parents have no choice but to try to accept it.

（同义词：**can do nothing but do sth.**，**have nothing to do but do sth.**，**can not but do sth.**，**there's nothing to do but do sth.**）

anything but 决不是

（考题）Life on the ship is anything but cruising.

nothing but 只是

（考题）I have nothing but praise for your devotion and your hard work.

last but one 倒数第二

but for 要不是

（考题）They would be far worse but for this outflow of bodies and inflow of dollars.

but that 要不是

（考题）When I hurried there I apologized for being late，and told him I'd come as quickly as I could，but that the car had needed a major repairs.

（注意：在使用 but for 和 but that 的句子里常用虚拟语气。but for 是介词，but that 后面跟从句）

butcher /ˈbʊtʃə/ *n.* 屠夫;肉食品商

butter /ˈbʌtə/ *n.* 黄油　*v.* 涂黄油于

butterfly /ˈbʌtəflaɪ/ *n.* 蝴蝶

button /'bʌtn/ *n*. 纽扣

buy /baɪ/ (bought，bought) *vt*. 购买

    buy sth. from sb. 向某人买某物

    buy sb. sth. /buy sth. for sb. 为某人买某物

    buy sth. for … 用…钱买某物

    （考题）Nothing pleased me quite so much as to buy a bargain lot of them on sale for several pounds.

by /baɪ/ *prep*. 在…旁；经过；到某时刻；以某种方式；以…为单位；（被动语态中）被、由某人

    （考题）Days go by unnoticed. How can I regain childhood when it was an illusion?

    by and by 不久以后

    by day(night) 白天/夜间

    by far 最（和形容词、副词最高级连用）

    （考题）This is, by far, the best suggestion we've got up to now.

    by oneself 自己、亲自；独立

    by the way 顺便说一下、还有件事

    by doing sth. 通过做某事…

    （考题）You can know the animal's behaviour by watching it closely.

    by ten o'clock 到 10 点为止、最晚十点

    （考题）By the time he reached the small boat，a thick white mist had spread over the surface of the water.

bye /baɪ/ *interj*. 再见

    Good-bye! 再见

    Bye-bye! 再见

cabbage /ˈkæbɪdʒ/ *n*. 卷心菜

cabin /ˈkæbɪn/ *n*. 舱房

cable /ˈkeɪbl/ *n*. 索;缆;电缆

   cable TV 有线电视

   by cable 电传

café /ˈkæfeɪ/ *n*. 咖啡馆;小餐馆

cafeteria /ˌkæfəˈtɪərɪə/ *n*. 自助餐厅

cage /keɪdʒ/ *n*. 笼子

cake /keɪk/ *n*. 蛋糕;饼、糕

calculate /ˈkælkjʊleɪt/ *vi*. 计算;估计

   (考题)It is roughly calculated that in 1997 alone, about 2 to 3 million people died of it.

   calculate on sb. /sth. 指望…

calculator /ˈkælkjʊleɪtə/ *n*. 计算器

   pocket calculator 袖珍计算器

calendar /ˈkælɪndə/ *n*. 日历

call /kɔːl/ *vt*. 大声说出;叫;打电话给;*vi*. 叫、喊;拜访;打电话 *n*.(一次)电话

   call sb. 叫某人;给某人打电话

   call sb. /sth. ... 把某人/物称为…;认为某人/物…

   (考题)Besides, everyone would call you crazy if you tried to kiss every bread roll before you ate them!

   call for ... 需要…;呼吁

   (考题)To call for a delay on commercial nanotech, critics of nanotech make use of the fact that no one is doing molecular manufacturing.

   call in(on sb.) 顺路拜访(某人)

   call sth. off 取消…

   call on sb. to do sth. 呼吁某人做某事

   (考题)The main purpose of the passage is to call on people to

fight against the worldwide water shortage and sanitation problem.

call sb.'s attention to ... 引起某人对···的注意

（考题）... he insisted that Macy's should stock the game and make an effort to call the public's attention to it.

call sth. to mind 想起某事

calm /kɑːm/ *adj.* 镇静的　*n.* 镇静、平静

（考题）If you are lost in the mountains, stay calm in the face of darkness, loneliness and the unknown.

vi. vt. （使）平静、镇静

（考题）It is thought that lighter, soft colours will calm the mind and aid concentration.

camel /ˈkæməl/ *n.* 骆驼

camera /ˈkæmərə/ *n.* 照相机

camp /kæmp/ *n.* 野营　*vi.* 野营、宿营

（考题）Altogether there are around 100 annual music festivals where people camp in the UK.

campaign /kæmˈpeɪn/ *n.* 战役；运动

（考题）The company is starting a new advertising campaign to attract new customers to its stores.

campus /ˈkæmpəs/ *n.* 校园

can¹ /kæn/ *v. aux.* 会；能够；可以

can² /kæn/ *n.* （美）罐头、听 = tin（英）　*v.* 把（食品等）装罐

canned food 罐头食品

canal /kəˈnæl/ *n.* 运河

the Suez Canal 苏伊士运河

the Panama Canal 巴拿马运河

the Grand Canal （中国）大运河

cancel /ˈkænsəl/ *vt.* 取消；删去

cancel sth. 取消···

（考题）... and you may cancel membership at any time after doing so.

cancer /ˈkænsə/ *n.* 癌

candidate /ˈkændɪdeɪt/ *n.* 候选人

candle /ˈkændl/ *n.* 蜡烛

candy /ˈkændɪ/ *n*. 糖果

cap /kæp/ *n*. 帽子

capable /ˈkeɪpəbl/ *adj*. 有能力的；有可能的

be capable of doing sth. 有能力做某事

（考题）... man-made bacteria would be widespread and capable of self-replicating

（辨析：capable 的主语可以是人，也可以是物，表示做某事的"能力、潜力、或可能"；able 一般指人，表示"具有完成某项工作的能力或机能"。）

capital /ˈkæpɪtl/ *n*. 首都；资本　*adj*. 首都的；资本的；主要的

capitalist /ˈkæpɪtəlɪst/ *adj*. 资本的；资本主义的

captain /ˈkæptən/ *n*. 船长；队长；上尉

capture /ˈkæptʃə/ *n*. 占领；俘房　*vt*. 俘获

car /kɑː/ *n*. 汽车；小汽车

carbon /ˈkɑːbən/ *n*. 碳

carbonic /kɑːˈbɒnɪk/ *adj*. 碳的

card /kɑːd/ *n*. 卡片

care /keə/ *n*. 照管；关怀；小心

take care of ... 照顾、照料…；关注

（考题）She takes great care of how she looks and has a great interest in fashion and the lifestyle of famous people.

take care to do sth. /that ... 注意…

（考题）There is a strong bad smell in the air even if you take care to be upwind of the cone.

with care 仔细地

vi. 关心；介意；照顾、护理

care for ... 照顾；喜欢

（考题）Often the elderly are disabled and cannot care for an animal by walking it or playing with it.

care about ... 在乎（多用于否定、疑问、条件句中）

（考题）People care a lot about making a mistake in a speech because they regard speech-making as a kind of performance rather than as an act of communication.

care how/who/why/where/what ... 在乎、介意（多用于否定、疑问、条件句中）

（考题）I don't care what Andrew thinks!

care to do sth. 介意、在乎做某事（否定、疑问、条件句中）

in care of ... 请…转交（信件）

career /kə'rɪə/ *n*. 生涯；职业

（考题）The useful skills developed through the study of philosophy have significant long-term benefits in career advancement.

careful /'keəfʊl/ *adj*. 小心的、仔细的

be careful about/of/with ... 小心、当心、注意…

（考题）Be careful of credit. Credit cards can help you buy necessary things and build a credit history, but they must be used responsibly, which means paying off your debt in time.

（考题）You can never be too careful with that.

be careful to do sth. 小心、注意做某事

be careful that ... 注意…

careless /'keəlɪs/ *adj*. 粗心的，疏忽的

be careless about/of/with ... 在…方面很粗心、不在意

cargo /'kɑːgəʊ/ *n*. （由船、飞机、车辆装载的）货物

carpenter /'kɑːpɪntə/ *n*. 木匠

carpet /'kɑːpɪt/ *n*. 地毯

carriage /'kærɪdʒ/ *n*. 四轮马车

carrot /'kærət/ *n*. 胡萝卜

carry /'kærɪ/ *vt*. 运载；传送；携带；担负

carry sth. 搬、运某物

carry ... away 把…搬走；打动某人

（考题）Normal people may get carried away by words.

carry (sth.) on 继续（…）

（考题）You've got a criminal record. If you carry on like this, you will end up in prison.

carry sth. out 执行…

（考题）Poe has also asked the National Park Service to carry out a "Children's Forest" project in every national park.

carry sth. through (to the end) 将某事进行到底

（考题）They are determined to carry the experiment through to the end.

cartoon /kɑː'tuːn/ *n*. 动画片;漫画

case /keɪs/ *n*. 事例;实例;情况

This/That is the case. 情况就是这样/那样。

(考题)Single-sex conditions are seen as leading to more extreme opinions，and possibly even as encouraging homosexuality，though there is no proof that this is the case.

in this/that case 在这/那种情况下

in some/most cases 在某些/大多数情况下

(考题)The causes of eating disorders are not clear. There may be genetic or biochemical factors in some cases.

in any case 在任何情况下、无论如何

(考题)Most people find it difficult to tell one from another in any case.

(同义词：**by all means, in one way or another, anyway, at any cost**)

in no case 决不

(同义词：**never, by no means, in no way, under no circumstances, on no condition**)

in the case of ... 就…而言

(考题)The application of science and technology to the development and production of weapons of mass destruction has created a real danger to the continued existence of the human race on this planet. We have seen this happen in the case of nuclear weapons.

in case of ... 万一(后面跟短语)

(考题)In case of fire，all exits must be kept clear.

in case ... 万一(后面跟从句)

(考题)Leave your key with a neighbor in case you lock yourself out one day.

cash /kæʃ/ *n*. 现金,现款

pay in cash 付现金(辨析：pay by cheque 用支票支付)

cashier /'kæʃɪə/ *n*. 出纳员;收银员

cassette /kə'set/ *n*. 磁带盒;胶卷暗盒

cast /kɑːst/ *v*. 扔;抛;投

(考题)They learned to use the shadows cast by the sun.

castle /ˈkɑːsl/ *n*. 城堡

a castle in the air 空中楼阁

casual /ˈkæʒuəl/ *adj*. 偶然的；随便的、不经意的

（考题）John was dismissed last week because of his casual attitude towards his job.

cat /kæt/ *n*. 猫

catalog (ue) /ˈkætəlɒg/ *n*. 目录(本、卡) *v*. 编目录

（考题）If the advertisement cannot give full details, catalogues are printed, and each group of goods to be sold together, called a "lot", is usually given a number.

catch /kætʃ/ (caught, caught) *vt*. 抓住；赶上；明白；染上

catch sb./sth. 抓住某人/某物

（考题）... they hardly know a time when computers weren't around, and they eagerly catch the chance to spend hours online, chatting with friends.

catch the train/bus/flight 赶上火车等

catch (a) cold 感冒

（同义词：have a cold, take a cold）

catch sb.'s eye/attention 引起某人的注意

（考题）The return address caught his attention.

catch fire 着火

（考题）The building around the corner caught fire last night. The police are now looking into the matter.

catch hold of 抓住

catch one's breath (因激动、惊讶等)屏住呼吸

catch up with sb./catch sb. up 追上某人

（考题）Trying to slow the Bismarck down so that their ships could catch up with her, the British fired at her form the air.

catch sb. doing sth. 发现某人在做某事

（考题）If one of my players were caught stealing, he'd be gone.

be caught in/by ... 突然遇到…

（考题）I got caught in the rain and my suit has been ruined.

cattle /ˈkætl/ *n*. 牛

cause /kɔːz/ *n*. 起因、原因

cause and effect 因果关系

（考题）Alzheimer's is a serious disease that is said to be the fourth or fifth leading cause of death for people over age 75.

vt. 使发生

cause sth. 引起、导致某事

（考题）Each year diseases related to inadequate water and sanitation kill between 2 and 5 million people and cause an estimated 80 percent of all sicknesses in the developing world.

cause sb. sth. /cause sth. to sb. 给某人造成、带来某事

（考题）Cars do cause us some health problems — in fact far more serious ones than mobile phones do.

cause sb. to do sth. 使某人做某事

cave /keɪv/ *n.* 山洞；地洞；洞穴

CD（compact disc）激光唱片；（计算机）光盘

cease /siːs/ *n.* 停止

    cease-fire 停火

    vi. vt. 停止

    cease (to do, doing) sth. 停止（做）某事

（考题）They have ceaced to trouble themselves with the matter.

ceiling /ˈsiːlɪŋ/ *n.* 天花板

celebrate /ˈselɪbreɪt/ *vt.* 庆祝

cell /sel/ *n.* 细胞

cement /sɪˈment/ *n.* 水泥

cemetery /ˈsemɪtərɪ/ *n.* 墓地、坟地

cent /sent/ *n.* 分（辅币单位）

centigrade /ˈsentɪɡreɪd/ *adj.* 摄氏的；百分度的

centimetre /ˈsentɪmiːtə/ *n.* 厘米（＝1/100 米）

central /ˈsentrəl/ *adj.* 中心的、中央的；主要的

centre /ˈsentə/ *n.* 中心、中央

century /ˈsentʃʊrɪ/ *n.* 世纪、百年

ceremony /ˈserəmənɪ/ *n.* 典礼

    the opening/closing ceremony 开/闭幕式

certain /ˈsɜːtən/ *adj.* 确实的；有把握的；某个、某些

（考题）Our feelings of well-being at any moment are determined to a certain degree by genes.

be certain of/about sth. 对某事有把握

(考题)They are not certain of the safety，so are going to make further researches about it.

be certain that ... 有把握

(考题)While no one is certain what causes these changes in the brain's nerve fibers，their effect is certain.

sb. is certain to do sth. 某人一定会做某事

It is certain for sb. to do sth. /that ... 肯定…

(考题)It seems certain that these "kings of the mountains" are moving.

(注意：在 sb. is certain to do sth. 中，可以用 sure 替换 certain；但在 It is certain ...这一结构中，不能使用 sure。)

for certain 有把握地、肯定地（同义词：for sure）

make sth. certain 弄清楚、使确凿

certainly /ˈsɜːtənlɪ/ *adv*. 无疑地；有把握地；当然；当然可以

certificate /səˈtɪfɪkɪt/ *n*. 证书；证明

chain /tʃeɪn/ *n*. 链条

chair /tʃeə/ *n*. 椅子

chairman /ˈtʃeəmən/((*pl*.) chairmen /ˈtʃeəmən/)*n*. 主席

chalk /tʃɔːk/ *n*. 粉笔

challenge /ˈtʃælɪndʒ/ *n*. 挑战

(考题)He travels widely and enjoys adventures and challenges.

vt. **challenge ...** 向…挑战

(考题)Since words had been out, our friendship was challenged.

champion /ˈtʃæmpɪən/ *n*. 冠军

championship /ˈtʃæmpɪənʃɪp/ *n*. 冠军称号；锦标赛

chance /tʃɑːns/ *n*. 机遇

by chance 碰巧

(考题)... they don't win by chance, but by means of logic and skills.

a chance to do/of doing sth. 做某事的机会

(考题)There are also those for whom hunting in tact otters a chance to prove themselves and risk death by design.

take a chance/take chances 碰运气、冒险

(the) chances are (that) ... 有可能…

（考题）Chances are you'll find the secret if you keep on trying.

change /tʃeɪndʒ/ *n*. 改变、变化

（考题）The change of blood pressure is not linked with the change of emotions.

vi. change（into ...）改变；变成…

（考题）The brain changes throughout our lives according to what we do with it.

vt. change sth. into ... 将某物改变成…

（考题）This practice was later changed into shaking hands among friends on meeting or leaving each other.

change sth. for ... 用某物交换…

change one's mind 改变主意

for a change 换换花样，改变一下

changeable /'tʃeɪndʒəbl/ *adj*. 易变的；可变的

channel /'tʃɒnəl/ *n*. 海峡；（电视）频道

the English Channel 英吉利海峡

chapter /'tʃæptə/ *n*. 章

character /'kærəktə/ *n*. 性质、特性；品质、性格

（考题）Whether it's inborn nature or developed character at work，too much control in the hands at the young isn't healthy for children or the family.

characteristic /ˌkærəktə'rɪstɪk/ *n*. 特征、特性、特色

（考题）Characteristics like strength are partly controlled by the animals' genes.

adj. 特有的

be characteristic of ... 表现了…的特点

（考题）It's characteristic of him. He always does things like that.

charge /tʃɑːdʒ/ *n*. 主管；费用；控告

be in charge of ... 负责…

（考题）Could I speak to whoever is in charge of International Sales，please?

be in sb. 's charge 由某人负责，管理

（考题）The improvement to the present system is in the charge of FCC.

put sb. in charge of ... 让某人负责…

take charge of ... 负责管理…

（考题）Kim has been invited to take charge of the staff meetings.

free of charge 免费

vt. 索价；充电；控告

charge sb. ... for sth. 因某物向某人索要…费用

（考题）They wanted to charge $5,000 for the car, but we managed to bring the price down.

charity /ˈtʃærɪtɪ/ *n.* 仁慈，慈善；救济物品；慈善组织

（考题）The famous charity's appeal to aid postwar Greece had been so successful it had been flooded with donations.

out of charity 出于仁慈、善心

charm /tʃɑːm/ *n.* 魅力

charming /ˈtʃɑːmɪŋ/ *adj.* 迷人的

chart /tʃɑːt/ *n.* 图表

chase /tʃeɪs/ *v.，n.* 追逐；驱赶

chase sb. 追赶、追逐某人

chase sb. from/out of 把某人赶出…

chat /tʃæt/ *vi. n.* 闲谈、聊天

chat with sb. about sth. 与某人闲聊某事

cheap /tʃiːp/ *adj.* 便宜的、廉价的

cheat /tʃiːt/ *v.* 欺骗；作弊

cheat sb. out of ... 骗走某人的…

cheat in the exam 考试作弊

check /tʃek/ *n.* 检查；核对；（美）支票

checklist 清单

medical check 体检

pay by check 用支票支付

v. 检查；核对

check ... 检查…；阻止、遏制…

（考题）Sky divers don't go up in an airplane without checking the parachutes beforehand.

check in 报到；检票进站；登记入住

check out 清点、检查；结账；离开

(考题)Come for the music and stay to check out some relevant books for the rest of the week!

checkout /ˈtʃekaʊt/ *n.* (超级市场等的)收银台

cheek /tʃiːk/ *n.* 面颊

cheer /tʃɪə/ *n.* 振奋；喝彩；情绪 *vt.* 使振奋、高兴；*vi.* 感到振奋、高兴；欢呼、喝彩

    cheer (sb.) up (使某人)高兴起来、振作起来！

    cheer (for) sb. 为某人欢呼、喝彩

cheerful /ˈtʃɪəfʊl/ *adj.* 愉快的、高兴的

cheese /tʃiːz/ *n.* 奶酪

chemical /ˈkemɪkəl/ *n.* 化学药品(常用复数) *adj.* 化学的

    chemical change 化学变化

    chemical reaction 化学反应

chemist /ˈkemɪst/ *n.* 药剂师；药商

chemistry /ˈkemɪstrɪ/ *n.* 化学

cheque /tʃek/ *n.* (英)支票

chess /tʃes/ *n.* 国际象棋

chest /tʃest/ *n.* 胸；胸部

chew /tʃuː/ *vt.* 咀嚼

chicken /ˈtʃɪkən/ *n.* 小鸡；鸡肉

chief /tʃiːf/ *n.* 首领；上司、头头 *adj.* 主要的

    chief engineer 总工程师

    chief manager 总经理

child /tʃaɪld/ (*pl.* children /ˈtʃɪldrən/) *n.* 孩子

    Cildren's Day 儿童节

childhood /ˈtʃaɪldhʊd/ *n.* 童年；幼年

childish /ˈtʃaɪldɪʃ/ *adj.* 孩子般的；幼稚的

chill /tʃɪl/ *n.* 寒冷；着凉 *adj.* 冷的

chimney /ˈtʃɪmnɪ/ *n.* 烟囱

china /ˈtʃaɪnə/ *n.* 瓷器

chocolate /ˈtʃɒklɪt/ *n.* 巧克力

choice /tʃɔɪs/ *n.* 选择、抉择

    make a choice 作出选择

(考题)No more hesitation. You have to make a choice now.

    have no choice but to do sth. 只能做某事

(考题)Parents have no choice but to try to accept it.

(同义词：**have no alternative but to do sth.，can do nothing but do sth.，have nothing to do but do sth.**)

choose /tʃuːz/ (chose，chosen) v. 选择、挑选

choose ... 选择…

(考题)Faced with the necessity for women to choose between home and workplace，Western society began to give particular attention to the role of women as homemakers with more energy than ever before.

choose to do sth. 选择做某事

(考题)Thinking is something you choose to do as a fish chooses to live in water.

chop /tʃɒp/ v. 砍、劈、斩 n. 排骨肉

chopsticks /'tʃɒpstɪks/ (pl.) n. 筷子

Christian /'krɪstʃən/ n. 基督教徒 adj. 基督教的

church /tʃɜːtʃ/ n. 教堂、礼拜堂;(常 C～)教会组织;教派

  go to church 做礼拜

cigar /sɪ'gɑː/ n. 雪茄烟

cigarette /sɪgə'ret/ n. 香烟、卷烟、纸烟

cinema /'sɪnɪmə/ n. 电影院

  go to the cinema 看电影

  (同义词：**go to the films, go to the movies**)

circle /'sɜːkl/ n. 圆;环状物 vt. 环绕;圈出 vi. 盘旋

  in political/economic circle 在政界/经济界

  circle ... 绕…运动

circular /'sɜːkjʊlə/ a. 圆(形)的、环形的;环行的、循环的

circumstance /'sɜːkəmstəns/ n. (常用复数)情况;环境

  (考题)More than anyone else，children are on the receiving end of their parents' improved circumstances.

  under ... circumstances 在…情况下

  under no circumstances 任何情况下都不能、绝不

  (见 case)

citizen /'sɪtɪzən/ n. 公民

city /'sɪtɪ/ n. 城市

civil /'sɪvl/ adj. 公民的;民用的

civil engineering 土木工程

civil law 民法

civilian /sɪˈvɪljən/ *n.* 平民　*adj.* 平民的

civilization /ˌsɪvɪlaɪˈzeɪʃən/ *n.* 文明；文化；教养

（考题）Throughout history, the language spoken by a powerful group spreads across a civilization.

civilize /ˈsɪvɪlaɪz/ *vt.* 使文明；使开化

claim /kleɪm/ *vt.* 宣称；要求（应得权利）；认领

claim to be/have done/be doing sth. 声称是/已经/正在…

（考题）Many firms already claim to be "customer-driven" or "consumer-centred".

claim that ... 声称…

（考题）Yesterday he proudly claimed in court that despite his complete lack of medical experience or qualifications, he had saved several people's lives.

claim sth. as ... /to be ... 声称某物…

（考题）A territory is an area that an animal, usually the male, claims as its own.

claim sth. 认领；要求得到

clap /klæp/ *vi.* 拍手；鼓掌　*vt.* 拍打

（考题）As the president ended his speech, we clapped politely and pushed back our chairs.

class /klɑːs/ *n.* 班级；课；等级

first-class 一流的；一等的

upper/middle/lower classes 上层/中层/下层社会

classic /ˈklæsɪk/ *n.* 经典作品；经典作家　*adj.* 经典的；古典的

（考题）As a leading publishing house, we are trying to make classics convenient for readers but it's not as if we're withdrawing the original versions.

classical /ˈklæsɪkəl/ *adj.* 经典的；古典的

（考题）Whether one listens to classical music or rock, whether one obeys the speed limit while driving, whether one encourages one's husband or wife to express his or her own ideas — all are influenced by attitudes.

classify /ˈklæsɪfaɪ/ *vt.* 归类，分类

classmate /ˈklɑːsmeɪt/ *n*. 同班同学

classroom /ˈklɑːsrʊm/ *n*. 教室

clean /kliːn/ *adj*. 清洁的、干净的　*vt*. 打扫

cleaner /ˈkliːnə/ *n*. 清洁工；吸尘器

clear /klɪə/ *adj*. 清楚的；清晰的；摆脱的

　be clear of/about sth. 对某事很清楚

　（考题）In choosing how to put out a fire, we should first be clear about when it breaks out.

　be/keep clear of ... 避开、摆脱…

　（考题）All streets must be kept clear of ice to ensure the traffic safety.

　It is clear that ... 显然…

　（考题）It becomes clear from the text that the driving force behind green products is public caring for environment.

　make ... clear (to sb.) （对某人）讲清楚、澄清某事

　（考题）He also made it perfectly clear that free food would be offered at all future events.

　vt. *vi*. 清除；(使)明朗

　clear sth. away 清除

　clear sth. of ... 把…从某物上清除、除去

　（考题）This detergent can clear your clothes of most of the dirt.

　clear ... off sth. 把…从某物上清除

　（考题）It snowed heavily last night and people are now clearing the snow off the streets.

　clear up 变得晴朗、开朗；收拾

　（考题）It shouldn't take long to clear up after the party if we all volunteer to help.

　clear sth. up 澄清某事；整理、收拾

　（考题）Something as simple as drinking some cold water may clear your mind and relieve pressure.

clerk /klɑːk/ *n*. 职员、办事员

clever /ˈklevə/ *adj*. 聪明的；灵巧的

click /klɪk/ *n*. 咔嗒声　*v*. (使)发出咔嗒声；(用鼠标)点击

cliff /klɪf/ *n*. 悬崖

climate /ˈklaɪmɪt/ *n*. 气候

（辨析：climate 是指某地在相当长的一段时间内总的气候状况，
而 weather 则表示某一时刻具体的天气情况。）

climb /klaɪm/ *v*. 爬；攀登

climber /ˈklaɪmə/ *n*. 爬山者；攀登者

clinic /ˈklɪnɪk/ *n*. 诊所；讲习所

clock /klɒk/ *n*. (时)钟

　　round-the-clock 昼夜不停的

　　round the clock 昼夜不停

　　（考题）And they can shop around the clock，buying something
　　simply by making a phone call.

　　work against the clock 拼命赶时间

　　set the clock 对时

　　wind the clock 上发条

clone /kləʊn/ *n*. 无性繁殖；克隆 *vt*. 使无性繁殖；克隆

close¹ /kləʊs/ *adj*. 接近的；亲密的；严密的　　*adv*. 接近、靠近

　　（考题）Photos record the beauties of nature. They can also bring
　　things close that are far away.

　　be close to ... 离…很近

　　（考题）If they are close to confessing a crime, the blue on the
　　wall might tip the balance.

　　keep a close watch on ... 对…严密监视

　　（考题）By paying closer attention to some important signs in
　　nature，we can become better prepared for any kind of
　　weather.

　　a close friend 亲密朋友

　　close relationship 亲密关系

　　close ties 紧密联系

　　close cooperation 密切合作

close² /kləʊz/ *vi*. 关，闭；*vt*. 关、闭某物

　　（考题）Last month pipes almost broke again and roads had to be
　　closed for a while.

　　close one's eyes to ... 对…视而不见

closed /kləʊst/ *adj*. 关闭的

　　be closed 关闭的；关门

　　（考题）And without a degree from a prestigious university, they fear that many of life's doors will remain forever closed.

cloth /klɒθ/ *n*. 布；织物

clothes /kləʊðz/ *n*. (*pl*.) 衣服

clothing /ˈkləʊðɪŋ/ *n*. (总称)衣服

cloud /klaʊd/ *n*. 云；烟尘

cloudy /ˈklaʊdɪ/ *adj*. 多云的

club /klʌb/ *n*. 俱乐部

clue /kluː/ *n*. 线索；提示

(考题)By using limited clues to provide us with a rapid opinion of other people or places, we may choose to limit our communication.

coach /kəʊtʃ/ *n*. (铁路)车厢；公共汽车；教练　*vt*. 训练、指导

(考题)The overly willful and unbending child may have trouble obeying teachers or coaches, for example, or trouble keeping friends.

coal /kəʊtʃ/ *n*. 煤

coast /kəʊst/ *n*. 海岸

coat /kəʊt/ *n*. (动物的)皮毛；上衣；外套

cock /kɒk/ *n*. 公鸡

code /kəʊd/ *n*. 密码；代号

　Zip Code, zip code 邮政编码(英)　**postcode**

coffee /ˈkɒfɪ/ *n*. 咖啡

coin /kɔɪn/ *n*. 硬币

coincidence /kəʊˈɪnsɪdəns/ *n*. 巧合

Coke /kəʊk/ *n*. 可口可乐

cold /kəʊld/ *adj*. 冷的、寒冷的　*n*. 伤风、感冒

　catch (a) cold 得了感冒

　have a cold 得了感冒

　get a cold 得了感冒

　take a cold 得了感冒

collapse /kəˈlæps/ *vi*. 塌下；崩溃

(考题)Wars break out as countries fight for food. A year later civilization has collapsed. No more than 10 million people have survived.

collar /ˈkɒlə/ *n*. 衣领；(动物)颈圈

the white/blue-collared 白领/蓝领

colleague /ˈkɒliːg/ *n*. 同事

collect /kəˈlekt/ *vt*. *vi*. 收集，采集；聚集

　　collect sth. 收集、汇集…

　　（考题）For storm chasing, the first thing storm chasers do is to collect information about a coming storm.

collection /kəˈlekʃən/ *n*. 收集；收藏品

　　（考题）The collection of happy actions broadly categorized as "honor" help you create this life of good feelings.

college /ˈkɒlɪdʒ/ *n*.（综合大学中的）学院；（独立的）学院

colour /ˈkʌlə/ *n*. 颜色

coloured /ˈkʌləd/ *adj*. 彩色的；涂色的

column /ˈkɒləm/ *n*. 柱、支柱，柱状物；印刷的纵列；专栏

comb /kəʊm/ *n*. 梳子　*vt*. 梳理

combination /ˌkɒmbɪˈneɪʃən/ *n*. 结合

　　（考题）His eyes were wet and there was a combination of love and respect on his face.

combine /kənˈbaɪn/ *v*.（使）结合

　　combine sth. with sth. 把…与…结合起来

　　（考题）... had the idea of combining the real excitement of a treasure hunt with clues found in a book when he wrote a children's story.

come /kʌm/（came，come）*vi*. 来

　　come about 发生；造成

　　come across 碰到、巧遇

　　（考题）Almost every day we come across situations in which we have to make decisions one way or another.

　　come around 来（看望某人）；到来

　　come down 跌落；下降

　　come from 来自；原因在于

　　（考题）Death will come mainly from accidents, murder and war.

　　come into being 出现；开始存在

　　come into effect/force 开始生效

　　come on 进行；上演；赶快，来吧

　　（考题）"Come on!" My friend Alex encouraged me to join him

as he jogged by my house every evening. "You'll feel great."

come out 出来；出版；结果、结局

（考题）Her 1998 book about the death of her work shot to the top of the New York Times best-selling list as soon as it came out.

come to (life/oneself) 苏醒

（考题）Frank suddenly came to life. The cigarette fell from his lips as he let out a shout that could be heard halfway down the street.

come to ... 说到…

（考题）Armstrong had no equal when it came to playing the American popular song.

come up to ... 朝…走来；没有辜负…

come up with 提出

（考题）If scientists come up with some sort of pill or diet that would slow aging, could we possibly make it to 150-or beyond?

come to do sth. （经过变化而）做某事

（考题）He came to realize the importance of the time with his family.

come ＋ adj. 变得…

（考题）The boy's dreams came true at last.

comedian /kəˈmiːdjən/ *n.* 喜剧演员

comedy /ˈkɒmɪdɪ/ *n.* 喜剧

comfort /ˈkʌmfət/ *vt.* 使舒适；安慰 *n.* 舒适；安慰

live in comfort 生活舒适

comfortable /ˈkʌmfətəbl/ *adj.* 舒畅的、舒适的

command /kəˈmɑːnd/ *n.* 指挥；*vt.* 指挥；掌握；博得

under sb.'s command 在某人指挥下

have a good command of ... 很好地掌握了…

（考题）Many people believed that the Bismarck could not be defeated because she was under Luetjens' command.

command sb. to do sth. 命令某人做某事

command that ... 命令（从句中虚拟语气）

（考题）He commanded that the building be searched again.

commander /kəˈmɑːndə/ *n.* 司令员，指挥官

comment /ˈkɒmənt/ *n.* 评论

  make a comment on sth. 对某事发表评论

  （考题）What's your comment on pop music?

  vt. **comment on/upon sth.** 对某事发表评论

  comment that ... 发表意见说…

commerce /ˈkɒməs/ *n.* 商业；贸易

commercial /kəˈmɜːʃəl/ *adj.* 商业的；营利的　*n.* 商业广告

commit /kəˈmɪt/ *vt.* 犯罪、干坏事；答应做某事；承担义务

  commit suiside 自杀

  commit a crime 犯罪

  commit/be committed to (doing) sth. 答应（做某事）

  （考题）He has committed to offering us more imformation.

  commit oneself to (doing) sth. 答应、承诺做某事

committee /kəˈmɪtɪ/ *n.* 委员会

common /ˈkɒmən/ *adj.* 一般的、普通的；共同的；通常的

  common sense 常识

  common knowledge 常识；众所周知的事

  common diseases 常见病

  common interests 共同利益

  have sth. in common 有共同之处

  （考题）What do these three books have in common?

communicate /kəˈmjuːnɪkeɪt/ *vi.* 通讯；交流

  communicate with sb. 与某人交流

communication /kəˌmjuːnɪˈkeɪʃən/ *n.* 传播；通讯；交流；交通（或通讯）工具

  means of communication 交流、通信手段

  （考题）Great cultural changes led to more open communication and a more democratic process that encourages everyone to have a say.

communist /ˈkɒmjʊnɪst/ *adj.* 共产主义的

  the Communist Party of China 中国共产党

community /kəˈmjuːnɪtɪ/ *n.* 社会；社区；团体

companion /kemˈpænɪən/ *n.* 伴侣、同伴

  （考题）It is such comforting companions I wish to keep.

company /ˈkʌmpənɪ/ *n.* 公司；陪伴、伙伴

(考题)I would miss the company of people because I know I'd like to have someone to share experiences with.

in company with sb. 和某人一起

in sb.'s company 陪伴某人

(考题)I really love your company but I also need some privacy. So please call before you come over.

keep company with sb. / keep sb. company 与某人相伴

comparative /kəmˈpærətɪv/ *adj.* 相比较而言、相对的

compare /kəmˈpeə/ *vt.* 比较；对照

compare ... with ... 拿…与…相比较

(考题)First unless we remember how short our own lives are compared with the whole human history，we are likely to think our own interests are much more important than they really are.

compare ... to ... 把…比喻成…

(考题)Some have even compared this power to that of a dog with an ability to find out the drugs hidden in the baggage.

can't compare with ... 无法与…相提并论

comparison /kəmˈpærɪsn/ *n.* 比较

beyond comparison 无法相比的

by comparison 比较起来、通过比较

(考题)By comparison，a fast food meal with a hamburger is a steal at $480.

in comparison with ... 与…相比

(考题)Both are based on the mistaken belief that one's self-respect relies on how well one performs in comparison with others.

There's no comparison between ... 没法相比

compete /kəmˈpiːt/ *vi.* 比赛、竞争

competition /ˌkɒmpɪˈtɪʃen/ *n.* 比赛、竞争

competitive /kəˈpetɪtɪv/ *adj.* 竞争(或比赛)性的；(商品等)有竞争力的

complain /kəmˈpleɪn/ *vt.* 抱怨；*vi.* 抱怨说

complain about/of sth. to sb. 向某人抱怨某事

(考题)Rather than a small town where English teachers often complain of feeling like a goldfish in a bond，many people choose to live in Tokyo.

complain that ... 抱怨说…

（考题）Many experts complain that media too often take advantage of the science fiction aspects of nanotech.

complaint /kəmˈpleɪnt/ *n*. 抱怨

make a complaint about sth. to sb. 向某人抱怨某事

complete /kəmˈpliːt/ *adj*. 完整的；全部的

（考题）The book is a complete introduction to all the best Indian films.

vt. **complete sth.** 完成某事

（考题）Radcliffe，who failed to complete the Olympic marathon and the 10,000m last August，said："Athens made me a stronger person and it made me care less about criticism."

completion /kəmˈpliːʃən/ *n*. 完成、完工

（考题）You can always agree upon a completion time with the supplier of the service.

complex /ˈkɒmpleks/ *adj*. 组合的；复杂的

（考题）Researchers find that，on average，wealthier people are happier. But the link between money and happiness is complex.

a complex sentence 复合句

complicated /ˈkɒmplɪkeɪtɪd/ *adj*. 复杂的

（考题）There is nothing more complicated than that about Americans tipping in restaurants.

compliment /ˈkɒplɪmənt/ *n*. 赞美

comply /kəmˈplaɪ/ *vi*. 符合；遵守

comply with ... 符合、遵守…

（考题）Those who do not comply with the law will be punished.

compose /kəmˈpəuz/ *vt*. 作文、创作（乐曲、诗歌等）；构成

compose sth. 创作…

（考题）Mussorgsky composed the piece in 1874 after the death，at the age of 39，of the artist Victor Hartmann.

be composed of ... 由…组成

composer /kəmˈpəuzə/ *n*. 作曲家

composition /kɒmpəˈzɪʃən/ *n*. 作文；乐曲；组成、构成

（考题）I wrote and arranged a lot of musical compositions since few had been written specially for solo percussionists.

compound /ˈkɒmpaʊnd/ *n*. 复合物；复合词 *adj*. 复合的

a compound sentence 并列句

comprehension /ˌkɒmprəˈhenʃən/ *n*. 理解（力）；包含；广泛性

comprehensive /ˌkɒmprəˈhensɪv/ *adj*. 广泛的；综合的；理解的；有理解力的

（考题）Reporters from around the globe provide you with a comprehensive world view.

compute /kəmˈpjuːt/ *v*. 计算

computer /kəmˈpjuːtə/ *n*. 计算机

conceal /kənˈsiːl/ *vt*. 隐藏

conceal sth. from sb. 向某人掩藏、掩盖某事

concentrate /ˈkɒnsəntreɪt/ *vi*. 集中；专心 *vt*. 将…集中用

concentrate (sth.) on ... （将…）集中在…

（考题）He decided to concentrate on positive emotions as a way to treat some of the symptoms of his disease.

concentration /ˌkɒnsənˈtreɪʃən/ *n*. 集中（注意力）；专心

（考题）It is thought that strong blues will stimulate clear thought and lighter, soft colours will calm the mind and aid concentration.

concept /ˈkɒnsept/ *n*. 概念；理论；想法

（考题）Green Olympics is one of the three concepts of the Beijing Games.

concern /kənˈsɜːn/ *n*. 关心

show/have concern about sth. 关心某事

（考题）In writing this passage, the author mainly intends to show his concern about children's lack of experience in nature.

vt. 与…有关；使关心；使担心 *vi*. 关心；担心；忧虑

concern sb. with sth. 使某人担心、关心某事

（考题）She concerned herself with current social problems.

be concerned with/about ... 为…担心

（考题）North America was mainly concerned with survival and beyond that, its own economic prosperity.

be concerned in ... 与…有关系、有牵连

so/as far as ... is concerned 就…而言

（考题）As far as I'm concerned，the story's only just begun.

concert /ˈkɒnsɜːt/ *n*. 音乐会

conclude /kənˈkluːd/ *v*. 结束；推论；缔结

　conclude sth. 结束某事；得出结论

　conclude that . . . 得出结论…

　（考题）After years of study，researchers have concluded that it's what's inside that matters，not just the size of the brain.

conclusion /kənˈkluːʃən/ *n*. 结束；结局；结论、推论

　（考题）Read the news from different views and draw your own conclusions on the stories shaping our world.

concrete /ˈkɒnkriːt/ *n*. 混凝土　*adj*. 混凝土的；具体的、实在的

condition /kənˈdɪʃən/ *n*. 环境；状况；条件

　（考题）The information of the global climate conditions in the past can be obtained through studying the ice and air caught in each layer.

　（考题）There doesn't seem to be any chance if the serious condition of our birds is not improved.

　in good/out of condition 处于完好/损坏状态

　（同义词：**in good working condition, in（good）order, out of order**；另见 **wrong**。）

　on condition that . . . 条件是…

　（考题）Dad told me I could drive him into a distant village called Mijas，on condition that I took the car in to be serviced at a nearby garage.

　on no condition 绝不可以（见 **case**）

　living/working conditions 生活/工作条件

　（注意：condition 在表示事物本身状况时，使用单数形式；而在表示外部条件时，是用复数形式。）

conduct /kənˈdʌkt/ *vt*. 进行；指挥；导电

　conduct sth. 进行、指导某事

　conduct . . . to/into/out of . . . 把…引导到/…

　（考题）Lauren Smith conducted her research by monitoring sharks' reaction to weather changes.

conductor /kənˈdʌktə/ *n*. （汽、电车上的）售票员；（乐队的）指挥；导体

conference /ˈkɒnfərəns/ n. (正式的)会议;讨论会

confess /kənˈfes/ vt. 承认;坦白

confess (doing) sth. to sb. 向某人承认、忏悔(做了)某事

(考题)If they are close to confessing a crime, the blue on the wall might tip the balance.

confess that ... 承认…

confidence /ˈkɒnfɪdəns/ n. 信任;信心

self-confidence 自信

(考题)I would have to ring doorbells, address adults with self-confidence, and persuade them by saying that no one, no matter how poor, could afford to be without the Saturday Evening Post in the home.

have/put/lack confidence in ... 对…有/缺乏信心

(考题)Your child may always seem to expect the worst to happen and lack confidence in his or her ability to deal with any challenge.

with confidence 有信心地

confident /ˈkɒnfɪdənt/ adj. 有信心的;自信的

be confident of/about ... /that ... 对…有信心;相信

(考题)But they also feel less confident about their parenting skills.

confirm /kənˈfɜːm/ vt. 证实;确认

confirm sth. 证实、肯定、批准某事

conflict /ˈkɒnflɪkt/ n. 冲突 vi. 争论;战斗

confuse /kənˈfjuːz/ vt. 使混乱;使困惑

confuse sb. 使某人糊涂、迷惑

(考题)This phenomenon confused scientists for years until a recent study found that people tend to sympathize with fellow humans.

be confused (about ...) (对…)感到困惑

(考题)Scientists are still confused about contagious yawning.

confuse sth. with sth. 混淆…与…

congratulate /kənˈɡrætjʊleɪt/ vt. 祝贺;向…道喜

congratulate sb. on sth. 就某事向某人表示祝贺

(考题)... his friends had come to congratulate him on his luck.

congratulation /kənˌgrætjuˈleɪʃən/ *n*. 祝贺、道喜；贺词

congratulations to sb. on sth. 就某事向某人祝贺

（注意：在向别人表示祝贺时，congratulation 用复数形式。）

congress /ˈkɒŋgres/ *n*. 代表大会；立法机关

connect /kəˈnekt/ *vt*. 连接；联系

connect sth. with/to sth. 使…相连接

（考题）According to Hugo Critchley, emotions are connected with states of internal responses.

conquer /ˈkɒŋkə/ *vt*. 攻克、征服

conquer sth. /sb. 征服…

（考题）By saying "The only way to cure is to conquer," Dr. Mootee suggests that an OCD sufferer must cure his illness by himself.

conscience /ˈkɒnʃəns/ *n*. 良心

conscious /ˈkɒnʃəs/ *adj*. 意识到的；神志清醒的

be conscious of/that ... 意识到、明白…

（考题）He's quite conscious of the possible outcome.

consequence /ˈkɒnsɪkwʊəns/ *n*. 结果；后果；重要（性）

consider /kənˈsɪdə/ *vt*. 认为；考虑

consider (doing) sth. 考虑（做）某事

（考题）However, if you can't afford these costs, then you should consider staying in hotels where the cheapest twin rooms with shared bathroom ...

consider ... as/(to be) ... 认为…是…/怎么样

（考题）Their study found that theobromine, found in cocoa, was nearly a third more effective in stopping coughs than codeine, which was considered the best cough medicine at present.

considerate /kənˈsɪdərɪt/ *adj*. 体谅他人的

It's considerate of sb. to do sth. 某人考虑得真周到

consideration /kənsɪdəˈreɪʃən/ *n*. 考虑

in consideration of ... 考虑到…

take sth. into consideration 对某事加以考虑

（同义词：take sth. into account；反义：leave sth. out of consideration/account）

consist /kənˈsɪst/ *vi*. 由…组成

consist of ... 由…组成

（考题）The brain consists of "grey matter" and it has been suggested that smaller brain appears to work faster.

（同义词：**be made up of , be composed of**）

consist in 在于、寓于…之中

（考题）Happiness does not necessarily consist in money.

constant /'kɒnstənt/ *adj .* 经常的、不断地

construct /kən'strʌkt/ *vt .* 建造；构建

consult /kən'sʌlt/ *vt .* 请教；查阅

consult sth ./sb. 查阅、请教

（考题）Not all hotels are equal, of course, and it's a good idea to consult a guidebook with a good reputation.

consult with sb . about sth. 与某人商讨某事

consume /kən'sjuːm/ *vt .* 消耗；耗尽 *vi .* 耗尽

consume sth. 消耗…

consumer /kən'sjuːmə/ *n .* 消费者

contact /'kɒntækt/ *n .* 接触；联系

（考题）Regular contact can remove the strange ideas about the opposite-sex and lead to more natural relationships.

be in/out of contact with sb. 与某人有/没有联系

（考题）... each member must fulfill a number of personal and occupational role and be in contact with many other members.

bring ... into contact with 使…与…接触

come/get in(to) contact with 与…建立联系

keep in contact with 与…保持联系

lose contact with 与…失去联系

（同义词：上列各短语中，可以用 touch 替换 contact。）

vt . 与…接触；与…联系

contact sb. 与某人联系、接触

（考题）Liz is someone I look up to but she hasn't spoken to me since last year and if she really cared for me, I'm sure she would have contacted me.

contain /kən'teɪn/ *vt .* 包含、含有；控制、遏制

contain sth. 包含、包括…；控制、遏制…

container /kən'teɪnə/ *n .* 容器；集装箱

contemporary /kən'tempərərɪ/ *adj*. 当代的；同一时代的

（考题）Clearly，he was a writer who knew how to interest contemporary children.

content /'kɒntənt/ *n*.（常 *pl*.）内容；目录

table of contents 目录

contest /'kɒntest/ *n*. 竞赛、比赛；争夺；竞争

a maths contest 数学竞赛

a speaking contest 演讲比赛

context /'kɒntekst/ *n*. 上下文；语境

continent /'kɒntɪnənt/ *n*. 大陆

the Continent 欧洲大陆

continental /ˌkɒntɪ'nentl/ *adj*. 大陆的

continual /kən'tɪnʊəl/ *adj*. 继续的；反复不断的

（考题）In Fleet Street the man was under continual pressure.

（辨析：continual 表示"反反复复的"相当于 at short intervals；而 continuous 则强调"持续不断的"，即 uninterrupted。）

continue /kən'tɪnjuː/ *vt*. 使继续；使连续　*vi*. 继续；连续

（考题）If your sleep problem continues for a few nights，you could suffer serious problems.

continue（to do /doing）sth. 继续（做）某事

（考题）As we continue to overheat our weak planet，it can only be hoped that other animal species will adapt as extraordinarily well to change as the desert elephant.

continue that . . . 继续说道…

contract /'kɒntrækt/ *n*. 合同

contrary /'kɒntrərɪ/ *n*. 相反、反面

（考题）Being too anxious to help an event develop often reaults in the contrary to our intention.

be contrary to . . . 与…相反

on the contrary 恰恰相反

（考题）I don't like that fellow. On the contrary，I don't even want to see him.

contrast /'kɒntrɑːst/ *n*. 对比、对照

by contrast 对比；与之相比

in contrast with（to）. . . 与…相比

（考题）In contrast，bringing the error to the clerk's attention causes different things to happen.

contribute /kən'trɪbjuːt/ *vt*. 贡献；捐助；*vi*. 贡献；捐款；促使

contribute (sth.) to sth. （将…）贡献、捐赠给…

contribute to ... 促使、助长…

（考题）Careless methods of production and lack of consumer demand for environment friendly products have contributed to the pollution problem.

contribution /ˌkɒntrɪ'bjuːʃən/ *n*. 贡献；捐献；捐助

make contributions to sth. 对…作出贡献

control /kən'trəʊl/ *n*. 控制、支配

beyond/out of control 失去控制、无法控制

（考题）Mr. Drexler himself thought that self-replicating machines could probably go out of control.

have/gain/take control of/over ... 取得对…的控制

I'm able to take control of the situation.

lose control of/over ... 失去对…的控制

（考题）He's got himself into a dangerous situation where he is likely to lose control over the plane.

have/bring sth. under control 控制住…

（考题）Men can do nothing without its permission，and it fastens its young round people's wrists so that everywhere men go they are still under its control.

vt. 控制

control sth. /sb. 控制住某事/某人

（考题）This kind of activity must be strictly controlled because even a slight movement in the wrong direction will lead to a mistake.

convenience /kən'viːnjəns/ *n*. 方便

（考题）Among all the conveniences of computerized testing， there are some limits.

to sb. 's convenience 对某人方便

convenient /kən'viːnjənt/ *adj*. 方便的；提供便利的

be convenient to sb. 对某人方便的

it is convenient for sb. to do sth. 某人做某事很方便

conversation /ˌkɒnvəˈseɪʃən/ *n.* 谈话、交谈

convey /kənˈveɪ/ *vt.* 运送、传送；传导；表达；转达

    convey ...（to ...） 把…运送、转达(给…)

    （考题）Through a range of surprising contrast, Mussorgsky manages to convey the spirit of the artist and his work.

convince /kənˈvɪːns/ *vt.* 使确信、说服

    convince sb.（of sth.） 使某人相信(某事)

    （考题）The best way to get rid of a negative self-image is to realize that your image is far from objective, and to actively convince yourself of your positive qualities.

    convince sb. that ... 使某人相信…

cook /kʊk/ *n.* 厨师　　*vt.* 烹调

cooker /ˈkʊkə/ *n.* 炊具

cool /kuːl/ *adj.* 凉的；凉爽的

cooperate /kəʊˈɒpəreɪt/ *vi.* 合作、协作；配合

    cooperate with sb. 与某人合作

cope /kəʊp/ *vi.* 对付、应付；处理

    cope with ... 应付、对付…

    （考题）And to cope with the British summer, the cardboard has been made waterproof.

    （见 attend to）

copy /ˈkɒpɪ/ *n.* 抄件、副本；拷贝　　*vt.* 抄写

    （考题）Our bodies synchronise and when we like the other person, we even copy his behivour.

corn /kɔːn/ *n.* 谷物；玉米

corner /ˈkɔːnə/ *n.* 角落；拐角　　*vt.* 将……逼入困境

    at/on/round the corner 在转角处(指外角)

    in the corner 在角落里(指内角)

    （考题）Whatever it was, it has become a good example of how a little mistake can trap you in a more serious moral corner.

corporation /ˌkɔːpəˈreɪʃən/ *n.* 法人(团体)；公司

correct /kəˈrekt/ *adj.* 正确的　　*vt.* 改正、纠正

corridor /ˈkɒrɪdɔː/ *n.* 走廊

cost /kɒst/ *vt.*（cost, cost）价钱为；化费

    cost（sb.）sth.（to do sth.） 花费(某人)…做某事

（考题）The Buddy devices will cost the average store about $160,000, and the Concierge will cost stores about $500 for each device.

（注意：cost 的主语是物。在表示"花了多少钱做某事"时，上述短语同 sb. spend ... on sth., sb. spend ... doing sth.）

n. 费用；成本

at a cost of ... 以…的代价、花了…钱

（考题）We offer morning or afternoon classes, both of which last three months and a half at a cost of 800 yuan.

at any cost/at all costs 不惜任何代价、无论如何

at the cost of ... 以…为代价

cotton /ˈkɒtən/ *n.* 棉花

cough /kɒf/ *v.*, *n.* 咳嗽

count /kaʊnt/ *n.* 数数

keep count of ... 数…的数量

（考题）Existing pedometers normally clip onto a belt or slip into a pocket and keep count of steps by measuring sudden movement.

vi. 数数；起作用 *vt.* 清点；计算

count sth. 数某物

（考题）Count your steps so that you know how far you have gone and note any landmarks such as tower blocks or hills which can help to find out where you are.

count sth./sb. as/among ... , count ... +*adj.* 认为某物/人…

（考题）He's never against you. you can surely count him as a support of your plan.

count on sb. (to do/doing sth) 指望、依靠某人（做某事）

（考题）He found no one here to count on to do the job.

counter /ˈkaʊntə/ *n.* 柜台

country /ˈkʌntri/ *n.* 国家；乡下

the country 乡下

countryside /ˈkʌntrɪsaɪd/ *n.* 农村地区、乡下

county /ˈkaʊntɪ/ *n.* 郡（英国最大的地方行政区）；县（美国）

couple /ˈkʌpl/ *n.* 夫妻；一对；一双

a couple of 一、两个；少数

courage /ˈkʌrɪdʒ/ *n*. 勇气

lose courage 失去勇气

pluck/summon up one's courage 鼓起勇气

course /kɔːs/ *n*. 过程；课程

（考题）Although many students have chosen to join the course with a reasonable motivation，we considered it important to note what seemed to encourage interest.

in the course of ... 在…的过程中

（考题）In the course of working my way through school，I took many jobs I would rather forget.

of course 当然、自然

in/during/over the course of ... 在…长的时间里

（考题）Or they might have been the result of dinosaurs getting stuck one after another over a course of a few centuries.

court /kɔːt/ *n*. 球场；法院

cousin /ˈkʌzen/ *n*. 堂（或表）兄弟；堂（或表）姐妹

cover /ˈkʌve/ *n*. 盖子；封面

read from cover to cover 从头读到尾

under the cover of ... 在…的掩护下

vt. 盖上；走完；付费用；占面积；涉及

（考题）The money comes straight out of your account，so you can spend as much as you like as long as you have enough money （or an agreed overdraft）to cover it.

（考题）Oceans cover three-quarters of the Earth's surface — that would make wave power seem ideal for creating energy throughout the world，though there are some weak points yet to overcome.

（考题）Movies to be shown in the festival cover different subjects.

cover ... with sth. 用某物盖上…

cow /kaʊ/ *n*. 母牛

crack /kræk/ *n*. 裂缝　*vi*. 裂缝；瑕疵；爆裂声

craft /krɑːft/ *n*. 工艺、手艺；船；（飞机等）航空器

crash /kræʃ/ *n*. 坠毁；爆裂声；*vi*. 怦然落地；坠毁

crawl /krɔːl/ *vi*.，*n*. 爬、爬行；匍匐前进

crazy /ˈkreɪzɪ/ *adj*. 发疯的；不切实际的

be crazy about ... 对…极其喜欢

（考题）I've always been crazy about traveling and diving and this led me to an interest in sharks.

cream /kriːm/ *n*. 奶油(食品)；奶油色

create /krɪ(ː)ˈeɪt/ *vt*. 创造；产生

（考题）Diet foods and diet pills contain zero calorie only because the diet industry has created chemicals to produce these wonder products.

creative /krɪˈeɪtɪv/ *adj*. 有创造力的

creature /ˈkriːtʃə/ *n*. 生物(动物或人)

credit /ˈkredɪt/ *n*. 信用；贷款；存款

credit card 信用卡

crew /kruː/ *n*. (车、船、飞机的)乘务员；团队

crime /kraɪm/ *n*. 犯罪行为

（考题）Campus crime mirrors the rest of the nation.

commit a crime 犯罪

criminal /ˈkrɪmɪnəl/ *n*. 罪犯　*adj*. 犯罪的；刑事的

crisis /ˈkraɪsɪs/ (*pl*. crises /ˈkraɪsiːz/) *n*. 危机；转折点、关键时刻

（考题）European countries, realizing crisis is at hand, are providing great encouragement for parents to create more babies in the 21st century.

economic crises 经济危机

critic /ˈkrɪtɪk/ *n*. 批评家，评论家

criticism /ˈkrɪtɪsɪzm/ *n*. 批评，批判

criticize /ˈkrɪtɪsaɪz/ *vt*. 批评，批判；指责，非难

criticize sb. for sth. 因某事批评某人

（考题）It does not mean taking one view against another view, as when someone criticizes another person for doing something wrong.

（见 accuse）

crop /krɒp/ *n*. 农作物；庄稼

be in/out of crop (土地)在耕种/没有耕种

cross /krɒs/ *n*. 十字形　*adj*. 易怒的；交叉的

cross talk 相声

the Red Cross 红十字会

vt. 穿过,越过

(考题) Before they were able to ride horses, humans had to cross land on foot.

crossroads 十字路口

crowd /kraʊd/ *n*. 群;人群

(考题) Because of the large quantity and high quality of his collection, a huge crowd of possible buyers gathered for the auction.

vt. 挤满 *vi*. 挤;聚集

be crowded with 挤满;拥塞

(考题) Although this is only a small town, it's crowded with tourists who come here all year round.

crown /kraʊn/ *n*. 王冠;国王;王位

(考题) ... but sometimes when it is cloudless, gray steam gathers around the top of the mountains which, in the last rays of the setting sun, will shine and light up like a crown of glory

cruel /krʊel/ *adj*. 残忍的、残酷的

be cruel to ... 对…残忍

cruelty /ˈkrʊeltɪ/ *n*. 残忍

crush /krʌʃ/ *vt*. 压碎;压倒

cry /kraɪ/ *n*. 叫喊;哭;哭声

(考题) "Bystander Apathy Effect" means on hearing a cry for help, people keep themselves to themselves

v. 叫喊;哭

(考题) But when you feel like crying, don't fight it. It's a natural-and-healthy-emotional response.

crystal /ˈkrɪstəl/ *n*. 水晶;结晶体 *adj*. 透明的;晶体的

cucumber /ˈkjuːkʌmbə/ *n*. 黄瓜

cultivate /ˈkʌltɪveɪt/ *vt*. 耕作;培植、培养

(考题) Unlike vitamin C, leadership skills can't be easily swallowed down. They must be carefully cultivated.

cultural /ˈkʌltʃərəl/ *adj*. 文化的

culture /ˈkʌltʃə/ *n*. 文化;文明

(考题) Art museums are places where people can learn about

various cultures.

cup /kʌp/ *n.* 杯子

cupboard /ˈkʌbəd/ *n.* 食橱；碗柜

cure /kjʊe/ *n.* 治疗；药物；治愈

（考题）Once an eating disorder has become firmly established，there is no easy cure.

cure for ... 治疗某种疾病/治某种疾病的药物

（考题）According to Professor Barnes，theobromine can be a more effective cure for coughs.

beyond cure 难以治愈

vi. vt. 治疗；治愈

cure sb. (of ...) 治好某人（的…）

（考题）It's time you cured the child of his bad habit.

cure ... 治愈…（疾病）

（考题）Charles Blackman's paintings come from his eagerness to cure his wife's illness.

curious /ˈkjʊerɪəs/ *adj.* 好奇的

be curious about ... 对…感到好奇

（考题）If you are curious about life and desire to dig deeper into it，you are a critical thinker.

be curious to do sth. 对做某事很好奇

（考题）... you may be curious to know what you usually do in a typical week，how you can get along with your fellow students，and so on.

current /ˈkʌrənt/ *adj.* 现时的；最近的

curtain /ˈkɜːtən/ *n.* 窗帘

curve /kɜːv/ *n.* 曲线；弧线；弯；

cushion /ˈkʊʃən/ *n.* 垫子；气垫

custom /ˈkʌstəm/ *n.* 习惯；风俗；

（考题）By mistake，President Clinton's advisers thought that Koreans have the same naming customs as the Japanese. Clinton had not been told that，in Korea，wives keep their family names.

traditions and customs 风俗习惯

the Customs 海关

customer /ˈkʌstəmə/ *n.* 顾客

cut /kʌt/ *n.* 切,割;裂口 *v.* (cut, cut) 切、割

    cut sth. down 压缩、减少…

    (考题) By describing the shortened classics as "a breath of fresh air", Ms. Weir speaks highly of the cut-down classics.

    cut in 插话

    cut sth. off 切断;阻挡、隔绝

    (考题) The Bismarck sailed into the Atlantic Ocean to cut off American supplies to Britain.

    cut sth. /sb. short 打断…

    a short cut 捷径

cycle /ˈsaɪkl/ *n.* 周期;循环;自行车 *vt.* 使循环 *vi.* 循环;骑自行车

cyclist /ˈsaɪklɪst/ *n.* 骑自行车的人

D

dad /dæd/ *n*. (口)爸爸

daily /'deɪlɪ/ *adj*. 每日的　*adv*. 每日地　*n*. 日报

 daily life 日常生活

 daily necessaries/necessities 日常必需品

dairy /'deərɪ/ *n*. 牛奶坊;乳品店　*adj*. 奶制的;乳品的

dam /dæm/ *n*. 水闸;坝

damage /'dæmɪdʒ/ *n*. 毁坏

 cause/do damage to ... 对…造成损坏

 (考题)The creativity of science has been employed in doing damage to mankind.

 vt. **damage sth.** 损坏某物

 (考题)Before they buy a product, they ask questions like these: "Will this shampoo damage the environment?" "Can this metal container be reused or can it only be used once?"

damp /dæmp/ *n*. 潮湿　*adj*. 潮湿的

dance /dɑːns/ *n*. *vi*. 舞蹈;跳舞

danger /'deɪndʒə/ *n*. 危险

 in danger (of ...) 处于(…)危险之中

 (考题)People with fair skin and freckles are more in danger of skin cancer.

 out of danger 脱离危险

 (考题)If you get frostbite, do not rewarm the affected area until you're out of danger.

dangerous /'deɪndʒərəs/ *adj*. 危险的、不安全的

 be dangerous to sb. 对某人危险

 (考题)The chemical wastes are dangerous to people in the area.

 It's dangerous for sb. to do sth. 某人做某事危险

dare /deə/ *vt*. *v. aux*. 敢

 dare sth. 敢于面对…

 dare to do sth. 敢做某事(偶有不用 to 的情况)

（考题）Only a brave man，or a very rich one，dares to buy and sell on the Stock Market.

dare sb. to do sth. 向某人挑战（要他做某事）

dare do sth. （用于否定、疑问或条件句，第三人称没有变化，但有过去时的形式 dared。）

（考题）How dare you say that?

I dare say 我敢说；我想

dark /dɑːk/ *adj*. 黑暗的、暗的　　*n*. 黑暗、暗处

（考题）I found the building was dark except for a single light in a ground floor window.

after/before dark 天黑前/后

in the dark 在黑暗中

（考题）But I knew he would be frightened alone in the dark.

darling /ˈdɑːlɪŋ/ *n*. 心爱的；亲爱的（称呼）*adj*. 心爱的、亲爱的

dash /dæʃ/ *n*. 短跑；破折号；*vi*. 猛冲；急忙赶往　*vt*. 掷

datum /ˈdeɪtəm/（*pl*. data /ˈdeɪtə/）*n*. 论据；资料；数据

date /deɪt/ *n*. 日期；约会

（考题）Some teens admit that asking someone for a date，or breaking up，can be easier in message form，though they don't want to do so.

out of date 过时的、落后的

up to date 符合现实的、跟得上变化的

（考题）This two-volume Guide features up-to-date and in-depth information about UK course options and institutions.

vt. **date sth.** 给…注上日期；确定某物的年代

date sb. 与某人约会

daughter /ˈdɔːtə/ *n*. 女儿

dawn /dɔːn/ *n*. 黎明，天亮

at dawn 黎明时分

day /deɪ/ *n*. 天；日子

all day (long) 一天到晚

（考题）In late afternoon I returned to my car and found that I'd left the lights on all day，and the battery was dead.

by day 在白天

day after day 日复一日

day and night 夜以继日

day by day 一天天地

(考题)We live day by day, but in the great things, the time of days and weeks is so small that a day is unimportant.

have a day off 休息一天

in the days to come 将来

one day 总有一天(同义词：**sooner or later，in the end**)

some day 将来有一天，某一天

(考题)It can be inferred that some day we might not worry about our power supply.

the other day 前几天,有一天

(考题)I'm sorry. I shouldn't have shouted at you the other day.

to this day 至今

(考题)This scar will be lasting, but to this day, I have never regretted what I did.

daylight /'deɪlaɪt/ n. 日光

dead /ded/ adj. 死的

deadline /'dedlaɪn/ n. 最后期限

deadly /'dedlɪ/ adj. 致命的、极其危险的；极度的 adv. 极其

(考题)The system, called Driver Alert, aims to reduce deadly road accidents by 20%—40% that are caused by tiredness.

deaf /def/ adj. 聋的

be deaf in the right/left (ear) 右耳/左耳聋了

deal¹ /diːl/ (dealt，dealt) vi. 处理；涉及

deal with 处理；对待；与…交往；与…有关

(考题)The text mainly deals with reducing their mental pressures

deal² /diːl/ n. 数量

a good/great deal of 大量(修饰不可数名词)

(考题)A great deal of money is spent on new and bigger aircraft and airports to deal with the vast increase in passengers travelling by air.

a great deal 大量的东西；大量地

dear /dɪə/ adj. 亲爱的；昂贵的

death /deθ/ n. 死；死亡

（考题）Even with healthier lifestyles and less disease, they say failure of the brain and organs will finally lead all humans to death.

（考题）With the 28 births and 10 deaths, the population of the village next year will be 1,018.

（注意：在表示"死亡"时,death 是不可数名词；但在表示某种类型的死亡或死亡人数时,则是可数名词。）

debate /dɪˈbeɪt/ v. n. 辩论；争论

debate with sb. on/about sth. 与某人辩论某事

debt /det/ n. 欠款,债务

in debt 欠债

（考题）The teenagers expected to be in debt when they finished university or training, although half said that they assumed the debts would be less than $10,000.

get/run into debt 陷入债务

decade /ˈdekeɪd/ n. 十年

decay /dɪˈkeɪ/ n. 腐烂；蛀蚀 vi. 腐败 vt. 使腐烂；使蛀蚀

deceive /dɪˈsiːv/ vt. 欺骗,蒙骗

deceive sb. (into . . .) 欺骗某人(使…)

decide /dɪˈsaɪd/ v. 决定

decide sth. 决定某事

（考题）Human brains were known to decide the final death.

decide to do sth. 决定做某事

（考题）The best way to defeat a passive self-image is to step back and decide to stress your successes.

decide what/how/when/where . . . to do sth. 决定做什么/如何做/何时做/何处做…

（考题）I can't decide where to go for the holiday — any ideas?

decide that . . . 决定…

（考题）But the carmakers haven't decided if they will put it into production because it would add several hundred dollars to the cost of their cars.

decide against (doing) sth. 决定不做某事/作出不利决定

decide on/upon sth. 对某事作出决定

decision /dɪˈsɪʒən/ n. 决定

come to/arrive at/reach/make a decision 作出决定

（考题）Most important of all，it is always wise to make decisions by compromise and agreement.

deck /dek/ *n.* 甲板、舱面

declare /dɪˈkleə/ *vt.* 宣布；申报

　declare sth. 宣布、申报…

（考题）If you have nothing to declare，go through the Green Channel.

　declare sth. … 宣布、宣称…如何

（考题）The moment the Olympic Games were declared open，the whole world cheered.

　declare that ... 宣布…

　declare war on ... 向…宣战

decline /dɪˈklaɪn/ *n.* 衰退、减弱

（考题）Maybe the decline is caused by the increasing availability of computes games.

　v. ... **decline** ... 变得衰弱

（考题）My eyesight is declining as I am getting old.

　decline (to do) sth. 婉言拒绝（做）某事

decorate /ˈdekəreɪt/ *v.* 装饰、装潢

decrease /dɪˈkriːz/ *n.* 减少；下降

（考题）The birthrate in Europe has been in a steady decrease since the 1960s.

　vi. vt. （使）减少

（考题）Within eight days of starting his "laugh therapy" program his pain began to decrease and he was able to sleep more easily.

deed /diːd/ *n.* 事情；行为

deep /diːp/ *adj.* 深的

deer /dɪə/ *n.* 鹿

defeat /dɪˈfiːt/ *n. vt.* 击败

　defeat ... 打败、击溃、战胜…

（考题）The best way to defeat a passive self-image is to step back and decide to stress your successes.

（辨析：defeat 的宾语是"击溃"的对象。win 的宾语则是赢得的物品、荣誉，或是比赛本身，如：the match，the prize。）

defence /dɪˈfens/ *n*. 防御,保卫;辩护

defend /dɪˈfend/ *vt*. 防守(球门);保卫

defend sb./sth. 保卫、保护某人/某物

(考题)But plants can defend themselves by using both physical and chemical means.

define /dɪˈfaɪn/ *vt*. 给…下定义

define sth. (as …) 给…下定义(为…)、把…解释为…

(考题)He defines creativity as "the ability to produce work that is both new (original) and appropriate (applicable to the situation)."

definite /ˈdefɪnɪt/ *adj*. 确定的

It is definite that … 一定、肯定会…

(同义词:**clear, certain, exact**)

definition /ˌdefɪˈnɪʃən/ *n*. 定义;释义

degree /dɪˈɡriː/ *n*. 程度;学位;度数

(考题)Most of my time was spent outside loading trucks with those heavy boxes in near-zero-degree temperatures.

take a degre 取得学位

(考题)We offer a wide choice of bachelor's degrees for international students, which includes: Arts, Communication Studies, Social Sciences, etc.

by degrees 一步一步地、逐渐地

to a … degree 达到…程度

(考题)To what degree it can be settled depends on your position, of course, and that is something only you can determine.

delay /dɪˈleɪ/ *n*. 推迟;延误

(考题)Critics of nanotech have made use of such images, calling for a delay on commercial nanotech until regulations are established.

vt. **delay (doing) sth.** 推迟(做)某事

(考题)Though many reasons other than Alzheimer's disease may cause memory loss, its early diagnosis and treatment may delay some of the most serious effects.

delay sb. 耽搁某人

（辨析：delay 表示由于受到阻碍或阻挡而减速或暂时停止，因而延期至某个不确定的时候；put off 较通俗口语化，强调"先搁一搁"，多数情况下后面说明更改在何时。）

delegate /ˈdelɪɡeɪt/ n. 代表

delete /dɪˈliːt/ vt. 擦去；删除

delicate /ˈdelɪkət/ adj. 纤细的；雅致的

delicious /dɪˈlɪʃəs/ adj. 美味的、可口的

delight /dɪˈlaɪt/ n. 高兴、愉快

　　take delight in ... 喜欢…

　　to sb.'s delight 使某人感到高兴的是

　　（考题）Then he would casually shoot the ball with either hand, to the delight of the fans.

　　vt. delight sb. 使某人高兴

　　（考题）Tales From Animal Hospital will delight all fans of the programme and anyone who has a lively interest in their pet, whether it be cat, dog or snake!

　　be delighted at/with/about/to do/that ... 很高兴…

　　（考题）I was delighted to have been able to do research work with the famour scientist. I know I can learn a lot from him.

deliver /dɪˈlɪvə/ vt. 交付；投递；作（演讲）；

　　deliver sth. (to sb.) 递交某物（给某人）

　　（考题）Mail carriers will be delivering some good news and some bad news this week.

delivery /dɪˈlɪvərɪ/ n. 投递；分送

demand /dɪˈmɑːnd/ n. 要求；需要

　　a demand/demands for sth. 对某物的需求

　　（考题）The demand for natural resources is becoming an increasingly serious problem for the future of mankind.

　　supply and demand 供求

　　vt. 要求；需求；查问

　　demand sth. (of sb.)（向某人）要求…

　　demand to do sth. 要求做某事

　　demand that ... 要求…（虚拟语气）

　　（考题）However, today, more and more consumers are choosing "green" and demanding that the products they buy should be safe for the environment.

demanding /dɪ'mɑːndɪŋ/ *adj*. 要求高的；费力的

（考题）As nanny, cook, cleaner, shopper, driver, and gardener, she has one of the most demanding jobs in Britain today.

democracy /dɪ'mɒkrəsɪ/ *n*. 民主

dentist /'dentɪst/ *n*. 牙医

deny /dɪ'naɪ/ *vt*. 否认；拒绝

deny (doing) sth. 否认（做过）某事

（考题）... women's rights are denied in some developing countries.

deny that ... 否认说…

deny sb. sth. 拒绝给某人…

（考题）The "solution" that some teens choose is to deny themselves all the time so as to keep temptation away.

depart /dɪ'pɑːt/ *vi*. 离开；出发；偏离

（考题）Asian children depart from their diet tradition.

department /dɪ'pɑːtmənt/ *n*. 部门；系

departure /dɪ'pɑːtʃə/ *n*. 离开

depend /dɪ'pend/ *vi*. 视…而定；依靠，依赖

depend on/upon ... 依赖、信赖…；取决于…

（考题）This would mean that everything would depend on luck since every pupil would depend on the efficiency, the values and the purpose of each teacher.

depend on sb. to do sth. 依赖某人做某事

（考题）Most of them depend on animals to eat their fruits and spread their seeds.

It all depends/That depends. 看情况、还很难说

（考题）— Will you go skiing with me this winter vacation? — It all depends.

dependent /dɪ'pendənt/ *adj*. 依靠的，依赖的

be dependent on/upon ... 依赖于…

（考题）They aren't dependent on "star" actors with enormous salaries.

deposit /dɪ'pɒzɪt/ *n*. 沉积物；存款；定金

make/pay a deposit on ... 支付…的定金

vt. 使沉淀;存放;储蓄 *vi.* 沉淀

deposit sth. 存放某物;沉淀某物

depress /dɪˈpres/ *vt.* 使抑郁,使沮丧;使不景气;按下

be depressed at/about/with/to do/that ... 因…而感到沮丧

depth /depθ/ *n.* 纵深;深(度)

(考题)Scientists from 10 nations have now almost completely drilled through a 3,000-meter depth of ice high in the Antarctic mainland.

in depth 深度;深入地

(考题)This two-volume Guide features up-to-date and in-depth information

describe /dɪsˈkraɪb/ *vt.* 描述,形容

describe ... (as ...) 描述…(成…)

(考题)*Dream of the Invisibles* describes young immigrants' feelings of both belonging and not belonging in their adopted country.

describe that ... 描述说…

(考题)By quoting the remark of a being from another planet, the author intends to describe why clocks can rule the planet Earth.

description /dɪsˈkrɪpʃən/ *n.* 描述、形容

(考题)It also includes a description of British soldiers burning Washington. D.C. in the war of 1812.

beyond description 无法形容

beggar description 难以描绘、无法形容

desert[1] /ˈdezət/ *n.* 沙漠、荒芜之地

desert[2] /dɪˈzɜːt/ *vt.* 离弃、抛弃

deserve /dɪˈzɜːv/ *vt.* 应该得到

deserve sth. 值得、应该得到

(考题)What comes first is to keep an open mind, becasue everyone's ideas deserve consideration and each group member can make his or her own contribution.

deserve to do sth. 值得做某事

(考题)What he did deserved to be understood.

sth. deserve doing 某事值得做

（注意：在 sth. deserve doing 中，动名词是主动的形式，被动的意思，如：The book deserves reading。如使用不定式，则是 The book deserves to be read。见 need。）

design /dɪ'zaɪn/ *n.* 图案；设计 *vt.* 设计

desire /dɪ'zaɪə/ *n.* 愿望、渴望

（考题）Professor Alex Michalos found that people feel less happy if the gap between reality and desire is bigger.

have a desire for sth. /to do sth. 渴望得到…/做某事

（考题）Children, he says in his book *From Defiance to Cooperation*, "have secret feelings of weakness" and "a desire to feel safe."

vt. **desire sth.** 渴望得到…

（考题）When it comes to friends, I desire those who will share my happiness, who possess wings of their own and who will fly with me.

desire (sb.) to do sth. 希望（某人）做某事

（考题）If you are curious about life and desire to dig deeper into it, you are a critical thinker.

desire that ... （虚拟语气）

desk /desk/ *n.* 书桌；办公桌

despair /dɪs'peə/ *n. vi.* 绝望

in despair 绝望地

desperate /'despərɪt/ *adj.* 不顾一切的；绝望的

despite /dɪs'paɪt/ *prep.* 不管；尽管

despite sth. 尽管…

（考题）Men and women always score similarly on intelligence tests, despite the difference in brain size.

despite the fact that ... 尽管…（这一事实）

（注意：despite 后面不直接跟从句，所以，常常使用 fact 再接一个同位语从句的结构。）

destination /ˌdestɪ'neɪʃən/ *n.* 目的地、终点；目标、目的

（注意："你的目的地是哪里"，在英语翻译中应该是 **What** is your destination，而不是 where。同样"What is the height of the building?"或"How high is the building?"）

destroy /dɪs'trɔɪ/ *vt.* 破坏；毁坏；消灭

destroy sth. 毁坏某物

（考题）The power of a big storm can throw a cow into the air or destroy a whole house in seconds.

（辨析：destroy 指造成的破坏、摧毁，有无法恢复的含义；damage 指某种功能或某种程度的损坏，程度较 destroy 轻。）

destruction /dɪs'trʌkʃən/ *n*. 破坏；毁灭

detail /'diːteɪl/ *n*. 细节

（考题）Many birdwatchers logged on to the website for details

in detail 详细地

detective /dɪ'tektɪv/ *n*. 侦探　*adj*. 侦探的

determination /dɪˌtɜːmɪ'neɪʃən/ *n*. 决心；顽强；确定

determine /dɪ'tɜːmɪn/ *vt*. 决定；使下决心　*vi*. 下决心；决定

determine sth. 决定某事

determine to do sth. /that … 决定做某事/…

（考题）My mother，dissatisfied with my father's plain workman's life，determined that I would not grow up like him and his people.

be determined to do sth. 决心做某事

（考题）By the time I left，I was determined never to go back there again.

determined /dɪ'tɜːmɪnd/ *adj*. 决意的；坚决的

develop /dɪ'veləp/ *vt*. 发展；开发　*vi*. 发展；生长、发育

（考题）Students develop friendships through groups，as well as learning more about other people's ideas.

development /dɪ'veləpmənt/ *n*. 发展

with the development of … 随着…的发展

device /dɪ'vaɪs/ *n*. 设计；装置

devote /dɪ'vəʊt/ *vt*. 奉献

devote … to (doing) sth. 把…奉献给…

（考题）As parents，we should devote some of our energies to taking our kids into nature.

be devoted to sth. 专心致志于、献身于…

（考题）He was devoted to the study of birds all his life.

dial /daɪəl/ *vt*. 拨号

dialect /'daɪəlekt/ *n*. 方言；行话

dialogue /ˈdaɪəlɒg/ *n*. 对话、对白

diamond /ˈdaɪəmənd/ *n*. 钻石、金刚石

diary /ˈdaɪərɪ/ *n*. 日记；日志

　keep a diary 记日记

dictate /ˈdɪkteɪt/ *v*. 口授；发号施令

dictation /dɪkˈteɪʃən/ *n*. 听写

dictionary /ˈdɪkʃənrɪ/ *n*. 词典、字典

die /daɪ/ *vi*. 死；熄灭；枯萎　*vt*. 遭受(接同源名词)某种形式的死亡

　(考题)For this busy man, it was a sort of alarm：after years of non-stop hard work, he might wear himself out and die an early death.

　die away 消失、平静

　die down 平息、熄灭

　die for . . . 为…而死；迫切想要…

　die from . . . 因…而死亡

　(考题)His doctor told him that he would lose the ability to move and eventually die from the disease.

　die of . . . 因(患某种疾病)而死亡

　(考题)What will people die of 100 years from now?

　die out 熄灭、灭绝

diet /ˈdaɪət/ *n*. 日常饮食；规定饮食

　(考题)Diet products make people believe that gain comes without pain, and that life can be without resistance and struggle.

　be/go on a diet 节食

differ /ˈdɪfə/ *vi*. 不同

　differ from . . . 与…不同

　(考题)Human facial expressions differ from those of animals in the degree to which they can be controlled on purpose.

　differ with sb. about/on sth. 在某事上与某人意见分歧

　(考题)Scientists also differ on what kind of life the super aged might live.

　differ from . . . in . . . 在…方面与…不同

difference /ˈdɪfərəns/ *n*. 差别；不同(之处)

make a difference between ... 对…区分对待

make no difference 没有影响

(考题) It makes a great difference whether we develop wood products or not.

different /ˈdɪfərənt/ *adj.* 不同的

be different from ... 与…不同

difficult /ˈdɪfɪkəlt/ *adj.* 困难的;艰难的

It is difficult for sb. to do sth. 某人做某事很困难

(考题) It's very difficult for the scientists to reach an agreement because different results can be got from the same fossils.

... be difficult to sb. ... 对某人来说难

(辨析:hard 强调体力上的困难,difficult 侧重智力及其他方面的困难,程度强于 hard。在修饰人时,difficult 有"难弄"的意思,而 hard 则有"严酷"的含义。)

difficulty /ˈdɪfɪkəltɪ/ *n.* 困难

have difficulty with ... 在…方面有困难

have difficulty (in) doing sth. 做某事有困难

(考题) Pre-storm low pressure makes the air so thin that birds have difficulty flying.

with/without difficulty 困难地/不费力地

dig /dɪg/ (dug, dug) *v.* 挖,掘

digest /dɪˈdʒest/ *vt.* 消化,吸收

digital /ˈdɪdʒɪtəl/ *adj.* 数字的;数字显示的

dignity /ˈdɪgnɪtɪ/ *n.* 尊严

with dignity 有尊严地、体面地

diligent /dɪˈlɪdʒənt/ *adj.* 勤勉的

be diligent at/in ... 在…方面很勤奋

dim /dɪm/ *adj.* 昏暗的;模糊不清的

dine /daɪn/ *vi.* 吃饭、用餐

dinner /ˈdɪnə/ *n.* 正餐;晚餐

dioxide /daɪˈɒksaɪd/ *n.* 二氧化碳

dip /dɪp/ *vt.* 浸;蘸

dip sth. in/into ... 将某物浸入…

dip into ... 随意翻阅;稍加尝试

diploma /dɪˈpləumə/ *n.* 奖状;毕业文凭

diplomat /ˈdɪpləmæt/ *n*. 外交官、外交家

direct /dɪˈrekt/ *adj*. 直接的

（考题）We can achieve knowledge either actively or passively. We achieve it actively by direct experience, by testing and proving an idea, or by reasoning.

vt. **direct sth.** 指导、指挥某事

（考题）In large universities, graduate students, called teaching assistants, usually direct discussion sections.

direct sb. to do sth. 指挥某人做某事

direct sb. to a place 指引某人到某处

direction /dɪˈrekʃən/ *n*. 方向；（常用复数）指引，说明

in the direction of ... 朝…的方向

（考题）This kind of activity must be strictly controlled because even a slight movement in the wrong direction will lead to a mistake.

director /dɪˈrektə/ *n*. 主管；董事；经理

dirt /dɜːt/ *n*. 污物；灰尘

dirty /ˈdɜːtɪ/ *adj*. 脏的

disabled /dɪsˈeɪb(ə)ld/ *adj*. 丧失能力的；有残疾的

disadvantage /ˌdɪsədˈvɑːntɪdʒ/ *n*. 不利地位，不利条件　*vt*. 使处于不利地位；损害，危害

（考题）According to the passage, the main disadvantage of using stereotypes is that they may make us miss some pleasant experience.

to sb.'s disadvantage 对某人不利

disagreeable /ˌdɪsəˈɡriːəbl/ *adj*. 不合意的；令人不快的

disappear /ˌdɪsəˈpɪə/ *vi*. 消失，消散

disappoint /ˌdɪsəˈpɔɪnt/ *vt*. 使失望

disappoint sb. (with sth. /by doing sth.) （因…）使某人失望

（考题）If all this disappoints you, it shouldn't.

be disappointed at/with/in ... 因…、对…感到失望

（考题）Should you choose to join us, we know that you will not be disappointed!

disappointment /ˌdɪsəˈpɔɪntmənt/ *n*. 失望

disapproval /ˌdɪsəˈpruːvəl/ *n*. 不赞成；非难

disapprove /ˌdɪsəˈpruːv/ *v*. 不赞成

　disapprove of sth. 不赞成某事

disaster /dɪˈzɑːstə/ *n*. 灾难、大祸

disc /dɪsk/ *n*. 圆盘物；唱片；磁盘

discipline /ˈdɪsɪplɪn/ *n*. 纪律

disco /ˈdɪskəʊ/ *n*. 迪斯科舞(曲)

disconcert /ˌdɪskənˈsɜːt/ *vt*. 挫败；扰乱

discourage /dɪsˈkʌrɪdʒ/ *vt*. 阻止、阻拦

　discourage sb. /sth. 使某人泄气/阻止某事

　(考题) The news that they failed their driving test discouraged him.

　(考题) Internationally，laws to discourage the use of plastic bags have been passed ...

　discourage sb. from doing sth. 劝阻某人做某事

discover /dɪsˈkʌvə/ *vt*. 发现；发觉；找到

　discover sth. 发现某物

　(考题) Only as this basic and often troublesome fear begins to dissolve can we discover a new meaning in competition.

　discover sb. doing sth. 发现某人做某事

　(考题) We couldn't believe our eyes when we discovered him smoking.

　discover ... to be ... 发现…如何

　(考题) To our surprise，we discovered him to be a thief.

　discover that ... 发现…

discovery /dɪsˈkʌvərɪ/ *n*. 发现；被发现的事物

　(考题) A great scientific discovery or a great work of art is surely the result of problem-solving activity.

discuss /dɪsˈkʌs/ *vt*. 讨论

　discuss (doing) sth. with sb. (与某人)讨论(做)某事

　(考题) I expect to hear more from you at staff meetings or at any other time you want to discuss an idea with me.

　discuss what/how/... to do 讨论做什么/如何做…

　discuss what/how/when/ ... 讨论…

　(注意：discuss 后面不能直接跟动词不定式。)

discussion /dɪsˈkʌʃən/ *n*. 讨论

（考题）In discussion of technological changes，the Internet gets most of the attention these days.

be under discussion 在讨论中

disease /dɪ'ziːz/ *n.* 疾病

（考题）... studies show that childhood events，besides genes，may well cause such midlife diseases as cancer，heart disease and mental illness.

catch/have/develop a disease 得病

an occupational disease 职业病

an endemic disease 地方病

a chronic disease 慢性病

a contagious disease 传染病

（辨析：disease 和 illness 都表示"患病"。illness 指的是因 disease 引起的患病状态，具体的疾病用 disease 更多。）

dish /dɪʃ/ *n.* 盘装菜肴；盘、碟

dishwasher /'dɪʃwɒʃə/ *n.* 洗碟机；洗碟工

dislike /dɪs'laɪk/ *n. vt.* 不喜爱；厌恶

have a dislike for/of/to ... 不喜欢…

（考题）A bookseller cannot always tell the truth about his books，and that gives him a dislike for them.

dislike (doing) sth. 不喜欢（做）某事

（考题）I don't dislike the work though I can't say I'm mad about it.

dismiss /dɪs'mɪs/ *vt.* 解散；打消；解雇 *vi.* 解散

（考题）After everything I'd done for the company，they dismissed me by text！

dismiss an idea 打消一个注意

disobey /dɪsə'beɪ/ *vt.* 不服从；违抗

disorder /dɪs'ɔːdə/ *n.* 杂乱，混乱；（身心机能的）失调，紊乱

（考题）The causes of eating disorders are not clear. There may be genetic or biochemical factors in some cases.

in disorder 混乱

disorderly /dɪs'ɔːdəlɪ/ *adj.* 混乱的；目无法纪的；骚乱的

display /dɪs'pleɪ/ *n.* 展示

on display 展出

vt. **display sth.** 展示、展现…；显示出…

（考题）Horsemen from different nations display their beautiful clothes and their fine horsemanship.

dissatisfy /dɪs'sætɪsfaɪ/ *vt.* 使不满意

dissatisfy sb. 使某人感到不满意

be dissatisfied with/at sth. 对…感到不满

（考题）My mother, dissatisfied with my father's plain workman's life, determined that I would not grow up like him and his people.

a dissatisfied look/expression 不满的表情

dissolve /dɪ'sɒlv/ *vi.vt.* （使）溶解；逐步消失

（考题）Only as this basic and often troublesome fear begins to dissolve can we discover a new meaning in competition.

（辨析：dissolve 常指"使溶解在液体中"，melt 则是"通过加热使物体由固态变为液态"，即"熔化、融化"。dissolve 偶尔也可替换 melt，如 Heat soon dissolved the candle。）

distance /'dɪstəns/ *n.* 距离

（考题）This geographical and cultural distance also prevents the grown-up children from providing response in time for their aged parents living by themselves.

at a distance 离开一定的距离

（考题）People can tell at a distance whether an individual has similar tastes by what he or she wears.

from a distance 从远处；离开一定距离

in the distance 在远处、远方

（考题）They watched the train until it disappeared in the distance.

distant /'dɪstənt/ *adj.* 远的

distinct /dɪs'tɪŋkt/ *adj.* 有区别的、不同的；明显的

be distinct from ... 与…不同

（考题）The new evidence makes it very clear that these people are a new species, distinct from modern humans.

distinguished /dɪs'tɪŋgwɪʃt/ *adj.* 卓越的、杰出的

distress /dɪs'tres/ *n.* 痛苦、不幸

（考题）More married men than women named their wife/husband as a best friend, most trusted person, or the one they would turn to in time of emotional distress.

in distress 在痛苦之中

vt. 使痛苦

be distressed at/about/to do ... 因…而痛苦、难过

district /ˈdɪstrɪkt/ *n*. 地区、地域

distrust /dɪsˈtrʌst/ *vt*. 不信任、怀疑

distruct sb. /sth. 不相信、信任某人/某事

n. 不信任

with distrust 怀疑地、不信任地

disturb /dɪsˈtɜːb/ *vt*. 扰乱、使不安

disturb sb. 打扰某人；使某人不安

（考题）The bad news really disturbed us.

disturb sth. 影响、扰乱、干扰某事

（考题）When you sleep late just one morning during the week，it may disturb your body clock.

disturbance /dɪsˈtɜːbəns/ *n*. 打扰、扰乱

ditch /dɪtʃ/ *n*. 沟；渠道

dive /daɪv/ *vi*. 跳水；潜水；跳下；深入；迅速把手伸进

（考题）Once she has fully studied her subjects，ready to dive into the book，she can spend twenty hours nonstop at her desk.

diver /ˈdaɪvə/ *n*. 潜水员

divide /dɪˈvaɪd/ *vi*. *vt*. （把）分开；除

（考题）... it makes a job easier to divide the group task among all group members.

divide ... into 把……分成

（考题）When there is research to be done，divide the topic into several areas，and this can explore the issue in a very detailed way.

divide ... by 2 以 2 来除…

division /dɪˈvɪʒən/ *n*. 分；分开；部门；除法

divorce /dɪˈvɔːs/ *n*. 离婚；脱离

（考题）Some experts believe that marriage without the couple's meeting each other first ends in divorce.

vt. **divorce sb.** 与某人离婚

dizzy /ˈdɪzɪ/ *adj*. 头晕目眩的

do /duː/ (did，done) *v*. 做、干

have sth. done 使…完成、做好

do away with 消除、处理

do well 做得好

（考题）Despite her love of reading，she did not do well in elementary school because she was too shy to participate.

do with 处理、安排；凑合

（考题）It still remain a problem how they will do with the nuclear wastes.

do without (...) 不用、不需要

do wrong/right 做得不对/对

make do with ... 凑合用

（考题）As he had no money for a new car，he had to make do with the old one.

That will do! 行、可以。

It will/won't do to do sth. 可以/不可以做某事

（考题）I'm afraid it won't do to put the box here in the rain.

doctor /ˈdɒktə/ *n*. 医生

document /ˈdɒkjʊmənt/ *n*. 文件；证件

dog /dɒg/ *n*. 狗

doll /dɒl/ *n*. 玩具娃娃

dollar /ˈdɒlə/ *n*. 元（美国、加拿大等国的货币单位）

dolphin /ˈdɒlfɪn/ *n*. 海豚

domestic /dəˈmestɪk/ *adj*. 家庭的；驯养的；国内的

dominant /ˈdɒmɪnənt/ *adj*. 占优势的；支配的

（考题）They then find themselves in conflict with another dominant pressure in society — to stay slim and trim.

donkey /ˈdɒŋkɪ/ *n*. 驴；笨蛋

donate /dəʊˈneɪt/ *vt*. 捐赠

door /dɔː/ *n*. 门

from door to door 挨家挨户

next door (to ...) （在…的）隔壁

out of doors 户外的、露天的

knock at the door 敲门

answer the door 开门

dormitory /ˈdɔːmɪtrɪ/ *n*. 寝室；〈美〉(学生)宿舍

dot /dɒt/ *n*. 点

double /ˈdʌbl/ *adj*. 两倍的；加倍的

(考题)Often, there is the double pressure to enjoy life through food and yet remain ultra-slim.

a double room 双人房间

vi. 加倍；对折　*vt*. 使加倍

sth. double 某物增加一倍

(考题)The hot sun had caused the dough to double in size and the fermenting yeast made the surface shake and sigh as though it were breathing.

double sth. 使某物增加一倍；使某物折叠

(考题)The average human life span cannot be doubled.

doubt /daʊt/ *n*. 怀疑、不相信

beyond doubt 毫无疑问

(考题)The popularity of the igloo is beyond doubt；it is now attracting tourists from all over the world.

in doubt 怀疑、犹豫

(考题)A visit to such school will leave you in no doubt that the children enjoy themselves.

no doubt = there is no doubt 无疑、肯定

(考题)Despite such a big difference in attitude towards what one eats, there is no doubt that people in the west regard the Chinese food as something special.

without (a) doubt 毫无疑问

Without doubt it was my work.

vt. 怀疑，不相信

doubt sth. 怀疑某事

(考题)"If people doubt the outcome of his two experiments," said Baker, "I suggest they repeat the experiments and see for themselves."

doubt whether/if ... 怀疑…

(考题)Watchers doubted if any of the vehicles could finish the race because they did not have any human guidance.

doubt that ... 不相信…

（注意：doubt that . . .表示对某事持怀疑态度，如：I doubt that he did it表示"我不认为是他做的"；而 I don't doubt that he did it则表示我不怀疑（即相信、认为）是他做的。）

down /daun/ *prep. adv.* 向下；在下

get/settle down to sth. 开始认真做某事

let sb. down 使某人失望、辜负了某人

（考题）Before the show, he treated us to dinner at a restaurant and taught us not to talk with our mouths full. We did not want to let him down.

up and down 上上下下、来来回回

（考题）On some services, prices went up and down at random.

upside down 颠倒

（考题）Some even ride upside down — their legs and feet straight up in the air — all at full speed.

down with . . . 打倒…

be down with 由于…病倒了

download /'daunləud/ *n. vt.*（计算机）下载

downstairs /ˌdaun'steəs/ *adv.* 往楼下；在楼下

downwards /'daunwədz/ *adj.* 向下地

dozen /'dʌzən/ *n.* 一打，十二个

a dozen . . . 一打…

dozens of . . . 几十个…、许多…

Dr /'dɒktə/ *n.*（Doctor 的缩略形式）博士；医生

draft /drɑːft/ *n.* 草稿；草案 *v.* 起草

drag /dræg/ *vt.* 拖；费力地走

drag sth. 拖、拉某物

. . . drag on . . . 慢慢地进行；拖得很长

（考题）Since I've got to be here, I try to enjoy myself — and I usually do, because of the other girls. We all have a good laugh. So the time never drags.

dragon /'drægən/ *n.* 龙

drain /drein/ *n.* 排水管；耗竭；消耗

be a drain on . . . 不断消耗…

vt. vi. **drain sth. away/off** 把…排掉

sth. drain away/off . . . 被排掉

drama /ˈdrɑːmə/ *n.* 戏剧；剧本

dramatic /drəˈmætɪk/ *adj.* 戏剧(性)的；给人深刻印象的

draw /drɔː/ (drew, drawn) *vt.* 拉，拖；拔；吸引；画；提取(存款等)
vi. 拉；绘画；有吸引力

　　draw a conclusion 得出结论

　　(考题)Read the news from different views and draw your own conclusions on the stories shaping our world.

　　draw sb.'s attention 吸引了某人的注意

　　(考题)The writer uses the two questions at the beginning of the passage to draw the readers' attention to the topic.

　　draw sth. from ... 从…中提取

　　(考题)If you carry the Servicecard or the Casheard, you can draw your money from cash machines conveniently.

　　draw near 接近、临近

　　draw to a close/an end 结束

　　(考题)In conversation he expressed little joy and it seemed that his life was drawing to a close.

drawer /ˈdrɔːə/ *n.* 抽屉

drawing /ˈdrɔːɪŋ/ *n.* 图画；素描(画)

　　(考题)In science and engineering classes, the instructors put tables and drawings on the blackboard.

dream /driːm/ *n.* 梦、睡梦　*vi.* *vt.* (dreamed，或 dreamt，dreamt) 做梦；梦想

　　dream of/about sth. 梦见…；渴望…

　　(考题)Most young architects, particularly those in big cities, can only dream about working in a building of their own.

　　dream that ... 梦见…

　　dream a ... dream 做了一个…的梦

dress /dres/ *n.* 女服；服装　*vi.* 穿衣　*vt.* 为…穿衣

　　(考题)Parents and kids today dress alike, listen to the same music, and are friends.

　　dress sb. 给某人穿衣服

　　be dressed in ... 穿着…

　　(考题)If all students are dressed in the same way, they will not pay too much attention to their clothing, ...

dress (sb.) up (替某人)打扮、装扮起来

(考题)... some believe that many city beggars dress up on purpose to look pitiable and actually make a good living from begging.

drift /drɪft/ *n.* 漂流 *vt. vi.* (使)漂流

drill /drɪl/ *n.* 训练;操练;钻孔 *vi.* 操练;钻孔

(考题)Scientists from 10 nations have now almost completely drilled through a 3,000-meter depth of ice high in the Antarctic mainland.

drink /drɪŋk/ (drank, drunk) *v.* 喝,饮 *n.* 饮料

drink sth. up 喝完…

drink to ... 为…而干杯

drip /drɪp/ *n.* 水滴 *vi.* 滴下

drive /draɪv/ (drove, driven) *v.* 开车;驱赶

(考题)Some people prefer to drive without wearing a safety belt because they believe the belt prevents them from escaping in an accident.

drive sb. to a place 开车送某人去某地

drive sb. out of/away/to ... 驱赶某人

(考题)If another animal has made a kill, they will drive it off and take the kill for themselves.

drive sb. to (do) sth. 逼迫某人做某事

(考题)The whole model is driven by advertisers' need to get in front of shoppers ...

drive sb. mad/crazy 使某人受不了、使发疯

n. 驾驶;车道;路程;魄力、动力

driver /ˈdraɪvə/ *n.* 驾驶员,司机

drop /drɒp/ *n.* 滴;下降

(考题)Drops in air pressure produce an effect on small animals in many ways.

v. (使)落下、掉下、滴下

drop in (on sb.) 顺道拜访(某人)

(考题)You may drop in or just give me a call. Either will do.

drop off 下降;掉下;睡着了

drop out 退出;掉队;退学

drown /draʊn/ v. (使)淹死;淹没;掩盖

(考题)The wall of water rushed towards southern Africa at 800 kilometers an hour. Cities on the African coast are totally destroyed and millions of people are drowned.

drug /drʌg/ n. 药物;麻醉品;毒品

drugstore /'drʌgstɔ:/ n. 药店;杂货店

drum /drʌm/ n. 鼓;鼓声

dry /draɪ/ adj. 干的;干旱的;枯燥无味的

(考题)Rain forests slightly farther away from the equator remain just as warm, but they have a dry season of three months or more when little rain falls.

vt. 使干 vi. 变干

(考题)For black tea, the young green leaves are first spread out on shelves to dry.

dry up 干涸

(考题)Over the centuries, the water dried up. Wind, sand, rain, heat and cold all wore away at the remaining rocks.

dry sth. up 使…变干

duck /dʌk/ n. 鸭

due /dju:/ adj. 应得的;到时的;适当的

(考题)She is due to complete her study and graduate later this year.

due to 由于;因为

(考题)It was reported that Mr. Evans' healthy long life was to a certain extent due to his mild temper.

(辨析: due to, owing to, because of 等都可以表示"由于"。但 due to 可以担任表语。)

duel /djʊəl/ n. 决斗 vi. 决斗

dull /dʌl/ adj. 乏味的;(色彩等)不鲜明的;无光泽的

dumb /dʌm/ adj. 哑的;无言的

dump /dʌmp/ vt. 倾倒(垃圾等)

dumpling /'dʌmplɪŋ/ n. 馄饨;汤团

during /'djʊərɪŋ/ prep. 在…期间

dusk /dʌsk/ n. 黄昏

dust /dʌst/ n. 灰尘、尘土

dusty /'dʌstɪ/ *adj*. 多尘的；灰蒙蒙的

duty /'djuːtɪ/ *n*. 责任、义务

（考题）But he never forgot the land of his birth, or the duty to share his fortune with others.

on duty 值日

off duty 下班

do one's duty 尽自己的责任

dynamite /'daɪnəmaɪt/ *n*. 炸药

dynasty /'dɪnəstɪ，'daɪnəstɪ/ *n*. 朝代、王朝

E

each /iːtʃ/ *pron.* 每一个　*adj.* 每一个；各个

（考题）Therefore, it is important for each person in our society to try to maintain a healthy and realistic self-image.

each other 互相、彼此

（考题）Through body language, humans give each other very subtle but clear signals that show emotions.

（辨析：each、every 都表示"每一个"。each 强调个体，指多数中的任何一个。each 可以作代词使用；every 则通过强调"每一个"而达到强调"所有、总体"，即 all 的目的。）

eager /ˈiːgə/ *adj.* 迫切的、渴望的

be eager for sth. 渴望得到某物

be eager to do sth. 渴望做某事

（考题）She is eager to get more knowledge of child development and to better understand how young children look at the world.

（同义词：**be keen to do sth.、be anxious to do sth.、long to do sth.、desire to do sth.、have a desire to do sth.**）

eagerness /iːgənɪs/ *n.* 迫切、渴望

（考题）In the story, Tim's mood changed from eagerness to nervousness

in one's eagerness to do sth. 迫切想做某事

with eagerness 迫切地

ear /ɪə/ *n.* 耳朵

have no ear for ... 没有欣赏…的能力

turn a deaf ear to sth. /sb. 对某事/某人置之不理

（考题）Many of them turned a deaf ear to his advice, even though they knew it to be valuable.

early /ˈɜːlɪ/ *adj. adv.* 早

earn /ɜːn/ *vt.* 赚；赢得

earn sth. 赚得、赢得某物

（考题）The author thinks modern hunters kill mainly to earn

people's admiration.

earn sb. sth. 为某人赢得某物

earn one's living 谋生

(考题) The young man made a promise to his parents that he would try to earn his own living after graduation.

earnest /ˈɜːnɪst/ *adj*. 认真的、诚恳的

earnings /ˈɜːnɪŋz/ *n*. 赚得的钱、收入

(考题) Teenagers tend to overestimate their future earnings.

earth /ɜːθ/ *n*. 地球；土地、泥土

the earth 地球

bring sb. back to earth 使某人回到现实中来

on earth 在世上；究竟

(考题) When the fragments landed in the southern part of the giant planet，the explosions were watched by scientists here on earth.

(辨析：earth 指地球表面，也可指种植植物的土壤；land 指地球表面上海面以外的陆地；ground 指地面、场地；field 指原野、田地；soil 指种庄稼的土地表层、土壤。)

earthquake /ˈɜːθkweɪk/ *n*. 地震

ease /iːz/ *n*. 容易、不费力；舒适、自在

be/put sb. at ease (使某人)自在、不拘束

(考题) But Einstein immediately put Hoffman at ease by saying，"Please go slowly. I don't understand things quickly."

with ease 轻易地

easily /ˈiːzɪlɪ/ *adv*. 容易地、轻松地；随意地

east /iːst/ *n*. 东方；东部　　*adv*. 朝东；向东

eastern /ˈiːstən/ *adj*. 东部的；向东的

eastward /ˈiːstwəd/ *adv*. 向东

easy /ˈiːzɪ/ *adj*. 容易的

be easy to sb. 对某人来说很容易

It's easy (for sb.) to do sth. (某人)做某事很容易

(考题)　this labeling makes it easy to send out information about fashion and price instantly.

Take it easy. 别紧张。放轻松点。

eat /iːt/ (ate，eaten) *vt*. *vi*. 吃

eat one's words 收回前言,自认失言

eat out 在外面吃饭

eat (sth.) up 吃光(…)

E-book *n*. 电子书籍

economic /ˌiːkənˈɒmɪk/ *adj*. 经济的;经济学的

(考题)These food-price increases, combined with increasing energy costs, will slow if not stop economic growth in many parts of the world and will even affect political stability.

economical /ˌiːkəˈnɒmɪkəl/ *adj*. 节省的、节约的

economy /ɪˈkɒnəmɪ/ *n*. 经济;节约

(考题)But a rapidly changing economy and frequent periods of high unemployment make it difficult for most of its members to be able to increase their savings greatly.

national economy 国民经济

edge /edʒ/ *n*. 边缘;*vt*. 给…加边;使锋利

edit /ˈedɪt/ *vi*. 编辑

edition /ɪˈdɪʃən/ *n*. 版本

a paperback edition 平装本

a pocket edition 袖珍本

a revised edition 修订本

an overseas edition 海外版

(考题)A special edition of a newspaper was rushed out and delivered all over the country.

editor /ˈedɪtə/ *n*. 编辑

chief editor 主编

editorial /edɪˈtɔːrɪəl/ *n*. 编辑的;社论

educate /ˈedjuːkeɪt/ *vt*. 教育

well-educated 受过良好教育的

(考题)I searched books for good expressions and sayings, pieces of information, ideas, themes — anything to enrich my thought and make me feel educated.

education /ˌedjuːˈkeɪʃən/ *n*. 教育

(考题)For students, the school uniform reminds them that their task for the six or seven hours they are in school is to get an education.

have a good education 受过良好教育

of good education 受过良好教育的

effect /ɪˈfekt/ *n*. 效果；影响

come/go into effect 生效

（考题）The new law will go into effect from the first day of next month.

have an effect on sth. 对某事有影响

（考题）It is found that the look of the package has a great effect on the "quality" of the product and on how well it sells.

in effect 实际上

（考题）I think it is a wonderful phrase，reminding us，in effect，to enjoy the moment：to value this very day.

be of no effect 没有作用

put/bring/carry sth. into effect 使…生效

take effect 生效

（考题）Don't worry. The medicine is taking effect now.

to no effect 没有作用

without effect 没有作用

effective /ɪˈfektɪv/ *adj*. 有效的

take effective measures 采取有效措施

efficient /ɪˈfɪʃənt/ *adj*. 有效率的、高效的

effort /ˈefət/ *n*. 努力

make an effort/efforts（to do sth.） 努力做某事

（考题）Beijing has made efforts to improve its air quality.

in one's effort to do sth. 努力做某事

（考题）Unless watched，she will walk in the streets in an effort to find her father，who died 30 years ago.

spare no effort 不遗余力

with effort 努力地

（考题）With effort，we can translate compassion into actions.

without effort 毫不费力、轻松

（考题）But a specially trained person can do this without much effort.

e. g.（exempli gratia）＝ for example 例如

egg /eɡ/ *n*. 蛋；鸡蛋

lay eggs 生蛋

eh /eɪ/ *interj*. 啊；嗯

eight /eɪt/ *num*. 八

eighteen /ˈeɪˈtiːn/ *num*. 十八

eighteenth /eɪˈtiːnθ/ *num*. 第十八

eighty /ˈeɪtɪ/ *num*. 八十

Einstein, Albert /aɪnsteɪn ælbət/ 阿尔伯特·爱因斯坦

either /ˈaɪðə, ˈiːðə/ *adv*. （否定句中）也；*adj*. *pron*. *adv*. （两个中的）任何一个

　　either ... or ... 或是…或是…；不是…，就是…
　　（见 both）

elaborate /ɪˈlæbərət/ *adj*. 精心制作的；复杂的

elder /ˈeldə/ *adj*. 年龄较大的；年长的　*n*. 上了年纪的人

　　elder brother/sister 哥哥/姐姐
　　（考题）You should respect your elders.

elderly /ˈeldəlɪ/ *adj*. 上了年纪的

　　（考题）Often the elderly are disabled and cannot care for an animal by walking it or playing with it.

elect /ɪˈlekt/ *vt*. 选举

　　elect sb. (as/to be) ... 选举某人为…
　　（注意：在 elect 后面担任补足语的名词前一般不使用冠词。如：He was elected mayor of the city.）

electric /ɪˈlektrɪk/ *adj*. 电的

　　electric light 电灯
　　electric current 电流

electrical /ɪˈlektrɪkəl/ *adj*. 与电有关的

　　an electrical engineer 电气工程师
　　（辨析：electric 表示以电为动力的设备，或是因电而产生的现象；electrical 则表示"电学的"、"有关电的"。）

electrician /ɪlekˈtrɪʃən/ *n*. 电工；电气工作人员

electricity /ɪlekˈtrɪsɪtɪ/ *n*. 电

electron /ɪˈlektrɒn/ *n*. 电子

electronic /ɪlekˈtrɒnɪk/ *adj*. 电子的

elegant /ˈelɪgənt/ *adj*. 优雅的；典雅的、有风度的

element /ˈelɪmənt/ *n*. 成分、元素

elementary /ˌelɪˈmentərɪ/ *adj*. 初级的；基本的

　　elementary school 小学

elephant /ˈelɪfənt/ *n*. 大象

elevator /ˈelɪveɪtə/ *n*. 电梯

eleven /ɪˈlevən/ *num*. 十一

eleventh /ɪˈlevənθ/ *num*. 第十一

eliminate /ɪˈlɪmɪneɪt/ *vt*. 消除；排除；淘汰

　　elimination match 淘汰赛

else /els/ *adj*. 其它的、别的

　　who/what else 别的什么人/东西

　　something/anything else 其它什么事

　　somewhere/anywhere else 别的什么地方

　　or else 或者

　　（注意：表示所有格使用 else's 这一形式，所以没有 whose else 的用法，而应说 Who else's；另外，也不说 which else。）

elsewhere /ˌelsˈweə/ *adv*. 在别处

e-mail, E-mail, email /ˈiːmeɪl/ *n*. 电子邮件

embarrass /ɪmˈbærəs/ *vt*. 使局促不安、使尴尬

　　（考题）I hope that my request will not embarrass anyone.

emerge /ɪˈmɜːdʒ/ *vi*. 出现；产生、被发现

　　emerge from … 从…出现、表现出来

emergency /ɪˈmɜːdʒɪnsɪ/ *n*. 紧急情况；急诊

　　（考题）In case of emergency, please call the Help Desk at 926-3736 and follow the procedures outlined on the voice message.

　　an emergency exit/door 紧急出口

　　emergency measures 紧急措施

　　emergency ward 急诊病房

emotion /ɪˈməʊʃən/ *n*. 情感；情绪、激动

　　（考题）If they associate you with this emotion of fear, they will become less functional around you

　　（辨析：emotion 指强烈的感情，如喜怒哀乐；feeling 指外部刺激在身体上的感觉，如寒冷饥饿等，也可指快乐、同情、失望等情绪和心情。复数形式 feelings 意思同 emotion。）

emotional /ɪˈməʊʃənəl/ *adj*. 易动感情的；感情强烈的

emperor /ˈempərə/ *n*. 皇帝；君主

emphasis /'emfəsɪs/ (*pl* . emphases) *n* . 强调；着重

　　lay/put/place emphases on ... 强调…

emphasize /'emfəsaɪz/ *vt* . 强调

　　（考题）Some companies have made the manufacturing of clean and safe products their main selling point and emphasize it in their advertising.

empire /'empaɪə/ *n* . 帝国

employ /ɪm'plɔɪ/ *vt* . 雇用；使用

　　（考题）... we can employ them at the emotional level, so they became fully devoted to the projects and provide some of their own motivation.

　　be employed in ... 忙于做某事

　　employ oneself in ... 忙于做某事

employee /ˌemplɔɪ'iː/ *n* . 雇员

employer /ɪm'plɔɪə/ *n* . 雇主

employment /ɪm'plɔɪmənt/ *n* . 雇用、就业

　　（考题）What makes this class differ from the lower class is, first, longer periods of employment — and therefore, more fixed incomes — and, second, employment in skilled or semiskilled occupations, not unskilled ones.

　　in/out of employment 有工作/失业

　　（注意："失业"的表达方法有这几种：be out of employment, be out of work, be out of a job, be unemployed, be jobless。）

empty /'emptɪ/ *adj* . 空的

　　be empty of 没有

　　vi . *vt* . 使空、倒掉

　　empty into 流入

　　（考题）All big rivers in the country empty into the Atlantic.

　　empty sth. out 把某物倒空

enable /ɪ'neɪbl/ *vt* . 使能够

　　enable sb. to do sth. 使某人有能力做某事

　　（考题）Tears also enable us to understand our emotions better; sometimes we don't even know we're sad until we cry.

enclose /ɪn'kləʊz/ *vt* . 围住、围起；封入（信封等）

　　（考题）When people are enclosed together, they are in what is

called a stress situation.

encourage /ɪnˈkʌrɪdʒ/ *vt.* 鼓励、激励；促进、有利于

encourage sb. to do sth. 鼓励某人做某事

（考题）He encourages buyers to bid higher figures，and finally names the highest bidder as the buyer of the goods.

encourage sth. 促进、激发、推动某事

（考题）Leadership means power，commands respect and，most important，encourages achievement.

encouragement /ɪnˈkʌrɪdʒmənt/ *n.* 鼓励；激励

end /end/ *n.* 结束；结尾；末端

at the end (of ...) 在(…)的末尾

come to an end 结束

（考题）The discussion will come to an end soon. It has taken too much time.

from beginning to end 从头至尾

in the end 最后、终于

put an and to sth. 结束某事

（考题）We should put an end to this kind of things.

to the end 到底

vi. vt. **end sth.** 结束某事

（考题）Men often take sudden action to end their marriage.

end (up) in sth. 以…为结果

（考题）If you carry on like this，you will end up in prison.

end up (by) doing sth. 最终会…，结果是…

（考题）Searchers often end up finding a car with no one in it.

endurance /ɪnˈdjʊərəns/ *n.* 忍受(力)；忍耐

beyond endurance 到无法忍受的地步

endure /ɪnˈdjʊə/ *vt. vi.* 忍受、忍耐；承受

endure sth. /sb. 忍受某事/某人

（考题）But we have a few that are in commercial use for 12 years and they have endured over 80,000 uses each，without need of repair.

(can't) endure to do/doing sth. 无法忍受做某事

（辨析：endure，bear，stand 都表示"忍受"，常可互换。endure 语气更为严肃、或是指较长时间的痛苦。）

enemy /'enɪmɪ/ *n.* 敌人

energetic /ˌenə'dʒetɪk/ *adj.* 精力充沛的

energize /'enədʒaɪz/ *vt.* 使有活力;供给能量

energy /'enədʒɪ/ *n.* 能量;活力;精力

（考题）But when they get excited about the work，all their energy gets poured into the job. That's a great force!

give/apply/devote one's energy to (doing) sth. 把精力投入到

with energy 努力地、精力充沛地

nuclear energy 核能

solar energy 太阳能

thermal energy 热能

engage /ɪn'geɪdʒ/ *vi.* *vt.* 从事、参加;约定;订婚

engage (oneself) in sth. 从事与

（考题）The scientist is engaging himself in the experiment.

be engaged in (doing) sth. 从事…忙于…

（考题）He's engaged in a conversation. Please don't bother.

be engaged to sb. 与某人订婚

engine /'endʒɪn/ *n.* 发动机、引擎

engineer /endʒɪ'nɪə/ *n.* 工程师

engineering /endʒɪ'nɪərɪŋ/ *n.* 工程学;工程

civil engineering 土木工程

electrical engineering 电气工程

mechanical engineering 机械工程

England /'ɪŋglənd/ *n.* 英格兰

English /'ɪŋglɪʃ/ *n.* 英语 *n.* 英国的;英语的

Englishman /'ɪŋglɪʃmən/ *n.* 英国人

enhance /ɪn'hɑːns/ *vt.* 增强、强化

（考题）Blue does enhance communication but I am not sure it would enhance truthful communication.

enjoy /ɪn'dʒɔɪ/ *vt.* 喜欢、欣赏;有权享受

enjoy (doing) sth. 喜欢(做)某事

（考题）Often，there is the double pressure to enjoy life through food and yet remain ultra-slim.

（考题）They enjoyed expressing their ideas and sharing them in

groups.

enjoy oneself 过得开心

enjoyable /ɪnˈdʒɔɪəbl/ *adj*. 有趣的、令人快乐的

enlarge /ɪnˈlɑːdʒ/ *vt*. 扩大、放大

（考题）He hoped to enlarge the forest on the farm.

enlargement /ɪnˈlɑːdʒmənt/ *n*. 扩大

enormous /ɪˈnɔːməs/ *adj*. 巨大的

enough /ɪˈnʌf/ *adj*. *adv*. 足够的　*n*. 足够、充分

（考题）My only concern is that you are not active enough in putting forward your suggestions.

（考题）By cramming，a student may learn the subject well enough to get by on the examination，but he is likely soon to forget almost everything he learned.

（注意：enough 在修饰形容词或副词时，要摆在后面，如：big enough，fast enough。但修饰名词时，前后均可。）

enroll /ɪnˈrəʊl/（enrol）*vt*. 招收、招募　*vi*. 入学、加入

ensure /ɪnˈʃʊə/ *vt*. 确保、保证

ensure sth. 确保某事

（考题）Whatever the task your group is assigned，a few rules need to be followed to ensure a productive and successful experience.

ensure sb. sth. 向某人保证某事

ensure that ... 保证、确保…

（考题）You have to ensure that everybody understands the importance of the job before you begin it.

（辨析：在表示"向某人保证某事"时，可使用 ensure. sb. sth.，或 assure sb. of sth.；另外，ensure 可直接跟宾语从句，而 assure 的用法是 assure sb. that ...。）

enter /ˈentə/ *vi*. *vt*. 进入；报名参加；输入

（考题）Just enter the start and the end of your journey and the Traveler will work out the quickest route.

enter（sb.）for sth. （替某人）报名参加…

（注意：表示进入某处时，enter 不使用介词 into。但在表示开始谈话、谈判、订立协定等意思时，常使用 into。如：The two countries have entered into a peace agreement.）

enterprise /'entəpraɪz/ *n*. 企业

entertain /entə'teɪn/ *vt*. 娱乐、招待

entertain sb. with sth. 用…招待某人

entertainment /entə'teɪmənt/ *n*. 娱乐、招待；娱乐活动

enthusiasm /ɪn'θju:zɪæzəm/ *n*. 热情、热心

with enthusiasm 热情地

（考题）When they were shown an unfamiliar human they wagged to the right，but with somewhat less enthusiasm.

enthusiastic /ɪn'θju:zɪ'æstɪk/ *adj*. 热心的、热情的

（考题）According to the OECD，being a regular and enthusiastic reader is of great advantage.

be enthusiastic about sth. 对…非常热心

entire /ɪn'taɪə/ *adj*. 整个的、全部的

（考题）As the parasites multiply，they take over the entire body.

（辨析：entire 和 whole 表示"总体、全部"，常可互换。但 entire 可修饰抽象概念，whole 则不可以。total 则是强调数量含义，指 "总和"。）

entitle /ɪn'taɪtl/ *n*. 标题、题名 *vt*. 使有权得到某物

（考题）The book entitled A History of Modern Indonesia has focused on its social and political aspects in modern times.

be entitled to (do) sth. 有权得到某物/做某事

entrance /'entrəns/ *n*. 进入；进口；入学

at the entrance to ... 在…的入口处

envelope /'envələʊp/ *n*. 信封

environment /ɪn'vaɪərənmənt/ *n*. 环境

to protect the environment 保护环境

envy /'envɪ/ *n*. *vt*. 嫉妒；羡慕

envy sb./sth 嫉妒某人/某事

（考题）Helen was much kinder to her youngest son than to the others，which，of course，made the others envy him.

envy sb. sth. 就某事嫉妒（羡慕）某人

（考题）All others envy him the good chance.

equal /'i:kwəl/ *adj*. 平等的；相等的；

be equal to ... 与…平等

（考题）When two cars traveling at 30 mph hit each other，an

unbelted driver would meet the windshield with a force equal to diving headfirst into the ground from a height of 10 meters.

n. 同等的人或事物

have no equal 无人能与之相提并论

(考题) Armstrong had no equal when it came to playing the American popular song.

equip /ɪˈkwɪpt/ *vt.* 配备

equip sb./sth. with sth. 给某人/物配备某物

be equipped with sth. 配备有某物

(考题) The ship is equipped with a lot of most advanced navigational aids.

equipment /ɪˈkwɪpmənt/ *n.* 设备

(考题) This laboratory has the most advance equipment and the most outstanding scientists in the world.

(注意: equipment 是设备的总称,一般用作不可数名词。偶尔也有复数的形式,如: military equipments。)

equivalent /ɪˈkwɪvələnt/ *adj.* 相当的、相等的; *n.* 相当的物体、数量等

be equivalent to ... 与…相当

erect /ɪˈrekt/ *vt.* 建起、树立

error /ˈerə/ *n.* 错误、过失; 误差

(考题) Still, it was a lot of learning by trial and error.

be in error about sth. 某事弄错了

escalator /eˈskəleɪtə/ *n.* 自动扶梯

escape /ɪsˈkeɪp/ *vi. vt.* 逃脱; 逃逸

escape from ... 从某处逃出

(考题) By trying to escape from present interests and imagine life far in the future, we may arrive at quite fresh ideas that we can use ourselves.

escape sth. 逃脱、摆脱某事

(考题) Although 40 percent said that the main reason for going away is to escape pressure from work, almost all said they worry more than they do at home.

escape doing sth. 避免了做某事、差一点做某事

(考题) The child narrowly escaped from being drowned.

escape sb. /sb. 's notice/sb. 's attention 逃脱了某人的注意

especially /ɪsˈpeʃəlɪ/ *adv*. 尤其、特别

（考题）Birds are especially good weather indicators because they also show the effect of a pressure drop in many ways.

（考题）Besides，she also enjoys reading articles written especially for young girls.

（辨析：especially 表示程度，意思是"尤其、特别"；有时也可表示"专门地、特地"的意思。这时，和 specially 的意思相同，如：He was especially glad to attend the party, which was specially given in his honor.）

essay /ˈeseɪ/ *n*. 散文、论文

（见 article）

essential /ɪˈsenʃəl/ *adj*. 必要的；根本的

be essential to/for sth. 对…来说是必不可少的

（考题）The reason for Marc's going home was that he realized his family was essential to him.

establish /ɪˈstæblɪʃ/ *vt*. 建立；确立

（考题）Once an eating disorder has become firmly established，there is no easy cure.

estimate /ˈestɪmeɪt/ *vt*. 估计；评价、评估

Mercer estimates London is 26 percent more expensive than New York these days.

n. 估计；估算

（考题）At a rough estimate，Nigeria is three times the size of Great Britain.

etc. /ɪtˈsetərə/（et cetera）等等

Europe /ˈjʊərəp/ *n*. 欧洲

European /jʊərəˈpiːn/ *adj*. 欧洲的

eve /iːv/ *n*. 前夜、前夕

Christmas Eve 圣诞夜

on the eve of ... 在…的前夜

even /ˈiːvən/ *adj*. 甚至

even if/even though 尽管、即使

（考题）Even if you do make an obvious mistake during a speech，that doesn't really matter.

event /ɪ'vent/ *n*. 事件；体育项目

a historic event 历史事件

eventual /ɪ'ventʃʊəl/ *adj*. 最后的，结果的

ever /'evə/ *adv*. 从来

for ever 永远（＝**forever**）

ever since 从…以来（＝**since then**）

everlasting /ˌevə'lɑːstɪŋ/ *adj*. 永久的、持久的

every /'evərɪ/ *adj*. 每一个

every other ... 每隔一个

every six hours 每六个小时

every now and then 每隔一段时间

（注意：every，all，both 等词的否定形式属于部分否定，分别表示"并不是每一个"、"并不是所有的"以及"并不是两者都"。如要表示全部否定的意义，则需要用 none，not any 以及 neither。）

（辨析：every 和 per 都表示"每一个"的意思。every 强调"所有中的每一个都不例外"，从不同的侧面表示"所有"的意思；而 per 则是强调"每一份、以每一个为单位"。）

everybody /'evərɪbɒdɪ/ *pron*. 每个人、人人

everyday /'evərɪdeɪ/ *adj*. 每天的、日常的；普通的

（辨析：everyday 是形容词。every day 则表示"每天"，担任时间状语。）

everyone /'evərɪwʌn/ *pron*. 每个人、人人

（辨析：everyone 表示每个人，后面不能接 of 引导的介词短语。如要表示"…中的每一个"，应使用 every one of ...。）

everything /'evərɪθɪŋ/ *pron*. 每样东西；每件事

everywhere /'evərɪweə/ *adv*. 到处；每个地方

evidence /'evɪdəns/ *n*. 证明、证据；现象

evident /'evɪdənt/ *adj*. 明白的、显然的

evil /'iːvəl/ *n*. 罪恶　*adj*. 罪恶的

evolution /ˌiːvə'luːʃən/ *n*. 演变、发展；进化、发展

evolve /ɪ'vɒlv/ *vi*. *vt*. 演变、发展、进化

（考题）Does Martin really believe that humans could evolve their way to longer life?

exact /ɪg'zækt/ *adj*. 精确的、确切的

（考题）In most years, more than five hundred million cases of

illness result from the disease，although exact numbers are difficult to assess because many people don't（or can't）seek care.

be exact in (doing) sth. 做事很精准

be exact to ... 完全符合…

to be exact 确切地说

exactly /ɪgˈzæktlɪ/ *adv*. 确切地、准确地

（考题）Most often，people do not fit exactly into a producer's size. Their clothing must be altered to make it fit better.

not exactly 不完全是这样

（考题）Well，not exactly，but ...

exam /ɪˈgzæm/ *n*. 考试、检查

pass an exam 通过一项考试

fail (in) an exam 没有考及格

sit for/take an exam 参加考试

examine /ɪˈgzæmɪn/ *vt*. 考试、审查

（考题）Researchers in Italy examined the tail wagging behaviour of 30 dogs，catching their responses to a range of stimuli with video cameras

examine sb. on sth. 在某方面考查某人

example /ɪgˈzɑːmpl/ *n*. 例子；榜样

for example 例如

take ... for exampl 以…为例

an example to sb. 是某人的榜样

（考题）He has done something great and is a good example to us all.

follow sb. 's example 学习某人的榜样

an example of ... 是…的例子

（考题）Every storm is an example of the power of nature.

（注意：example 在表示"榜样"时，后面的介词用 to；表示"例子"时，介词用 of。）

excellent /ˈeksələnt/ *adj*. 优秀的、极好的

except /ɪkˈsept/ *prep*. *conj*. 除…之外

except sth. 除了…之外，其它的

except that ... 除了、要不是

（考题）I cannot remember anything about it except that it was about a tiger.

except for sth. 要不是、除了

（考题）When I arrived to collect，I found the building was dark except for a single light in a ground floor window.

do nothing except/but do sth. 只能做某事

（考题）You don't have to do anything except to be with them and be yourself.

（辨析：except 表示"除了…之外，其它的"，即提到的人或物被排除在外。except 用于同类的人或物，如：I know everyone here except that girl. everyone 和 that girl 是同类的。except for 则指不同类的事物，如：Your furniture is very good except for its color. 其中 furniture 和 color 属于不同类的事物。而 except that 后面跟的是从句。另见 besides。）

exception /ɪkˈsepʃən/ *n*. 例外

with the exception of ... 除…之外

I agree with most of Raj Persaud's opinions about the doubtful value of tipping，but with one exception.

without exception 毫无例外地

exchange /ɪksˈtʃeɪndʒ/ *n*. 交换

in exchange for sth. 交换某物

（考题）It's good to do whatever we can for our animals who in exchange for a little love fill our existence with their attention.

vt. 交换

（考题）For example，she has been learning how to exchange messages with people.

exchange A for B 用 A 换 B

（同义词：change sth. for sth. ，trade sth. for sth. ）

excite /ɪkˈsaɪt/ *vt*. 使激动、使兴奋

excited /ɪkˈsaɪtɪd/ *adj*. 激动的、兴奋的

be excited at/about sth. 为某事而激动

excitement /ɪkˈsaɪtmənt/ *n*. 激动、兴奋

in excitement 激动地

（考题）... and often the birthday boy or girl gets lost in wild excitement.

to sb. 's excitement 使某人感到激动的是

exclaim /ɪksˈkleɪm/ *vi*. *vt*. 惊叫；惊叫着说出

exclude /ɪksˈkluːd/ *vt.* 排除在外;不让进来

excursion /ɪkˈskɜːʃən/ *n.* 短途旅行;远足

excuse /ɪkˈskjuːz/ *n.* 原谅;借口、理由

（考题）For us ten-year olds, "being out in the woods" was just an excuse to do whatever we feel like for a while.

make/find/have an excuse for sth. 找借口

vt. 原谅;允许离开

excuse sb. for (doing) sth. 原谅某人做了某事

（考题）Each person excuses himself by thinking someone else will help, so that the more "other people" there are, the greater the total shifting of responsibility.

excuse sb. from doing sth. 免除某人做某事的义务

executive /ɪgˈzekjʊtɪv/ *n.* 管理者、行政官 *adj.* 管理的

CEO（chief executive officer）首席执行官

exercise /ˈeksəsaɪz/ *n.* 练习;锻炼; *vi. vt.* 锻炼;运用、行使

exhaust /ɪgˈzɔːst/ *vt.* 耗尽;使筋疲力尽

exhibit /ɪgˈzɪbɪt/ *n.* 展览品

exhibition /eksɪˈbɪʃən/ *n.* 展览;展览会

exist /ɪgˈzɪst/ *vi.* 存在

（考题）This variety didn't exist in the horse population before domestication.

existence /ɪgˈzɪstəns/ *n.* 存在

be in existence 存在

come into existence 出现、产生

exit /ˈeksɪt/ *n.* 出口;退场

expand /ɪkˈspænd/ *vi. vt.* 扩大、展开

expect /ɪkˈspekt/ *vt.* 期待;预料

expect sb./sth. 期待某人/物

expect to do sth. 期待做某事

（考题）And children expect to take part in the family decision-making process. They don't want to "rock the boat".

expect sb. to do sth. 期待某人做某事

（考题）Your child may always seem to expect the worst to happen and lack confidence in his or her ability to deal with any challenge.

expect that ... 期待…

（考题）We expected that he would help us, but he didn't.

expectation /ˌɪkspek'teɪʃən/ *n.* 期望；预计

（考题）Many place their expectations on their children, hoping that they at least will rise in the ladder of success, American style.

beyond expectation(s) 出乎预料

（考题）Merlin succeeded beyond expectation.

come up to sb.'s expectation(s) 没有辜负某人的期望

（考题）People feel less happy if their income is below their expectation.

expense /ɪk'spens/ *n.* 花费、开销；费用

household expenses 家庭开销

living expenses 生活开销

traveling expenses 旅行开销

expensive /ɪk'spensɪv/ *adj.* 价格昂贵的

experience /ɪk'spɪərəns/ *n.* 经验、经历

（考题）She says she will be looking for a job which will give her the chance to enrich her experience of shark research.

（考题）By telling his own experiences, the author tries to show the importance of expressing thanks.

vt. 经历

（考题）What feeling will you likely experience should a loved one suffer from Alzheimer's disease?

（注意：表示"经验"时，一般做不可数名词。但表示某种经验时，可有复数的形式，如：He's a man of an experience of forty years at sea. 表示"经历"时，是可数名词。）

experienced /ɪk'spɪərənst/ *adj.* 有经验的

be experienced in (doing) sth. 做某事有经验

（考题）As I was not experienced in cooking, I thought if a dozen was good, two dozen would be better, so I doubled everything.

experiment /ɪk'sperɪmənt/ *n.* 实验；试验

do/make/perform/carry out an experiment on sth. 做有关…的实验

expert /'ekspɜːt/ *n.* 专家、行家

be an expert in/on/at sth. 是某方面的行家

（考题）Alan Beck，an expert in human-animal relationship，and Nancy Edwards，a professor of nursing，are leading the animal-assisted study concerning ...

adj. 拿手的、善于

This teacher is quite expert in teaching children.

explain /ɪk'spleɪn/ *vt.* 解释；说明

（考题）Of all the reasons that explain their loneliness，a large geographical distance between parents and their children is the major one.

explain sth. to sb. 向某人解释某事

（考题）I explain to my parents that I need some free time.

explain that ... 解释说

explain what/how/... to do 解释做什么/如何做/…

（考题）"Please explain why you're so late，" his boss said.

explanation /ˌeksplə'neɪʃən/ *n.* 解释、说明

give an explanation for sth. 对某事做出解释

explode /ɪk'spləʊd/ *vi. vt.* 爆炸；使爆炸

exploit /'eksplɔɪt/ *vt.* 剥削；开发

explore /ɪk'splɔː/ *vt.* 勘探；探险

（考题）When there is research to be done，divide the topic into several areas，and this can explore the issue in a very detailed way.

explosive /ɪk'spləʊsɪv/ *n.* 炸药

export /ɪk'spɔːt/ *vt.* 出口、输出　*n.* 出口；出口产品

import and export 进出口

expose /ɪk'spəʊz/ *vt.* 使暴露、使接触

expose sth. to sth. 使暴露在…

（考题）It will ignite if it is exposed to the air for long.

express[1] /ɪk'spres/ *n.* 快车；快递

an express mail 快件

express[2] /ɪk'spres/ *vt.* 表达

（考题）Many and different are the faces of art，and together they express the basic need and hope of human beings.

expression /ɪk'spreʃən/ *n.* 表达；表情；词组

（考题）Aphasics seem to understand human expressions better，

though they cannot understand words.

(考题)I searched books for good expressions and sayings, pieces of information, ideas, themes — anything to enrich my thought and make me feel educated.

without expression 毫无表情地

extend /ɪkˈstend/ *vi.* *vt.* 伸出;延伸、延长;扩大、给予

(考题)By extending a "proven" marketing method, a parent can profit in several ways.

extension /ɪkˈstenʃən/ *n.* 延长、扩大;分机

extensive /ɪkˈstensɪv/ *adj.* 广阔的;广泛的;巨大的

extensive reading 泛读

extent /ɪkˈstent/ *n.* 广度;宽度;长度;范围

to a large/certain/some extent 在很大/一定/某种程度上

(考题)It was reported that Mr. Evans' healthy long life was to a certain extent due to his mild temper.

extinct /ɪkˈstɪŋkt/ *adj.* 灭绝的

extinction /ɪkˈstɪŋkʃən/ *n.* 灭绝

extinguish /ɪkˈstɪŋgwɪʃ/ *vt.* 使熄灭;扑灭

extinguisher /ɪkˈstɪŋgwɪʃə/ *n.* 灭火机

extra /ˈekstrə/ *adj.* 额外的、另加的

(考题)You have to pay some extra money when you pay for services in the UK.

extraordinary /ɪkˈstrɔːdɪnərɪ/ *adj.* 非同寻常的、特别的

extreme /ɪkˈstriːm/ *adj.* 极端的、极度的;过分的

eye /aɪ/ *n.* 眼睛;目光;

catch sb.'s eye 吸引了某人的目光

(考题)Something strange suddenly caught my eye.

close/shut one's eyes to sth. 不理会某事、视而不见

keep an eye on sth. 照看、关照、注意某事

(考题)However, when teenage children have the use of the car, their parents can't keep an eye on them.

see sth. with one's own eyes 亲眼看到某事

eyebrow /ˈaɪbraʊ/ *n.* 眼眉毛

eyesight /ˈaɪsaɪt/ *n.* 视力

F

fable /ˈfeɪbl/ *n.* 寓言

face /feɪs/ *n.* 脸、面孔

  lose face 丢面子

  save face 保全面子

  make a face/make faces 做鬼脸

  face to face 面对面地

  in (the) face of ... 在…的面前

  vt. **face sth.** 面对、正视某事；面朝…方向

  （考题）When asked to choose the biggest challenge they face, 31% of them quoted involving parents and communicating with them as their top choice.

  vi. **face to ...** 面朝…方向

  （考题）His room faces to the sea and he likes to sit by the window, looking far into the blue sea in fine weather.

  be faced with sth. 面临、遇到某事

  （考题）These internal states are acquired throughout life from situations one is faced with in the home, in the streets, and in the school.

facility /fəˈsɪlɪtɪ/ *n.* 方便、便利；(*pl.*)设备、设施；熟练

  teaching facilities 教学设施

  （考题）As a university student you can get first-class research facilities with trained teachers to help, support and advise you in your study.

  do sth. with facility 熟练地做某事

fact /fækt/ *n.* 事实；实际

  in fact 实际上

  as a matter of fact 实际上

factor /ˈfæktə/ *n.* 因素

factory /ˈfækt(ə)rɪ/ *n.* 工厂

fail /feɪl/ *vi. vt.* 失败；衰退；不及格；未能做到

（考题）If these drugs should fail, nobody knows what would come next.

fail in (doing) sth. （做）某事失败了

fail to do sth. 未能做某事

（考题）No matter how famous the product's origin is, if it fails to impress consumers with its own qualities, it begins to resemble an exercise in self-promotional marketing.

failure /ˈfeɪljə/ *n*. 失败；失败的人或事

    end up in failure 以失败告终

    heart failure 心脏衰竭

    power failure 电力中断

faint /feɪnt/ *adj*. 虚弱的；微弱的　*vi*. 昏厥

fair¹ /feə/ *adj*. 公平的；合理的

    play fair 公平竞争；公正办事

fair² /feə/ *n*. 定期集市；博览会、商品交易会

fairly /ˈfeəli/ 公平地、诚实的；相当地

（考题）You have to be a fairly good speaker to hold listeners' interest for over an hour.

fairy /ˈfeəri/ *n*. 仙女

faith /feɪθ/ *n*. 信任；信心；信念

    have faith in ... 对…有信心、信任…

（考题）Throughout this painful experience, the kindness of strangers brought back my faith in humanity

fake /feɪk/ *n*. 假货、赝品

fall¹ /fɔːl/ (fell, fallen) *vi*. 落下；跌落

    fall apart 破碎，破裂

    fall behind 落后

    fall into 落入；进入某种状态

In particular, he showed that all games fall into two classes: games of 'perfect information', like chess, and games of 'imperfect information', like poker.

    fall over 跌倒

    fall ＋*adj*. 变得…；进入某种状态

（考题）I have such a terrible time falling asleep every night that I'm always tired and it's affecting my schoolwork.

fall² /fɔːl/ *n*. 秋天

false /fɔːls/ *adj*. 错误的、非真实的；伪造的

   take a false step 犯错

   false teeth 假牙

   a false friend 虚心假意的朋友

   a false impression 错误的印象

fame /feɪm/ *n*. 名声；名望

familiar /fəˈmɪlɪə/ *adj*. 熟悉的

   be familiar with sth. /sb. 很熟悉某事/某人

   (考题)One advantage of design museums is that they are places where people feel familiar with the exhibits.

   ... be familiar to sb.... 对某人来说是很熟悉的

   (考题)Though they haven't been here long, the environment is already familiar to them

family /ˈfæmɪlɪ/ *n*. 家庭

   a big family 一大家子人

   family name 姓

   family life 家庭生活

   family planning 计划生育

   (注意：family 是个集合名词，如看作一个整体，动词用单数形式；但如强调家庭成员，则动词用复数的形式。)

   (辨析：family 指组成家庭的成员；home 指日常居住的环境场所；house 则指的是房屋建筑。)

famous /ˈfeɪməs/ *adj*. 著名的

   be famous for ... 因…而著名

   (考题)At that time, New Orleans was famous for the new music of jazz and was home to many great musicians.

   (辨析 famous 语气较为正式，所指影响的深度和广度超过 well-known；well-known 常有"有点名气"的译法；distinguished 指在科技文化领域有名气、成就，杰出的人。)

fan /fæn/ *n*. 扇子；迷、狂热者

fancy /ˈfænsɪ/ *n*. 想象；幻想（力）   *adj*. 想象出来的

   have a fancy for sth. 热衷于某事

   take a fancy to ... 喜欢上…

   vt. *vi*. **fancy (doing) sth.** 幻想(做)某事

fantastic /fænˈtæstɪk/ *adj*. 幻想的；奇异的；极好的

far /fɑ:/ *adj*. 远的　*adv*. 远处、在远处

as far as 一直到；就…而言

What would have happened had Bob walk farther，as far as the river bank?

as (so) far as . . . is concerned 就…而言

As far as I'm concerned，the story's only just begun.

by far（和比较级连用）远比…；（和最高级连用）最

far from 远离；远不是…

（考题）The best way to get rid of a negative self-image is to realize that your image is far from objective，and to actively convince yourself of your positive qualities.

so far 到目前为止

（注意：far 的比较及和最高级有 farther，further 和 farthest，furthest 两种形式。farther 和 farthest 表示距离"更远"、"最远"；further 和 furthest 则表示程度。）

fare /feə/ *n*. 车费

farewell /ˈfeəwel/ *n*. 分别；告别　*adj*. 告别的

（注意：farewell 表示长期的分别，不可数名词；但表示告别时，是可数名词，如：It was a painful farewell。）

farm /fɑ:m/ *n*. 农场

farmer /ˈfɑ:mə/ *n*. 农民、农夫

fascinate /ˈfæsɪmeɪt/ *vt*. 使着迷、吸引

be fascinated with/by sth. 被…所吸引、对…入迷

fashion /ˈfæʃən/ *n*. 时髦；流行式样；方式、样子

（考题）Having already achieved great wealth and public recognition，many celebrities see fashion as the next frontier to be conquered.

be in/come into fashion（变得）时尚的、流行的

be/go out of fashion 过时的、不时髦的

old-fashioned 老式的、过时的

fashionable /ˈfæʃənəbəl/ *adj*. 时髦的、流行的

fast /fɑ:st/ *adj*. 快的；牢固的　*adv*. 快地；酣畅地

be fast asleep 熟睡

make sth. fast 绑牢紧、挽紧某物

fasten /ˈfɑːsn/ *vt*. 绑牢、挽紧、加固

（考题）Ladies and gentlemen，please fasten your seat belts. The plane is taking off.

fat /fæt/ *adj*. 肥胖的 *n*. 脂肪、肥肉

fatal /ˈfeɪtl/ *adj*. 致命的；极其危险的

（考题）You have to overcome your fatal weakness if you want to succeed.

fate /feɪt/ *n*. 命运

father /ˈfɑːðə/ *n*. 父亲

　　our fathers 我们的祖先

　　like father，like son 有其父必有其子

　　Father Christmas 圣诞老人

fault /fɔːlt/ *n*. 缺点、错误

　　it's sb.'s fault to do sth./that ... ⋯是某人的错

（考题）"I don't think it's my fault that the TV blew up. I just turned it on，that's all，" said the boy.

　　be at fault for sth. 在某事上有错

（考题）Parents are at fault for the change in their children.

　　find fault with ... 对⋯挑刺找茬、挑毛病

（考题）He is such a man who is always finding fault with other people.

faulty /ˈfɔːltɪ/ *adj*. 有故障的、有毛病的

favour /ˈfeɪvə/ *n*. 好感、偏爱；帮助、优惠

　　ask a favour of sb. 请求某人帮助

　　be in favour with sb./be in sb.'s favour 受到某人的宠爱

　　be in favour of (doing) sth. 赞成（做）某事

（考题）Strangely enough，few head teachers seem to be in favour of mixed-ability school football teams.

　　do a favour for sb./do sb. a favour by doing sth. 帮助某人

　　in sb.'s favour 对某人有利

favourite /ˈfeɪvərɪt/ 特别喜爱、偏爱的 *n*. 特别喜爱的人或物

fax /fæks/ *n*. 传真机 *v*. 传真

fear /fɪə/ *n*. 恐惧、害怕

　　for fear of .../for fear that ... 担心、唯恐、以防⋯

（考题）He got to the station early，for fear of missing his train.

in/with fear 惊恐地

（考题）People tend to associate leadership with fear.

in fear of sth. 害怕、担心

vt. **fear (to do) sth.** 害怕（做）某事

fear that ... 害怕、担心…

（考题）Some parents fear that close contact with members of the opposite sex is dangerous for teenagers.

feasible /ˈfiːzɪbl/ *adj.* 可行的、行得通的

（同义词：practicable）

feather /ˈfeðə/ *n.* 羽毛

Birds of a feather flock together 物以类聚，人以群分

feature /ˈfiːtʃə/ *n.* 特写；特征

（考题）Another convenient feature of the EoL is that you'll be able to pick the level of detail you want to see to match your interest，age and knowledge.

vt. 以…为特征的；刊载…

（考题）This fully updated book features the latest information about study opportunities

February /ˈfebrʊərɪ/ *n.* 二月

fee /fiː/ *n.* （会费、入场费等）费用；酬金；小费

feed /fiːd/ （fed，fed）*vt. vi.* 喂、养

feed sb. (on ...) （用…）喂养某人

（考题）Hunting is not a cruel and senseless killing — not if you respect the thing you kill，not if you kill to enrich your memories，not if you kill to feed your people.

feed sb. with ... 喂某人吃…

（考题）People like to feed animals in the zoo with all kinds of fruit.

feed on ... 以…为食；用…喂养

（考题）This kind of animals feeds on grass.

feed sth. back (to sb.) 向某人反馈某信息

be fed up (with sth.) （对某事）受够了、腻了

（考题）People are fed up with diet products.

feedback /ˈfiːdbæk/ *n.* 反馈

feel /fiːl/ （felt，felt）*link* *v.* 感到、觉得 *vt. vi.* 感到；摸

feel ＋ _adj._ 感到…

feel as if/though 觉得好像

（考题）She felt as if someone were running after her.

feel like sth. 感觉像…

（考题）The steel floors of the trucks were like ice，which made my feet feel like stone.

feel like (doing) sth. 想、喜欢（做）某事

（考题）But when you feel like crying, don't fight it. It's a natural-and-healthy-emotional response.

feel sth. 摸、触摸某物

feel sb. do (doing) sth. 觉得某人在做某事

（考题）I just felt someone stealing into my room in the dark.

feel that . . . 觉得、认为…

（考题）For many years, the bright red color of tomatoes and carrots on the thin bottle makes you feel that it is very good for your body.

feeling /ˈfiːlɪŋ/ _n._ 感觉；感情

（考题）Art museum exhibits，on the other hand，would most probably fill visitors with a feeling that there is something beyond their understanding.

hurt/wound sb.'s feelings 伤害某人的感情

（见 emotion）

fellow /ˈfeləʊ/ _n._（口）家伙；人；伙伴

female /ˈfiːmeɪl/ _adj._ 女性的 _n._ 女子、女人

ferry /ˈferɪ/ _n._ 渡船

fertile /ˈfɜːtaɪl/ _adj._ 肥沃的；丰富的

fertilizer /ˈfɜːtɪlaɪzə/ _n._ 肥料

festival /ˈfestɪvəl/ _n._ 节日；汇演

fetch /fetʃ/ _vt._（去）拿、取；叫某人来

fever /ˈfiːvə/ _n._ 热度、发烧

few /fjuː/ _adj._ 很少的、几乎没有的

a few 一些、几个（修饰可数名词）

quite a few 不少、相当多

（注意：few 表示否定的语气，而 a few 则表示肯定的语气。这个不取决于具体的数字，而取决于说话者的语气。little 和 a little 的

区别同样如此。如身上带了 200 元钱,但想买的东西价格为 100 元,就可以说 I have a little money with me. I can buy it. 如果身边带了 500 元,可要买的东西需要 2000 元,尽管 500 元多于 200 元,可这时也只能说 Sorry, I have little money with me. I can't buy it today.）

fiction /ˈfɪkʃən/ *n.* 小说;虚构的事情

field /fiːld/ *n.* 田地;场地;领域

battle field 战场

track and field events 田径比赛

field hospital 野战医院

fierce /fiəs/ *adj.* 凶猛的;激烈的

fifteen /ˈfɪfˈtiːn/ *num.* 十五

fifth /fɪfθ/ *num.* 第五

fight /faɪt/ *n.* 战斗

(考题)It is a fight between human beings and nature.

vi. vt. (fought, fought) **fight (against)** ... 与…进行斗争

(考题)But when you feel like crying, don't fight it. It's a natural-and-healthy-emotional response.

(考题)The main purpose of the passage is to call on people to fight against the worldwide water shortage and sanitation problem.

fight with ... 与…进行斗争;与…并肩战斗

(考题)In the following years, the white explorers began to fight with the Indians for their land.

fight for sth. 为…而斗争

figure /fɪg/ *n.* 数字;外形;轮廓;人影

(考题)Karen is but one of about 30 million people now living with HIV/AIDS, a figure larger than the combined populations of Australia.

v. 算出;想象

figure sth. in 把某物计算进去

figure sth. out 算出,想出、弄清

(考题)They figure out that the area where summer temperatures can fall to −40℃, has at least 900,000 years of snowfalls, kept as nearly as the growth rings of a tree.

file /faɪl/ 档案;存档的文件;文件夹、档案柜

fill /fil/ *v.* 装满;使充满

fill sth. with ... 用…把某物装满

(考题)It's good to do whatever we can for our animals who in exchange for a little love fill our existence with their attention.

fill ... into sth. 用…装满某物

be filled with ... 装满了某物

(同义词: **be full of sth.** 也可表达同样的意思。)

fill the need of ... 满足…的要求

fill up (in, out) a form 填写表格

(考题)Collecting information about pre-employment and filling out an application form are closely connected.

film /fɪlm/ *n.* 电影

final /ˈfaɪnl/ *adj.* 最后的、最终的;决定性的 *n.* 决赛

the semi finals 半决赛

the finals 决赛

finance /ˈfaɪnæns/ *n.* 财政;金融;资金

financial /faɪˈnænʃəl/ *adj.* 财政的;金融的

find /faɪnd/ (found, found) 找到;发现

find sth. /sb. 找到某物/人

find sb. do/doing sth. 发现某人做某事

(考题)I was surprised to find him taking a walk alone in the garden so late at night.

find sb. /sth. ... 发现某人/物…

(考题)The aim of the competition was to find two strangers prepared to marry without having met each other.

find that ... 发现…

find it easy (for sb.) to do sth. 发现(某人)做某事很容易

(考题)But few business people find it comfortable to admit that they are taking a chance.

find sth. out 弄明白、查明某事

(考题)To help concerned parents, Carter promised to visit campuses and talk to experts around the country to find out major crime issues and effective solutions.

fine¹ /faɪn/ *adj.* 好的;晴朗的;细微的

fine arts 美术(绘画、雕刻、建筑、音乐等)

fine² /faɪn/ *n.* 罚款 *vt.* 处以罚款

find sb. for (doing) sth. 因(做)某事而罚某人的款

(考题) Albert was fined for breaking the American security rules.

finger /ˈfɪŋgə/ *n.* 手指

finger alphabet/language 手势语

have a finger in the pie 染指、插一手

finish /ˈfɪnɪʃ/ *vi.* *vt.* 结束、完成

sth. finish 某事结束了

finish (doing) sth. 做完某事

(考题) But be sure you finish exercising at least 4 hours before bedtime — working out later than that could leave you too excited to fall asleep easily.

fire /faɪə/ *n.* 火

catch (take) fire 着火

(考题) Paper is easy to catch fire.

make a fire 生火

on fire 烧着了

(考题) By that time, a large part of the city was on fire.

play with fire 玩火、做冒险的事

put/set sth. on fire 把某物烧掉

(考题) It still remains a secret who set the bridge on fire.

set fire to sth. 点燃、烧掉某物

(考题) Before leaving, they set fire to the house.

vi. 燃烧；开火；解雇

fire at sb. 朝某人开枪

be fired 被解雇

(考题) Should you be fired, your health care and other benefits will not be immediately cut off.

fireworks /ˈfaɪəwɜːks/ *n.* 烟花；礼花

firm /fɜːm/ *n.* 商行 *adj.* 坚定的；牢固的

as firm as a rock 坚如磐石

with firm steps 以稳健的步伐

first /fɜːst/ *n.* 第一个 *adj.* 第一的、最早的 *adv.* 最初、起先

at first 开始、最初

（同义词：at the beginning）

first-class/first-rate 一流的、优秀的

firsthand 第一手的、原始的

first aid 急救

be the first to do sth. 是第一个做某事的

for the first time 第一次

first and foremost 首先、第一

（辨析：first 强调"初次、首先"，在列举所述内容时可以和 firstly 互换；firstly 指所列多项内容的第一项，接下来是 secondly；first of all 也表示"首先"，但语气较强；above all 强调"最重要的、高于其它的"；at first 则表示"在开始阶段、最初"。）

fish /fɪʃ/ *n*. 鱼　*v*. 钓鱼

　　go fishing 钓鱼

fisherman /ˈfɪʃəmən/ *n*. 渔夫；捕鱼人

fit /fɪt/ *v*. 与…适合、匹配

　　... fit (sb./sth.) 某物适合（某人/某物）

　　fit sb. for ... 使某人适合…

　　fit into sth. 可放进某物；适合

　　（考题）Most often, people do not fit exactly into a producer's size.

　　fit in with ... 与…相适合、相和谐、相匹配

　　adj. 适合的；健康的

　　be fit for sth./to do sth. 适合（做）某事

　　（考题）These clouds protect the forest from the daytime heat and night-time cold of nearby deserts, keep temperatures fit for plant growth.

　　keep fit 保持健康

　　（考题）Either way, it's not only good fun, but a great way to keep fit.

fix /fɪks/ *vt*. 修理；安装

flag /flæg/ *n*. 旗子、旗帜

　　the national flag 国旗

　　signal flag 信号旗

flame /fleɪm/ *n*. 火焰

（考题）As put forward in the various official texts，the Olympic symbols of ancient Olympia，the Olympic flame and the Marathon race are bridges between the ancient and the modern Olympic Games.

be in flames 在燃烧

flash /flæʃ/ n. 闪光、闪现； vi. 闪光、闪现 vt. 突然发出

flat /flæt/ n. 一套公寓房间 adj. 平的；平坦的

flesh /fleʃ/ n. 肌肉；果肉

flexible /ˈfleksɪbl/ adj. 易弯曲的；柔韧的；灵活的

flight /flaɪt/ n. 飞行；航班

float /fləʊt/ vi. 漂、浮 vt. 使浮起

flood /flʌd/ n. 洪水

floor /flɔː/ n. 地板；表面

Florida /ˈflɔːrɪdə/（美国）佛罗里达州

flour /flaʊə/ n. 面粉

flow /fləʊ/（flew，flown）vi. 流动 n. 流；流量

flower /flaʊə/ n. 花

flu /fluː/ n. 流行性感冒

fluent /fluːənt/ adj. 流利的

speak fluent English 说流利的英语

fly /flaɪ/（flew，flown）vi. 飞；乘飞机 vt. 使飞翔；驾驶飞机

（考题）How I wish I could fly!

（考题）I'm flying to Paris next Monday.

fly into a temper/rage/passion 大发脾气、勃然大怒

n. 苍蝇

focus /ˈfəʊkəs/ n. 焦点

in (out of) focus 焦点对准（没有对准）

vi. vt. **focus on sth.** 集中在某事上

（考题）What I do is to focus on the value of the stories that people can translate into their own daily world of affairs.

focus one's attention/thoughts on . . . 把注意力集中到…

（考题）In meditation，people sit quietly and focus their attention on their breath.

fog /fɒg/ n. 雾

foggy /ˈfɒgɪ/ adj. 有雾的

fold /fəʊd/ *vt.* *vi.* 折叠(某物)

　　fold sth. up 把某物折叠起来

　　a folded chair/bed/bike 折叠椅(床、自行车等)

folk /fəʊk/ *n.* 人们　*adj.* 民间的

　　folk music 民间音乐

　　folk songs 民歌

　　folk custom 民间习俗

follow /ˈfɒləʊ/ *vt.* *vi.* 跟随；遵循

　　follow …跟着

　　(考题)His failure to follow Korean customs gave the impression that Korea was not as important to him as Japan.

　　follow sb.'s orders/advice 服从某人的命令/采纳某人建议

　　(考题)We will naturally follow their advice.

　　be followed by ... 后面跟着…

　　(考题)The couple are now on a Caribbean honeymoon followed by journalists.

　　as follows 如下

　　(考题)Like the sample of non-profits noted as follows, some organizations are large, others small-scale; some operate worldwide, others are devoted to certain areas in Africa, Asia, or Latin America.

following /ˈfɒləʊɪŋ/ 接下来的；下列的

　　the following day 第二天

fond /fɒnd/ *adj.* 喜爱的

　　be fond of (doing) sth. 喜欢(做)某事

　　(考题)The British love to think of themselves as polite, and everyone knows how fond they are of their "pleases" and "thank yous".

food /fuːd/ *n.* 食物

　　frozen food 冷冻食品

　　health food 健康食品

　　food chain 食物链

fool /fuːl/ *n.* 愚人、傻瓜　*vt.* 愚弄

　　be fool enough to do sth. 傻到做某事

　　make a fool of sb. 捉弄、愚弄某人

April Fools' Day 愚人节

vt. 愚弄

fool sb. into (doing) sth. 欺骗使某人做某事

（考题）... in most cases, the normal people were fooled by words, but the aphasics were not.

foolish /ˈfuːlɪʃ/ *adj.* 愚蠢的、傻的

　It's foolish of sb. to do sth. 某人做了某事真傻

foot /fʊt/ (*pl.* feet) *n.* 脚；英尺

　at the foot of ... 在…脚下

　on foot 步行

　stand on one's own feet 自立

　by the foot 以英尺为单位

football /ˈfʊtbɔːl/ *n.* 足球

for /fɔː/ *prep.* 为了；因为；一段时间；为代价；目的地

　for example (instance) 例如

　for certain (sure) 肯定地、有把握地

　（考题）And if you don't know for sure, it's very unlikely that you can find out.

　for ever 永远、总是

　（考题）Rainy days at home when you were ill seemed to last for ever.

　for the sake of 为了…

　be for sth. 赞成某事

　（考题）I don't know who of them are for the plan and who are against it.

　but for 要不是…

　（考题）They would be far worse but for this outflow of bodies and inflow of dollars.

　for a long time/for long 很长时间

　（注意：for 引导的时间状语不能修饰表示非延续性动作的动词，如 finish, stop, leave 等。）

forbid /fəˈbɪd/ (forbade, forbidden) *vt.* 禁止；不让

　forbid (doing) sth. 禁止（做）某事

　（考题）What you said sounds reasonable. But the law forbids doing so.

forbid sb. to do sth. 不让某人做某事

（考题）All ships are forbidden to enter the military area.

forbid sb. sth. 不让某人进入、使用某物

force /fɔːs/ *n*. 力量、力气；军队

（考题）The major market force rests in the growing population of white-collar employees, who can afford the new service.

be in/come into force 有效、生效

by force 使用暴力

vt. **force sb. to do sth.** 强迫某人做某事

（考题）He mixed a spoonful of instant chocolate into a glass of cold water, and his impatience forced him to finish the drink in gulps.

force ... into sth. 强迫…进入某物

（考题）They forced a small amount of special water into the birds' bodies so that they could measure the amount of energy burnt during the flight.

force sb. into doing sth. 强迫某人做某事

forceful /ˈfɔːsfʊl/ *adj*. 强有力的；坚强的

forecast /ˈfɔːkɑːst/ *n*. 预报；预测

the weather forecast 天气预报

forehead /ˈfɒrɪd/ *n*. 前额

foreign /ˈfɒrɪn/ *n*. 外国的；不熟悉的；不适合的

be foreign to sb. 对某人不适合、不熟悉

（考题）If you are traveling where customs are really foreign to your own, please do as the Romans do.

forest /ˈfɒrɪst/ *n*. 森林

forever /fəˈrevə/ *adv*. 永远

forget /fəˈget/ (forgot, forgot 或 forgotten) *vt*. *vi*. 忘记

forget (doing) sth. 忘了（做过）某事

（考题）Time makes one forget the past.

forget to do sth. 忘了做某事

（考题）Never forget to wear the safety belt while driving.

forgetful /fəˈgetfʊl/ *adj*. 健忘的

forgive /fəˈgɪv/ (forgave, forgiven) *vt*. 原谅

forgive sb. for (doing) sth. 原谅某人做了某事

（考题）New-comers to Britain could be forgiven for thinking that queuing rather than football was the true national sport.

fork /fɔːk/ *n*. 餐叉；叉状物

form /fɔːm/ *n*. 形式；方式；表格

　in the form of . . . 以…的形式

　（考题）The auctioneer's services are paid for in the form of a percentage of the price the goods are sold for.

　（辨析：form 可以指抽象的形式，也可指具体的形状；而 shape 则侧重外形、轮廓，指具体的形状。）

　vt. **form . . .** 形成某物

　（考题）. . . those children who were unable to form normal emotional ties with others did not experience contagious yawning, which showed that humans communicate regularly without words.

formal /ˈfɔːməl/ *adj*. 正式的

former /ˈfɔːmə/ *adj*. 从前的、过去的；(两者中)前者

　the former president 前总统

　the former . . . , the latter . . . 前者…，后者…

　（考题）As for this, there is a great difference between human beings and insects. The former make every possible effort to avoid being discovered，while the latter quickly draw attention to themselves.

forth /fɔːθ/ *adv*. 向前

　and so forth 等等（同 **and so on**）

　back and forth 来来回回

　put/bring sth. forth 提出某事

　（考题）No matter what objects they select，artists are to bring forth new forces and forms that cause change.

fortunate /ˈfɔːtʃənət/ *adj*. 幸运的

fortune /ˈfɔːtʃən/ *n*. 幸运、运气；财富

　（考题）One thousand dollars a month is not a fortune but would help cover my living expenses.

　make a fortune 发财

　try one's fortune 碰运气（同 **try one's luck**）

　（辨析：fortune 往往至于人生有较大关系的运气；而 luck 常指偶

然的一次机会。)

forward(s) /ˈfɔːwəd(z)/ *adv*. 向前

（考题）... and this discovery could be a huge step forward in treating this problem.

put sth. forward 提出某事（同 put forth）

（考题）My only concern is that you are not active enough in putting forward your suggestions.

look forward to (doing) sth. 期待、盼望（做）某事

（考题）Though I knew I wouldn't tell her about my parents' situation，I was looking forward to getting out of the house.

found /faʊnd/ *vt*. 建立、创立

foundation /faʊnˈdeɪʃən/ *n*. 基础；创建；基金会

lay a solid foundation for ... 为…打下坚实的基础

founder /ˈfaʊndə/ 创建者、缔造者

fourteen /ˈfɔːˈtiːn/ *num*. 十四

fountain /ˈfaʊntɪn/ *n*. 泉水、喷泉；源泉

fox /fɒks/ *n*. 狐狸

frame /freɪm/ *n*. 框架

France /frɑːns/ *n*. 法国

frank /fræŋk/ *adj*. 坦率的、直率的；公开的

to be frank 坦率地说

frankly /ˈfræŋklɪ/ *adv*. 坦率地、直率地；公开地

frankly speaking 坦率地说

free /friː/ *adj*. 自由的；空闲的；免费的；未被占用的

be/feel free from ... 没有…的、不受…影响的

be free of ... 没有…的、离开…的、

（考题）The food is free of pesticides，and you are generally supporting family farms instead of large farms.

be free to do sth. 可随意做某事

free of charge 免费

set sb. /sth. free 释放某人/物

（考题）If you try to persuade people that you yourself are a psychiatrist after you are set free，I shall make sure that you are given a much longer sentence.

vt. 使自由

free sb. from/of ... 使某人摆脱…

(考题)Once you free your mind of this，you will find it much easier to give your speech freely.

freedom /ˈfriːdəm/ *n.* 自由

freeze /friːz/ (froze，frozen) *vi. vt.* (使)结冰、冰冻

  freezing point 冰点

  frozen food 冷冻食品

French /frentʃ/ *adj.* 法国的　*n.* 法语

frequent /ˈfriːkwənt/ *adj.* 时常的；经常性的

fresh /freʃ/ *adj.* 新鲜的；新来的

  fresh air 新鲜空气

  fresh water 淡水

Friday /ˈfraɪdɪ/ *n.* 星期五

fridge /frɪdʒ/ *n.* 冰箱

friend /frend/ *n.* 朋友

  make friends with sb. 与某人交朋友

friendly /ˈfrendlɪ/ *adj.* 友好的；朋友般的

  be friendly to sb. 对某人很友好

friendship /ˈfrendʃɪp/ *n.* 友谊

frighten /ˈfraɪtən/ *vt.* 使害怕

(考题)If a stranger should enter your territory and threaten you，you might shout. Probably this would be enough to frighten him away.

  be frightened to death 怕得要死

frog /frɒg/ *n.* 青蛙

from /frɒm/ *prep.* 从…起；来自…

  apart from 除…之外

(考题)The owners of the watches were admired and set apart from the crowd.

  far from 远不是（见 far）

(考题)Money spent on electronic equipment is far from enough.

  from bad to worse 越来越糟，每况愈下

  from morning till/to night 从早到晚

  from now/then on 从现在/那时起

(考题)From then on，I've always tried to keep an open mind

about those strange old wives' tales because they do have some truth to them.

from ... to ... 从…到…

front /frʌnt/ *n*. 前面、前部；前线

 in front of sth. 在某物的前面

 in the front of sth. 在某物内的前部

fruit /fruːt/ *n*. 水果

fry /fraɪ/ *v*. 油煎、油炸；炒

fuel /ˈfjuːəl/ *n*. 燃料；燃油

fulfil(l) /fulˈfɪl/ *vt*. 完成；满足；履行

 (考题)We always make plans but seldom fulfil them.

 fulfil the task/need/requirement/one's desire 完成任务/满足需求/符合要求/实现愿望

 (考题)They need homework, too, if they are to fulfill their academic potential.

full /ful/ *adj*. 满的；完整的、完全的

 be full of 充满了(同：**be filled with**)

 be full up 吃饱了

 full-time 全部时间的、专职的

 (辨析：part-time 部分时间的、兼职的；spare-time 业余时间的)

 in full 完整的；全部的

fun /fʌn/ *n*. 乐趣；有趣的人或事

 have fun (in) doing sth. 从…中得到乐趣

 It's (great, a lot of, much) fun doing/to do sth. 做…很快乐

 (考题)It's great fun to explore new places — it feels like an adventure, even when you know you're not the first to have been there.

 for fun 为了开心、为了好玩

 make fun of 拿某人开玩笑、取笑

 (注意：fun 是不可数名词，前面不能使用不定冠词，也不能有复数的形式)

function /ˈfʌŋkʃən/ *n*. 功能、作用

 (考题)Besides its main function the noise-killing system can make a car light.

 vi. 发挥功能，起作用

（考题）Fear causes the thinking brain to shut down，making the person unable to function at his or her best.

fund /fʌnd/ *n.* 基金、一笔专款；资金、钱款（常用复数）

funeral /ˈfjuːnərəl/ *n.* 葬礼

　　the funeral march 葬礼进行曲

funny /ˈfʌnɪ/ *adj.* 有趣的；滑稽可笑的、古怪的

　　（考题）Each of us appears，sometimes in a funny way，in the other's dreams.

fur /fɜː/ *n.* 毛皮；皮毛

furnish /ˈfɜːnɪʃ/ *vt.* 为…装备、配备

　　furnish . . . with sth. 为…配备某物

　　（考题）The house is furnished with everything we may need in daily life.

　　furnish sth. to . . . 为…提供、配备某物

furniture /ˈfɜːnɪtʃə/ *n.* 家具

further /ˈfɜːðə/ *adj. adv.* 进一步；更多

　　（考题）Each of these is further divided into 3 skill levels（easy，medium and difficult）so younger children can fairly compete against teenagers and adults.

　　further information 进一步的消息

　　till further notice 直到进一步通知

　　go further 继续走；往下说

furthermore /ˈfɜːðəˈmɔː/ *adv.* 此外，而且

future /ˈfjuːtʃə/ *n.* 将来；未来

　　in future 今后、以后

　　（考题）When Holowka says，"It's going to be big"，she means that green buildings will become popular in future.

　　in the future 将来；未来

　　（考题）Large department stores are busy setting up their own TV channels to encourage TV shopping in the future.

　　in the near/immediate future 不久以后

G

gain /geɪn/ *n*. 获得；受益

（考题）Diet products make people believe that gain comes without pain, and that life can be without resistance and struggle.

vt. *vi*. **gain sth.** 获得某物

（考题）Whenever we take honorable action we gain the deep internal rewards of goodness and a sense of nobility.

gain in (doing) sth. 在…中得以增强

gallery /ˈgælərɪ/ *n*. 走廊；画廊、艺术品陈列馆

gamble /ˈgæmbl/ *n*. *v*. 赌博

gamble sth. on ... 把某物押在…上

game /geɪm/ *n*. 游戏；比赛；猎物

gang /gæŋ/ *n*. 一伙人（常指坏人）；（从事某种工作的）班组

a gang of ... 一群…

gap /gæp/ *n*. 空隙，裂口；缺口；距离

（考题）Professor Alex Michalos found that people feel less happy if the gap between reality and desire is bigger.

the generation gap 代沟

garage /ˈgærɑːdʒ/ *n*. 车库；汽车修理厂

garbage /ˈgɑːbɪdʒ/ *n*. 垃圾

garden /ˈgɑːdən/ *n*. 花园；园子

gas /gæs/ *n*. 气体；煤气；毒气

gasoline /ˈgæsəliːn/ 汽油

gate /geɪt/ *n*. 大门

gather /ˈgæðə/ *vt*. *vi*. 收集、汇拢；集聚；聚集、集合

gather sth. 收集某物

gather (...) round （使）聚在周围

（考题）You should try to gather your friends around you to rebuild a happy family atmosphere.

gather (sth.) together (把某物)聚在一起

(考题)You will sometimes see birds settling in trees or gathering together on a wire close to a building.

gather strength 积聚力量

(见 collect)

gay /geɪ/ *adj*. 快乐的;色彩鲜艳的;放荡不羁的

gaze /geɪz/ *n. vi*. 注视、凝视

gaze at sth. 凝视

gene /dʒiːn/ *n*. (遗传)基因

general /ˈdʒenərəl/ *adj*. 一般的;普遍的;总的   *n*. 将军;上将

the general idea 大概情况

(考题)It is based on the general idea that people have the ability to change the way they think and behave.

general knowledge 普通知识、常识

as a general rule 一般说来

in genera l 一般说来、通常;总的来说

(考题)"In general," writes Rubin in her new book, "women's friendships with each other rest on shared emotions and support, but men's relationships are marked by shared activities."

generally /ˈdʒenərəlɪ/ *adv*. 通常;一般

generally speaking 一般说来

(考题)Generally speaking, when taken according to the directions, the drug has no side effect.

generation /ˌdʒenəˈreɪʃən/ *n*. 一代、一辈

(考题)You are what you eat and fats are a main food for Asia's fast-food generation.

the generation gap 代沟

generous /ˈdʒenərəs/ *adj*. 慷慨的、大方的

It's generous of you to do sth. 你真慷慨这样做

genius /ˈdʒiːnɪəs/ *n*. 天才;天分

(考题)Any fool can make soap, but it takes a genius to sell it.

have a genius for sth. 有某方面的天分

gentle /ˈdʒentl/ *adj*. 柔和的;温和的;细微的

(考题)In fact greyhounds love people and are gentle with

children.

gentleman /ˈdʒentlmən/ *n.* 有风度、有教养的男人

（考题）For everybody, England meant gentlemen, fair play, and good manners.

geography /dʒiˈɒɡrəfɪ/ *n.* 地理

geology /dʒiˈɒlədʒɪ/ *n.* 地质学

germ /ɡɜːm/ *n.* 细菌；病菌

German /ˈdʒɜːmən/ *adj.* 德国的 *n.* 德语；德国人

Germany /ˈdʒɜːmənɪ/ *n.* 德国

gesture /ˈdʒestʃə/ *n.* 手势

（考题）There are also more visible changes in our gesture and facial expressions.

v. 打手势；用手势表示

（考题）The policeman gestured for cars to leave the place.

get /ɡet/（got，got）*v.* 得到；到达；变得

get sth. 得到某物

（辨析：在表示"得到"时，get 是最普通用语；acquire 表示通过自己的技能、知识去获得；gain 强调通过努力获得有益、有利的东西；obtain 指有计划、通过努力而获得。）

get sb. to do sth. 使某人做某事

（考题）He found it hard to get anyone to help him here.

get sth. done 使某事被做好

get to know/understand/realize . . . 变得了解（明白）

（考题）We get to know the characters and see them grow and develop week after week.

get + adj. 变得…

（考 题）Children get fat because they don't move, and eventually, they don't want to move because they're fat.

（同义词：**become，turn，grow，go，come** 等。）

get about/around（消息等）传开

get along/on（with sb. /sth.）（与某人相处/从事某事）的情况…

（考题）Many teenagers can't get along well with their parents nowadays.

get away（from . . .） 摆脱（…）；逃离

get back（to a place） 返回（某地）

get down to (doing) sth. 开始认真对待、从事某事

（考题）Would you like a cup of coffee or shall we get down to business right away?

get on 上车

get off 下车

get to (a place) 达到某地

（同义词：**come to** ，**arrive at/in, reach** 都可表示"到达"的意思。其中 reach 是及物动词，后面没有介词。）

get through 完成；通过

（考题）Don't lose heart. It's only something you have to get through on your way through life.

get up 起床

get-together /ˈɡetˈtəɡeðə/ *n* . 聚会

ghost /ɡəʊst/ *n* . 鬼魂

giant /ˈdʒaɪənt/ *adj* . 巨大的　　*n* . 巨人

gift /ɡɪft/ *n* . 礼物；天赋

（考题）Our exploration of London was a memorable gift to both of us.

have a gift for sth. 有…的天赋

girl /ɡɜːl/ *n* . 女孩

give /ɡɪv/ (gave, given) *v* . 给

give sth. to sb. /give sb. sth. 被某物给某人

give sth. away 分发；泄露；出卖

（考题）He didn't only give away money to the poor，but also spent a lot of time looking after them.

give sth. back (to sb.) 归还

give in (to sth. /sb.) （向某事/某人）屈服

（考题）Chief Joseph tried to lead his people to Canada，winning several battles against the soldiers during their flight. But finally，he was forced to give in.

give off 散发（气味、烟雾等）

（考题）Cars use lots of gas and give off pollution.

give one's regards/greeting/wishes to sb. 向某人表示问候（祝愿）

give rise to 引起；促进

（考题）Why do more choices of goods give rise to anxiety?

give (sth.) up 放弃(某物)

(考题)Babbage always had new ideas but gave them up easily.

give way (to . . .) (给…)让路

glad /glæd/ *adj*. 高兴的、乐意的

be glad to do sth./that . . . (为做某事)感到很高兴

be glad at/about/of sth. 为某事感到高兴

glance /glɑːns/ *n*. 一眼、一瞥

take/have a glance at sth./sb. 看某物/某人一眼

(考题)When he came out, he paid his bill and left without another glance in my direction.

at a glance 一看就

vi. 看一眼、一瞥

glance at sth./sb. 看某物/某人一眼

(注意:就像 look 和 see 的关系一样,glance 表示看的动作,而这"看一眼"的结果是 get (catch) a glimpse of sth.)

glass /glɑːs/ *n*. 玻璃;玻璃杯

glasses /ˈglɑːsɪs/ *n*. 眼镜

global /ˈgləʊbəl/ *adj*. 球状的;全球的、全世界的

globe /gləʊb/ *n*. 地球、全球;地球仪

the globe 地球

glorious /ˈglɔːrɪəs/ *adj*. 光荣的、辉煌的

glory /ˈglɔːrɪ/ *n*. 光荣、荣耀、荣誉

glove /glʌv/ *n*. 手套

glue /gluː/ *n*. 胶水

go /gəʊ/ (went, gone) *vi*. 去、走

go after sth./sb. 追求

(考题)She's always busy. I really don't know what she's going after.

go against 违背

(考题)I won't go against his instructions. It's not good for me.

go ahead (with sth.) 继续做某事

go all out to do sth. 全力以赴做某事

(考题)Don't worry. We'll go all out to finish the job ahead of time.

go around 到处走走；传播

（考题）The news soon got round.

go bad（食物）变坏了

go mad 发疯

go in for sth. 爱好、喜欢某物

（考题）I don't go in for rock 'n' roll. It's much too noisy for my taste.

go on with sth. /doing sth. 继续做某事

go on to do sth. 继续做下一件事情

go over 检查、审查；复习

go through 通过、经历

（考题）If you are not sure of your duty free allowances，or if you have something to declare，go through the Red Channel.

go to a place 去某地

（辨析：go 表示"离此地而去"，而 come 表示"到这里来"。如只能说 go there，come here，而不能替换使用。）

go without (sth.) 没有、不用（常含勉强之意）

go wrong 出故障

goal /gəʊl/ *n.* 目标；目的；球门；进球

achieve one's goal 实现目标

goat /gəʊt/ *n.* 山羊

god /gɒd/ *n.* 神；God 上帝

Oh, God! /My God! 天哪！

God knows! 上帝可以作证！

God bless you! 愿上帝保佑你！

goddess /'gɒdɪs/ *n.* 女神

gold /gəʊld/ *n.* 金子、黄金

golden /'gəʊdən/ *adj.* 金子般的；极好的

a golden opportunity 极好的机会

golden age 黄金时代、鼎盛时期

golden rule 良好的准则、金科玉律

golden wedding 金婚纪念

golf /gɒlf, gɔːlf/ *n.* 高尔夫球

good /gʊd/ *adj.* 好的

be good at (doing) sth. 擅长(做)某事

(考题)People poor at one thing can be good at another.

be good for … 对…有好处

a good deal of 大量的、许多(修饰不可数名词)

(考题)I have spent a good deal of time painting as an artist.

a good many 许多(修饰可数名词)

(考题)But for a good many people in the world，in rich and poor countries，choice is a luxury，something wonderful but hard to get，not a right.

do a good job (of …) 干得漂亮

(考题)Having said that she didn't do a good job，I don't think I am abler than her.

it's no good doing sth. 做某事没有好处、没有用处

(见 use)

have a good time 过得很开心

for good (and all) 永远

n. 好处、有利的事

do good to sb. /do sb. good 对某人有好处

(考 题) Sometimes，however，two kinds of animals come together in a partnership which does good to both of them.

goodbye, good-bye /gʊd'baɪ/ *interj.* 再见

goodness /'gʊdnɪs/ *n.* 善良、好意；仁慈；

Thank goodness! 谢天谢地

goods /gʊdz/ *n.* 货物

goose /guːz/ *n.* (*pl.* geese /giːs/) 鹅

gossip /'gɒsɪp/ *n.* 闲话、流言蜚语；爱说闲话的人　*vi.* 说闲话、搬弄是非

gossip about sb. /sth. 议论某人/某事

govern /'gʌvən/ *vt.* 统治、管理

government /'gʌvənmənt/ *n.* 政府

the loca/central government 地方/中央政府

grab /græb/ *vt. vi.* 抓住；抢走

grab sth. 抓住、抢夺某物

grab at sth. /sb. 设法抓住

graceful /ˈgreɪsfʊl/ *adj.* 优雅的

gracious /ˈgeɪʃəs/ *adj.* 和蔼可亲的、彬彬有礼的

   Good gracious! 天哪！

grade /greɪd/ *n.* 等级；年级

gradual /ˈgrædjʊəl/ *adj.* 逐渐的、逐步的

graduate /ˈgrædjʊeɪt/ *n.* 毕业生 *vi.* 毕业

   graduate from 从…毕业

graduation /ˌgrædjʊˈeɪʃən/ *n.* 毕业

grain /greɪn/ *n.* 谷物

gram /græm/ *n.* 克

grammar /ˈgræmə/ *n.* 语法

grand /grænd/ *adj.* 宏伟的；盛大的；壮丽的

grandfather /ˈgrændfɑːðə/ *n.* (外)祖父

grant /grɑːnt/ *vt.* 授予；同意；承认

   grant sb. sth. /grant sth. to sb. 同意给某人某物

   take it for granted 认为是理所当然的

   (考题) But now they seem to take it for granted that they can show up any time they like.

   n. 补助金、津贴

grape /greɪp/ *n.* 葡萄

grasp /grɑːsp/ *vt.* 抓住；掌握、领悟

   grasp sth. 抓住某物；理解…

   (考题) But the brain recordings showed that the less experienced mediators tended to grasp the first number and hang onto it, so they missed the second number.

   n. 抓住；掌握、领悟

   have a good grasp of sth. 很好地掌握、理解…

grass /grɑːs/ *n.* 草；草地

grateful /ˈgreɪtfʊl/ *adj.* 感激的

   be grateful to sb. for (doing) sth. 因某事感激某人

gratitude /ˈgrætɪtjuːd/ *n.* 感激

   with gratitude 感激地

grave /greɪv/ *n.* 坟墓

gravity /ˈgrævɪtɪ/ *n.* 严肃、认真；重力；引力

specific gravity 比重

great /greɪt/ *adj*. 伟大的;巨大的;绝好的

Greece /griːs/ *n*. 希腊

greedy /ˈgriːdɪ/ *adj*. 贪婪的

    be greedy for sth. 渴望…

green /griːn/ *adj*. 绿色的;未成熟的;环保的　*n*. 绿色

Greek /griːk/ *adj*. 希腊的　*n*. 希腊人;希腊语

greet /griːt/ *vt*. 问候、打招呼

greeting /ˈgriːtɪŋ/ *n*. 问候、招呼

grey /greɪ/ *adj*. 灰色的　*n*. 灰色

grief /griːf/ *n*. 忧伤、悲哀;令人悲痛的事

grocery /ˈgrəʊsərɪ/ *n*. 杂货店

ground /graʊnd/ *n*. 地面;场地

group /gruːp/ *n*. 组、群　*vt*. 分组;归类;聚集

grow /grəʊ/ (grew, grown) *vt*. *vi*. 种植;生长;成长;变得

    (考题)As prices and building costs keep rising, the "do-it-yourself"(DIY) trend in the U. S. continues to grow.

    grow into . . . 长成…

    (考题)The seeds lying on the forest floor then grow into new trees.

    grow up 长大成人

    (考题)You have grown up and you should learn to take care of yourselves.

    grow + adj. 变得…(见 become)

    (考题)People learn a sense of direction as they grow older.

grown-up /ˈgrəʊnʌp/ *n*. 成年人

growth /grəʊθ/ *n*. 生长;增长

    (考题)Holiday Inns and McDonald's, both saw unmatched growth in the 1960s.

guarantee /ˌgærənˈtiː/ *n*. 保证

    (考题)I'm planning to hold a party in the open air, but I can make no guarantees because it depends on the weather.

    vt. **guarantee sth.** 确保、保证…

    guarantee sth. for . . . 保修某物…(时间)

（考题）The car is guaranteed for two years.

guarantee to do sth. 保证做某事

guard /gɑːd/ *n.* 卫兵

be on guard 站岗

v. **guard against . . .** 提防…

（考题）We have taken measures to guard against the spread of the disease.

guard sb./sth. against (from) . . . 保护某人/物不受…伤害

guess /ges/ *n.* 猜测、猜想

have/make a guess at . . . 猜测

（考题）Who would agree that a scientist will become famous if he makes the wildest guess at longevity?

vt. *vi.* **guess (at) sth.** 猜测

guess that . . . 估计、猜想…

（考题）I guess I am a really restless spirit. I like traveling, so when the chance came, I jumped at it.

guest /gest/ *n.* 客人

guidance /ˈgaɪdəns/ *n.* 指引；指导

（考题）But the Grand Challenge, as it was called, just proved how difficult it is to get a car to speed across an unfamiliar desert without human guidance.

guide /gaɪd/ *n.* 指导；指引；向导 *v.* 引导；指导

（考 题）We miss the guide telling us where to go, the food providing us with strength, the quiet giving us wisdom.

guide sb. (through/to . . .) 引导某人…

（考题）Here are some basics that will help guide them their entire lives

guilty /ˈgɪltɪ/ *adj.* 有罪的；内疚的

be guilty of (doing) sth. 犯有做…的过失

（考题）I'm guilty of never having read Anna Karenina, because it's just so long.

guilt /gɪlt/ *n.* 罪；罪责；内疚

guitar /gɪˈtɑː/ *n.* 吉他

gulf /gʌlf/ *n.* 海湾

gum /gʌm/ n. 口香糖

gun /gʌn/ n. 枪；炮

guy /gaɪ/ n. 家伙；人

gymnasium /dʒɪmˈneɪzɪəm/ (pl. gymnasia) n. 体育馆

H

habit /ˈhæbɪt/ *n*. 习惯

　be in the habit of doing sth. 有做某事的习惯

　（考题）She was in the habit of scratching other children.

　have a habit of doing sth. 有做某事的习惯

　get/fall into the habit of doing sth. 养成做某事的习惯

　from/by/out of habit 出于习惯

hair /heə/ *n*. 头发；毛发

　have one's hair cut 剃头

hairdresser /ˈheədresə/ 美发师

half /hɑːf/ *adj*. *adv*. 一半

　（考题）He didn't say anything that was false，but he left out important information on purpose. That's called a half-truth. Half-truths are not technically lies, but they are just as dishonest.

　half-time 半场休息

　n. 一半

　by half（减少）一半（辨析：**by halves** 不彻底、做到一半）

　cut sth. in half/into halves 将某物一切为二

　half a/an . . . 半个…

　（注意表示"几个半"时 half 的用法：two hours and a half/ two and a half hours 两个半小时，动词用复数形式；但如果是 one and a half 则动词用单数形式。）

halfway /ˈhɑːfweɪ/ *adv*. 半途；不彻底　*n*. 半途

　（考题）. . . both the students and the teachers lost interest by about halfway through the ten weeks.

hall /hɔːl/ 大厅；礼堂

hamburger /ˈhæmbɜːgə/ *n*. 汉堡包

hammer /ˈhæmə/ *n*. 榔头、锤子　*v*. 捶击

hand /hænd/ *n*. 手

　at hand 在手头；即将到来

　European countries，realizing crisis is at hand，are providing great encouragement for parents to create more babies in the 21st century.

by hand 手工的

（考题）... so that the watch never needs to be wound by hand.

give/lend a hand（to sb.）帮助某人

hand in hand 手挽手地、齐心协力

（考题）Activities of the mind and higher-order reasoning are processes of deep and careful consideration. They take time, and do not go hand in hand with the fast speed in today's world.

in hand 手头上的、在手上的

（考题）With a checklist of criteria in hand, the Dallas family looked around the country visiting half a dozen schools.

in the hand of 由某人负责

（考题）Many people say they are environmentally friendly but they don't take matters in their own hands.

join hands 携手合作

live from hand to mouth 勉强维持生活

on hand 手头（有事要做）

on the one hand, ..., on the other hand 一方面，另一方面

（考题）Being drawn to overeating on the one hand and self-denial on the other can bring about anorexia or bulimia — or both.

shake hands with sb. 与某人握手

v. **hand sth. down** 将某物传下去

hand sth. in 上交

（考题）Writing increased as a problem as students discovered difficulties in writing papers that they were now expected to hand in.

hand sth. out 分发

hand sth. over to sb. 将某物移交给某人

（考题）Now hand over you work to others and have a good rest.

handbag /ˈhændbæg/ *n*. 手提包

handkerchief /ˈhæŋkətʃiːf/ *n*. 手帕

handle /ˈhændl/ *vt*. 拿、搬；处理、管理

（考题）Lots of stores, hotels, and restaurants are needed to

handle the crowds.

handsome /'hænds∧m/ *adj*. 英俊的、漂亮的

handwriting /'hænd,raɪtɪŋ/ *n*. 笔迹；书法

hang¹ /hæŋ/（hung，hung）*vt*. *vi*.（将某物）挂起、吊起；

（考题）He loves the painting so much that he hung it on the wall of his bedroom.

hang about/around 待着不走

（考题）There were the older jazz musicians who hung around our house when I was young.

hang on 坚持；紧抓不放

hang² /hæŋ/（hanged，hanged）*vt*. 吊死、绞死

hang sb. for ... 因…而绞死某人

happen /'hæpən/ *vi*.（偶然）发生；碰巧

sth. happen to sb. 某人发生了某事

It (so) happens that ... 碰巧…

happen to do sth. 碰巧做某事

（注意：happen 是不及物动词，尽管中文说"发生了变化"，可英语中一定是"some changes happened"；表达类似意思的还有 take place，occur，come about。）

happily /'hæpɪlɪ/ *adv*. 幸福地、快乐地

happiness /'hæpɪnɪs/ *n*. 幸福

happy /'hæpɪ/ *adj*. 幸福的、快乐的

harbour /'hɑːbə/ *n*. 港口；港湾

hard /hɑːd/ *adj*. 难的；努力的；硬的；严厉的

be hard on sb. 对某人很严厉

adv. 努力地；艰难地

work hard 努力工作

（辨析：注意下列词组的区别：with hard work 通过努力工作；by working hard 通过努力工作；hard-working 勤劳的。）

hardly /'hɑːdlɪ/ *adv*. 几乎不

（考题）As the first generation to grow up in a wired world, they hardly know a time when computers weren't around, and they eagerly catch the chance to spend hours online, chatting with friends.

can hardly do sth. 几乎不能做某事

hardly ... when ... 刚…，就…

（同义词：**no sooner ... than ...** 也表示同样的意思。）

（辨析：hardly 是表示否定意义的副词。因此，含有 hadly 的句子应看成是否定句。表示否定意义的副词还有 rarely，scarcely，seldom 等。）

hardship /'hɑːdʃɪp/ *n*. 艰难、艰苦

hardworking /'hɑːd͵wɜːkɪŋ/ *adj*. 勤劳的、勤奋的、努力的

harm /hɑːm/ *n*. 伤害

　　do harm to ... 对…造成伤害、有害

　　（考题）Stereotypes can do more harm than good to people.

　　vt. 伤害

　　（考题）Criminals are more likely to harm women.

harmful /'hɑːmfʊl/ *adj*. 有害的

　　be harmful to ... 对…有害

　　（考题）Often，this waste produced by major industries and people is harmful to both nature and human life.

harmony /'hɑːmənɪ/ *n*. 和谐、一致；和睦；

　　be in/out of harmony with ... 与…和谐/不和谐一致

harvest /'hɑːvɪst/ *n*. 丰收　*v*. 收获；收割

hat /hæt/ *n*. 帽子

hate /heɪt/ *vt*. 憎恨、讨厌；不喜欢；遗憾

　　hate (doing) sth. 不喜欢（做）某事

　　（考题）I hate coming home every evening and a pile of junk mail in my post box.

　　hate to do sth. 不喜欢、不愿意做某事

　　（考题）I hate always to be told what to do and what not to do.

　　hate sb. to do sth. 不愿意某人做某事

hatred /'heɪtrɪd/ *n*. 憎恨、痛恨；怨愤

　　have a hatred for 痛恨

have /hæv/ （had，had）*vt*. 有

　　have sb. do sth. 让、叫某人做某事

　　（考题）You don't have to do it yourself. You can have someone do it for you.

　　have sth. done 使某事被完成

　　（考题）The radio doesn't work. Have it repaired，please.

have sb. doing sth. 允许、容忍某人做某事

（考题）I won't have you doing it again. It's so rude.

have (got) to do sth. 不得不做某事

（考题）They have to finish the job today, don't they?

Hawaii /hɑːˈwaɪiː/ *n.* 夏威夷

head /hed/ *n.* 头

 head-on 迎面的(相撞等)

 lose one's head 惊慌失措

 take/put sth. into (out of) sb.'s head 使某人打消/有某种想法

 use one's head 动脑筋

 vt. 率领；*vi.* 朝…方向

（考题）They sent out a task force headed by their best battleship

 head/be headed for … 朝…去

（考题）When a storm is coming, most people leave the area as quickly as possible and head for safety.

headache /ˈhedeɪk/ *n.* 头疼；令人头疼的事

 have a headache 头痛

headline /ˈhedlaɪn/ 大字标题、新闻提要

headmaster /ˈhedmɑːstə/ *n.* (中小学)校长

headphone /ˈhedfəʊn/ *n.* 耳机

headquaters /ˈhedˌkwɔːtəz/ *n.* 总部；指挥部；大本营

health /helθ/ *n.* 健康

（考题）Obesity is a major public health concern, so why shouldn't we change the law regarding unhealthy food ads?

 be in good/poor health 健康状况良好/不好

healthy /ˈhelθɪ/ *adj.* 健康的；有利于健康的

heap /hiːp/ *n.* 一堆、大量

 a heap of … 一大堆…

hear /hɪə/ (heard, heard) *vt. vi.* 听见；

 hear sb. do (doing) sth. 听到某人(在)做某事

（考题）Sometimes you hear people say that you can't love others until you love yourself.

 hear that … 听说…

 hear about/of 听说(有关…的事)

（考题）10 or 12 years ago, you would have heard about the

coming age of computing.

hear from sb. 收到某人的来信

（考题）I wonder why Jenny hasn't written us recently. We should have heard from her by now.

heart /hɑːt/ *n.* 心、心脏

　　heart trouble 心脏病

　　heart attack 心脏病发作

　　heart rate/rhythm 心律

　　have sth. in one's heart 把某事摆在心上、想着某事

（考题）I had a hurt in my heart for this kind of human soul, all alone in the world.

　　heart and soul 全心全意地

　　learn sth. by heart 牢牢记住某事

　　in one's heart 在内心

　　lose heart 灰心、泄气

　　good/kind/warm/stone-hearted 心地善良…/热心肠/铁石心肠

heartbreak /ˈhɑːtbreɪk/ *n.* 悲痛、伤心；令人伤心的事

heat /hiːt/ *n.* 热　*vt.* 加热

heated /ˈhiːtɪd/ *adj.* 热烈的；激烈的

　　a heated argument/discussion 激烈的争论/讨论

heater /ˈhiːtə/ *n.* 取暖器；加热装置

heaven /ˈhevən/ *n.* 天堂、天国（常大写）；天空（常复数）

heavily /ˈhevɪlɪ/ *adv.* 重的；大的（雨雪等）；厉害的

height /haɪt/ *n.* 高度

　　… in height 高度为…

helicopter /ˈhelɪkɒptə/ *n.* 直升飞机

hello /ˈheləʊ, heˈləʊ/ *interj.* 嗨、喂（见面时打招呼）

　　say hello to sb. 与某人打招呼

help /help/ *n.* 帮助　*vi. vt.* 帮助；克制、忍住

　　… helps …能起作用、有帮助

（考题）If you plan to sell on eBay, it helps to include a picture of the item.

　　help sb. with/to do/do sth. 帮助某人做某事

　　help (to) do sth. 有助于做某事

（考题）Television wildlife programmes have helped to fuel the

new trend.

be of great help 有帮助

come to sb.'s help 来帮某人的忙

（类似短语还有：**come to sb.'s aid/assistance/rescue**）

with the help of ... 在…的帮助下

can't help doing sth. 忍不住做某事

（考题）Following the waterfront of the city after sunset, you couldn't help stopping and listening to the sweet silence, interrupted only by the screaming seabirds and leaving fishing boats.

helpful /ˈhelpful/ *adj*. 有帮助的

be helpful to sb. 对某人有帮助

（考题）His books were interesting and helpful to adults.

be helpful for sb. to do sth. 对某人做某事有帮助

hen /hen/ *n*. 母鸡

hence /hens/ *adv*. 因此；所以

here /hɪə/ *adv*. 在这里

here and there 到处

Here we are. 我们到了。

Here you are. 给你（这就是你要的东西）。

hero /ˈhɪərəu/ *n*. 英雄；男主角

hers /hɜːz/ *pron*. 她的

herself /hɜːˈself/ *pron*. 她自己

hesitate /ˈhesɪteɪt/ *v*. 犹豫

hesitate to do/in doing sth. 做某事犹豫不决

（考题）He hesitates in doing everything.

（考题）If you have trouble, don't hesitate to let me know.

hesitate about what/whether/how ... to do sth. 犹豫该做什么/是否该做/如何去做

hesitation /ˌhesɪˈteɪʃən/ *n*. 犹豫不决

do sth. without (a moment's) hesitation 毫不犹豫

do sth. with much hesitation 犹豫不决地做某事

（考题）He agreed to come with much hesitation.

hide /haɪd/ (hid, hidden) *vt*. *vi*. 藏；隐藏；掩盖

hide sth. (from sb.) （向某人）隐藏、掩盖某事

go into hiding 躲藏起来

high /haɪ/ *adj*. 高的

highlight /ˈhaɪlaɪt/ *n*. 最显著的、最突出的部分　*vt*. 使显著,强调

highly /ˈhaɪlɪ/ *adv*. 高地;非常地

　　think/speak highly of . . . 对…看法很好、评价很高

　　(考题)He thinks highly of what they have got to offer.

highrise /ˈhaɪraɪz/ *n*. 高层建筑;高楼大厦

highway /ˈhaɪweɪ/ *n*. 公路;主要干道

hijack /ˈhaɪdʒæk/ *vt*. 劫持;拦路抢劫

hill /hɪl/ *n*. 小山

himself /hɪmˈself/ *pron*. 他自己

hint /hɪnt/ *n*. 暗示

　　give sb. a hint of sth. 就某事给某人一个暗示

　　v. **hint (to sb.) that . . .** 对某人暗示说

　　hint at sth. 含蓄地说到某事

　　(考题)No one knew what he hinted at.

hire /haɪə/ *n*. 租用

　　(考题)Those three rules used for the goods you buy can also be
　　used for the goods you get on hire, or for the goods you get as
　　part of a service.

　　vt. 租用;雇佣

　　(考题)It cost 2 pence to hire a machine and an attendant.

　　(辨析:hire 常表示较短期的租用;而 rent 往往表示较长时间的
　　租用,尤其是租房。let 则表示"出租房子等"。)

historic /hɪsˈtɒrɪk/ *adj*. 有历史意义的

historical /hɪsˈtɒrɪkəl/ *adj*. 历史的;过去的

　　(考题). . . it seems not that far off from historical accounts but
　　his choice of facts: other things that could be said of the man
　　are not said.

　　(辨析:historic 强调"有历史意义的",而 historical 表示"历史上
　　的、过去的"。a historic event 表示"有历史意义的事件",而 a
　　historical event 仅表示"一件过去发生的事"。)

history /ˈhɪst(ə)rɪ/ *n*. 历史

　　(注意:一般是不可数名词,但在表示"一段"或"某种"历史时,可
　　使用不定冠词。)

hit /hɪt/ (hit, hit) *vt.* 击、打、敲；撞上；打击

（考题）But what if our own planet is hit by a comet?

hit sb. in the face/stomach (on the head/nose) 打某人某部位

hit on/upon sth. 想到、发现、碰上…

hitech /'haɪtek/ *n.* 高科技、尖端技术

hobby /'hɒbɪ/ *n.* 兴趣、嗜好

hold /həʊld/ (held, held) *vt. vi.* 抓住、握住；持有；保持；举行

（考题）I have taught many children who held the belief that their self-worth relied on how well they performed at tennis and other skills.

hold back 控制；阻碍

（考题）Colleges must report crime statistics by law, but some hold back for fear of bad publicity, leaving the honest ones looking dangerous.

hold off 推迟

hold on 坚持

（考题）Hold on, Allen thought. Keep your eyes open. Breathe. Keep awake.

hold on to sth. 牢牢抓住

hold sb. responsible for sth. 让某人对某事承担责任

hold out 坚持、维持

（考题）In addition, promising drugs hold out hope of better health and longer life.

hold water 能成立、有道理

n. **catch/get/take hold of** 抓住

（考题）An immediate anxiety took hold of him

hole /həʊl/ *n.* 洞

holiday /'hɒlɪdeɪ/ *n.* 假日；假期

be/go on holiday 在（去）休假

（考题）More American people take their troubles with them on holiday, according to a new survey.

in the holidays 在假期里

（考题）In the summer holidays, the library will have special hours on weekends.

public holidays 公共假日

national holidays 国定假日

（辨析：holiday 指假日、节日、休息日，可用单、复数；festival 指喜庆节日。而 vacation 指机关、学校时间较长的正式假期。）

hollow /ˈhɒləʊ/ *n*. 洞；窟窿　　*adj*. 空的、空心的；虚伪的

holy /ˈhəʊlɪ/ *adj*. 神圣的；上帝的

　the Holy Bible 圣经

home /həʊm/ *n*. 家　　*adv*. 在家

　be (feel) at home 无拘束、自在

　at home and abroad 国内外

　home-made 国产的

homesick /ˈhəʊmsɪk/ *adj*. 想家的、思乡的

homework /ˈhəʊmwɜːk/ *n*. 家庭作业

honest /ˈɒnɪst/ *adj*. 诚实的；正直的

　to be honest 老实说、说实话

honestly /ˈɒnɪstlɪ/ *adv*. 诚实地；坦率地

（考题）... but I can honestly say that without Mrs. Parks, I probably would not be standing here as Secretary of State.

　honestly (speaking) 老实说、坦率地说

honesty /ˈɒnɪstɪ/ *n*. 诚实、正直

honey /ˈhʌnɪ/ *n*. 蜂蜜；亲爱的

honeymoon /ˈhʌnɪmuːn/ *n*. 蜜月、新婚之月

honour /ˈɒnə/ *n*. 荣誉

　do honour to sb. /do sb. honour 向某人表示敬意

　in honour of ab. 向某人表示敬意；为了某人

（考题）Washington, a state in the Unite States, was named in honour of one of the greatest American presidents.

　It is an honour to do sth. 很荣幸能做某事

hornourable /ˈɒnərəbl/ *adj*. 值得尊敬的；体面的、光荣的

hook /hʊk/ *n*. 钩子　　*v*. 钩住

hope /həʊp/ *vt*. 希望

　hope to do sth. 希望做某事

Young adult filmmakers all hope to show their works in international festivals like Sundance and Toronto.

　hope that ... 希望…

I can only hope that this will not lead to further problems.

（辨析：hope 的宾语从句表示可能实现的愿望，使用陈述语气。另见 wish。）

hope for sth. 期盼某物

hope for the best 期待最好的

n. 希望；期望

in hopes/in the hope of/that ... 希望…

The Second World War was the golden age of queuing, and people joined any line in the hope that it was a queue for something to buy.

beyond hope 没有希望

with no /without hope of ... 没有…的希望

With no hope for cure and no way to reduce her pain and suffering from the terrible disease, the patient sought her doctor's help to end her life.

hopeful /ˈhəʊpful/ *adj*. 有希望的；抱有希望的

horizon /həˈraizn/ *n*. 地平线

horn /hɔːn/ 喇叭

horrible /ˈhɒrəbl/ *adj*. 可怕的、恐怖的；令人讨厌的

horror /ˈhɒrə/ *n*. 恐怖、恐惧

    in horror 惊恐地

    to sb.'s horror 使某人感到恐惧的是

horse /hɔːs/ *n*. 马

hospital /ˈhɒspitl/ *n*. 医院

    be in hospital 住院

host /həʊst/ *n*. 主人、东道主

    the host country 东道国

    v. **host ...** 主办…

（考题）Every January, Breckenridge hosts the International Snow Sculpture Championships.

hostage /ˈhɒstidʒ/ *n*. 人质

hostess /ˈhəʊstis/ *n*. 女主人

    air hostess 空姐

hot /hɒt/ *adj*. 热的；激烈的

hotel /həʊˈtel/ *n*. 旅馆

hour /haʊə/ *n*. 小时

by the hour 以小时为单位

（考题）Cleaning women usually get paid by the hour.

for hours 好几个小时

the rush hours 交通繁忙时刻

house /haʊs/ *n*. 房子

household /ˈhaʊshəʊd/ 一家人；家庭生活

（考题）You can get nearly all kinds of household goods in this shop.

housewife /ˈhaʊswaɪf/ *n*. 家庭主妇

housework /ˈhaʊswɜːk/ *n*. 家务活

hovercraft /ˈhɒvəkrɑːft/ *n*. 气垫船

how /haʊ/ *adv*. 怎样、如何

How are you? 你好吗？（需要具体答复）

How do you do? 你好。（回答：How do you do?）

How about (doing) sth.? 做某事如何？

（同义词：**What about (doing) sth.?**）

How much is it? 价格是多少？

（同义词：**What's the price? How much does it cost?**）

however /haʊˈevə/ *adv*. 无论如何；仍然 *conj*. 不论

（注意下列用法的转换：However hard he tried/Though he tried hard/No matter how hard he tried/Hard as he tried，...）

huge /hjuːdʒ/ *adj*. 巨大的；庞大的

huge amounts of 大量的（修饰不可数名词）

human /ˈhjuːmən/ *adj*. 人的；人类的 *n*. 人

（同 human being）

（考题）The new evidence makes it very clear that these people are a new species, distinct from modern humans.

humanity /hjuː(ː)ˈmænɪtɪ/ *n*. 人类（总称）；人道；人性

（考题）Throughout this painful experience, the kindness of strangers back my faith in humanity.

humble /ˈhʌmbl/ *adj*. 低下的；卑微的

humour /ˈhjuːmə/ *n*. 幽默；心情

be in a good/bad humour 心情好/坏

（同义词：**be in a good temper/mood**）

a sense of humour 幽默感

hunger /ˈhʌŋə/ *n*. 饥饿；渴望

have a hunger for sth. 渴望得到

hungry /ˈhʌŋgrɪ/ *adj*. 饿的；使人饥饿的；渴望的

go hungry 挨饿

be hungry for 渴望得到

hunt /hʌnt/ *n*. 狩猎；追寻　*v*. 狩猎；追寻；

hunt for sth. 搜索、追寻

（考题）He agreed such caves would be perfect places to hunt for life escaping from the bitterly cold, radiation-soaked, dry surface.

hunter /ˈhʌntə/ *n*. 猎人

hurry /ˈhʌrɪ/ *n*. 匆忙

be in a hurry (to do sth.) 正忙着（要去做某事）

do sth. in a hurry 匆忙做某事

vt. *vi*. （使）匆忙

hurry (sb.) up （催某人）快点

（注意：在否定句中，一般不使用 up。如：Don't hurry him。）

hurry off/away/home/there/into the room 匆忙离开、赶到…

hurt /hɜːt/ *n*. 疼痛；伤害

（考题）I had a hurt in my heart for this kind of human soul, all alone in the world.

vi. *vt*. （hurt, hurt）痛；使痛苦；伤害

（考题）Giving credit is more effective than even the most constructive criticism, which often hurts rather than helps.

husband /ˈhʌsbənd/ *n*. 丈夫

hut /hʌt/ *n*. 小屋；棚屋

hydrogen /ˈhaɪdrədʒən/ *n*. 氢

I

I /aɪ/ *pron*. 我

ice /aɪs/ *n*. 冰　*v*. (使)结冰

    ice cream 冰淇淋

    iced drink 冰镇饮料

idea /aɪˈdɪə/ *n*. 注意、念头；意见

have an/no idea (about sth.) 了解/不了解某事

    (考题) People in Los Angeles, California, have no idea of distance on the map; they measure distance in time, not miles.

    give sb. an idea about sth. 向某人介绍某事

    (考题) Franchising may give you the idea that as a franchisor, you need only relax in the rocking chair.

    It's a good idea to do sth. 做某事是个好主意

    (考题) Not all hotels are equal, of course, and it's a good idea to consult a guidebook with a good reputation.

    come up with an idea 突然想到一个注意

ideal /aɪˈdiːl/ *adj*. 理想的；完美的

    (考题) Oceans cover three-quarters of the Earth's surface — that would make wave power seem ideal for creating energy throughout the world.

identification /aɪˌdentɪfɪˈkeɪʃən/ *n*. 识别、鉴定；身份

identify /aɪˈdentɪfaɪ/ *vt*. 鉴定；辨别

    (考题) In the research, the teenagers were presented with the terms of four different loans but 76 per cent failed to identify the cheapest.

    identy sb./sth. as ... 辨认出某人/某物为…

idle /ˈaɪdl/ *adj*. 闲着的；无所事事的；无聊的　*v*. 闲待的

    idle away the time 消磨时光

    (同义词: **kill time, pass the time**)

if /ɪf/ *conj*. 如果、假定

    as if 好像(同义词: **as though**)

（考题）We say this to one another as if our tireless efforts were a talent by nature and an ability to successfully deal with stress.

even if 即便

（考题）Even if you don't have a timepiece of some sort nearby, your body keeps its own beat.

if any 如果说有的话

（考题）Set your sights more realistically by comparing yourself with family and friends, if anyone.

if need be 如果需要的话

if only 但愿、要是…就好了

（辨析：if 是引导条件状语最普通的用词，表示"如果、要是"；in case 强调"万一"；as long as 或 so long as，on condition that 以及 provided that 强调"在一定的条件下"。）

ignorance /ˈɪɡnərəns/ *n*. 无知、愚昧；不了解

ignorant /ˈɪɡnərənt/ *adj*. 无知的、愚昧的；不了解的

（考题）A study involving 8,500 teenagers from all social backgrounds found that most of them are ignorant when it comes to money.

be ignorant of/about sth. 对某事不了解

ignore /ɪɡˈnɔː/ *vt*. 不理、不顾；忽视

ignore sth. 忽视、不顾

（考题）Time is something from which we can't escape. Even if we ignore it, it's still going by, ticking away, second by second, minute by minute, hour by hour.

（辨析：ignore 常有故意的含义；neglect 强调"疏忽、不留心"而未能注意到；overlook 则表示由于粗心而"忽略"。）

ill /ɪl/ *adj*. 有病的；坏的；恶意的　*adv*. 坏、恶劣地、无情地

be/fall ill 生病了

speak ill of 说坏话

illegal /ɪˈliːɡəl/ *adj*. 非法的

（考题）If we have illegal immigrants coming in, many local workers will lose their jobs.

illegible /ɪˈledʒɪbl/ *adj*. （字迹）模糊的、难以辨认的

illness /ˈɪlnɪs/ *n*. 疾病（见 disease）

illustrate /ˈɪləstreɪt/ *vt*. （用实物、图片等）说明、解释

illustrate sth. 给某物配插图；用插图说明

illustrate that ... 说明…

（考题）The three facts presented in the passage are used to illustrate that safe drinking water should be a primary concern.

illustration /ˌɪləsˈtreɪʃən/ *n*. 解释、说明；插图

image /ˈɪmɪdʒɪ/ *n*. 影像；形象；概念

（考题）Finally, lighthouses have a romantic attraction, summed up by the image of the oil-skin coated keeper climbing his winding stairs to take care of the light to warn ships and save lives.

imaginary /ɪˈmædʒɪnərɪ/ *adj*. 想象出来的；虚构的

（考题）I had the lonely child's habit of making up stories and holding conversations with imaginary persons ...

（辨析：imaginary 强调"想象出来的"；imaginative 表示"有想象力的"；imaginable 表示"可以想象出来的"。）

imagination /ɪˌmædʒɪˈneɪʃən/ *n*. 想象；想象力

（考题）So set you imagination free when you think about the future.

imagine /ɪˈmædʒɪn/ *vt*. 想象；设想

imagine (sb.) doing sth. 想象（某人）做某事

（考题）The designers imagine using surface space for public parks and using underground space for flats, offices, shopping, and so on.

imagine sb. (to be) ... 想象某人…

imagine that ... 想象…

（考题）It is exciting to imagine that the advance in technology may be changing the most basic condition of human existence.

imitate /ˈɪmɪteɪt/ vt 模仿；仿效

immediate /ɪˈmiːdɪət/ *adj*. 即刻的、立即的；直接的、紧挨的

（考题）They find immediate gains from the opportunity to expand markets on the basis of reputation alone.

immediately /ɪˈmiːdɪətlɪ/ *adv*. 立即、马上

immediately after 一…就…（同 as soons as）

immigrant /ˈɪmɪɡrənt/ *n*. 移民

immigrate /ˈɪmɪɡeɪt/ *v*. 移居

immigrate to a place 移居某地

impact /ˈɪmpæck/ *n.* 冲击；影响、作用

（考题）Green building means reducing the impact of the building on the land.

have/make an impact on ... 对…产生影响

（考题）Rice said she and others, who grew up when the political activities of Parks held public attention, might not have realized her impact on their lives.

vi. 撞击；影响

impact on sb./sth. 对某人/事产生影响

impatient /ɪmˈpeɪʃənt/ *adj.* 不耐烦的、没有耐心的

be impatient with sb. 对某人不耐心

imperial /ɪmˈpɪəriəl/ *adj.* 帝国的

impersonal /ɪmˈpɛːsənl/ *adj.* 非个人的；不通人情的

implement /ˈɪmplɪmənt/ *n.* 工具 *vt.* 实现、执行

farm implement 农具

household implement 家用器具

implication /ˌɪmplɪˈkeɪʃən/ *n.* 含义；暗示

（考题）As our survey shows, a consumer power has great implications for companies, because it is changing the way the world shops.

imply /ɪmpˈlaɪ/ *vt.* 暗示；有…的含义

imply sth. 暗示某事

imply that ... 暗示说…

（考题）The judge's remark implied that York would be more severely punished if he pretended to be a psychiatrist.

importance /ɪmˈpɔːtəns/ *n.* 重要；重要性

be of great importance 很重要

important /ɪmˈpɔːtənt/ *adj.* 重要的

be important to sb. 对某人很重要

It's important for sb. to do sth. 某人做某事很重要

It is important that sb.（should）do sth. 某人做某事很重要

（考题）It was very important that her house should remain at all times clean and tidy.

（注意：在 important, necessary, good, wrong, decisive 等表示

判断意义的形容词后的从句中,使用虚拟语气。)

impose /ɪmˈpəʊz/ *vt*. 强加于

impose ... on sb. 将…强加于某人

(考题)You shouldn't have imposed your idea on others.

imposing /ɪmˈpəʊzɪŋ/ *adj*. 给人深刻印象的;壮观的、雄伟的

impossible /ɪmˈpɒsɪbl/ *adj*. 不可能的

It's impossible for sb. to do sth. 某人不可能做某事

do the impossible 做不可能的事

Nothing is impossible. 一切都有可能。

impress /ɪmˈpres/ *vt*. 留下印记;留下印象

impress sb. with sth. 给某人留下某印象

(考题)No matter how famous the product's origin is, if it fails to impress consumers with its own qualities, it begins to resemble an exercise in self-promotional marketing.

impress sth. on sb. (或 onsb.'s mind)给某人留下某印象

be impressed with/by sth. 对某事留下印象

impression /ɪmˈpreʃən/ *n*. 印象

give/leave sb. an impression of ... 给某人留下…印象

(考题)Leave the interviewer a bad impression, and often he will assume you have a lot of other unsatisfactory characters.

first impression 第一印象

(考题)First impressions are lasting ones.

improve /ɪmˈpruːv/ *vt*. *vi*. (使)改进、改善

(考题)... but to learn about and experience another culture that helped improve my own understanding of life and the world.

improvement /ɪmˈpruːvmənt/ *n*. 改进、改善

make improvements to sth. 对…加以改进

(考题)The plan comes from the Warning Alert and Response Network Act, a 2006 federal law that requires improvements to the nation's emergency alert system.

in /ɪn/ *prep*. 在…里;在…方面;过…时间

inaccessible /ˌɪnækˈsesəbl/ *adj*. 无法进入的;无法到达的;难以接近的

... be inaccessible to sb. 某人无法进入、接近…

inadequate /ɪnˈædɪkwɪt/ *adj*. 不充分的；不适当的

be inadequate for/to 不够/适合

（考题）The food supply is inadequate to a city of millions of people.

inch /ɪntʃ/ *n*. 英寸

incident /ˈɪnsɪdənt/ *n*. 事件；事变

include /ɪnˈkluːd/ *vt*. 包括；包含

including /ɪnˈkluːdɪŋ/ *prep*. 包括；包含

（考题）So many other exercises, including walking, lead to almost the same results painlessly, so why jog?

（注意：表达同样的意思，还可使用过去分词，但注意词序：..., walking included。）

income /ˈɪnkʌm/ *n*. 收入；所得

income tax 所得税

incomplete /ɪnkəmˈpliːt/ *adj*. 不完全的、不完整的

inconvenient /ɪnkənˈviːnɪənt/ *adj*. 不方便的

increase /ɪnˈkriːz/ *vt. vi*. （使）增加；增长

increase sth.（to...，by...） 增加某物（至…，增幅为…）

（考题）If their marketing plans succeed, they will increase their sales by 15 percent.

... increase（to...，by...）... 增加（到…，增幅为…）

（考题）So although they may eat the same volume of food, their calorie intake has increased.

indeed /ɪnˈdiːd/ *adv*. 确实；真正

independence /ˌɪndɪˈpendəns/ *n*. 独立；自主

independent /ˌɪndɪˈpendənt/ *adj*. 独立的；自主的

be independent of 独立于、不依靠

India /ˈɪndɪə/ *n*. 印度

Indian /ˈɪndɪən/ *adj*. 印度的；印第安人的 *n*. 印度人、印第安人

indicate /ˈɪndɪkeɪt/ *vt*. 指示、表示；象征

（考题）The bell indicating the end of the period rang, interrupting our heated discussion.

individual /ˌɪndɪˈvɪdjʊəl/ *adj*. 个人的；各自的 *n*. 个人

（考题）The world is going to be a loosely coupled set of individual small devices, connected wirelessly ...

individual sports 个人项目

indoors /ˌɪnˈdɔːz/ *adv.* 在室内

industrial /ɪnˈdʌstrɪəl/ *adj.* 工业的

industrialize /ɪnˈdʌstrɪəlaɪz/ *vt.* 工业化

industry /ˈɪndʌstrɪ/ *n.* 工业；行业；勤奋；勤劳

    the trourist industry 旅游业

    （考题）Diet foods and diet pills contain zero calorie only because the diet industry has created chemicals to produce these wonder products.

inevitable /ɪnˈevɪtəbl/ *adj.* 不可避免的

inexact /ˌɪnɪgˈzækt/ *adj.* 不精确的；不准确的

infant /ˈɪnfənt/ *n.* 婴幼儿

infect /ˈɪnfect/ *v.* 传染；感染

    infect sb./sth. 感染某人/某物

    be/get infected 受到感染

    （考题）The doctor suspected that he had been infected with HIV, the virus that leads to AIDS.

infer /inˈfɜː/ *vt.* 推论；推断

    infer ... from ... 从…推论

inferior /ɪnˈfɪərɪə/ *adj.* 低等的；劣质的；地位低的

    be inferior to 比…差、比…地位低

influence /ˈɪnfluəns/ *n.* 影响

    have an influence on ... 对…产生影响

    （考题）Emotions have delicate influence on fellow humans.

    under the influence of ... 在…的影响下

    vt. 影响

    influence sb./sth. 对某人/物产生影响

    （考题）Particulars of a situation may influence an individual's action.

influential /ˌɪnfluˈenʃəl/ *adj.* 有影响的

inform /inˈfɔːm/ *vt.* 通知；通告

    inform sb. (of sth.) (that ...) 通知某人(某事)

    （考题）Bill's aim is to inform the viewers that cigarette advertising on TV is illegal

    inform sb. what/how/where ... to do sth. 通知某人做…

（考题）I'd like to be informed in time when to begin the job.

inform sb. that ... 通知某人…

keep sb. well informed 使某人及时得到信息

（考题）I'd like to be kept well informed of what is going on there.

informal /ɪnˈfɔːməl/ *adj.* 非正式的

information /ˌɪnfəˈmeɪʃən/ *n.* 信息；情报；资料

   gather/collect information 收集资料

informative /ɪnˈfɔːmətɪv/ *adj.* 能提供消息的；增长见识的

inhabitant /ɪnˈhæbɪtənt/ 居民

inherit /ɪnˈherɪt/ *vt.* 继承；遗传

   inherit sth. from sb. 从某人处继承某物

initial /ɪˈnɪʃəl/ *afj.* 开始的；最初的

inject /ɪnˈdʒekt/ *vt.* 注射

injection /ɪnˈdʒekʃən/ *n.* 注射

injure /ˈɪndʒə/ *vt.* 受伤

   injure sb. 伤害某人

   be/get injured 受伤

（考题）They wanted to find out whether a certain amount of physical exercise would injure those suffering from heart problems.

（注意：表示身体某一部分受伤的方法：He is injured in the head/back/should, etc.）

（辨析：injure 往往指事故中受伤，伤员是 the injured。也表示伤害感情，如：It injured my feelings；wound 指战斗中受的刀伤枪伤，因此受伤的士兵称为 the wounded（soldiers）；hurt 指肉体上的疼痛，或感情、精神上受到伤害，如：It hurts me when you talk like that.）

injury /ˈɪnjʊərɪ/ *n.* 伤害

ink /ɪŋk/ *n.* 墨水

   in ink 用墨水书写

inn /ɪn/ *n* 小旅店；客栈

inner /ˈɪnə/ *adj.* 内部的、里面的；n. 内部、里面

innocent /ˈɪnəsənt/ *adj.* 清白的；无辜的；无罪的

input /ˈɪnpʊt/ *n.* 输入；投资　*vt.* 输入（计算机）

inquire /ɪn'kwaɪə/ *vi*. *vt*. 询问;打听

inquire about sth. 打听某事

(考题)Please go and inquire about the next flight to Tokyo.

inquire after sb. 问候某人

inquire into sth. 调查、了解某事

(考题)The police are inquiring into the murder，but nothing has come out.

inquiry /ɪn'kwaɪərɪ/ *n*. 询问、打听

make inquiries about sth. 询问某事

insect /'ɪnsekt/ *n*. 昆虫

insecticide /ɪn'sektɪsaɪd/ *n*. 杀虫剂;杀虫药

insert /ɪn'sɜːt/ *vt*. 插入

inside /'ɪnsaɪd/ *prep*. 在…里面、内部 *adv*. 在里面 *n*. 内部

insist /ɪn'sɪst/ *vi*. *vt*. 坚持认为;主张

insist on (doing) sth. 主张(做)某事

insist that ... 主张;坚持说

(考题)One strict mother insisted that her son，right from a child，should stand up whenever anyone entered the room，open doors and shake hands like a gentleman.

(考题)Some teens admit that asking someone for a date，or breaking up，can be easier in message form，though they don't want to do so. But they insist there's no harm.

(注意：insist 后的从句如表示"坚持认为、主张"，使用虚拟语气；如表示坚持对某事的陈述，则使用陈述语气。)

(辨析：insist on doing sth. 表示坚持认为应该做某事，是一种主张，如：He insisted on having a meeting to discuss the problem；而 persist in doing sth. 表示"坚持不懈地做某事"，是一种行为，如 He persists in reading English every day。)

inspect /ɪn'spect/ *vt*. 检查

inspect sth. 检查某物

(考题)When people come to visit the Gallery，they should have all their carried items inspected at the entrance.

inspire /ɪn'spaɪə/ *vt*. 鼓舞;激励;使有灵感

inspire sb. to do sth. 鼓励、激励某人做某事

(考题)The author mainly intends to inspire children to keep the sense of wonder about things around.

inspire sth. 激发、引起某事

（考题）The primary purpose of the project is to inspire a strong desire for discovery among the students.

install /ɪnˈstɔːl/ *vt.* 安装

instance /ˈinstens/ *n.* 例子

　for instance 例如（同义词：for example）

instant /ˈinstənt/ *adj.* 即刻的；速溶的　*n.* 一会儿

　the instant ... 一……，就……

　（同义词：the moment ... ,the minute ... ,as soon as ... ）

instead /ɪnˈsted/ *adv.* 代替；顶替

　instead of ... 代替……；而不是……

　（考题）You can share other members' troubles and successes, give your children some attention, or just sit down for a moment instead of rushing through life aimlessly.

instinct /ˈinstiŋkt/ *n.* 本能；直觉

institute /ˈinstɪtjuːt/ *n.* 学院；研究院

instruct /ɪnˈstrʌkt/ *vt.* 教；指引、指导；指示

　instruct sb. to do sth. 指示某人做某事

　（考题）A computer can only do what you have instructed it to do.

　instruct sb. in ... 教某人……（学科）

instruction /ɪnˈstrʌkʃən/ *n.* 指示、命令；指导；说明

　（考题）How much instruction the students get depends on their level of skill in listening, speaking, reading and writing.

instrument /ˈinstrəmənt/ *n.* 仪器；工具；乐器

insult /ˈinsʌlt/ *n.* 侮辱　*vt.* 侮辱

　（考题）This was the last straw. She could not take another insult.

　insult sb. 侮辱某人

insurance /ɪnˈʃʊərəns/ *n.* 保险

insure /ɪnˈʃʊə/ *v.* 给……保险

　insure sb. /sth. against ... 给某人/物保……险

　（考题）The house is insured against fire and theft.

intellect /ˈintəlekt/ *n.* 才智；智力

intelligence /ɪnˈtelɪdʒəns/ *n.* 智力、理解力；消息、情报

    an intelligence test 智力测试

    IQ=intelligence quotient 智商

intelligent /ɪnˈtelɪdʒənt/ *adj.* 聪颖的；有智力的

intend /ɪnˈtend/ *vt.* 打算、计划

    intend to do (doing) sth. 打算做某事

    （考题）She didn't intend to steal when she went into the store.

    intend to have done sth. 本打算要做某事

    （考题）I don't know how to express what it is like to watch the once handsome man you love and intend to live with forever dying slowly.

    intend sb. to do sth. 打算让某人做某事

    be intended for ... 为…而准备的（同义词：be meant for ...）

    be intended as 起某种作用

    （考题）The ten pieces that make up pictures at an exhibition are intended as symbols rather than representations of the paintings in the exhibition.

intention /ɪnˈtenʃən/ *n.* 动机；意图；目的

interest /ˈɪntrɪst/ *n.* 兴趣；利息；利益（常用复数）

    have/take/find/feel (an) interest in sth. 对某事感兴趣

    in the interest of ... 符合…的利益；对…有利

    v. 使有兴趣

    （考题）What he saw and heard there interested everyone.

interested /ˈɪntrɪstɪd/ *adj.* 感兴趣的

    be interested in sth. 对某事感兴趣

interesting /ˈɪntrɪstɪŋ/ *adj.* 有趣的

interfere /ɪntəˈfɪə/ *vi.* 妨碍；干扰；干预

    interfere with sb. /sth. 妨碍；干扰某人/某事

    （考题）He is doing the job in his own way. He doesn't like to be interfered with.

    interfere in sth. 干涉、干预某事

    （考题）No country has the right to interfere in other country's internal affairs.

intermediate /ɪntəˈmiːdɪət/ *adj.* 中间的；中等的

international /ɪntəˈnæʃənəl/ *adj.* 国际的

Internet /ˈɪntənet/ *n.* 因特网

interpret /ɪnˈtɜːprɪt/ *v*. 翻译；口译；解释

interpreter /ɪnˈtɜːprɪtə/ *n*. 译员

interrupt /ˌɪntəˈrʌpt/ *vt*. 打断；打扰

　interrupt sb./sth. 打断、干扰某人/某事

　（考题）They had interrupted their research to accept an invitation to take part in an unusual experiment: "an interesting week of poetry."

interval /ˈɪntəvəl/ *n*. 间隔；幕间休息

　at intervals 每隔一段时间/距离

　（考题）There will also be electric signs at frequent intervals.

interview /ˈɪntəvjuː/ *n*. 会面；面试　*vt*. 采访；面试

into /ˈɪntʊ/ *prep*. 进入

introduce /ˌɪntrəˈdjuːs/ *vt*. 介绍；引进

　introduce ... (to ...) 把…介绍给…

　（考题）They have just introduced new lessons in how to manage debts.

　introduce ... into ... 引进…

　（考题）The new technology is introduced into China from some European countries.

introduction /ˌɪntrəˈdʌkʃən/ *n*. 介绍；引进

intruder /ɪnˈtruːdə/ *n*. 入侵者；闯入者

invade /ɪnˈveɪd/ *v*. 侵略；侵入

invent /ɪnˈvent/ *vt*. 发明；创造

　invent sth. 发明某物

　（考题）They invent new ways to meet these needs and build models of their creations.

invention /ɪnˈvenʃən/ *n*. 发明

inventor /ɪnˈventə/ *n*. 发明者；发明家

invest /ɪnˈvest/ *vi. vt*. 投资；投入

　invest (sth.) in ... （将某物）投资于…

　（考题）How should one invest a sum of money in these days of inflation?

investigate /ɪnˈvestɪgeɪt/ *vi. vt*. 调查；侦查；检查

　investigate (sth.) 调查（某事）

　（考题）Broadly, we investigate the world's lakes and rivers and the creatures which inhabit them.

investment /ɪnˈvestmənt/ *n*. 投资；投入

invisible /ɪnˈvɪzəbl/ *adj*. 看不见的；无形的

invitation /ˌɪnvɪˈteɪʃən/ *n*. 邀请；请柬

　accept/decline an invitation 接受/婉拒邀请

invite /ɪnˈvaɪt/ *vt*. 邀请

　invite sb. to sth. 邀请某人参加…

　（考题）If it were not for the fact that she can't sing, I would invite her to the party.

　invite sb. to do sth. 邀请某人做某事

　（考题）Then invite her to join you for a day at a spa. Let her try various looks until she's comfortable in her own skin.

inviting /ɪnˈvaɪtɪŋ/ *adj*. 诱人的、吸引人的

　（考题）That's why the round yellow M signs of McDonald's are inviting to both young and old.

involve /ɪnˈvɒlv/ *vt*. 牵涉、涉及；包含

　（考题）And parent-child activities, from shopping to sports, involve a feeling of trust and friendship that can continue into adulthood.

　involve sb. in sth. 将某人牵扯进某事

　be/get involved in sth. 牵涉到某事

　（考题）The number of people involved is so big that they have great potential to influence government decisions affecting the environment.

　be involved with sb. 与某人有牵连

　（考题）In the 1850s, Douglass was involved with the Underground Railroad, the system set up by antislavery groups to bring runaway slaves to the North and Canada.

iron /aɪən/ *n*. 铁；*vt*. 熨、烫

irregular /ɪˈregjʊlə/ *adj*. 不规则的

island /ˈaɪlənd/ *n*. 岛

isolate /ˈaɪsəleɪt/ *vt*. 使隔离；使孤立

　（考题）They had only basic ways of creating light, and yet they found a way of using this simple technology in isolated places to save ships from hitting rocks.

isolate ... from ... 将…与…隔离开

(考题)The disaster area has been isolated from the outside in case some infectious diseases will spread.

issue /ˈɪsjuː/ *n*. 问题；一期（书报）；发行

(考题)When there is research to be done, divide the topic into several areas, and this can explore the issue in a very detailed way.

v. 发行、发出

issue sth. 发行、颁布…

(考题)America will be the first country to issue forever stamps.

Italian /ɪˈtælɪən/ *adj*. 意大利的；n. 意大利语；意大利人

Italy /ˈɪtəlɪ/ *n*. 意大利

item /ˈaɪtəm/ *n*. 项目；节目；产品；新闻

item of interest 令人感兴趣的消息、内容

(考题)The first question presented is of medium difficulty. If the test taker answers correctly, the next item will be more difficult.

its /ɪts/ *pron*. 它的

itself /ɪtˈself/ *pron*. 它自己

J

jacket /ˈdʒækɪt/ *n.* 短上衣；茄克衫

jail /dʒeɪl/ *n.* 监狱　*v.* 关入监牢

　　be in/put into/sent to jail 被关进牢房

jam /dʒæm/ *n.* 果酱；堵塞

　　traffic jam 交通堵塞

　　v. 堵塞；(把…)塞进、挤进

　　(考题)Sometimes there are so many animals that they jam the roads.

January /ˈdʒænuərɪ/ *n.* 一月

Japan /dʒəˈpæn/ *n.* 日本

Japanese /dʒæpəˈniːz/ *adj.* 日本的　*n.* 日本人；日语

jar /dʒɑː/ *n.* 罐子；大口瓶

jaw /dʒɔː/ *n.* 颌、下巴

jazz /dʒæz/ *n.* 爵士乐

jealous /ˈdʒeləs/ *adj.* 羡慕的；嫉妒的

　　be jealous of 羡慕、嫉妒

jeans /dʒiːnz/ *n.* 牛仔裤；紧身工作裤

jeep /dʒiːp/ *n.* 吉普车

jet /dʒet/ *n.* 喷气式飞机；射流　*v.* 喷射

jewel /ˈdʒuːel/ *n.* 宝石；首饰

job /dʒɒb/ *n.* 工作；事情

　　be out of a job 失业

　　(考题)Now that she is out of a job, Lucy has been considering going back to school, but she hasn't decided yet.

　　(同义词：**be out of work, be unemployed, be jobless**)

　　do a good job (of ...) 干得漂亮

　　(考题)Use energy-efficient ceiling fans either alone or with air conditioning ceiling fans do a great job of circulating air.

　　(辨析：为谋生而从事的工作是 job，或 work。正式长期的工作是 occupation。post 和 position 指具体的职位、岗位。)

jog /dʒɒg/ *v.* 慢跑

(考题)My friend Alex encouraged me to join him as he jogged by my house every evening. "You'll feel great."

join /dʒɔɪn/ *vi.* *vt.* 加入;参加

join sb. (in doing sth.) 加入到某些人中(做某事)

(考题)Join us for a wonderful holiday in one of Europe's most wonderful corners.

join ... (团体、组织等)加入…

join in (doing) sth. 参加做某事

(考题)After reading the ad, one will probably join in the tour because the price offered is reasonable and the sights are beautiful.

join sth. 与某物连接、交会

(考题)A railway joins the two cities.

join battle 参战

join forces(with sb.) 合力

join hands (with sb.) 携手合作

joint /dʒɔɪnt/ *n.* 连接处;关节 *adj.* 联合的;共同的

(考题)The main purpose of the passage is to call on people to take joint action in support of some nonprofit water organizations.

joint effort 共同努力

joint exploration 共同开发

joint meeting 联席会议

joint venture 合资企业

joke /dʒəʊk/ *n.* 笑话;玩笑

make/have a joke 说笑话;开玩笑

play a joke on sb. 开某人的玩笑

(考题)The writer felt "ashamed" because he played a joke on an outstanding athlete.

do sth. in joke 闹着玩的、不当真(同义词:do sth. for fun)

Journal /'dʒɜːnəl/ *n.* 杂志;期刊;日记

journalist /'dʒɜːnəlɪst/ *n.* 记者

journey /'dʒɜːnɪ/ *n.* 旅行

make/take a journey (to a place) 去某地旅行

Have a pleasant jouney! 一路顺风！旅途愉快！

joy /dʒɔɪ/ *n*. 欢乐；高兴

（考题）There's more room for joy in her life — and it wasn't just writing.

to sb.'s joy（to the job of …） 使某人感到高兴的是

with joy 高兴地

（考题）It was with great joy that he received the news that his lost daughter had been found.

judge /dʒʌdʒ/ *n*. 裁判；法官 *v*. 判断；评判；审判

judge sth. 判断某事

（考题）The lack of right male role models in many of their lives means that their peers are the only people they have to judge themselves against.

judge that … 判断、认为…

judge … ＋*adj*./*n*. 认为…如何

（考题）Each team hopes that when the time is up, its sculpture will be judged the best.

judge from … 根据…判断

judgement /ˈdʒʌdʒmənt/ *n*. 判断；审判；判断力

（考题）We make use of stereotypes as convenient ways to make quick judgements about situations and people around us.

in sb.'s judgement 在某人看来

juice /dʒuːs/ *n*. 果汁

July /dʒuˈlaɪ/ *n*. 七月

jump /dʒʌmp/ *n*. 跳、跳跃

high jump 跳高

long jump 跳远

vi. *vt*. 跳、跳跃；跳过

jump at sth. 欣然接受

（考题）I guess I am a really restless spirit. I like traveling, so when the chance came, I jumped at it.

jump over 跳过、越过；省去

（考题）Diet products allow us to jump over the thinking stage and go straight for the scale instead.

jump to one's feet 跳起身来

jump the line 插队

June /dʒuːn/ *n*. 六月

jungle /dʒʌŋgl/ *n*. 丛林

the law of the jungle 弱肉强食的法则

(考题)The law of the jungle has begun to operate at bus stops, with people using their arms to push others out of the way.

junior /'dʒuːnjə/ *adj*. 较年轻的;地位、级别较低的;

(考题)This is a junior school. You should go to a senior school for girls of your age.

be junior to ... 比…年轻/地位低

jury /'dʒuərɪ/ *n*. 陪审团

just /dʒʌst/ *adj*. 正义的;正当合理的

(考题)Ours is a just cause and it will surely win.

adv. 正好、恰恰

Just a minute/moment. 请稍等。

just as 正像、就像…那样

(考题)Just as laughing has many health advantages, scientists are discovering that so, too, does crying.

just now 刚才

just then 就在那时

just the same 同样

(考题)My body had long since used up all its energy, but it went on running just the same.

Just think ... 真想不到…

justice /'dʒʌstɪs/ *n*. 正义;公平

justify /'dʒʌstɪfaɪ/ *vt*. 使正当;证明有道理

justify sth. 证明某事合理

be justified in doing sth. 做某事有道理

K

keen /kiːn/ *adj.* 渴望的；锋利的；敏锐的

    be keen on sth. 对…很感兴趣、喜爱

    （考题）Most boys are keen on detective stories.

    be keen to do sth. 迫切想做某事（见 be eager to do sth.）

keep /kiːp/ （kept，kept）*v.* 保持；保存；管理；使…

    keep sth. 保存某物

    keep sb./sth. … （*adj.，prep，adv.*）使某人/物…

    （考题）To keep your brain young and plastic you can do one of a million new activities that challenge and excite you.

    keep （sb.） doing sth. （使某人）不停做某事

    （考题）It'll be easier if you keep turning the map so it follows the direction you're traveling in.

    keep sb. from doing sth. 阻止某人做某事

    （考题）A special protein keeps it from freezing.

    keep （on） doing sth. 反复、持续做某事

    （考题）Keeping on doing good deeds brings us peace of mind，which is important for our happiness.

    keep + *adj.* 保持…

    （考题）Nothing other than jogging can help people keep fit.

    keep at … 坚持、不停做某事

    keep （sb.） away from … （使某人）远离、避开…

    （考题）What is worse，keeping your child away from what they fear can turn that feeling into a phobia.

    keep sth. in mind 牢记某事

    （考题）It is important to keep in mind that you are in a national park where wildlife exists.

    （同义词：**bear sth. in mind, learn sth. by heart**）

    keep one's word/promise 信守诺言

    keep to sth. 遵守、坚持

    keep up with … 跟上

（考题）She wanted me to "make something" of myself, and decided I had better start young if I was to have any chance of keeping up with the competition.

keeper /ˈkiːpə/ *n.* 看守人

kettle /ketl/ *n.* 水壶

key /kiː/ *n.* 钥匙；答案；(作定语)重要的、关键的

　key to ...... 的答案

（考题）Teams and watchers knew there might be no winner at all, because these vehicles were missing a key part — drivers.

keyboard /ˈkiːbɔːd/ *n.* 键盘

kick /kɪk/ *vt.* 踢

kid /kɪd/ *n.* 小孩；欺骗、哄骗　*vi. vt.* 哄骗；戏弄

kidnap /ˈkɪdnæp/ *vt.* 绑架；诱拐

kill /kil/ *vt.* 杀死；去除

（考题）Therefore, by producing a perfect copy of the noise and delaying it by half a wave cycle, we can kill the unwanted noise.

　kill time 消磨时间(见 idle away the time)

　Kill two birds with one stone. 一箭双雕、一举两得

kilogram /ˈkɪləɡræm/ *n.* 千克、公斤

kilometer /ˈkɪləmiːtə/ *n.* 千米、公里

kind¹ /kaɪnd/ *adj.* 和蔼的、仁慈的；好心的

　It's kind of you to do (have done) sth. 多谢你…

　be kind enough to do sth. 劳驾、费心做某事

（考题）Would you be kind enough to get things ready for the meeting within two days?

　be so kind as to do sth. 劳驾、费心尊某事

kind² /kaɪnd/ *n.* 种类

　this kind of ... (或 **... of this kind**)这种…

　all kinds of ... 各种各样的

　a kind of ... 某种、一种…

　of a/the same kind 同样种类的

kindergarten /ˈkɪndəˌɡɑːtən/ *n.* 幼儿园

kindly /ˈkaɪndlɪ/ *adl.* 和蔼的可亲的；亲切的　*adv.* 和蔼可亲地

　Would you kindly do ...? 能麻烦你做…吗?

（考题）Would you kindly take the letter to Jimmy?

kindness /'kaɪndnɪs/ *n*. 和蔼可亲;好意

king /kɪŋ/ *n*. 国王

kingdom /'kɪŋdəm/ *n*. 王国

kiss /kɪs/ *n*. 吻

(考题)A goodbye kiss to a husband or wife at the age of 85, for example, may bring far more complex emotional responses than a similar kiss to a boy or girl friend at the age of 20.

vt. 吻;用吻表示

kiss sb. 吻某人

kiss sb. good-bye 与某人吻别

kitchen /'kɪtʃən/ *n*. 厨房

kite /kaɪt/ *n*. 风筝

kitten /'kɪtən/ *n*. 小锚

knee /niː/ *n*. 膝盖

be/go down on one's knee 跪下

kneel /niːl/ *vt*. 跪下

knife /naɪf/ *n*. 小刀

knock /nɒk/ *vi*. *vt*. 敲;打;碰撞

knock (sth.) on/against sth. (使某物)撞上某物

knock at the door 敲门

(考题)I think we are knocking at the door of immortality.

knock sth. down 拆卸;撞倒

(考题)She had been knocked down by a car and fainted. When she came to in hospital, York was standing over her.

knock off 下班

knock sth. off 减价;匆匆做完

(考题)If you buy more than ten, they knock 20 pence off the price.

knock sb. out 击败;使昏迷

knock sth. over 打翻;撞倒

know /nəʊ/ (knew, known) *vi*. *vt*. 知道;认识

know sb./sth. 认识某人/知道某事

know about sb./sth. 听说,了解某人/某事

(考题)I don't know him, but I have long known about him.

know how to do sth. 知道如何做某事

know that ... 知道…

It is known that ... 人们知道…

（考题）It's widely known that you value more anything that needs your effort in the first place.

（注意：在表示"知道、了解、认识"时，know 一般不用完成时态，除非强调"知道、认识了多长一段时间"。比较：Have you learned the news? 但 Do you know the news?）

knowledge /ˈnɒlɪdʒ/ *n*. 知识

common knowledge 常识；众所周知的事

have a good knowledge of ... 对…很了解

（考题）You will also have a better knowledge of methods of solving the international problems.

beyond one's knowledge 是某人不知道的

knowledgeable /ˈnɒlɪdʒəbl/ *adj*. 知识渊博的；在行的

（考题）But as people become more knowledgeable about these problems they will go and get help.

Korea /kəˈrɪə/ *n*. 朝鲜；韩国

Korean /kəˈrɪən/ *adj*. 朝鲜的；韩国的；朝鲜语；朝鲜人

L

lab /læb/ *n.* (laboratory) 实验室

    language lab 语言实验室

label /ˈleɪbl/ *n.* 标签

    (考题) It is becoming increasingly common for brand names to be placed on the outside of clothes, and this labeling makes it easy to send out information about fashion instantly.

    vt. 给…贴标签

    lable sb. /sth. as … 把某人/物看成…

labour /ˈleɪbə/ *n.* 劳动;劳动力

    (考题) For the labour importing countries, the flow of labour may lead to greater money inflows.

    manual labour 体力劳动

    mental labour 脑力劳动

lack /læk/ *n.* 缺乏

    for/from/because of/due to lack of … 由于缺乏…

    (考题) Your eating habits will be broken due to lack of sleep.

    vt. vi. 缺乏

    lack sth. 缺乏某物

    (考题) Your child may always seem to expect the worst to happen and lack confidence in his or her ability to deal with any challenge.

    be lacking in sth. 缺乏某物

    (考题) They are diligent, but they are lacking in experience.

    sth. is lacking 缺乏某物

lady /ˈleɪdɪ/ *n.* 女士;夫人

lake /leɪk/ *n.* 湖

lamb /læm/ *n.* 羔羊;小羊

lamp /læmp/ *n.* 灯

land /lænd/ *n.* 陆地、大地;土地

    (考题) Green building means "reducing the impact of the

building on the land".

by land（交通）由陆路

vi. 降落、着陆；上岸

（考题）One of its engines had gone wrong, but, to everyone's relief, the plane landed safely.

landlord /ˈlændlɔːd/ *n.* 地主；房东

lane /leɪn/ *n.* 小道；弄堂；车道

a fast lane 一根快车道

language /ˈlæŋgwɪdʒ/ *n.* 语言

large /lɑːdʒ/ *adj.* 大的

at large 在逃的、逍遥法外的；总体说来

by and large 总的说来

laser /ˈleɪzə/ *n.* 激光

last /lɑːst/ *adj.* 最后的；刚过去的；*adv.* 最后的

last but not least 最后但同样重要的

n. 最后

at last 最后、终于

to the last 到最后

（考题）They were determined to hold on to the last.

v. 持续、维持

last (sb.) ...（时间） 维持某人…时间

（考题）Their success as designers might last only a short time, but fashion — like celebrity — has always been temporary.

late /leɪt/ *adj.* 晚的、迟到的；已故的　*v.* 晚

（考题）It's not a good habit to "sleep late and rise late".

be late for ...（做某事）迟到了

lately /ˈleɪtlɪ/ *adv.* 最近；近来

（考题）Farmers, as we all know, have been having a hard time of it lately, and have turned to new ways of earning income from their land.

later /ˈleɪtə/ *adj. adv.* 更晚的（地）；较晚的（地）

（考题）Educators feel that multitasking by children has a serious effect on later development of study skills.

later on 后来；将来、过些时候

（考题）Once you have confirmed your answer, you cannot go

back to change it if, later on, you realize that your answer was wrong.

sooner or later 早晚

latest /ˈleɪtɪst/ *adj*. 最晚的；最新的

　　the latest news 最新消息

　　(考题) He also takes advantage of the latest developments of color photography to help both the eye and the memory when he improves his painting back in his workroom.

latter /ˈlætə/ *adj*. 后面的；后面提到的　*n*. (两者中的)后者

　　the former . . . , the latter . . . 前者…，后者…

　　(考题) The former make every possible effort to avoid being discovered, while the latter quickly draw attention to themselves.

laugh /lɑːf/ *vi*. *vt*. 笑；*n*. 笑声

　　laugh at . . . 嘲笑…

　　laugh sth. off 一笑置之，不当回事

laughter /ˈlɑːftə/ *n*. 笑；笑声

launch /lɔːntʃ/ *n*. 发射　*vt*. 发射；(使)船下水

　　(考题) Most of the danger of space flight is in the launches and landings.

laundry /ˈlɔːndrɪ/ *n*. 洗衣店

lavatory /ˈlævətərɪ/ *n*. 厕所

law /lɔː/ *n*. 法律；法规；定律

　　against the law 违法

　　(考题) It's against the law to make false statements so they try to mislead you with the truth.

　　break the law 违法

　　(考题) When he was young, Arthur Bonner broke the law and ended up in prison.

　　natural law/law of nature 自然法则

lawn /lɔːn/ 草坪

lawyer /ˈlɔːjə/ *n*. 律师

lay /leɪ/ (laid, laid) *vt*. 放下，铺放；布置；产蛋

　　(考题) In the deserts of the southwestern United States, cliffs and deep valleys were formed from thick mud that once lay beneath a sea more than millions of years ago.

lay sth. down 放下;制定;献出

lay sth. out 布置

(考题)Such tools as laser beams and power planes help lay out a house better and make more precision cuts on the wood.

lay the table 摆餐桌

(辨析:lay 是及物动词,过去时和过去分词为 laid, laid;lie 是不及物动词,表示"躺下"。过去时和过去分词为 lay, lain;但 lie 表示"说谎"时,过去时和过去分词为 lied, lied。)

layer /ˈleɪə/ *n.* 层

lazy /ˈleɪzɪ/ *adj.* 懒惰的;懒散的

lead /liːd/ (led, led) *v.* 领导;引导;通向;导致

lead ... in (doing) sth. 领导某人做某事

lead sb. to do sth. 诱使、导致某人做某事

lead sb. to a place 带某人去某处

(考题)Even with healthier lifestyles and less disease, they say failure of the brain and organs will finally lead all humans to death.

lead to sth. 通往、导致…

(考题)Honorable thoughts lead to honorable actions. Honorable actions lead us to a happier existence.

n. **take the lead** 带头;领先

leader /ˈliːdə/ *n.* 领袖;领导人

leadership /ˈliːdəʃɪp/ *n.* 领导

under the leadership of 在…的领导下

leaf /liːf/ *n.* 树叶;书页 *vi.* 翻书页

turn over a new leaf 从头做起

leaf through a book 翻阅一本书

leaflet /ˈliːflɪt/ *n.* 传单;散页宣传品;小册子

league /liːg/ *n.* 联盟;协会;社团

leak /liːk/ *v.* 漏、泄漏;渗漏

(考题)A new house should have straight walls and the roof must not leak.

lean /liːn/ (leaned,或 leant, leant) *vi. vi.* (使)靠、倚

lean forward 俯身向前

lean (sth.) against/on ... （将某物）靠在…上

leap /liːp/ *vi*. 跳、跃 *vt*. 跳过、越过

learn /lɜːn/ （leanred，或 learnt, learnt）*vi*. *vt*. 学习

　learn (sth.) (from sb.) （向某人）学习（某事）

　learn (how) to do sth. from sb. 向某人学如何做某事

　（考题）Everyone should learn always to think of others.

　learn that ... 了解到…

　（考题）So it came as no surprise to learn that researchers believe crying and laughing come from the same part of the brain.

　learn of/about ... 了解到有关…的事

　（考题）Art museums are places where people can learn about various cultures.

　learn a lesson from ... 从…中吸取教训

　（辨析：学习某种技能技巧或动作用 learn 而不用 study。study 强调带有研究性质的学习，以理论知识学习为主。）

leanred /ˈlɜːnɪd/ *adj*. 有学问的

learner /ˈlɜːnə/ *n*. 学者；学习者

learning /ˈlɜːnɪŋ/ *n*. 学识、学问

least /liːst/ *adj*. 最少的、最小的 *n*. 最少，最小

　at least 至少

　not in the least 一点也不

　to say the least 至少

　least of all 最不…

leather /ˈleðə/ *n*. 皮革

leave /liːv/ *vi*. *vt*. 离开；遗忘；使处于某种状态 *n*. 请假

　leave (a place) (for ...) 离开（某地）（去某地）

　leave sb. doing sth. (*adj*., *prep*., etc.) 使某人…

　（考题）Students who perform poorly on the exam are left feeling that it is all over.

　leave sth. to sb. 把某物留给某人

　leave sth. with sb. 把某物留在某人处

　leave sb. alone/to himself 不要打扰某人

　（考题）If left to himself, he would have whistled life away in perfect satisfaction; but his wife was always mad at him for his idleness.

n. ask for leave 请假

lecture /ˈlektʃə/ *n.* 讲座；讲演

    go to/attend/ be present at a lecture 听讲座

    give a lecture on sth. 就…举办讲座

lecturer /ˈlektʃərə/ *n.* 讲演者

left /left/ *adj.* 左边的   *adv.* 向左地 左边地   *n.* 左侧

    on the left 在左边

    turn to the left/turn left 向左转

    left-handed 使用左手的、左撇子

leg /leg/ *n.* 腿

legal /ˈliːgəl/ *adj.* 法律上的；合法的

leisure /ˈleɪʒə/ *adj.* 空闲的

    at leisure 有空的

    leisure time 空闲时间

    （考题）Most people on this island are recreational fishers, and obviously fishing forms an actual part of their leisure time.

lemon /ˈlemən/ *n.* 柠檬

lend /lend/ (lent，lent) *vt.* 借出

    lend sb. sth. /lend sth. to sb. 将某物借给某人

    lend sb. a hand 帮助某人

length /leŋθ/ *n.* 长度

    at length 最终；冗长的；细致的

    in length 长度为

    （考题）The tunnel in construction is the top one in length in the world.

lesson /lesn/ *n.* 课；教训

    take lessons 上课

    learn a lesson from ... 从…吸取教训

    teach sb. a lesson 给某人一个教训

    （考题）But last Sunday, one aged gentleman appeared to teach me a valuable lesson.

let /let/ (let，let) *vt.* 让；出租

    let sb. do sth. 让某人做某事

    let sb. /sth. ＋prep., adv. etc. 让某人/物…

    （注意：如宾语补足语是动词不定式，也可用 allow sb. to do sth.

表示；但如果宾语补足语是介词短语、副词等结构时，则不能用 allow。另外，主动语态中省去的动词不定式 to 在被动语态中要还原。）

（辨析：注意这两句话意思的不同：Let's do sth. , shall we? 我们（一起）去做某事，好吗？ Let us do sth. , will you? 你可以让我们去做某事吗？ 因此，反意疑问句的形式不同。）

let alone 不用说；不要打扰

let go/let sth. go/let go of sth. 放开…、松手

（考题）As thoughts go through their minds, they let them go. Breathe. Let go. Breathe. Let go.

let ... in (into ...) 让…进来

let ... out 泄漏；发出（喊声等）；出租

（考题）The cigarette fell from his lips as he let out a shout that could be heard halfway down the street.

let me see 让我想想

letter /ˈletə/ n. 信；字母

level /ˈlevəl/ n. 水平；高度；层次 adj. 平的；相等的

（考题）One characteristic of the EoL is that it provides different levels of information.

at a high level 在高水平上

（考题）The surface of Mars is exposed to high levels of space radiation.

liberate /ˈlɪbəreɪt/ vt. 解放；使获得自由

liberty /ˈlɪbɜːti/ n. 自由

librarian /laɪbˈreərɪən/ n. 图书管理员

library /ˈlaɪbrərɪ/ n. 图书馆

licence /ˈlaɪsəns/ 执照

lid /lɪd/ n. 盖子；vt. 盖盖子

lie /laɪ/ (lay, lain) vi. 躺下；卧倒；

lie in 在于；寓于…之中（同义词：consist in）

（考题）On one level, we are not allowing our brain to admit that our weight problems lie not in actually losing the weight, but in controlling the consumption of fatty, high-calorie, unhealthy foods.

lie + adj. , etc. 处于某种状态

（考题）We would also demonstrate that we cannot lie trusted，since we advertise our dishonor by telling our family and friends.

vi．（lied，lied）说谎

n．**tell a lie/tell lies** 说谎

（见 lay）

life /laɪf/ *n*．生活；生命

live/lead a ... life 过着…的生活

in one's life 一生中

（考题）In her later life，Elizabeth Taylor devoted herself to doing business and helping others.

between life and death 生死攸关

everyday life 日常生活

life-long 一生的

come to life 苏醒

（考题）During the heat of the day，a visitor may see very few signs of living things，but as the air begins to cool in the evening，the desert comes to life.

bring sb. to life 使苏醒

（考题）I found the old news pictures really interesting — they helped to bring to life the stories the people were telling.

give/devote one's life to/lay down one's life for ... 为…献出生命

（考题）And so the little women had grown up and lived happily with their children，enjoying the harvest of love and goodness that they had devoted all their lives to.

lift /lɪft/ *n*．电梯；搭车　*vt*．提升、提起

give sb. a lift 让某人搭车

light¹ /laɪt/ *adj*．轻的

light² /laɪt/ （lighted，lighted 或 lit，lit）*vt*．*vi*．点燃

light (sth.) up 点燃；照亮；（使）容光焕发

（考题）... but sometimes when it is cloudless，gray steam gathers around the top of the mountains which，in the last rays of the setting sun，will shine and light up like a crown of glory.

n．光线；光亮

bring sth. to light 使公之于众

come to light 为人所知

（注意：表示"照明"时，light 的过去式常用 lit，如：a well-lit room；表示"点着的"则常用 lighted，如：lighted cigarette。）

lightning /ˈlaɪtnɪŋ/ *n*. 闪电　*adj*. 闪电般的；迅速的

like¹ /laɪk/ *prep*. 像…一样

　　look like … 看上去像…

　　feel like (doing) sth. 喜欢（做）某事

　　（考题）I was so angry and I just didn't feel like looking for another job.

　　（辨析：在表示"像…一样"时，like 是介词，后面不跟从句；但 as 是连词，后面使用从句；作介词使用时，as 表示"作为"。试比较下面两句句子的不同含义：As the mother, she takes good care of the child 以及 She takes good care of the child like the mother.）

like² /laɪk/ *v*. 喜欢

　　like (to do, doing) sth. 喜欢（做）某事

　　（考题）They do need regular exercise but they like to run for a short burst and then get back on the bed or a comfortable seat.

　　（考题）Estrella likes being busy and getting to know people from all over the world.

　　like sb. to do sth. 想要某人做某事

　　would like (to do) sth. 想要（想做）某事

　　would like sb. to do sth. 想要某人做某事

　　as you like 随你的便

　　（考题）The money comes straight out of your account, so you can spend as much as you like as long as you have enough money (or an agreed overdraft) to cover it.

　　if you like 如果你喜欢的话

likely /ˈlaɪklɪ/ *adj*. 可能的

　　It is likely for sb. to do sth. 某人有可能做某事

　　sb. is likely to do sth. 某人有可能做某事

　　（考题）Therefore, with the gentle waves touching all round the lighthouse, the visitor is likely to think it is a world preferable to the busy and noisy modern life.

　　（考题）The more exposed young people are to financial issues,

and the younger they become aware of them, the more likely they are to become responsible, forward-planning adults who manage their finances confidently and effectively.

adv. 可能地

sb. will likely do sth. 某人有可能做某事

（考题）They don't think anyone will likely to help you.

limit /'lɪmɪt/ *n.* 限制、限度

a limit to/of sth. 某事的限制

（考题）Some experts say that scientific advances will one day enable humans to last tens of years beyond what is now seen as the natural limit of the human life span.

to the limit 最大限度

without limit 无限制的

vt. 限制、限定

limit sth.（to ...） 将某事限制（在…）

（考题）They are also trying to limit the amount of waste industries are allowed to produce.

line /laɪn/ *n.* 线；路线；行

in line with 与…相一致

hold the line 请别挂电话

read between the lines 从字里行间去了解

v.（使）排成行；划线

line sth. 沿…排列

（考题）Steaming, hot remains from recent eruptions begin to line the path as you near the active summit：the McKenney Cone.

line up 排队

link /lɪŋk/ *n.* 联系；连接

（考题）But the link between money and happiness is complex.

vt. 使连接；汇合、碰头

link ...（with sth.）（用某物）连接…

（考题）Emotions are closely linked with states of internal responses.

lion /'laɪən/ *n.* 狮子

lip /lɪp/ *n.* 嘴唇

liquid /ˈlɪkwɪd/ *n.* 液体

list /lɪst/ *n.* 表;清单

listen /ˈlɪsn/ *vi.* 听

  listen to ... 听…

  listen to sb. do (doing) sth. 听某人做某事

  (考题)Specialists use dogs to listen to children reading because they think dogs can provide encouragement for shy children.

literature /ˈlɪtərɪtʃə/ *n.* 文学

litre /ˈliːtə/ *n.* 升(容量单位)

litter /ˈlɪtə/ *n.* 废物、垃圾   *v.* 乱放、乱扔;把弄得脏乱

  Don't litter/No litter 不得乱丢杂物

little /ˈlɪtl/ *adj.* 小的;很少的   *adv.* 很少、几乎没有   *n.* 少量

  a little 一些

  little 很少、几乎没有(修饰不可数名词。另见 few)

  (考题)It makes but little difference whether you own a farm or not.

  little by little 一点一点地

  not a little 相当,不是一点点(见 bit)

live /lɪv/ *v.* 生活;居住

  live a ... life 过…样的生活

  live by doing sth. 靠…生活

  (考题)Malaria parasites live by eating the red blood cells they infect.

  live up to 符合;不辜负

  (考题)The WTO cannot live up to its name if it does not include a country that is home to one fifth of mankind.

lively /ˈlaɪvlɪ/ *adj.* 充满活力的;生动的

liver /ˈlɪvə/ *n.* 肝脏

load /ləʊd/ *n.* 负荷;装载物

  (考题)Cut your air conditioning load and reduce pollution by planting leafy trees around your home and fixing reflective bricks on your roof.

  vi. 装货   *vt.* 给…装货、装载

  load ... with sth. 把某物装上…

  load sth. into/onto ... 将某物装上…

be loaded with ... 装有…

（考题）Just looking at his bench loaded with tools and pieces of leather，I knew he was a skilled craftsman.

loaf /ləʊf/ *n.* 一只面包

loan /ləʊn/ *n.* 贷款；借出（物）*vt.* 借出

loan sb. sth. /loan sth. to sb. 将某物借给某人

local /ˈləʊkəl/ *adj.* 当地的

locate /ləʊˈkeɪt/ *vt.* 确定位置；使位于…

locate sth. 确定某物的位置

（考题）Doctors can put a tiny chip under the skin that will help locate and obtain a patient's medical records.

be located ... 位于…（同义词：be situated ...）

location /ləʊˈkeɪʃən/ *n.* 位置、地点

lock /lɒk/ *n.* 锁

keep sth. under lock and key 将某物严加保管

vt. **lock sth. up** 把某物锁好

locker /ˈlɒkə/ *n.* 柜子

log /lɒg/ *n.* 原木、木料

logical /ˈlɒdʒɪkəl/ *adj.* 逻辑的；符合逻辑的

lonely /ˈləʊnlɪ/ *adj.* 寂寞的；感到孤单的

Jogging is also a lonely pastime.

（见 alone）

long /lɒŋ/ *adj.* 长的　*n.* 一段长时间

long before 很久以前

before long 不久以后

（考题）You may start out slow, but before long you're pretty quick.

as/so long as 只要（引导条件状语从句）

no longer 不再；已不

（考题）If pop music is no longer your only favourite，and you are considering a relaxing holiday where the scenery is breathtaking and the sound of the sea is live music to your ears, come and stay with us.

vi. **long for sth.** 渴望得到某物

（考题）The last sentence in the text implies that most of the

people long for a peaceful world.

long to do sth. 渴望做某事

（考题）You will go away enriched, longing to come back.

long for sb. to do sth. 渴望、期待某人做某事

look /luk/ *n*. 看一下；表情

have/take a look (at sth.) 看一下

vi. 看 link *v*. 看起来

look about/around 环顾

look at ... 看…

look back on/to sth. 回顾

（考题）It's all part of growing up. It happens to everyone, and some day you will look back on all of this and say, "Hard as it was, it make me who I am today.

（同义词：**think back to sth.**, **trace back to sth.**, **recall sth.**）

look down on/upon 轻视、看不起

look for 寻找

look into sth. 朝里看去；调查某事

（考题）It allows us to look into the future and explore the cities of the next century and the way we'll be living then.

look on 旁观

look out (of ...)（从…里）朝外望去

look on ... as ... 把…看作…

（考题）... people look on work as a path to ever-increasing consumption rather than a way to realize their own abilities.

（同义词：**consider ... as/to be ...**, **thnik of ... as**, **think ... to be ...**, **regard ... as ...**）

look out (for ...) 注意、当心(…)

（考题）— Look out for the glass! — It's OK. I'm wearing shoes.

look through sth. 浏览；复习；核查

look to sb (to do sth.) 依赖、指望某人(做某事)

look sth. up (in ...)（在…中）查找(资料、信息等)

（考题）If you don't know his telephone number, you can look it up in the telephone directory.

look ＋ adj. 看起来…

loose /luːs/ *adj*. 松的；松散的

loosen /ˈluːsən/ vt. 松开、解开

lose /luːz/ (lost，lost) vt. 丢失；失去；vi. 输

lose sth. 丢失某物

（考题）As the disease progresses，patients might lose the ability to move and may be unable to speak or move at all.

lose one's way 迷路

be/get lost 迷路

（考题）But make sure not to get lost or waste time going round in circles.

lose heart 丧失信心

lose one's temper 发脾气

（考题）Martha shouldn't have lost her temper with her supervisor.

lose oneself in (doing) sth. 全神贯注地做某事

loss /lɒs/ n. 遗失；丢失；损失

be at a loss 茫然、不知所措

be at a loss for sth. (to do sth.) 不知该说什么（该做什么）

（考题）She is at a loss to explain it.

lot /lɒt/ n. 许多；命运；签

a lot of/lots of 许多（修饰可数或不可数名词,但一般用在肯定句中）

a lot=a lot of things 很多东西（相当于名词）

（考题）We have our differences，but we have a lot in common.

a lot=greatly，much 大量地,极大地,非常地（相当于副词）

（考题）Computer people talk a lot about the need for other people to become "computer-literate."

loud /laʊd/ adj. 响亮的   adv. 响亮地、大声地

（考题）Throwing their hats into the air，the fans of the winning team let out loud shouts of victory.

（考题）Say it loud enough that the other tables nearby can hear you.

（注意：loud 也可做副词使用。另见 aloud）

loudly /ˈlaʊdlɪ/ adv. 大声地

（考题）The children talked so loudly at dinner table that I had to struggle to be heard.

love /lʌv/ n. 爱、热爱；爱好

have (a) love for ... 热爱…

（考题）I was so moved by her spirit to help others and her endless love for every human being that after I graduated from high school, I too wanted to try her kind of work.

be/fall in love with sb. 爱上某人

vt. **love sb./sth.** 爱、喜欢某人/某物

love to do/doing sth. 喜欢做某事

（考题）Some joggers say, "I love being out there with just my thoughts".

lovely /ˈlʌvlɪ/ *adj.* 可爱的；美好的

lover /ˈlʌvə/ *n.* 爱人、情人；爱好者

low /ləʊ/ *adj.* 低的、矮的；卑鄙的　*adv.* 低、低下

（考题）Water is the best cooling material because it is low in cost and easy to get.

be/feel low (in spirits) 情绪低下

（考题）Blamed for the breakdown of the school computer network, Alice was in low spirits.

run low 快用完了

lower /ˈləʊə/ *adj. adv.* 较低、更低　*vt.* 使更低

loyalty /ˈlɔɪəltɪ/ *n.* 忠诚

luck /lʌk/ *n.* 运气

（考题）... he found it by logic, not by luck.

try one's luck 碰运气

wish sb. good luck 祝某人好运

（考题）When you can pat yourself on the back, you'll know you're well on your way. Good luck!

lucky /ˈlʌkɪ/ *adj.* 幸运的

luggage /ˈlʌɡɪdʒ/ *n.* 行李

lump /lʌmp/ *n.* 块、团、堆

a lump of ... 一块…

lunch /lʌntʃ/ *n.* 午饭

lung /lʌŋ/ *n.* 肺

luxury /ˈlʌkʃərɪ/ *n.* 奢侈

（考题）But for a good many people in the world, in rich and poor countries, choice is a luxury, something wonderful but hard to get, not a right.

M

machine /məˈʃiːn/ *n*. 机器

   a sewing machine 缝纫机

   a washing machine 洗衣机

machinery /məˈʃiːnərɪ/ *n*. 机械；机器（总称）

mad /mæd/ *adj*. 发疯的、发狂的

   be mad at/about/with ... 因…而气得要命、狂怒

   （考题）If left to himself, he would have whistled life away in perfect satisfaction; but his wife was always mad at him for his idleness.

   be mad about ... 喜欢得要命

   （考题）I don't dislike the work though I can't say I'm mad about it.

   drive sb. mad 把某人气得发狂

   go/get mad 发狂

   （考题）She just gets mad or bursts into tears.

madam /ˈmædəm/ *n*. 夫人；女士（招呼妇女的尊称）；太太

magazine /ˌmæɡəˈziːn/ 杂志；期刊

magic /ˈmædʒɪk/ *adj*. 有魔力的；n. 魔法

magnificent /mæɡˈnɪfɪsənt/ *adj*. 壮丽的；宏伟的

maid /meɪd/ *n*. 女佣、女仆

mail /meɪl/ *n*. 邮件；邮寄

   by mail 用邮寄的方式

   （考题）Advance booking can be received by mail.

   by air mail 航空邮件

   by ordinary mail 普通邮件

   by registered mail 挂号邮件

   by express mail 特快邮件

   vt. **mail sth. to sb.** 将某物邮寄给某人

   （考题）If you prefer some other selection, or none at all, just mail the answer card always provided by the date specified.

main /meɪn/ *adj*. 主要的

mainland /ˈmaɪnlænd/ *n.* 大陆

maintain /meɪˈteɪn/ *vt.* 维持；保养；坚持认为

maintain sth. 保持、保养…

（考题）Therefore, it is important for each person in our society to try to maintain a healthy and realistic self-image.

maintain that ... 坚持认为、坚持说

（考题）Some people maintain that watching violence on TV is one of the major causes of aggressive behaviour and crime in society.

major /ˈmeɪdʒə/ *adj.* 主要的；重大的；

（考题）In fact, the scientific community is deeply divided over whether self-replication machines are possible. If they are, major dangers could exist.

n. 主修、专业

（考题）They sought a university that offered the teenager's intended major, one located near a large city, and a campus where their daughter would be safe.

vi. **major in ...** 主修…专业

（考题）On the other hand, people who major in subjects like literature or history usually have to read and write more than science majors do.

majority /məˈdʒɒrɪtɪ/ *n.* 多数；半数以上

（考题）While most people use little white lies to make life easier, the majority of Americans care about honesty in both public and personal life.

make /meɪk/ (made, made) *vt.* 制造、制作；使…如何

make sth. (for sb.)/make sb. sth. 为某人制作某物

（考题）Quietly, the graying of America has made us a very different society — one in which people have a quite different idea of what kind of behavior is suitable at various ages.

make sb./sth. ... 使某人/某物成为、变得…

（考题）Athens made me a stronger person and it made me careless about criticism.

make sb. do sth. 使某人做某事

（考题）You made me feel important and showed me that I could

make a difference.

make it ... for sb. to do sth. 使某人做某事变得更为…

（考题）... as modern gadgets have made it unnecessary for them to learn special skills to do their work.

be made of ... 由…制作（原材料）

be made from ... 由…制作（已变化，看不出原材料的模样）

make for ... 朝…走去

make oneself heard/understood 让别人听到你/明白你意思

make it（口）对付；成功；做到

make sth. out 弄明白、看清楚…

make sure（certain）that ... 使确凿；核实

（考题）Make sure you're in the right channel when you reach Passport Control.

make the best of ... 充分利用…

（考题）Creative people can make the best of what they have.

make（a）difference 有关系、有影响

（考题）It makes a great difference whether we develop wood products or not.

make an effort/make efforts to do sth. 努力做某事

（考题）... he insisted that Macy's should stock the game and make an effort to call the public's attention to it.

make up 组成、构成；创造；补足；化妆；构成、占比例

（考题）Americans have to use annoying 2-or-3-cent stamps to make up postage differences.

make use of ... 利用…

（考题）We make use of stereotypes as convenient ways to make quick judgements about situations and people around us.

be made up of ... 由…组成

（考题）Their search led to some really strange thing made up of a protein never before seen in the blood of a fish.

make up for ... 弥补；偿还

（考题）And making up for lost sleep during the week by sleeping in on weekends doesn't really work.

male /meɪl/ *adj*. 男性的　*n*. 男人

man /mæn/ *n*. 人；男人

manage /'mænɪdʒ/ *vi*. 对付;设法办到   *vt*. 管理;设法完成;

manage sth. 管理、经营…

(考题)They have just introduced new lessons in how to manage debts.

manage to do sth. 设法、努力做某事

(考题)How was it that he managed to get the information?

(注意: manage 的过去时后面跟动词不定式时,表示"做成功了某事";而将来时只是表示"设法做到"。)

manager /'mænɪdʒə/ *n*. 经理

mankind /mæn'kaɪnd/ *n*. 人类

man-made /'mænmeɪd/ *adj*. 人造的

manner /'mænə/ *n*. 方式;态度;(*pl*.)礼貌、举止;(*pl*.)风俗

(考题)In England, clothes, hairstyles, people's pronunciation and the manner of speaking are all clues to our social group.

in a . . . manner 用…的方法

have good/bad/no manners 懂礼貌/不懂礼貌、没有规矩

(考题)He is a child without manners.

mansion /'mænʃən/ *n*. 大厦、大楼

manufacture /mænj'ufæktʃə/ *n*. *vt*. 生产;制造

many /'menɪ/ *adj*. 许多

a great/good many 许多(后面名词用复数形式)

(考题)But all of us are called upon daily to make a great many personal decisions.

many a 许多(后面名词用单数形式)

map /mæp/ *n*. 地图   *vt*. 绘制…的地图

March /mɑːtʃ/ *n*. 三月

march /mɑːtʃ/ *n*. 行军;行进;进行曲 *vi*. 行军;行进

margin /'mɑːgɪn/ *n*. 书页的空边;边缘;余地

write sth. in the margin 在页边上写…

by a narrow margin 以微弱多数、勉强地

mark /mɑːk/ *n*. 记号;分数;

(考题)But for some, it is also a mark of social position and for young people, a sign of becoming an adult.

below/up to the mark 不符合/符合标准

give full marks for . . . 对…大加赞赏

on your marks 各就各位(赛跑时口令)

vt. **mark ...** 标志着…；在…上留下标记

(考题) The Summit was to mark the 25th anniversary of President Nixon's journey to China, which was the turning point in China-U.S. relations.

market /ˈmɑːkɪt/ *n.* 市场；*vt.* 销售、经销

come/put on the market 上市；出售

(考题) It is not just the availability of the goods that is the problem, but the speed with which new types of products come on the market.

black market 黑市

market economy 市场经济

market research 市场调研

marriage /ˈmærɪdʒ/ *n.* 婚姻；结婚

(考题) We have enough problem getting young people to take marriage seriously without this. Marriage should always be about love.

marry /ˈmærɪ/ *vt.* (与某人)结婚；嫁出女儿；主持婚礼

marry sb. 与某人结婚

(考题) In 1984, at the age of 23, she married Bill.

be/get married to sb. 与某人结婚

(考题) The old couple have been married for 40 years and never once have they quarreled with each other.

marvelour /ˈmɑːvələs/ *adj.* 令人惊讶的；绝妙的

mask /mɑːsk/ *n.* 面具；口罩

mass /mæs/ *n.* 大量；大堆；物体的质量

mass production 批量生产

mass destruction 大规模杀伤

(考题) The application of science and technology to the development and production of weapons of mass destruction has created a real danger to the continued existence of the human race on this planet.

master /ˈmɑːstə/ *n.* 主人；掌握；大师

(考题) This creature is the real master of Earth and men are its slaves.

(考题)My grandmother was a master at making quilts.

have a master of . . . 掌握了…

a master's degree 硕士学位

vt . 控制；掌握

(考题)People should work harder to master computer use.

masterpiece /ˈmɑːstəpis/ *n .* 杰作

match /mætʃ/ *n .* 比赛；对手

be a good match/no match for . . . 是/不是…的对手

(考题)But even in his cornered panic, he was no match for the two athletic men.

vt ., vi . **match . . .** 与…相匹敌；与…相配

(考题)Whatever the case, it has been noted that the values they hold do not necessarily match what they actually do.

match with . . . 与…相匹配

mate /meɪt/ *n .* 伙伴；同事

material /məˈtɪərɪəl/ *n .* 材料

mathematical /mæθɪˈmætɪkəl/ *adj .* 数学的；精确的

mathematics /mæθɪˈmætɪks/ *n .* 数学

matter /ˈmætə/ *n .* 物质；事情；麻烦事

(考题)It's a matter of great importantce and deserves attention.

a matter of . . . 是…的事情

(考题)The animal is, in fact, playing a very dangerous game with its environment, a game in which it must make decision — a matter of life or death.

as a matter of fact 实际上、其实

(考题)As a matter of fact, I'm merely an employee — the lowest kind of employee.

no matter what/how/when . . . 不论…

(考题)No matter where he is going to what he is doing, he is never on time.

What's the matter? 怎么了？

vi . **It doesn't matter whether** 是否…无关紧要

. . . matters 要紧、起作用

(考题)Reading for fun matters because children who are keen on reading can report lifelong pleasure and loving books is an excellent indicator of future educational success.

mature /məˈtjʊə/ *adj.* 成熟的；到期的　*v.* (使)成熟

(考题)A lot of the material is really mature，Ms. Gardner said，talking about films ...

maximum /ˈmæksɪməm/ *n.* 最大限度　*adj.* 最大程度的

(考题)The fine for disobeying the rule of road closures is a maximum of ＄5,000 fine and/ or six months in prison.

May /meɪ/ *n.* 五月

may /meɪ/ *v.*，*aux.* 可以

mabe /ˈmeibi:/ *adv.* 或许、可能

(考题)This guy's a winner，right？Maybe，maybe not.

(注意：maybe 是副词，不能和 may be 相混淆。)

mayor /meə/ *n.* 市长

meal /miːl/ *n.* 膳食；一餐

mean /miːn/ (meant，meant) *vt.* 意味着；打算

mean (doing) sth. 指的是…；意味着…

(考题)News photos mean history in a sense.

mean to do sth. 打算做某事

(考题)She meant to joke with her husband.

mean sb. to do sth. 想要某人做某事

(考题)We are meant to understand the difference of a warning commander in the body of a fat little Frenchman.

mean that ... 意味着、意思是…

(考题) Diet foods can indirectly harm our bodies because consuming them instead of healthy foods means we are preventing our bodies from having basic nutrients.

be meant for ... 用来…的；为…准备的

(考题)Put into use in April 2000，the hotline was meant for residents reporting water and heating supply breakdowns.

mean what one says/promises 说话算数

(考题)She wanted to know if the teacher meant what she had said.

What do you mean by doing ... 你这么做是什么意思？

(注意：mean to do sth.表示"打算、旨在做某事"；而 mean doing sth.则表示"等于、意味着做某事"。两者含义不同。)

meaning /'mi:nɪŋ/ *n*. 意思；意义；

（考题）The meaning of the word "volunteer" may be a little different in different countries, but it usually means "one who offers his or her services".

means /mi:nz/ *n*. 手段；方法

（考题）The SAT is an excellent test in many ways, and the score is still a useful means of testing students.

by means of 以某种方法、手段

（考题）... they don't win by chance, but by means of logic and skills.

by all means 无论如何；当然（见 case）

by no means 决不（见 case）

（考题）... though it is by no means unwise to compare your observations with those of other group members.

meantime /'mi:n'taɪm/ *adv*. 与此同时；在这段时间里

in the meantime 与此同时

（考题）Adults are often surprised by how well they remember something they learned as children but have never practised in the meantime.

meanwhile /'mi:n'waɪl/ *adv*. 与此同时；在这段时间里

（考题）Toronto, meanwhile, is Canada's most expensive city but fell 35 places to take 82nd place worldwide.

measure /'meʒə/ *n*. 措施；度量

take measures to do sth. 为…采取措施

（考题）Sadly, it is often only after someone has died or become seriously ill that governments will take measures to reduce levels of harmful waste.

v. **measure sth.** 度量、衡量…

（考题）The civilization of a city can be measured by this.

meat /mi:t/ *n*. 肉

mechanic /mɪ'kænɪk/ *n*. 技工；机械工人

mechanical /mɪ'kænɪkəl/ *adj*. 机械的

（考题）Today, you are offered the same kind of watch with improvement. It has a 24-jewel mechanical movement, the kind desired by watch collectors.

medal /ˈmedəl/ *n*. 奖牌

medical /ˈmedɪkəl/ *adj*. 医学的；医疗的

medicine /ˈmedɪsɪn/ *n*. 医学；药物

medium /ˈmiːdɪəm/（*pl*. mediums，media）*n*. 媒介；媒体、传媒

mass media 或 **media** 传媒工具（一般是用复数）

（考题）Don't compare yourself with the models and actors in the media.

adj. 中等的、适度的

（考题）Each of these is further divided into 3 skill levels（easy，medium and difficult）so younger children can fairly compete against teenagers and adults.

meet /miːt/（met，met）vt.，vi. 相遇；迎接；满足　*n*. 聚会（运动会等）

meet ... 遇到、会面、迎接…

（考题）To meet friends here，it usually has to be in a pub，and it can be difficult to go there alone as a woman. The cafes are not terribly nice.

meet the need/expectation/standard/hope ... 满足、实现…

（考题）The Medical Centre is open five days a week，including student holidays with four doctors and nurses to meet your medical needs.

meet with ... 遇到、碰见…；遭遇…

（考题）The fast developing situation has greatly increased the chances that people will meet with a lot of unexpected things.

make both ends meet 入能敷出、收支相抵

meeting /ˈmiːtɪŋ/ *n*. 会议；相聚

melon /ˈmelən/ *n*. 瓜（西瓜、甜瓜等）

melt /melt/ *vi*. *vt*. （使）融化、溶化

（考题）The Ice Age was a long period of time in which four great glaciers pushed southward to cover almost all the upper half of North America，and then melted away.

member /ˈmembə/ *n*. 成员

memo /ˈmiːməʊ/（*pl*. ～s）*n*. 备忘录　＝memorandum

memorable /ˈmemərəbl/ *adj*. 值得纪念的

（考题）... our exploration of London was a memorable gift to

both of us.

memorandum /ˌmeməˈrændəm/ *n*. 备忘录

memorial /mɪˈmɔːrɪəl/ *n*. 纪念物；纪念仪式 *adj*. 纪念的

（考题）My husband and I would like to set up a memorial to him, somewhere on campus.

memorize /ˈmeməraɪz/ *vt*. 记住

memorize ... 记住…

（考题）It is a good way for us to memorize new words by seeing them repeatedly.

memory /ˈmemərɪ/ *n*. 记忆；纪念；回忆；存储器

（考题）Why is memory so important to us? Why do we all seek to freeze in time the faces of our children, our parents, our lovers, and ourselves? Will they mean anything to anyone after we've gone?

have a good/poor memory 记性好/差

（考题）... my family members had a poor memory.

from memory 凭记忆

in memory of ... 纪念…

to the memory of ... 纪念…

（考题）... people collected money for a headstone in front of the baby's grave, carved with the words: "To the memory of an unknown child."

mend /mend/ *vt*. 修理、修补

mental /ˈmentl/ *adj*. 智力的；精神的

（考题）When people suffer from Alzheimer's disease, their families and friends will experience mental sufferings.

mention /ˈmenʃən/ *vt*. 提及、提到

mention sth. /that ... 提到…

（考题）Why hasn't anyone mentioned their family? I'd be lost without my husband and two kids. They're the most important for me.

the above mentioned 上述

not to mention ... 更不用提…

（考题）That accident cost the driver plenty — a thousand dollars for the new engine — not to mention the charges for driving without a license and attempting to run away.

Don't mention it. 不用客气(回答别人感谢时)

menu /'menju:/ *n.* 菜谱

merchant /'mɜːtʃənt/ *n.* 商人

mercy /'mɜːsɪ/ *n.* 慈悲、宽容、怜悯

  show mercy to sb. 对某人表示怜悯

  (考题)We can only show mercy to the unfortunate man who had to stop his car soon after setting out from a country village to drive to London.

  have mercy on sb. 对某人表示怜悯

  at the mercy of ... 任…摆布

  without mercy 无情地

mere /mɪə/ *adj.* 仅仅的

  (考题)Swedish parents can take their paid leave as they wish，men use a mere 12% of it; 60% of fathers do not take even a single day off work.

merry /'merɪ/ *adj.* 快乐的、欢乐的

mess /mes/ *n.* 零乱、混乱；困境

  be in a mess 乱七八糟、处境尴尬

  get (sb.) into a mess (使某人)陷入狼狈处境

  make a mess (of ...) 把…弄得乱七八糟

  (考题)Margaret gets angry with people who work in the office because they always make a mess in their offices.

  v. 弄脏、弄乱

message /'mesɪdʒ/ *n.* 信息；口信；消息

  (考题)The Queen's broadcast is a personal message to the Commonwealth countries.

  carry a message 含有、表达信息

  (考题)No wonder greeting cards today carry the message，"To my mother，my best friend."

  give sb. a message 给某人带个口信

  leave/take a message 留个/记个口信

messenger /'mesɪndʒə/ *n.* 送信者；通信员

metal /'metl/ *n.* 金属

method /'meθəd/ *n.* 方法；办法

a method to do/of doing sth. 做某事的方法

（考题）Another method of extinguishing fire is by cutting off the oxygen.

metre, meter /'miːtə/ *n*. 米（公制长度单位）

microphone /'maɪkrəfəʊn/ *n*. 扩音器；话筒

microwave /'maɪkrəweɪv/ *n*. 微波　*adj*. 微波的

　a microwave oven 微波炉

midday /'mɪdeɪ/ *n*. 中午

middle /'mɪdl/ *adj*. 中间的　*n*. 中部、中间

　in the middle of ... 在…的中间

midnight /'mɪdnaɪt/ *n*. 午夜

might /maɪt/ *v*. *aux*.（may 的过去时形式）可能、也许

　n. 力量、力气

　with all one's might 竭尽全力

mild /maɪld/ *adj*. 和缓的；温和的

mile /maɪl/ *n*. 英里

milestone /'maɪlstəʊn/ *n*. 里程碑

military /'mɪlɪtəri/ *adj*. 军事的

milk /mɪlk/ *n*. 奶；牛奶　*vt*. 挤奶

mill /mɪl/ *n*. 磨坊、磨；工场

million /'mɪljən/ *num*. 百万

millionaire /ˌmɪljə'neə/ *n*. 百万富翁

mind /maɪnd/ *n*. 头脑、智力

（考题）Tell a story and tell it well，and you may open wide the eyes of a child，open up lines of communication in a business，or even open people's mind to another culture.

　be in sb.'s mind 有…想法；想着

　be on sb.'d mind 担心…

（考题）I will never know what was on his mind at the time，nor will anyone else.

　be of one/the same mind 想法一致

（考题）She and I agree that，at certain times，we seem to be parts of the same mind

　in sb.'s mind 在某人看来

（考题）In my mind，attending my dream university would be the

only way to realize my dream of becoming a best writer.

keep/bear sth. in mind 牢记…

（考题）From the passage we learn that uniforms in general help the wearers keep their duties in mind.

keep an open mind to ... 对…持开放、欢迎态度

（考题）Keep an open mind to everyone's ideas.

call/bring sth. (back) to sb.'s mind（使某人）回想起某事

change sb.'s mind 改变某人的想法

（考题）One day，I told my mother I'd changed my mind. I didn't want to make a success in the magazine business.

have ... in mind 想着…

have sth. on one's mind 有心事；为…担心

（考题）They're expected to be rebellious and selfish，but actually they have other things on their minds.

make up one's mind to do sth. 下决心做某事

v. 介意、反对

mind ... 当心、提防…

mind (sb.'s) doing sth. 介意（某人）做某事

（考题）— Do you mind my smoking here? — Yes，better not.

would you mind if/what ... 如果…，你介意吗？

（考题）— Do you mind if I open the window? — I'd rather you didn't. I feel a bit cold.

mind one's own business 管好自己的事

never mind 没关系、不要紧（回答别人道歉时用）

（考题）— Oh dear! I've just broken a window. — Never mind. It can't be helped.

mine¹ /maɪn/ *pron*. 我的

mine² /maɪn/ *n*. 矿；矿井 *v*. 采矿

mineral /ˈmɪnərəl/ *n*. 矿物 *adj*. 矿物的；含有矿物质的

mini /ˈmɪnɪ/ *n*. 极小的、微型的（用于和名词构成复合词）

  minibus 面包车

  miniskirt 超短裙

minimum /ˈmɪnɪməm/ *n*. 最少量 adj.最少量的、最低程度的

ministrer /ˈmɪnɪstə/ *n*. 部长；牧师

ministry /ˈmɪnɪstrɪ/ *n*. （政府的）部

minor /ˈmaɪnə/ *adj.* 次要的

minority /maɪˈnɒrɪtɪ/ *n.* 少数;少数民族

minus /ˈmaɪnəs/ *prep.* 减去

minute /ˈmɪnɪt/ *n.* 分钟

    in a minute 很快、马上

    the minute ... 一…就…

    (同义词:as soon as,the moment,immediately after)

miracle /ˈmɪrəkl/ *n.* 奇迹

mirror /ˈmɪrə/ *n.* 镜子

miserable /ˈmɪzərəbl/ *adj.* 痛苦的、悲惨的;可怜的

misery /ˈmɪzərɪ/ *n.* 不幸;苦难

miss /mɪs/ *vt.* 失去;错过;想念;未能赶上(交通工具)

    miss sth. 错失、未打中、未赶上;发觉丢失

    (考题)Don't miss the chance to realize your dream.

    (考题)This is Life, all right, but we do treat it like a rehearsal and, unhappily, we do miss so many of its best moments.

    miss sb. /sth. 想念、留恋…

    (考题)We miss the guide telling us where to go, the food providing us with strength, the quiet giving us wisdom.

    miss doing sth. 错过、差点就…

    (考题)I wouldn't miss getting up at six every day to go to work, though!

    sth. is missing 缺少了…

    (考题)She had excellent grades, but she always thought that something was missing.

Miss /mɪs/ *n.* 小姐

missing /ˈmɪsɪŋ/ *adj.* 失踪的;缺失的

    (辨析:在表示"缺少、缺失"时,miss用现在分词的形式missing,但lose用过去分词的形式lost。)

mission /ˈmɪʃən/ *n.* 任务;使命;使团

mistake /mɪsˈteɪk/ *n.* 错误

    by mistake 错误地、无心出错

    (考题)By mistake, President Clinton's advisers thought that Koreans have the same naming customs as the Japanese.

    make a mistake 犯错误

（考题）Even if you do make an obvious mistake during a speech，that doesn't really matter.

there's no mistake about ... 不会出错

vt.（mistook，mistaken）**mistake ... for ...** 错把…当成…

（考题）George Washington，she writes，mistook her for the wife of a French man，and praised her excellent English.

mister /'mɪstə/ *n*. 先生

mistress /'mɪstrɪs/ *n*. 主妇；女主人

misunderstand /ˌmɪsʌndə'stænd/ *vt*.（misunderstood）误解

misunderstanding /ˌmɪsʌndə'stændɪŋ/ *n*. 误解

（考题）There is generally a misunderstanding among the Chinese that westerners are usually open and straightforward，while the Chinese are rather reserved in manner.

mix /mɪks/ *vt*.（使）混合

mix (sth.) (up) with sth.（把…）与…混合起来

（考题）As the glaciers melted，rocks，soil and other things that had mixed with the ice and snow were left.

（考题）Don't mix up the two solutions. It's dangerous.

mixture /'mɪkstʃə/ *n*. 混合物；混合剂

（考题）In the rest of the country lived the Saxons，actually a mixture of Anglos，Saxons，and other Germanic and Nordic peoples.

mobile /'məubaɪl/ *adj*. 流动的；可移动的

（考题）What would I miss least? My mobile phone — I'd like to be completely quiet — at least for a little while.

model /'mɒdəl/ *n*. 模型；模特

moderate /'mɒdərɪt/ *adj*. 不过分的；温和的；适量的

（考题）Such a diet is based primarily on grain products，fruits，and vegetables，with moderate amounts of meat and dairy products and with small amounts of snacks and desserts.

modern /'mɒdən/ *adj*. 现代的、摩登的；现代化的

modern times 现代

modernize /'mɒdənaɪz/ *vt*. 使现代化

modest /'mɒdɪst/ *adj*. 谦虚的

moment /'məumənt/ *n*. 时刻；一会儿

at any moment 随时

（考题）Our feelings of well-being at any moment are determined to a certain degree by genes.

at the moment 此刻；当时

（考题）— You haven't lost the ticket, have you? — I hope not. I know it's not easy to get another one at the moment.

for the moment 暂时、一时

（考题）The classroom is big enough for the moment, but we'll have to move if we have more students.

（同义词：**for the time being, for the present**）

for a moment/for a few moments 一会儿时间

（考题）The youths waited for a few moments, and then ran quickly and quietly towards Mrs Riley.

in a moment/in a few moments 很快、马上

（同义词：**in a minute, in no time, at once, right away**）

the moment 一⋯⋯就⋯⋯

（考题）The moment I arrived at Kathy's farm, I loved it and I knew I wanted to stay.

（见 minute）

Monday /ˈmʌndɪ/ *n*. 星期一

money /ˈmʌnɪ/ *n*. 钱

  make/earn money 挣钱

  money market 金融市场

  money bag 钱袋

  money-order 汇票

  money-maker 会赚钱的人

monitor /ˈmɒnɪtə/ *n*. 监视器；班长　*vt*. 监听；监视

（考题）If her studies prove the theory, scientists may be able to monitor the behaviour of sharks to predict bad weather.

monkey /ˈmʌŋkɪ/ *n*. 猴子

month /mʌnθ/ *n*. 月

monthly /ˈmʌnθlɪ/ *adj*. 每月的　*n*. 月刊

monument /ˈmɒnjʊmənt/ *n*. 纪念碑

mood /muːd/ *n*. 心情；情绪

  be in a good/bad mood 情绪好/不好

（考题）Here, all I need to put me in a good mood is a hot bath and one of Kathy's wonderful dinners.

（同义词：**be in a good humour, be in a good temper, be in high spirits**）

be in no mood/not in the mood for/to do sth. 对…没有兴趣

moon /muːn/ *n*. 月亮

moonlight /ˈmuːnlaɪt/ *n*. 月光

mop /mɒp/ *n*. 拖把 *v*. （用拖把）拖

moral /ˈmɒrəl/ *adj*. 道德的上；有道德的

（考题）It is a way the novelist uses to show the moral nature of a character.

more /mɔː/ *adj*. 更多的；较多的 *adv*. 更

more and more 越来越多

（考题）... and as more and more men were drawn into industry, domestic service became increasingly a female job.

the more ... , the more ... 越…，就越…

（考题）... so that the more "other people" there are, the greater the total shifting of responsibility.

what's more 还有、不仅如此（见 addition）

more or less 多少、或多或少

（考题）The idea of family seems to be more or less non-existent in England.

more than... 超过…

（考题）In fact, it has already happened more than once in the history of the earth.

no more than ... 仅仅、只有…

（考题）A year later civilization has collapsed. No more than 10 million people have survived.

no more/not any more 不再

（考题）He used to smoke a lot, but no more now.

once more 再一次

moreover /mɔːˈrəuvə/ *adv*. 而且；此外

（见 addition）

morning /ˈmɔːnɪŋ/ *n*. 早晨；上午

mosquito /məsˈkiːtəu/ *n*. 蚊子

most /məust/ *adj.* 最多的　*adv.* 最

　　at (the) most 最多、至多

　　(考题)Researchers are working on treatments that lengthen the life span of mice by 50 percent at most.

mostly /'məustlı/ *adv.* 主要地；大部分

　　(考题)Exploring was a more popular idea back then than it is today. History seemed to be mostly about explorers.

motel /'məutel/ *n.* 汽车旅馆

mother /'mʌðə/ *n.* 母亲

motion /'məuʃən/ *n.* 运动；移动；提案

　　(考题)No one can fail to stand in awed admiration of the great discoveries of history — Newton's laws of motion

　　(考题)Everything in the universe is in constant motion.

motor /'məutə/ *n.* 电动机、马达

motorcycle /'məutəˌsaɪkl/ *n.* 摩托车

mountain /'mauntən/ *n.* 山

mountainous /'mauntɪnəs/ *adj.* 有山的；多山的

mouse /maus/ (*pl.* mice) *n.* 老鼠；鼠标

mouth /mauθ/ *n.* 嘴

　　keep one's mouth shut 保守秘密、不说话

　　live from hand to mouth 勉强糊口

move /mu:v/ *n.* 走动；运动；搬迁

　　be on the move 在活动状态

　　(考题)But now they are on the move, heading northwards in countless millions towards Central and North America, and moving at the alarming speed of 200 miles a year.

　　vt. 移动某物；感动　*vi.* 移动

　　move ... 移动…；提议…；打动、感动…

　　(考题)... while the Opposition Leader, Mark Latham, recently announced that his party would move to protect children from unhealthy food advertisements.

　　(考题)We were deeply moved by his story.

movement /'mu:vmənt/ *n.* 运动；移动；活动

　　(考题)The early experiences of Rosa Parks (1913—2005), long known as the "mother of the civil rights movement," were not different from those of many African-Americans at that time.

movie /ˈmuːvɪ/ *n*. 电影

    go to the movies 看电影（见 cinema）

mow /muː/ *vt*. 割（草、庄稼等）

    m. p. h. 每小时英里 = miles per hour

Mr. /ˈmɪstə/ *n*. 先生（用于男子姓名前）

Mrs. /ˈmɪsɪz/ *n*. 夫人、太太（用于已婚妇女姓名前）

Ms. /mɪz/ *n*. 女士

much /mʌtʃ/ *adj*. *adv*. 很多　　*n*. 许多，大量

    as much as . . . 多达…

    （考题）Some people are paying as much as 500 Swedish kronor in taxes a year for the right to keep their dog.

    too much 过分了

    They eat too much for lunch

    how much is . . . 价格是多少

    （同义词：**What's the price of . . . ? What does it cost? How much do I have to pay for . . . ?**）

    much the same 几乎相同的

    （考题）The medicine，made up of the basic building materials of life，will build new brain cells，heart cells，and so on — in much the same way our bodies make new skin cells to take the place of old ones.

    see much of . . . 常常见到…

    so much for . . . 到此结束、就讲这些

mud /mʌd/ *n*. 泥；泥浆

muddy /ˈmʌdɪ/ *adj*. 泥泞的

multiple /ˈmʌltɪpl/ *n*. 倍数　　*adj*. 多样的；多重的；多倍的

    multiple purposes 多重目的

    multiple interests 兴趣广泛

    multiple choice 多项选择

    multiple injuries 多发性伤害

    the least/lowest common multiple 最小公倍数

multiply /ˈmʌltɪplaɪ/ *vt*. 乘；使相乘　　*vi*. 增多；繁殖

    multiply sth. by . . . 用…乘以某数

    （考题）As the parasites multiply，they take over the entire body.

mum /mʌm/ *n*. 妈妈

murder /'mɜːdə/ *n*. 谋杀 *vt*. 谋杀

muscle /'mʌsl/ *n*. 肌肉

museum /mjuː'zɪəm/ *n*. 博物馆

mushroom /'mʌʃruːm/ *n*. 蘑菇

music /'mjuːzɪk/ *n*. 音乐

musical /'mjuːzɪkəl/ *adj*. 音乐的

musician /mjuː'zɪʃən/ *n*. 音乐家

must /mʌst/ *v*. *aux*. 必须；应当

    must be (doing) ... 一定是/在做…

    must have done ... 一定做过…

    （注意：must 用在表示推测的肯定句中；如果是否定句，则应使用
    can't 或 couldn't。）

my /maɪ/ *pron*. 我的

myself /'maɪself/ *pron*. 我自己

mysterious /mɪs'tɪərɪəs/ *adj*. 神秘的

    （考题）Why was it so much more mysterious now?

mystery /'mɪstərɪ/ *n*. 神秘的事物；奥秘

N

nail /neɪl/ *n*. 钉子;指甲

name /neɪm/ *n*. 姓名

    by name 用名字、按名字叫

    Mr. Breen knew them all by name.

    by the name of ... 名叫…的

    (考题)... there lived many years ago, a simple, good-natured fellow by the name of Rip Van Winkle.

    in the name of ... 以…的名义

    vt. 叫出名字;命名;提名…(为…)

    name sb. /sth. (...) 给…起名(为…)

    (考题)So far, scientists have named about 1. 8 million living species, and that's just a small number of what probably exists on Earth.

    (考题)She was named "mother of the civil rights movement".

    name sb. /sth. after ... 以…为某人/某物命名

    (考题)The island was named after its discoverer.

namely /ˈneɪmlɪ/ *adv*. 即、也就是

    (考题)Although on the whole Asians tend towards thinness, culture — namely Asians' hospitality — is a reason for the fatness of today's generation.

nap /næp/ *n*. 午睡、小睡 *vi*. 小睡、打盹

    take a nap 睡午觉、打个盹

napkin /ˈnæpkɪn/ *n*. 餐巾;(英)尿布

narrow /ˈnærəʊ/ *adj*. 狭窄的

nasty /ˈnɑːstɪ/ *adj*. 龌龊的、肮脏的

nation /ˈneɪʃən/ *n*. 国家;民族

national /ˈnæʃənəl/ *adj*. 国家的;民族的

    the national anthem 国歌

    the national flag 国旗

nationality /ˌnæʃəˈnælɪtɪ/ *n*. 民族;国籍

native /'neɪtɪv/ *adj*. 本地的；土生土长的；*n*. 本地人

（考题）Mostly borrowed from English and Chinese, these terms are often changed into forms no longer understood by native speakers.

be native to ... …本地产的

natural /'nætʃərəl/ *adj*. 自然的

（考题）... philosophy can best be described as the study of both social and natural sciences.

It is natural for sb. to do sth. 某人做某事不足为奇

（考题）It's natural to like watching other people. They're interesting.

It is natural that ... …不足为奇

the natural world 自然界

natural resources 自然资源

natural law 自然法则

natural disaster 自然灾害

natural science 自然科学

natural ability 本能

（考题）I had a natural ability with words and a power of facing unpleasant facts

naturalist /'nætʃərəlɪst/ *n*. 自然主义者；博物学家

naturally /'nætʃərəli/ *adv*. 自然地；自然而然地

nature /'neɪtʃə/ *n*. 大自然、自然界；性格；性质

（考题）By paying closer attention to some important signs in nature, we can become better prepared for any kind of weather.

（注意：nature 在表示"自然界"时，前面不使用定冠词。）

（考题）Throughout the history of the arts, the nature of creativity has remained constant to artists.

by nature 天生；生就的

（考题）The child has a talent for languages by nature.

in nature 实际上

naughty /'nɔːtɪ/ *adj*. 淘气的，顽皮的

naval /'neɪv(ə)l/ *adj*. 海军的

navy /'neɪvɪ/ *n*. 海军

near /nɪə/ *prep.* 在…附近 *adj.* 近的;较近的;亲密的 *adv.* 附近;接近 *vi.* 接近

(考题)As the day of the party came near, Merlin began to think how to make a grand entrance at the party.

(辨析:near 和 close 意义相同,但在某些短语中不能替换,如:in near future, the near distance 以及 a close friend 等。)

nearby /ˈnɪəbaɪ/ *adj. adv.* 附近(的)

(考题)These clouds protect the forest from the daytime heat and night-time cold of nearby deserts, keep temperatures fit for plant growth.

nearly /ˈnɪəlɪ/ *adv.* 几乎;差不多

(考题)Malaria has five thousand genes, and its ability to change rapidly to defend itself and resist new drugs has made it nearly impossible to control.

not nearly 远不、远非(同义词:far from)

(考题)Women are thought to be weaker, slower and not nearly as skilled in sport.

(辨析:almost, nearly, practically, virtually 意思相同,但语气逐个增强。almost 和 nearly 使用得也更频繁。)

neat /niːt/ *adj.* 整洁的;简洁的

necessary /ˈnesɪsərɪ/ *adj.* 必须的;必要的

it's necessary (for sb.) to do sth. (某人)有必要做某事

(考题)It's necessary to have specialized equipment and machinery to study the past climate.

be necessary to ... 对…来说是必须的

(考题)... who will only fill up the healing silence necessary to those darkest moments in which I would rather be my own best friend.

it's necessary that ... (从句中常用虚拟语气)

(考题)Don't you think it necessary that he not be sent to Miami but to New York?

if (it is) necessary 如果有必要的话

(考题)We can get you a sunrise over the sea, if necessary, but not a sunset.

n. 必需品

daily necessaries 日用必需品

neck /nek/ *n.* 颈、脖子

need /niːd/ *n.* 需要;需求

there's need for sth. 需要某物

（考题）"For every advance in business," she says, "there is a greater need for communication."

there's (no) need for sb. to do sth. 某人需要/不需要做某事

（考题）With forever stamps, there will be no need to worry about rate changes.

have need of sth. 需要某物

be in need of sth. 需要某物

（考题）Never before has this city been in greater need of modern public transport than it is today.

supply and need 供求

meet the need(s) 满足需求

v. aux. 需要

need (not) do sth. （用于疑问、否定或条件句中）

（考题）Now you need never get lost again!

vt. 需要

need sth. 需要某物

（考题）Children need risk if they are to grow up self-sufficient and confident.

need to do sth. 需要做某事

（考题）We need to know the answers or where to get them quickly.

sth. need doing/sth. need to be done ... 需要…

（考题）As a result of the serious flood, two-thirds of the buildings in the area need repairing.

（考题）Staff training needs to be improved.

（见 deserve、want）

needle /'niːdl/ *n.* 针

negative /'neɡətɪv/ *adj.* 否定的

（考题）Sometimes, something that is considered to be negative turns out to be an advantage on the job.

neglect /nɪ'ɡlekt/ *vt.* 忽视

neglect (to do, doing) sth. 忽视（做）某事

    neglect one's duty 玩忽职守

negotiate /nɪˈɡəʊʃɪeɪt/ *vi*. *vt*. 谈判；商谈

    negotiate sth. with sb. 与某人谈判某事

neighbour /ˈneɪbə/ *n*. 邻居

neighbourhood /ˈneɪbəhʊd/ *n*. 邻近地区；街坊、邻居（总称）

    in the neighbourhood 在这一地区、附近

neither /ˈnaɪðə/ *pron*. *conj*. *adv*. （两者中）任何一者都不

    neither ... nor ... 既不…，也不…

    （考题）Neither the volunteers nor the researchers knew who received which pill.

    I don't ... , neither does he. 我不…，他也不。

    （考题）Of the making of good books there is no end；neither is there any end to their influence on man's lives.

    （同义词：**Nor does he**.）

    （辨析：再 neither/nor does he 中，使用的是倒装结构，说的是另外一个人。如果不倒装，则表示附和前面的意思，说的是同一个人。如：— He doesn't know English. — Neither he does. He doesn't know even A, B, C.）

nephew /ˈnevjuː/ *n*. 侄子；外甥

nerve /nɜːv/ *n*. 神经

nervous /ˈnɜːvəs/ *adj*. 神经紧张的

    be nervous about sth. 对…感到紧张

    （考题）Human right supporters are nervous about the possibilities of such technology.

net /net/ *n*. 网；网状物

network /ˈnetwɜːk/ *n*. 网状组织；网络

never /ˈnevə/ *adv*. 决不；从不

nevertheless /ˌnevəðəˈles/ *adj*. 不过；仍然；然而

    （考题）It is roughly calculated that in 1997 alone, about 2 to 3 million people died of it. Nevertheless, there are fresh reasons for optimism in the battle against AIDS.

New Zealand /njuːˈziːlənd/ *n*. 新西兰

new /njuː/ *adj*. 新的

    be new to ... 对…来说是新的

(考题)"Are you new to this neighborhood?" I explained that I was, in fact, new to the entire state.

New Year's Day 元旦

New Year's Eve 除夕

newcomer /'njuːkʌmə/ *n*. 新来的人

news /njuːz/ *n*. 新闻；消息

newspaper /'njuːspeɪpə/ *n*. 报纸

next /nekst/ *adj*. 下一个；其次的

    next to... 与…相邻；紧挨着…

    (考题)I heard the garbage truck pull up to the sidewalk next to me.

    next to nothing 几乎没有

    next door (to...) (在…的)隔壁

nice /naɪs/ *adj*. 好的；令人愉快的；和蔼的

niece /niːs/ *n*. 侄女；外甥女

night /naɪt/ *n*. 夜晚

    at night 在晚上

    (考题)For occasional reading — in your bath, for example, or late at night when you are too tired to go to bed — there is nothing as good as a very old picture story-book.

    by night 夜里、夜间

    over night 夜里、夜间

    stay (for) the night 留下过夜

    (考题)One evening, a passer by asked to stay for the night.

nine /naɪn/ *num*. 九

nineteen /'naɪn'tiːn/ *num*. 十九

ninety /'naɪntɪ/ *num*. 九十

ninth /naɪnθ/ *num*. 第九

no /nəʊ/ *adj*. 不，不是；没有；*adv*. 不

    no longer 已不；再不

    (考题)Reality show will probably survive — it's just no longer so easy to make a successful one.

    no other than 正是；就是

    no sooner ... than ... 刚…就…

    (考题)He had no sooner got to the lab than he set out to do the experiment. (见 hardly)

no better than …不比…强

Though he has learned to play the piano much longer, he plays no better than I.

(辨析：no better than 常用来指不好的人或事，表示"差不多、一点儿也不比…强"的意思；而 not better than 并不带感情色彩，仅表示"不比…更好、没有胜过…"。)

no such 没有这样的…

(考题)It may help you to know that there is no such thing as a perfect speech.

(注意：在 no such ... 中，没有不定冠词 a。)

noble /ˈnəʊbl/ *adj*. 高尚的；显贵的；崇高的

(考题)He said the noble way of pronouncing vowels had gradually lost ground as the noble upper-class accent over the past years.

nobody /ˈnəʊbʊdɪ/ *pron*. 没人

nod /nɒd/ *vi*. *vt*. 点头；点头表示

nod to sb. 朝某人点头

nod off 睡着了

(考题)It may not be that the students who nod off at their desks are lazy.

n. 点头

(考题)As I came in, he greeted me with a nod.

noise /nɔɪz/ *n*. 噪声；吵闹声

make noise 发出噪声

(考题)They don't need a lot of space, don't make a lot of noise, and don't eat a lot for their size.

noisy /ˈnɔɪzɪ/ *adj*. 吵闹的；有噪声的

(考题)... the visitor is likely to think it is a world preferable to the busy and noisy modern life.

none /nʌn/ *pron*. 没有任何人；没有任何东西

(考题)We looked at many places, but none was satisfactory.

"How many did you sell, my boy?" my mother asked. "None."

(注意：在 of ... 结构前用 none，no one；在回答 how many 的提问时，用 none 而不是 no one。)

have none of 不接受;不容许

none but 只有

(考题)None but the strongest can win the match.

none other than 正是

none too 一点也不;不太

(考题)I was offered 2,000 dollars a month. Considering the high living cost there, it is none too high.

nonfiction /ˌnʌnˈfɪkʃən/ *n*. 非小说类作品

nonsense /ˈnɒnsəns/ *n*. 胡说;废话

talk nonsense 胡说八道

non-stop /ˈnɒnstɒp/ *adj*. 中途不停的

noodle /ˈnuːdl/ *n*. 面条

noon /nuːn/ *n*. 中午

nor /nɔː/ *conj*. *adv*. 也不;也没有

neither … nor … (两者)既不…,又不…;都不

(见 neither)

north /nɔːθ/ *n*. *adj*. 北方(的)

northeast /ˌnɔːθˈiːst/ *n*. 东北 *adj*. 东北的 *adv*. 在东北;向东北

northwest /ˌnɔːθˈwest/ *n*. 西北 *adj*. 西北的 *adv*. 在西北;向西北

nose /nəʊz/ *n*. 鼻子

not /nɒt/ *adv*. 不

note /nəʊt/ *n*. 笔记;便条;纸币

I wrote them a note to say thanks.

make a note (notes) of … 记下来;记住

take note of 注意到;提及

(考题)Next time you chat with a friend, take note of how you're sitting — it's pretty likely that you will be the same.

take notes of 记录

vt. 注意到;记下;谈到

note sth. /sb. do sth. /that … 注意到某物/人…

(考题)These old people will keep a diary to note their feelings and activity before and after AIBO.

(考题)Many leaders note that the most efficient way to get a

good performance from others is to treat them like heroes.

notebook /ˈnəʊtbʊk/ *n*. 练习本;笔记本

nothing /ˈnʌθɪŋ/ *pron*. 没有东西

for nothing 免费;白白地;无缘无故地

(考题)He was always looking for something for nothing.

have nothing to do (with ...) (与…)没有关系

(考题)Sorry, I can tell you nothing. I have nothing to do with him.

mean a lot/much/nothing to ... 对…很有/没有意义

(考题)Your help means a lot to us. We can't finish the task without it.

nothing but 仅仅、只有

(考题)I have nothing but praise for your devotion and your hard work.

have nothing to do but do sth. 只能做…

(见 have no choice but to do sth.)

do nothing about ... 对…无能为力;对…无所作为

(考题)Dick could do nothing about bad traffic.

to say nothing of ... 更不用说…了

notice /ˈnəʊtɪs/ *n*. 通知;注意到

take notice of ... 注意到…

(考题)For hours, the secretary took no notice of them, hoping that the couple would finally become disappointed and go away.

at ... (time)'s notice 提前…通知

bring ... to sb.'s notice 使某人注意某事

come to sb.'s notice 引起某人的注意

until further notice 直至另行通知

vt. 注意到

notice sth./that ... 注意到…

(考题)The scientists and engineers noticed one similarity between science and poetry.

notice sb. do/doing sth. 注意到某人做某事

(考题)Nobody noticed the thief slip into the house because the lights happened to go out.

noun /naʊn/ *n*. 名词

novel /ˈnɒv(ə)l/ *n*. （长篇）小说

November /nəʊˈvembə/ *n*. 十一月

now /naʊ/ *adv*. 现在

　　up to/till now 直到现在

　　now that ... 既然

　　（考题）Now that she was gone，I felt I had known her.

　　now and then 不时地、时而；偶尔

　　（考题）As a first-year student，the boy was not able to do much but wave his long skinny arms and shoot a basket now and then.

　　now and again 不时、时而；偶尔

　　（考题）Running a house takes a lot of time and most husbands don't understand this. For example，my husband only puts a shelf up now and again.

　　from now on 从今以后

　　just now 刚才；眼下、现在

　　right now 立刻，马上；现在

　　（考题）The committee is discussing the problem right now. It will hopefully have been solved by the end of next week.

nowadays /ˈnaʊədeɪz/ *adv*. 现在；近来

　　（考题）Young people nowadays are too careless about marriage.

nowhere /ˈnəʊweə/ *adv*. 任何地方都不

nuclear /ˈnjuːklɪə/ *adj*. 核的；原子能的

　　nuclear weapons 核武器

number /ˈnʌmbə/ *n*. 数字；号码

　　a (large/good/huge) number of 一些/许多（修饰可数名词）

　　（考题）A growing number of scientists are seriously thinking about it.

　　in large numbers 大量地

numerous /ˈnjuːmərəs/ *adj*. 许多的

nurse /nɜːs/ *n*. 护士；保育员　*v*. 护理；喂奶

nursery /ˈnɜːsərɪ/ *n*. 托儿所

nursing /ˈnɜːsɪŋ/ *n*. 看护、护理工作

nut /nʌt/ *n*. 坚果；干果

nutrient /ˈnjuːtrɪənt/ *n*. 营养物

nutrition /njuːˈtrɪʃən/ *n*. 营养

O

obey /əˈbeɪ/ *vt.*, *vi.* 服从;听从

　　obey (sb./sth.) 服从、听从;遵守(…)

　　(考题)...it is a rule to obey and a principle to follow.

object /ˈɒbdʒəkt/ *n.* 物品;目标;宾语

　　(考题)When sunlight strikes an object, some of the energy is absorbed and some is reflected.

　　v. /ɒbˈdʒekt/ 反对;反对说

　　object to (doing) sth. 反对(做)某事

　　(考题)I don't mind her criticizing me, but it is how she does it that I object to.

　　object to do sth./that ... 反对做某事/反对说…

objection /əbˈdʒekʃən/ *n.* 反对

objective /əbˈdʒektɪv/ *adj.* 客观的　　*n.* 目的;目标

　　(考题)The best way to get rid of a negative self-image is to realize that your image is far from objective, and to actively convince yourself of your positive qualities.

oblige /əˈblaɪdʒ/ *vt.* 迫使

　　oblige sb. to do sth. 迫使某人做某事

　　(考题)The promise I had made obliged me to do my best.

　　be obliged to do sth. 不得不做某事

　　be obliged to sb. (for sth.) (因某事)感激某人

observation /ɒbzəˈveɪʃən/ *n.* 观察;注意

observe /əbˈzɜːv/ *vt.* 观察;遵守

　　observe sth. 观察、注意…;遵守…

　　(考题)Though having lived abroad for years, many Chinese still observe the traditional customs.

　　observe sb. do/doing sth. 观察某人做某事

　　observe that ... 注意到…

obstacle /ˈɒbstək(ə)l/ *n.* 障碍;障碍物

obtain /əbˈteɪn/ *vt.* 得到;获得

（考题）Doctors can put a tiny chip under the skin that will help locate and obtain a patient's medical records.

obvious /ˈɒbvɪəs/ *adj.* 显而易见的；清楚的

（考题）It is obvious that if students value highly their test scores, then a great amount of their self-respect is put in the number.

occasion /əˈkeɪʒən/ *n.* 场合；时刻

（考题）In the past, however, big meals were only hosted on special occasions as people were more careful with money.

on the occasion of ... 在…的场合

take the occasion to do sth. 利用这个机会做某事

occasional /əˈkeɪʒənəl/ *adj.* 偶尔的

occupation /ɒkjʊˈpeɪʃən/ *n.* 占领；职业（见 job）

occupy /ˈɒkjʊpaɪ/ *vt.* 占领；占据

be occupied in/with (doing) sth. 忙于做某事

occupy oneself in/with sth. 忙于做某事

occur /əˈkɜː/ *vi.* 发生；出现；突然想到

（考题）Don't allow doubts to occur in it.

... occur to sb. 某人突然想到…

it occurs to sb. to do sth. /that ... 某人突然想到…

（考题）They don't see men succeeding in society so it doesn't occur to them that they could make something of themselves.

ocean /ˈəʊʃən/ *n.* 洋、海洋

October /ɒkˈtəʊbə/ *n.* 十月

odd /ɒd/ *adj.* 古怪的；零散不成对的；奇数的

of /ɒv/ *prep.* …的

off /ɒf/ *prep. adv.* 离开、脱开；中断

offend /əˈfend/ *vt.* 冒犯；得罪

offend sb. 冒犯某人

（考题）Sorry, but I really didn't mean to offend him.

be/get offended 生气

offer /ˈɒfə/ *vt.* 提供；提出

offer sth. (to sb.)/offer sb. sth. 向某人提供某物

（考题）We may decide not to go to certain places because we believe they will not offer something we enjoy.

offer to do sth. （主动）提出做某事

（考题）I have offered to paint the house in exchange for a week's accommodation.

    n. 提供；报价

（考题）He asks the crowd assembled in the auction-room to make offers, or "bids", for the various items on sale.

office /ˈɒfɪs/ *n*. 办公室

officer /ˈɒfɪsə/ *n*. 军官；官员；(船舶)驾驶员

official /əˈfɪʃəl/ *adj*. 官方的；正式的 *n*. 官员

often /ˈɒfən/ *adv*. 时常；经常

oil /ɔɪl/ *n*. 油 *vt*. 给…加油

O.K. /ˌəʊˈkeɪ/ *adj*. *adv*. *interj*. 好；可以；行啊

old /əʊld/ *adj*. 老年的；旧的

    how old 几岁

    the old 老年人

Olympic /əʊˈlɪmpɪk/ *adj*. 奥林匹克的

    the Olympic Games 奥林匹克运动会

Olympics /əʊˈlɪmpɪks/ *n*. 奥林匹克运动会

omit /əˈmɪt/ *vt*. 省略；遗漏

on /ɒn/ *prep*. *adv*. 在…上；关于

once /wʌns/ *adv*. 一次；曾经、一度 *conj*. 一旦

（考题）In fact, it has already happened more than once in the history of the earth.

（考题）Because they once dominated the earth

    all at once 突然

（考题）Then all at once he found himself at the ranch gate.

    at once 立刻

    once again/more 再一次

    once in a while 偶尔

    once … 一旦

（考题）Once an eating disorder has become firmly established, there is no easy cure.

oneself /wʌnˈself/ *pron*. 自己；亲自

one-sided /wʌnˈsaɪdɪd/ *adj*. 一边的；片面的

only /ˈəʊnlɪ/ *adj*. *adv*. 只有；仅仅

    if only … 但愿(句中用虚拟语气)

not only . . . , but also . . . 不但…,还…

(考题)In addition，the portable computers can connect students to not only the Internet，but also libraries and other resources.

only too 非常

(考题)I am only too glad to meet you here

(辨析：only too 和 too 常有不同的含义。too . . . to do sth. 这一句型表示"太…,以至不能…"。)

onto /ˈɒntʊ/ *prep*. 到…上面

open /ˈəʊpən/ *adj*. 开着的；打开的 *vt*. 打开 *vi*. 开

(be) open to . . . 对…开放；对…持开放态度

(考题)In the second half of the century，however，chances of other service work also opened up to women，from sales jobs in shops to teaching and nursing.

in the open (air) 在室外

(考题)Most performances at British festivals are given in the open air.

opener /ˈəʊpənə/ *n*. 开罐头工具

opera /ˈɒpərə/ *n*. 剧；歌剧

operate /ˈɒpəreɪt/ *vt*. 操作；掌管；vi. 运行、工作；动手术

(考题)A new regular bus service to Tianjin Airport started to operate two months ago.

operate sth. 操纵、运营…

operate on sb. 给某人动手术

operation /ɒpəˈreɪʃən/ *n*. 运行；操作；管理；手术

be in operation 运作之中

come into operation 生效

perform an operation on sb. 给某人动手术

(考题)Franchising refers to a business operation in which a successful parent company sells the right，the guidance to a business under its name.

operator /ˈɒpəreɪtə/ *n*. 操作员；报务员；话务员

opinion /əˈpɪnjən/ *n*. 看法、意见

in sb.'s opinion 在某人看来

(考题)Therefore，in his opinion，the most important skill for children to learn is to discover things on their own.

opponent /ə'pəʊnənt/ *n*. 对手

opportunity /ˌɒpə'tjuːnɪtɪ/ *n*. 机会

    an opportunity of doing/to do/for... 一个…的机会

    (考题)The purpose is to provide an opportunity to try out new ideas and to think through difficulties with fellow learners.

oppose /ə'pəʊz/ *vt*. 反对

    oppose sth. 反对…

    (考题)There are groups of people who oppose this view and who do not believe either in examinations or in any controls in school or on teachers.

    as opposed to 与…相对

    (考题)Communication is making a space for discussion and talking about how you feel as opposed to just saying what the other person did wrong.

    be opposed to sth. 反对…

opposite /'ɒpəzɪt/ *adj*. 对立的;对面的 *adv*. 对面、对过

    (考题)So I took the train going in the opposite direction, and then switched back to the downtown train.

    n. 对立物,对面

    (考题)I am sure they thought he was very generous. But I thought he was the opposite.

oppress /ə'pres/ *vt*. 压迫;压制

or /ɔː/ *conj*. 或者;否则

oral /'ɔːrəl/ *adj*. 口头的;口的

orange /'ɒrɪndʒ/ *n*. 桔子;橙子

orchestra /'ɔːkɪstrə/ *n*. 管弦乐队

order /'ɔːdə/ *n*. 次序;秩序;整齐;命令

    be in good order 有次序、整齐;处于完好状态

    (考题)You can do these tests in any order you like, or you can do all the tests with a formal or informal text.

    keep sth. in good order 保持整齐有序;使处于完好状态

    be/go out of order 出故障

    (考题)Their service systems frequently go out of order.

    in order to do sth. /in order that... 为了…

    (考题)Since fuel, oxygen and heat must be present in order for fire to exist，one or more of these things must be removed or reduced to extinguish a fire.

vt．命令；订购

order sb. to do sth. 命令某人做某事

（考题）Certainly，most of the world's great religions order us to be open-hearted and share what we have with those less fortunate than ourselves.

orderly /ˈɔːdəlɪ/ *adj*．整齐的、有序的

ordinary /ˈɔːdɪnərɪ/ *adj*．普通的、平常的

organ /ˈɔːgən/ *n*．组织；器官

organization /ˌɔːgənaɪˈzeɪʃən/ *n*．组织；机构

organize /ˈɔːgənaɪz/ *vt*．组织

origin /ˈɒrɪdʒɪn/ *n*．起源

（考题）You are encouraged to keep records of the sources used by each person，which helps you trace back to the origin of the problems that may happen unexpectedly.

original /əˈrɪdʒɪnəl/ *adj*．最初的；原始的　　*n*．原文；原来的版本

（考题）Mr. Crockatt seems to imply that shortening the classics does harm to the original.

orphan /ˈɔːfən/ *n*．孤儿　　*adj*．孤儿的

orphanage /ˈɔːfənɪdʒ/ *n*．孤儿院

other /ˈʌðə/ *adj*．别的；其他的　　*n*．别的（人或物）

each other 互相

other than 除了

（考题）Animals，other than service animals，are not permitted in the Gallery.

otherwise /ˈʌðəwaɪz/ *adv*．否则；不然

ought /ɔːt/ *v. aux*．应该

ought to do sth. 应该做某事

（考题）I thought she ought to be able to give up some of this strictness.

ought to have done sth. 本该做某事

（考题）— I'll tell Mary about her new job tomorrow. — You ought to have told her last week

（同义词：**should have done sth.**）

ounce /aʊns/ *n.* 盎司(英制重量单位);一点点

our /aʊə/ *pron.* 我们的

ours /aʊəz/ *pron.* 我们的

ourselves /aʊə'selvz/ *pron.* 我们自己

out /aʊt/ *adv.* 向外;出去;来源;离开

　out of ... 出去;缺乏、失去;源自

　(考题)Then one evening in June last year, she received a text message telling her she was out of work.

outcome /'aʊtkʌm/ *n.* 结果

outdoor /'aʊtdɔː/ *adj.* 户外的

　(考题)Thanks to technology, a growing army of children prefer video games to old outdoor sports.

outdoors /'aʊtdɔːz/ *adv.* 户外地

　(考题)People who spend a lot of time outdoors have observed that, before a storm, field mice come out of their holes and run around.

outer /'aʊtə/ *adj.* 外面的;外部的

outline /'aʊtlaɪn/ *n.* 梗概;轮廓;*vt.* 简要介绍;绘出轮廓

　(考题)In case of emergency, please call the Help Desk at 926-3736 and follow the procedures outlined on the voice message.

outlook /'aʊtlʊk/ *n.* 景色;前景;观点

　an outlook on ... 对…的看法

　(考题)His outlook on the matter is very pessimistic.

output /'aʊtpʊt/ *n.* 产量;输出

outside /'aʊtsaɪd/ *prep.* 在…的外面　*adv.* 在外面

outstanding /ˌaʊt'stændɪŋ/ *adj.* 突出的;出众的、杰出的

outward /'aʊtwəd/ *adj.* 向外的　*adv.* 向外

over /'əʊvə/ *prep.* 在…上方　*adv.* 越过;上方;超过;结束

　(考题)The dinosaurs were on the earth for over 160 million years.

　all over ... 遍及…

　(考题)Laptop computers are popular all over the world.

　all over again 重新;再一次

　over and over (again) 再一次

　(考题)I'm not interested in hearing recycled versions of the

same genre over and over.

... be over …结束

（考题）As soon as school was over, I should start ringing doorbells, selling magazines.

overall /ˌəʊvəˈrɔːl/ *adj.* 总的

overcoat /ˈəʊvəkəʊt/ *n.* 外衣；大衣

overcome /ˌəʊvəˈkʌm/（overcame, overcome）*vt.* 克服

overcome sth. 克服…（困难、情绪、习惯等）

（考题）If we fail to help children to overcome fears, they will grow up lacking self-confidence.（同义词：get over sth.）

overflow /ˌəʊvəˈfləʊ/ *vi.* 泛滥

overhead /ˈəʊvəhed/ *adj.* 在头顶上的　*adv.* 在头顶上

overlook /ˌəʊvəˈlʊk/ *vt.* 忽视；俯瞰；监视

overnight /ˌəʊvəˈnaɪt/ *adv.* 彻夜

overseas /ˌəʊvəˈsiːz/ *adj.* 在海外的　*adv.* 在海外、在国外

overtake /ˌəʊvəˈteɪk/（overtook, overtaken）*vt.* 追越、超过

（考题）Still, I was close enough to overtake her if she tired, so I didn't give up hope completely.

owe /əʊ/ *vt.* 欠…；把…归功于…

owe sth. to sb. 欠某人某物；把…归功于…

（考题）— "How much do I owe you?" she asked. — "Nothing," I said.

（考题）I must owe my success to you. Without your help, I couldn't have made it.

owing /ˈəʊɪŋ/ *adj.* 欠着的、未付的

owing to ... 由于…

（考题）Officials say that few patients are infected with the virus owing to the effective prevention.

（同义词：due to ... , because of ...）

（注意：owing to 不能担任表语，due to 则可以。）

own /əʊn/ *adj.* 自己的 pron. 自己的　*vt.* 拥有

of one's own 属于自己的

（考题）When it comes to friends, I desire those who will share my happiness, who possess wings of their own and who will fly with me.

on one's own 独自地

（考题）I'd like to have someone to share experiences with. I'd go mad on my own.

owner /ˈəʊnə/ *n.* 主人、拥有者

ox /ɒks/ *n.* 公牛

oxygen /ˈɒksɪdʒɪn/ *n.* 氧；氧气

P

pace /peɪs/ *n*. 一步；速率

  at a ... pace 以…的速度

  （考题）I'm walking two miles three times a week at a fast pace, and that feels good.

  keep pace with ... 跟得上…

  （考题）If you walk that fast, we can't keep pace with you.

Pacific /pəˈsɪfɪk/ *adj*. 太平洋的

  the Pacific 太平洋

pack /pæk/ *vt*. 把…打包、整理　*vi*. 打包、装箱

package /ˈpækɪdʒ/ *n*. 包；包裹

packet /ˈpækɪt/ *n*. 小包、小盒

  a packet of cigarettes 一包香烟

page /peɪdʒ/ *n*. 页

pain /peɪn/ *n*. 疼痛

  （考题）The fire caused great pain and loss, but after it London was a better place: a city for the future and not just of the past.

  spare no pains to do sth. 努力、不遗余力做某事

  take pains to do sth. 努力、不遗余力做某事

  （同义词: **spare no efforts to do sth.**）

  （考题）You take special pains when you are eating in public.

  with/without pain 痛苦地/没有痛苦地

  （考题）Diet products make people believe that gain comes without pain, and that life can be without resistance and struggle.

painful /ˈpeɪnfʊl/ *adj*. 疼痛的；痛苦的

paint /peɪnt/ *n*. 油漆　*vt*. 打油漆；绘画

  paint sth. (...) 油漆…（成…）

painting /ˈpeɪntɪŋ/ *n*. 绘画；绘画作品；油画

pair /peə/ *n*. 一双、一对、一副

  a pair of ... 一双（对、副）…

palace /ˈpælɪs/ *n*. 宫殿

pale /peɪl/ *adj*. 苍白的;灰白的

pan /pæn/ *n*. 平锅

panda /ˈpændə/ *n*. 熊猫

panic /ˈpænɪk/ *n*. 恐慌、惊慌

   be in panic 在恐慌之中

   cause panic 引起恐慌

   (考题)Most of it will miss our planet, but two fragments will probably hit the southern part of the earth. The news has caused panic.

pants /pænts/ *n*. (pl) 裤子(美);短裤

paper /ˈpeɪpə/ *n*. 纸;报纸;文件

   (注意:表示"纸"时是不可数名词。)

parade /pəˈreɪd/ *n*. 游行

paragraph /ˈpærəɡrɑːf/ *n*. 段落

parallel /ˈpærəlel/ *adj*. 平行的 *n*. 平行线 *vt*. 使平行

   be parallel to ... 与…平行

parcel /ˈpɑːsəl/ *n*. 包裹;小包

pardon /ˈpɑːdən/ *vt*. 原谅 *n*. 原谅、宽恕

   parden sb. for (doing) sth. 原谅某人做了某事

   I beg your pardon. 请原谅;对不起,请再说一遍。

   (注意:在表示"请再说一遍"时,parden 用升调。)

parent /ˈpeərənt/ *n*. 父亲、母亲 *adj*. 起源的、母体的

   a parent company 母公司

park /pɑːk/ *n*. 公园 *vi*. 停车

parking /ˈpɑːkɪŋ/ *n*. 停车;停车位;停车场

   No parking! 不准停车

   parking lot 停车场

parrot /ˈpærət/ *n*. 鹦鹉

part¹ /pɑːt/ *n*. 部分;部件;角色;作用

   (考题)All employees are shown how their part is important in making the park a success.

   for sb.'s part 就某人而言

   in part 部分地

   (考题)How often do we tell white lies? It depends in part on our age，education，and even where we live.

play a part in ... 在…中起作用；扮演角色

（考题）At first，the producers of the movie told Taylor that she was too small to play the part of Velvet.

take part in (doing) sth. 参加…

（考题）And children expect to take part in the family decision-making process. They don't want to "rock the boat".

part² /pɑːt/ *vi*. 分手；分别 *vt*. 使分开

part with/from sb. 与某人分手、分别

（考题）We parted with each other in London.

participant /pɑːˈtɪsɪpənt/ *n*. 参加者

participate /pɑːˈtɪsɪpeɪt/ *vi*. 参加

participate in (doing) sth. 参加(做)某事

（考题）And your actors won't go on strike. And why do people participate in them? Well，for fame and money of course.

particular /pəˈtɪkjʊlə/ *adj*. 特定的；具体的；特别的

be particular about sth. 对…很挑剔、很讲究

n. 细节；特点

（考题）An auction is usually advertised beforehand with full particulars of the articles to be sold and where and when they can be viewed by potential buyers.

in particular 特别地

（考题）We even have different words for some foods，meat in particular，depending on whether it is still out in the fields or at home ready to be cooked.

particularly /pəˈtɪkjʊləlɪ/ *adv*. 特别；尤其

partner /ˈpɑːtnə/ *n*. 合作者；合伙人；搭档

party /ˈpɑːtɪ/ *n*. 聚会；政党；一方

pass /vt*. 经过；传递；通过；及格 *vi*. 经过；考及格 *n*. 传递

（考题）Runners in a relay race pass a stick in one direction. However，merchants passed silk，gold，fruit，and glass along the Silk Road in more than one direction.

pass away 消磨掉；去世

pass by 从旁边经过

（考题）The Lake of Geneva，lying among the Alps，is a true

inland sea，making possible a wide range of pleasant boat trips，
you can relax and watch the beautiful scenes pass by.

pass sth. down 传下来

pass sth. on（to sb.） 传递某物（给某人）

pass the time 消磨时光

（考题）Alfred Butts invented the game "Lexico" when he was
playing word games to pass the time.

（同义词：**kill time，idle away the time**）

pass through ... 通过、穿过…；经历

（考题）All passengers must pass through the Customs after
Passport Control.

passage /ˈpæsɪdʒ/ *n.*（文章的）一段、一节

passenger /ˈpæsɪndʒə/ *n.* 乘客、旅客

passer-by /ˈpɑːsəbaɪ/ *n.* 过路人

passion /ˈpæʃən/ *n.* 热情；激情

（考题）Peterson aroused the local residents' passion for music.

passport /ˈpɑːspɔːt/ *n.* 护照

password /ˈpɑːswəd/ *n.* 口令；密码

past /pɑːst/ *prep.* 过、经过

（考题）But something happened on the way as Marc walked past
all the familiar landscape of the neighborhood.

adj. 过去的、以前的

（考题）Everything about my past life suddenly seemed
meaningless.

n. **in the past** 过去、以前

（考题）In the past，appearing on television wasn't for ordinary
people.

pat /pæt/ *vi.* 轻拍、轻打

path /pɑːθ/ *n.* 路、小径、小道

patience /ˈpeɪʃəns/ *n.* 耐心、忍耐

（考题）However，with the special patience and superstition of a
schoolboy，I looked at every word of the text.

have patience with ... 对…有耐心

lose patience with/over ... 对…失去了耐心

（考题）These old people are our main customers，and it's not

hard to lose patience over their slowness.

patient /ˈpeɪʃənt/ *adj.* 有耐心的　*n.* 病人

be patient with/to do . . . 对…有耐心

（考题）The British are always patient when they wait in line

Many people no longer have the patience to stand in a queue.

patriotic /ˌpætrɪˈɒtɪk/ *adj.* 爱国的

pattern /ˈpætən/ *n.* 模式；花样

pause /pɔːz/ *n.* 暂停、中止

（考题）After a long pause，the door opened. A small woman in her eighties stood before me.

vi. 暂停；中止

（考题）Dave paused to reach for the fishing pole and gear box on the bench where he had left them the night before.

pave /peɪv/ *vt.* 铺（路）

pave the way for . . . 为…铺平道路

pavement /ˈpeɪvmənt/ *n.* 人行道

pay /peɪ/（paid，paid）*vt.* 支付；付出　*vi.* 支付；回报　*n.* 报酬

pay sb. . . . / pay . . . to sb. 付给某人…

（考题）But the next day, he asked me to pay him S200 for what he had done.

pay（. . .）for . . . 为（…）付出…

（考题）You need to pay the difference for the special fitting and better skill that you are receiving.

pay attention to . . . 注意、关注…

（考题）. . . but we pay attention only to those that are important to us.

it pays to do sth. 做…是有好处、有回报的

peace /piːs/ *n.* 和平；平和；宁静

（考题）Unlike Cole who insists on a feeling of loneliness and the idea of finding peace in nature，Leslie paints what he actually sees.

at peace 处于平静、宁静状态

at peace with sb. 与…和平相处

peace of mind 心灵的安宁

（考题）Keeping on doing good deeds brings us peace of mind，

which is important for our happiness.

peaceful /'piːsfʊl/ *adj*. 和平的;平静的;和谐的

（考题）... the suburbs of big cities are peaceful and quiet.

peach /piːtʃ/ *n*. 桃子

peak /piːk/ *n*. 山峰;顶点

peanut /'piːnʌt/ *n*. 花生;花生米

pear /peə/ *n*. 梨

pearl /pɜːl/ *n*. 珍珠

peasant /'pezənt/ *n*. 农民

peculiar /pɪ'kjuːlɪə/ *adj*. 奇怪的;独特的

（考题）There is a peculiar flavour about the unexpected books you pick up in that kind of collection.

be peculiar to ... 具有…特征的;特有的

pen /pen/ *n*. 钢笔

pencil /'pensl/ *n*. 铅笔

penny /'penɪ/ *n*. 便士(英国货币单位)

people /'piːpl/ *n*. 人民;人们;民族

（考题）Before 1066, in the land we now call Great Britain lived peoples belonging to two major language groups.

（注意：在表示"人们"时,people 代表复数的概念,因此,不能加 s。a people 或 peoples 表示"民族"。）

per /pə/ *prep*. 每,每一

（考题）Current U. S. foreign aid for drinking water and sanitation budgets only one dollar per year per American citizen. （见 every）

percent /pə'sent/ *n*. 百分之一

percentage /pə'sentɪdʒ/ *n*. 百分比;所占比例

perfect /'pɜːfɪkt/ *adj*. 完美的;十足的;熟练的　*vt*. 使完善

（考题）Sea is a perfect choice for a truly memorable holiday!

perform /pə'fɔːm/ *vi*. 表现;表演 vt. 表演…;表现出;操纵

（考题）Students who perform poorly on the exam are left feeling that it is all over.

（考题）The increasingly popular "design museums" that are opening today, however, perform quite a different role.

performance /pə'fɔːməns/ *n*. 表演;操作;业绩

（考题）People care a lot about making a mistake in a speech because they regard speech-making as a kind of performance rather than as an act of communication.

performer /pəˈfɔːmə/ *n*. 表演者；操作者

perhaps /pəˈhæps/ *adv*. 也许；可能

（考题）Teens are becoming isolated, less skillful at person-to-person relationships, and perhaps numb to the cheatings that are so much a part of the e-mail world.

（辨析：perhaps 的意思是"或许"，表示"有疑问，不能肯定"；probably 的意思是"很可能"；possibly 的口气较 probably 弱，强调"有这种可能"，常和 will，may，might 等连用。否定句中则常和 can't，couldn't 连用。）

period /ˈpɪərɪəd/ *n*. 一段时间；句号

permanent /ˈpɜːmənənt/ *adj*. 长久的；永久性的

permission /pəˈmɪʃən/ *n*. 允许、准许、许可

　　with/without permission 得到/未获得许可

　　ask for permission 请求批准

permit /pəˈmɪt/ *vt*. 允许；许可

permit (doing) sth. 允许（做）…

（考题）Marriage between different classes was not permitted in the country at that time.

　　permit sb. to do sth. 允许某人做某事

（考题）The computer permits me to reach out into the world and do almost anything I want to do.

　　permit of ... 有…的余地

　　（见 allow）

　　n. 许可证

（考题）You can't run an Internet café without a permit.

persevere /ˌpɜːsɪˈvɪə/ *v*. 坚持；坚韧

　　persevere in (doing) sth. 坚持（做）某事

persist /ˈpɜːsɪst/ *vi*. 坚持；固执地做…　*vt*. 坚持说

　　persist in (doing) sth. 坚持做某事

　　persist that ... 坚持说…

（注意：表示"坚持、努力"时，persevere 和 persist 意思相同。但如果表示"固执地坚持某种不良行为、不好习惯"时，只能使用

persist。)

person /ˈpɜːsen/ *n*. 人

in person 亲自

（考题）You can get the watch either in person or by mail at an affordable price.

personal /ˈpɜːsən(ə)l/ *adj*. 个人的；私人的

personality /ˌpɜːsəˈnælɪtɪ/ *n*. 个性

（考题）Whether or not we are slaves of time today depends on our culture and personality.

persuade /pəˈsweɪd/ *vt*. 说服；劝说

persuade sb. to do sth. 说服某人做某事

（考题）They are persuaded by gunner magazines with stories honoring the chase and the kill.

persuade sb. that ... 使某人相信

（考题）And by me time I reached the last word, pleased, I persuaded myself that I had read The Republic, and seriously crossed Plato off my list.

（注意：persuade sb. to do sth. 表示已经说服对方答应做某事。否则，只能使用 try to persuade 或 want to perduade）

（同义词：**bring/talk/win sb. over to (doing) sth**.）

pet /pet/ *n*. 宠物；玩赏的动物

petrol /ˈpetr(ə)l/ *n*. 汽油

phenomenon /fɪˈnɒmɪnən/ *n*. 现象

philosophy /fɪˈlɒsəfɪ/ *n*. 哲学

phone /fəʊn/ *n*. 电话

make a phone call to sb. 给某人打电话

vt. **phone sb.** 给某人打电话

（同义词：**call sb. ,give sb. a ring/call,ring sb. up**）

photo /ˈfəʊtəʊ/ *n*. 照片（phtograph）

photographer /ˈfəʊtɒɡrəfə/ *n*. 摄影者

photographic /ˌfəʊtəˈɡræfɪk/ *adj*. 摄影的；摄影般的

photography /fəˈtɒɡrəfɪ/ *n*. 摄影；摄影术

phrase /freɪz/ *n*. 短语；词组

physical /ˈfɪzɪk(ə)l/ *adj*. 物理的；自然的；本身的

physician /fɪˈzɪʃən/ *n*. （内科）医生

physicist /ˈfɪzɪsɪst/ *n*. 物理学家

physics /ˈfɪzɪks/ *n*. 物理学

physiology /fɪzɪˈɒlədʒɪ/ *n*. 生理学

piano /ˈpiænəʊ/ *n*. 钢琴

play the piano 弹钢琴

pick /pɪk/ *vt*. 采摘；挑选

pick sth. out 选出；认出

（考题）This picture was taken a long time ago. I wonder if you can pick out my father.

pick sth. up 拣起；学会；接人；收听到；整理；加快；

（考题）The wind had picked up, and angry, dark clouds rolled across the sky.

（考题）I drove Dad into Mijas, and promised to pick him up at 4 pm, then dropped off the car at the garage.

pick oneself up（跌倒后）站立起来；振作起来

（考题）But if you want to be a leader, you must learn to fail — and not die a thousand deaths. Pick yourself up and start all over again.

picnic /ˈpɪknɪk/ *n*. *vi*. 野餐

go on a picnic 去野餐

picture /ˈpɪktʃə/ *n*. 图片

get/have a clear picture of ... 对…有清楚的了解

（考题）When someone tells you something that is true, but leaves out important information that should be included, he can give you a false picture.

go to the pictures 看电影

pie /paɪ/ *n*. 馅饼

piece /piːs/ *n*. 块、条、张（表示不可数名词的数量单位）

pig /pɪg/ *n*. 猪

pigeon /ˈpɪdʒən/ *n*. 鸽子

pile /paɪl/ *n*. 堆；叠

a pile of 一堆；一碟；一摞

pill /pɪl/ *n*. 药丸；药片

pilot /ˈpaɪlət/ *n*. 飞行员；领航员；引水员

pin /pɪn/ *n*. 别针；发卡

pine /paɪn/ *n*. 松树

pink /pɪŋk/ *adj*. 粉红色的 *n*. 粉红色

pint /paɪnt/ *n*. 品脱(容量单位,等于1/8加仑)

pioneer /ˌpaɪəˈnɪə/ *n*. 先驱;开拓者

the Young Pioneer 少先队

pipe /paɪp/ *n*. 管道;烟斗

pity /ˈpɪtɪ/ *n*. 同情;可怜;可惜的事

(考题)It was a pity that the great writer died with his works unfinished.

for pity's sake 请帮个忙

have/take pity on sb. 可怜某人

pizza /ˈpiːtsə/ *n*. 匹萨饼

place /pleɪs/ *n*. 地方、地点

in place 到位;适当

(考题)The permits were stopped suddenly three months ago by the government until new safeguards could be put in place to prevent misuse of the information superhighway

out of place 偏离位置;不适当;不协调

in the place of/take the place of 取代、代替…

(考题)The medicine, made up of the basic building materials of life, will build new brain cells, heart cells, and so on-in much the same way our bodies make new skin cells to take the place of old ones.

take place 发生

(考题)Conversations on subjects such as sex and drugs would not have taken place a generation ago.

vt. 放下;使处于

(考题)You've placed me in a very difficult situation.

plain /pleɪn/ *n*. 平原 *adj*. 明白的;简单的

(考题)People don't have to learn computer terms, but the experts have to explain plain in language. The computers are becoming "people-literate."

plan /plæn/ *n*. 计划

make a plan for/to do sth. 计划做某事

vt. 计划

plan to do sth. 计划、打算做某事

（考题）If you plan to sell on eBay，it helps to include a picture of the item.

as planned 按计划

（考题）To complete the project as planned，we'll have to work two more hours a day.

plane /pleɪn/ n. 飞机

planet /'plænɪt/ n. 行星

plant /plɑːnt/ n. 植物；工厂 vt. 种植

plantation /plɑːn'teɪʃən/ n. 种植园

plastic /'plæstɪk/ adj. 塑料的；n. 塑料（表示材料常用复数）

plate /pleɪt/ n. 盘子、碟子

platform /'plætfɔːm/ n. 站台；月台

play /pleɪ/ vi. vt. 玩；打（球）；弹奏

play the piano 弹钢琴（表示演奏乐器时有定冠词）

play basketball（体育项目前没有定冠词）

play with sb. /sth. 与某人玩/玩弄…

（考题）Johnny，you mustn't play with the knife，you may hurt yourself.

play a role/part in 起作用；扮演角色

（考题）I watched one of those TV dramas about a hospital and suddenly I felt like playing one of the roles myself.

n. 剧

（考题）They are going to put on a short play in the English evening.

player /'pleɪə/ n. 比赛者；运动员

playground /'pleɪɡraʊnd/ n. 操场

pleasant /'plezənt/ adj. 令人愉快的、惬意的；友善的

（考题）Everyone says the parent-teacher conference should be pleasant, civilized, a kind of dialogue where parents and teachers build partnership.

（考题）Mars has all the materials for a colony to produce or make everything it needs，and Mars is far more pleasant than the other planets in the outer space.

please /pliːz/ vt. 使高兴；请

（考题）In the past I wanted to please everyone，but now I am going to listen even more to the people around me.

pleased /pliːzd/ *adj*. 感到高兴的、喜欢的

be pleased about/with sth. /sb. 对…感到高兴

（考题）The manager is pleased with Kim's hard work and his suggestions.

be pleased to do sth. 很乐意做某事

（考题）The head of the Library said he was pleased to see the American and Chinese students talking and laughing together.

pleasure /ˈpleʒə/ *n*. 愉快；高兴

（考题）If you find pleasure in deep thinking about different ideas，characters，and facts，you are a critical thinker.

give/bring pleasure 带来快乐、欢乐

（考题）Roses require a good deal of care，and if it weren't for the pleasure they give，it wouldn't be worth the work.

It's my pleasure（回答感谢时）不客气；我很高兴这样做

（考题）— Thank you for joining in our conversation tonight. — It's my pleasure.

with pleasure 高兴地；（回答请求时）没问题；很乐意

（考题）— Would you take this along to the office for me? — With pleasure.

plentiful /ˈplentɪfʊl/ *adj*. 足够的；大量的

plenty /ˈplentɪ/ *n*. 充足；大量

plenty of 大量的；充足的

（考题）Many tours are timed so that you arrive at the cone of the volcano in plenty of time for sunset and the full contrast between the erupting red lava and the darkening sky.

plug /plʌg/ *n*. 电插头；塞子　*v*. 塞上

plug in 插上插头

plunge /plʌndʒ/ *vi*. *vt*. 猛地浸入、跳入

plus /plʌs/ *prep*. 加；加上；*n*.（符号）

（考题）If someone gave me $5 for something that cost $3.25，I handed over three quarters and a dollar and said，"75 cents makes four dollars，plus one dollar makes five."

p. m. 下午（post meridiem）

pocket /ˈpɒkɪt/ *n*. 口袋

poem /ˈpəʊɪm/ *n*. 诗；诗篇

poet /ˈpəʊɪt/ *n*. 诗人

poetry /ˈpəʊɪtrɪ/ *n*.（总称）诗、诗歌

point /pɔɪnt/ *n*. 点；要点；小数点

  a point of view 观点

  （考题）But I was not a good reader. Merely bookish. I lacked a point of view when I read.

  at the point 在这一时刻

  （考题）Newton is shown as a gifted scientist with very human weaknesses who stood at the point in history where magic ended and science began.

  off the point 偏题

  be on the point of doing sth. 正要做某事

  make a point of/make it a point to ... 特别注意

  （考题）Now，whenever I visit a friend's home，I make it a point to speak to the elder child first.

  strong point 长处、优点

  weak point 短处、弱点

  （考题）Everyone has his strong points and shortcomings.

  vi. *vt*. **point at/to ...** 指着…

  （考题）Mum pointed at a big chair by the door and I knew she wanted me to sit down.

  （注意：point to 侧重"朝…的方向指去"，如 point to a building in the distance；而 point at ... 强调指的具体位置、是一个较近而明确的目标，如：point at a mark in the map。）

  point sth. at/to sb. 用…对着、瞄着某人

  （考题）Todd quickly turned round and pointed a gun at the man. "Hands up and get out!"

  point to sth. 让人注意；指出

  （考题）Multimillion-pound spending on binoculars, bird food and boxes point to the increasing numbers of birdwatchers.

  point sth. out 指出

  （考题）The proposal pointed out Toronto's rich variety of national groups.

poison /ˈpɔɪzən/ *n*. 毒药；毒物

poisonous /ˈpɔɪzənəs/ *adj*. 有毒的

pole /pəul/ *n*. 杆；电线杆；极点

   the North/South Pole 北极/南极

police /pəˈliːs/ *n*. 警察(总称，复数动词)

policeman /pəˈliːsmən/ *n*. 警察

policy /ˈpɒlɪsɪ/ *n*. 政策

   the open-door policy 开放政策

polish /ˈpɒlɪʃ/ *vt*. 磨光；擦亮

polite /pəˈlaɪt/ *adj*. 有礼貌的；有教养的

political /pəˈlɪtɪkəl/ *adj*. 政治的

politician /pɒlɪˈtɪʃən/ *n*. 政治家；政客

politics /ˈpɒlɪtɪks/ *n*. 政治；政治学

   go into politics 进入政界

   play politics 耍手腕

pollute /pəˈluːt/ *vt*. 污染；弄脏

   (考题)Many cities around the world today are heavily polluted. Careless methods of production and lack of consumer demand for environment friendly products have contributed to the pollution problem.

pollution /pəˈluːʃən/ *n*. 污染

pond /pɒnd/ *n*. 池塘

pool /puːl/ *n*. 水池；水塘

   swimming pool 游泳池

poor /puə/ *adj*. 穷的；可怜的；差劲的、蹩脚的

   be poor at (doing) sth. 不善做某事

   (考题)People poor at one thing can be good at another.

   the poor 穷人

pop /pɒp/ *adj*. 大众的；流行的

   pop music 流行音乐

popular /ˈpɒpjulə/ *adj*. 大众的；流行的

   (考题)Laptop computers are popular all over the world.

   be popular with/among ... 受…的欢迎

   (考题)Smart and pretty, Kate is very popular among her friends.

population /ˌpɒpjʊˈleɪʃən/ *n*. 人口;人口总数

（考题）Habitat loss will continue with our increasing population, but can we slow the loss of wildlife caused by shooting?

pork /pɔːk/ *n*. 猪肉

port /pɔːt/ *n*. 港口

portable /ˈpɔːtəbl/ *adj*. 便携的

porter /ˈpɔːte/ *n*. 门卫;搬运工人

portion /ˈpɔːʃən/ *n*. 部分

portrait /ˈpɔːtrɪt/ *n*. 肖像;画像

Portugal /ˈpɔːtjʊgəl/ *n*. 葡萄牙

Portuguese /ˌpɔːtjʊˈgiːz/ *adj*. 葡萄牙的 *n*. 葡萄牙人;葡萄牙语

position /pəˈzɪʃən/ *n*. 位置;方位;地位;职位

positive /ˈpɒzɪtɪv/ *adj*. 积极的;明确的、肯定的

（考题）If you find that believing in yourself is a challenge, it is time you built a positive self-image and learned to love yourself.

possess /pəˈzes/ *vt*. 拥有;占有

possess sth. 拥有某物

（考题）Everybody possesses a sense of direction from birth.

possibility /ˌpɒsəˈbɪlɪtɪ/ *n*. 可能;可能性

（考题）Every new venture has the possibility of making or losing money.

there's possibility for sb. to do sth. 某人有可能做某事

possible /ˈpɒsɪbl/ *adj*. 有可能的

it's possible for sb. to do sth. /that ... 有可能…

（考题）Is it possible that love, hope, faith, laughter, confidence, and the will to live have positive treatment value?

as ... as possible 尽可能…地

（考题）The auctioneer therefore has a direct interest in pushing up the bidding as high as possible.

possibly /ˈpɒsɪblɪ/ *adv*. 可能

（考题）I'm sorry, but I can't possibly start until Monday. Will that be all right?

（见 perhaps）

post /pəʊst/ *n*. 柱子;职位;岗位;*vt*. 邮寄;张贴

post office 邮局

postage /'pəʊstɪdʒ/ *n*. 邮资

postal /'pəʊstəl/ *adj*. 邮政的；邮局的

postcard /'pəʊstkɑːd/ *n*. 明信片

postcode /'pəʊstkəʊd/ *n*. 邮政编码（美：Zip Code）

postman /'pəʊstmən/ *n*. 邮递员

postpone /'pəʊstpəʊn/ *vi*. 推迟、延期

  postpone (doing) sth. 推迟做某事

  （同义词：**delay**，**put off** 见 **deley**）

pot /pɒt/ *n*. 罐、壶

potato /pə'teɪtəʊ/ *n*. 土豆

potential /pə'tenʃəl/ *adj*. 有潜力的　*n*. 潜力；潜在的可能性

  （考题）The number of people involved is so big that they have great potential to influence government decisions affecting the environment.

pound /paʊnd/ *n*. 英镑；（英制重量单位）磅

pour /pɔː/ *vi*. *vt*. 倒出；流出

  pour (sth.) into （将某物）倾入…；流入

  （考题）Many industries and governments build simple landfills to store waste，and often just pour waste chemicals into nearby bodies of water.

poverty /'pɒvətɪ/ *n*. 贫穷；穷困

  （考题）Dikembe Mutombo grew up in Africa among great poverty and disease.

  live in poverty 过穷苦的日子

powder /'paʊdə/ *n*. 粉末；粉；炸药

power /paʊə/ *n*. 能量；电力；能力；力气；权力

  （考题）Every storm is an example of the power of nature. It is the greatest show on Earth.

  power station/plant 发电厂

  power grid 电网

  power supply 电力供应

  power failure 停电

  come into/to power 执政、上台掌权

  in power 执政、掌权

  vt. 提供动力

（考题）The turbine can then power an electrical generator to produce electricity.

powerful /ˈpaʊəfʊl/ *adj*. 强大的；强有力的；大功率的

powerless /ˈpaʊəlɪs/ *adj*. 无力量的；软弱的；无能力的

practical /ˈpræktɪkəl/ *adj*. 实际的；事实的；可行的

（考题）Paying the housewives may not be practical, but the government should recognize the value of housework, perhaps through the tax.

practice /ˈpræktɪs/ *n*. 实践；练习

（考题）I have watched, very carefully and with great respect and admiration, the theory and practice of selling satisfaction and serving millions of people on a daily basis, successfully.

out of practice 疏于练习

put into practice 用于实践

（考题）The underlined phrase in the last paragraph "on the way" means to be put into practice.

practise /ˈpræktɪs/ *vi*. *vt*. 实践；练习（美：practice）

practise (doing) sth. 练习做某事

（考题）As a new driver, I have to practise parking the car in my small garage again and again

praise /preɪz/ *vt*. 赞扬；表扬 *n*. 赞扬；称赞

praise sb. for (doing) sth. 因某事表扬某人

（考题）Mrs Collins praised the designers for using colours in the cells.

n.（考题）I have nothing but praise for your devotion and your hard work.

pray /preɪ/ *vt*. 祈求；祈祷

pray (to sb.) for sth. 为某事（向某人）祈祷

（考题）Mivna missed him very much and prayed for his return.

pray to do sth. 祈求做某事

pray that ... 祈求某事

precious /ˈpreʃəs/ *adj*. 珍贵的；贵重的

predict /prɪˈdɪkt/ *vt*. 预言；预报

predict sth. 预报…

（考题）Research by a British biology student suggests that sharks could be used to predict storms.

predict that ... 预言…

（考题）Experts predict modern kids will have poorer health than their parents — and they say a lack of outside play is surely part of it

prefer /prɪˈfɜː/ *vt.* 宁愿；更喜欢

prefer (doing) sth. to (doing) sth. 比起…来更喜欢…

（考题）Thanks to technology, a growing army of children prefer video games to old outdoor sports.

prefer to do sth. rather than do sth. 比起…更喜欢做某事

（考题）The estates prefer to employ women pickers because they are more careful.

prefer that ... 希望、但愿…（从句中用 should 或动词原形）

would prefer that ... 宁愿、倒希望（从句中使用动词的过去时或过去完成时表示虚拟语气）

pregnant /ˈpregnənt/ *adj.* 怀孕的；妊娠的

preparation /ˌprepəˈreɪʃən/ *n.* 准备

make preparations for/to do sth. 为…做好准备

in preparation for ... 为…做好准备

（考题）For the rest of the time you are working on your own, doing the necessary reading in preparation for tutorials or writing seminar papers.

prepare /ˌprɪˈpeə/ *vi. vt.* 准备

prepare sth. 准备…

（考题）He prepared a proposal on the subject and presented it to the city's Executive committee, asking for their support.

prepare for sth. 为…做准备

（考题）— What's that terrible noise? — The neighbors are preparing for a party.

prepare to do sth. 准备做某事

prepare sb./oneself for/to do sth. 使某人/自己为…做好准备

（考题）It is desirable that boys and girls grow up together, go to school together, and prepare themselves for a society that does not value sexual separation.

be/get prepared for/to do sth. 为…做好准备

（考题）He got well-prepared for the job interview，for he couldn't risk losing the good opportunity.

presence /'prezəns/ *n*. 出席；在场

in the presence of . . . sb. 某人在场时

（考题）"Well，well，why don't you say anything?" said he，as if it was ridiculous in his presence to respect any one but himself，Napoleon.

present¹ /'prezənt/ *adj*. 出席；在场

be present at . . . 出席…

（考题）The number of people present at the concert was much smaller than expected. There were many tickets left.

vt. **present sth. to sb.** 向某人赠送、提供…

（考题）The three facts presented in the passage are used to illustrate that safe drinking water should be a primary concern.

n. 礼物

（考题）They are my birthday presents from my friends.

present² /'prezənt/ *adj*. 现在；目前；此刻

（考题）These rivers were miles wide at first. Through the years they settled into their present channels.

n. **at present** 目前；现在

（考题）At present people who could get to that point are not in good health at all.

for the present 暂时；目前（见 moment）

presently /'prezəntlɪ/ *adv*. 不久；一会儿

preserve /prɪ'zɜːv/ *vt*. 保护；保存

（考题）At minus 130℃，a living cell can be preserved for a thousand years.

president /'prezɪdənt/ *n*. 总统；主席；总裁；董事长

press /pres/ *v*. 按、压；催促

press sth. 按、揿、挤、压…

（考题）This operation will press the leaves for juices which give the tea both its colour and taste.

press sb. to do sth. 催促、逼迫某人做某事

be pressed for sth. 缺乏…

. . . presses（时间、资金等）紧迫

n. 按压；报刊；出版社

（考题）At the press of a button, a microcomputer locks all other floors' chute door and sets the recycling container turning until the right box comes under the chute.

（考题）The music press has so much to introduce these days, and jazz is just a small fraction of it.

press conference 记者招待会

pressure /ˈpreʃə/ *n*. 压力

（考题）Often, there is the double pressure to enjoy life through food and yet remain ultra-slim.

under the pressure of ... 在…的压力下

（考题）That means that they are under an unusual amount of pressure or stress.

pretend /prɪˈtend/ *vt*. 假装

pretend to do sth. 假装做某事

（考题）The judge's remark implied that York would be more severely punished if he pretended to be a psychiatrist.

pretend that ... 假装…

（考题）But the smiles on our faces disappeared as the pilot tossed the plane around, pretending he was going to hit the ground.

pretty /ˈprɪtɪ/ *adj*. 美丽的；漂亮的

（考题）Pretty women are more likely to be helped.

adv. 相当地

（考题）Next time you chat with a friend, take note of how you're sitting — it's pretty likely that you will be the same.

prevent /prɪˈvent/ *vt*. 阻止；阻碍

prevent sth. 阻止某事

（考题）In their natural state, the spreading branches overhead shut out sunlight and prevent the growth of plants on the forest floor.

prevent sb. (from) doing sth. 阻止某人做某事

（考题）These gases act like the glass of a greenhouse in that they allow energy from the Sun to enter but prevent energy from leaving. They are therefore called greenhouse gases.

（同义词：**stop sb. (from) doing sth. , keep sb. from doing sth.** 。

注意：prevent 和 stop 后的介词 from 可以省略，但 keep 后面不能省略，否则，意思就成了"使某人不停地做某事"。）

prevention /prɪˈvenʃən/ *n.* 阻止；预防

（考题）Officials say that few patients are infected with the virus owing to the effective prevention

preview /ˈpriːvjuː/ *vt.* 预习

previous /ˈpriːvɪəs/ *adj.* 先前的；原先的

price /praɪs/ *n.* 价格

（考题）The auctioneer's services are paid for in the form of a percentage of the price the goods are sold for.

at a ... price 以…的价格

（考题）The charity shop is a British institution, selling everything from clothes to electric goods, all at very good prices.

at any price 以任何代价；无论如何

at the price of ... 以…为代价

beyond/above/without price 极其珍贵的，无价的

（同义词：priceless）

vt. （考题）The first six shortened editions, all priced at £6.99 and advertised as great reads "in half the time", will go on sale next month

pride /praɪd/ *n.* 骄傲；自豪

take pride in ... 为…感到骄傲

（考题）We can learn from the first letter that Joan Edward takes pride in her friends.

with pride 骄傲地

（考题）"See what I can do?" he said with pride. "Only three of us in Paris can do this kind of work."

primary /ˈpraɪmərɪ/ *adj.* 首要的；最初的；基本的

（考题）Safe drinking water should be a primary concern.

primary school 小学

prince /prɪns/ *n.* 王子

princess /prɪnˈses/ *n.* 公主；王妃

principal /ˈprɪnsɪpəl/ *adj.* 重要的；主要的

principle /ˈprɪnsɪpəl/ *n.* 原理；原则

（考题）... it is a rule to obey and a principle to follow.

in principle 原则上

print /prɪnt/ *vt*. 印刷

prison /ˈprɪzən/ *n*. 监狱

　be in prison 坐牢

　put sb. into prison 送某人去坐牢

prisoner /ˈprɪzənə/ *n*. 囚犯；俘虏

private /ˈpraɪvɪt/ *adj*. 私人的；私有的

（考题）As a particular form of problem solving, these creative acts are based on the broad knowledge gained in the past, whether this be of the "public" sort known to science, or of the "private" sort known to the artist.

　in private 私下里

prize /praɪz/ *n*. 奖；奖品

probable /ˈprɒbəbl/ *adj*. 有可能的；也许；大概

（考题）It's probable that traders along the Silk Road needed to remember the entire trade route.

probably /ˈprɒbəblɪ/ *adv*. 也许；大概；很有可能

（考题）The selection would be made by people who themselves are probably selected by some computer.

（见 perhaps）

problem /ˈprɒbləm/ *n*. 问题；习题

（考题）The commonest problem was information "storage failure". People often forget what they have done, will do or even are doing.

　have problem doing sth. 做某事会有困难

（考题）People who experience habitual loneliness have problems socializing and becoming close to others.

　no problem 没有问题

（考题）— Sorry to trouble you, but could I ask a quick question?
— No problem.

procedure /prəˈsiːdʒə/ *n*. 程序；手续

proceed /prəˈsiːd/ *v*. 继续；进行之中

process /ˈprəʊses/ *vt*. 加工；处理　*n*. 过程

（考题）When you think critically, you take control of your

thinking processes.

in process 在进行中

in the process of . . . 在…的过程中

produce /prə'djuːs/ *vt*. 生产；制造；制作

（考题）The TV companies like reality shows because they are cheap to produce and attract younger viewers

n. 产品

（考题）Organic produce is always better.

product /'prɒdʌkt/ *n*. 产品

production /prə'dʌkʃən/ *n*. 生产

productive /prə'dʌktɪv/ *adj*. 多产的；富有成效的

（考题）Group work is necessary, and is usually more productive than working alone.

prefession /prə'feʃən/ *n*. 职业

（考题）The schools admit that not all children will be successful in the profession for which they are being trained.

by profession 职业

professional /prə'feʃənəl/ *adj*. 职业的；专业的

（考题）... in a country like America, money is everything. It is more important than friendship, honour or professional morality.

professor /prə'fesə/ *n*. 教授

profit /'prɒfɪt/ *n*. 利润；收益

    at a profit 获利

    with profit 获益地

    gross profit 总利润；毛利

    net profit 净利

    make a profit 赢利

（考题）After all, if you are going to be ruled by time, why not invest in air antique clock and perhaps make a future profit?

profitable /'prɒfɪtəbl/ *adj*. 有利的；有收益的

programme /'prəʊɡræm/ *n*. 节目；程序

pregress /'prəʊɡres/ *n*. 进步；进展

（考题）One of the latest technical progress is the use of an electronic scanner which can read all the contents of your shopping basket or trolley in just a few seconds.

in progress 在进行中

(考题)The investigation of the murder is in progress.

(同义词：**go on,under way,underway,in process**)

make progress 取得进步

(考题)With the study of philosophy，you can make progress in your career development.

vi. /prəʊˈgres/ 进步；进展

(考题)The construction is progressing as scheduled.

progressive /prəˈgresɪv/ *adj*. 进步的；前进的

prohibit /prəˈhɪbɪt/ *vt*. 禁止；阻止

prohibit (doing) sth. 禁止…

(考题)Smoking is prohibited. Food and drink are not permitted outside the food service areas.

prohibit sb. from doing sth. 阻止某人做某事

project /ˈprɒdʒekt/ *n*. 工程；方案

promise /ˈprɒmɪs/ *n*. 许诺，允诺

(考题)We have so easily been attracted by the promise and potential of diet products that we have stopped thinking about what diet products are doing to us.

break one's promise 违背诺言

make a promise 做出承诺

(考题)The young man made a promise to his parents that he would try to earn his own living after graduation.

keep/stick to one's promise 信守诺言

(考题)For six years now Bonner has kept his promise to stay out of prison.

v. **promise sth.** 答应…；预示着…

(考题)Don't promise anything unless you are one hundred percent sure.

promise sb. sth. 答应某人…

promise to do sth. 答应做某事

(考题)He promised to spare more time to stay with his son.

promise (sb.) that ... 答应(某人)…

(考题)— Say，Jane，will you come with me to the game Friday?

— Thanks, Bob, but I promised Mary I'd go with her.

promote /prə'məut/ *vt.* 增强；提升；促进；

promote sth. 提升、发展、促进…

（考题）The study has shown that meditation is good for the brain. It appears to reduce pressure and promote a sense of well-being.

pronounce /prə'nauns/ *vt.* 发音

pronunciation /prəˌnʌnsɪ'eɪʃn/ *n.* 发音

proof /pruːf/ *n.* 证明；证据　*adj.* 耐、防…的

bullet-proof 防弹的

fire-proof 防火的

shock-proof 防震的

water-proof 防水的

proper /'prɒpə/ *adj.* 适当的；合适的

properly /'prɒpəlɪ/ *adv.* 适当地；合适地

property /'prɒpətɪ/ *n.* 财产；性质

proportion /prə'pɔːʃən/ *n.* 比例

proposal /prə'pəuzəl/ *n.* 提议；建议；动议

make/put forward a proposal 提出一项建议

（考题）… he prepared a proposal on the subject and presented it to the city's Executive committee.

propose /prə'pəuz/ *vt.* 建议；提议

propose (doing) sth. 建议（做）某事

（考题）I propose making some alterations in the plan according to the present conditions.

propose to do sth. 提议做某事

（考题）They proposed to set about doing the job immediately.

propose that …（从句中用虚拟语气）

prospect[1] /'prɒspekt/ *n.* 前景；希望；

in prospect 可以期望的；即将出现

prospect[2] /'prɒspekt, prə'spekt/ *v.* 勘探；探寻

protect /prə'tekt/ *vt.* 保护

protect sb./sth. 保护某人/某物

（考题）We are all interested in equality, but while some people try to protect the school and examination system in the name of equality, others, still in the name of equality, want only to destroy it.

protect sb. from/against ... 保护某人不受…

(考题) It has been proved that eating vegetables in childhood helps to protect you against serious illnesses in later life.

protection /prəˈtekʃən/ *n*. 保护

protein /ˈprəʊtiːn/ *n*. 蛋白质

protest /prəʊˈtest/ *n*. 抗议；反对 *vi*. *vt*. 反对；提出异议

(考题) Four students ... have made up their minds to ring the bell nonstop for two weeks as a protest.

protest against/at/about sth. 对…提出抗议

proud /praʊd/ *adj*. 骄傲；自豪

be proud of ... 为…而感到骄傲、自豪

(考题) York was proud of the fact that he could perform some duties of a doctor.

prove /pruːv/ (proved, proved 或 proven) *vt*. 证明

prove ... 证明…

(考题) Riis believed that poverty caused crime, and he used photos to help him prove his point.

prove sb. /sth. (to be) ... 证明某人/某物…

(考题) But we think it will prove to be good business for the merchants, as well as tourist attraction.

prove that ... 证明…

(考题) The experiment has proved that there really is an unknown element that caused the phenomenon.

link *v*. **prove + *adj*.,** *n*. …被证明…

(考题) What he discoverd has proved true.

proverb /ˈprɒvɜːb/ *n*. 谚语；成语；格言

provide /prəˈvaɪd/ *vt*. 提供；供给

provide sb. with sth. 向某人提供某物

(考题) By using limited clues to provide us with a rapid opinion of other people or places we may choose to limit our communication.

provide sth. for sb. 向某人提供某物

(考题) We take jobs to stay alive and provide homes for our

families always making ourselves believe that this style of life is merely a temporary state of affairs along the road to what we really want to do.

provided/providing that ... 只要、如果…

（考题）You can add as many users as you want, provided they each have a Windows account.

（注意：provide 和 supply 都表示"提供"。supply 可以有双宾语的用法。另外，在表示"商店供应商品"时，一般用 supply。）

province /ˈprɒvɪns/ n. 省；领域、范围

psychological /ˌsaɪkəˈlɒdʒɪkəl/ adj. 心理（学）的

psychology /saɪˈkɒlədʒɪ/ n. 心理学

public /ˈpʌblɪk/ n. 公众；民众 adj. 公众的；公共的

（考题）All these efforts to serve the public well have made Walt Disney Productions famous.

in public 公开地

（考题）You take special pains when you are eating in public.

publication /ˌpʌblɪˈkeɪʃən/ n. 出版、发行；出版物

publish /ˈpʌblɪʃ/ vt. 出版；发行

pudding /ˈpʊdɪŋ/ n. 布丁（西餐中的甜食）

pull /pʊl/ vt. 拉

（考题）This way you can avoid sharing the high way with mobile homes which can be pulled by cars.

pull ahead 向前

pull away 开车离开；挣脱；

（考题）The traffic lights went green and I pulled away.

pull sb./sth. down 使变得虚弱；拆毁

（考题）Houses standing in the direction of the fire were pulled down.

pull in （火车、汽车）驶进站

（考题）Todd saw the headlights coming at him and a car pulled in for gas.

pull out (of) 离站；退出

pull through 渡过难关；康复

（考题）We're glad that he has pulled through.

pull up 停车

(考题)I heard the garbage truck pull up to the sidewalk.

pullover /ˈpʊləʊvə/ *n*. 毛线套衫

pump /pʌmp/ *n*. 泵 *vt*. 泵水;打气

punctuation /ˌpʌŋktʃuˈeɪʃən/ *n*. 标点

punish /ˈpʌnɪʃ/ *vt*. 惩罚;处罚

punish sb. for (doing) sth. 因(做)某事而惩罚某人

(考题)Laws that punish parents for their little children's actions against the laws get parents worried.

pupil /ˈpjuːpl/ *n*. 小学生;学生

purchase /ˈpɜːtʃəs/ *n*. *vt*. 购买

make purchases 购物

pure /pjʊə/ *adj*. 纯的;完美的

purple /ˈpɜːpl/ *adj*. 紫色的 *n*. 紫色

purpose /ˈpɜːpəs/ *n*. 目的;意图

(考题)This would mean that everything would depend on luck since every pupil would depend on the efficiency, the values and the purpose of each teacher.

on purpose 故意地

(考题)Human facial expressions differ from those of animals in the degree to which they can be controlled on purpose.

purposeful /ˈpɜːpəsfʊl/ *adj*. 有目的的

purse /pɜːs/ *n*. 钱包

pursue /pəˈsjuː/ *vt*. 追逐;追捕;继续

(考题)I wanted to be a biologist, but I didn't pursue my dream. You know what you want. Go fulfill it

push /pʊʃ/ *v*. 推

(考题)A boy would try to climb a barrier before him or push it down while a girl would attract help from others.

push sth. ... 把某物推得…

(考题)The law of the jungle has begun to operate at bus stops, with people using their arms to push others out of the way.

put /pʊt/ (put, put) *vt*. 放下

put sth. aside/away 放到一边;储存;搁置

(考题)It is a time for us to take a rest, to put our work aside, trusting that there are many others taking care of the world.

（考题）It is wise to have some money put away for old age.

put ... down 放下；镇压；责怪

（考题）I just wish all the people that have put me down had said：
"I believe in you. You'll succeed."

put forward/forth 提出；建议

（考题）US lawmakers have put forth four bills on nanotech research and development.

put sth. into use/practice/operation 加以运用

（考题）Nanotech should not be put into wrong use in the military field.

put off 关掉；推迟；

（考题）— I have been told the sports meet might be put off. — Yes，it all depends on the weather.

put on 穿上；上演；开电源

（考题）Every year，the managers leave their desks and business suits and put on special service clothes.

put out 熄灭；扑灭；公布

put up 举起；提出；建起

（考题）Cardboard tents can be easily put up and removed by users.

put up with ... 容忍

（考题）I can put up with many things，but not with people who steal.

puzzle /ˈpʌzl/ *vt*. 使迷惑；使困惑

（考题）Unlike the average art museum visitors，design museum visitors seldom feel frightened or puzzled

be puzzled at/about ... 对⋯感到迷惑

（考题）They become puzzled about the student's correct last name.

be puzzled what/how to do sth. 不知该如何做

Q

qualification /ˌkwɒlɪfɪˈkeɪʃən/ *n.* 资格；资格证明

（考题）Yesterday he proudly claimed in court that despite his complete lack of medical experience or qualifications, he had saved several people's lives.

qualified /ˈkwɒlɪfaɪd/ *adj.* 合格的；胜任的；

be qualified for sth. /to do sth. 胜任做某事

（考题）Michael Fish is not qualified for his job.

qualify /ˈkwɒlɪfaɪ/ *vt.* 使有资格；使胜任

qualify sb. as ... 使具有…的资格

quality /ˈkwɒlɪtɪ/ *n.* 质量；品质

（考题）Testing helps manufacturers to be sure of a product's quality.

be of good/high quality 质量好

（考题）Goods must be of proper quality, must be as described on the package and must be fit for any particular purpose made known by the seller.

be of poor/low quality 质量差

quantity /ˈkwɒntətɪ/ *n.* 数量

large/small quantity of ... 大量的/少量的…

（考题）Because of the large quantity and high quality of his collection, a huge crowd of possible buyers gathered for the auction.

（注意：这一短语可修饰可数名词,也可修饰不可数名词）

quarrel /ˈkwɒrəl/ *n.* 争吵

have a quarrel with sb. about sth. 与某人争吵某事

vi. **quarrel with sb. about sth.** 与某人争吵某事

（考题）He accidentally let out he had quarreled with his wife and that he hadn't been home for a couple of weeks.

quarter /ˈkwɔːtə/ *n.* 四分之一；一刻钟

queen /ˈkwiːn/ *n.* 女王；王后

question /ˈkwestʃən/ *n.* 问题

    in question 讨论中的

    (考题)The problem in question must be paid due attention to.

    out of question 没问题

    out of the question 不可能的

    (考题)I can't afford the price, so it's out of the question for me to buy the car this year.

    vt. 询问

    question sb. on/about sth. 就某事询问某人

    question sth. 对…提出疑问

    (考题)Only philosophy questions the nature of the concepts used in a discipline, and its relation to other disciplines.

queue /kjuː/ *n.* 排队　*vi.* 排队

    stand in a queue 排队

quick /kwɪk/ *adj.* 快的、迅速的　*adv.* 快地、迅速地

    (考题)Practice makes a quick mind.

    be quick at (doing) sth. 在(做)某事方面很迅速

    (考题)The government is quick at taking action this time.

    be quick to do sth. 做某事很迅速

quiet /kwaɪət/ *adj.* 安静的;平静的　*n.* 安静;宁静

    peace and quiet 安宁;清静

quilt /kwɪlt/ *n.* 被子

quit /kwɪt/ (quitted 或 quit, quit) vi., *vt.* 离开;停止(工作等);辞职

    quit (doing) sth. 停止做某事

    (考题)Margaret quit her job as a nurse because she needed the right time to look after her children.

    quit work 辞职

    quit school 辍学

quite /kwaɪt/ *adv.* 很;十分

quote /kwəut/ *vt.* 引用;援引

    quote sth. 引用…

    quote sb. 引用某人的话

    (考题)He always quotes famous people in his speech.

R

race /reɪs/ *n*. 赛跑；人种；种族 *vi*. 比赛；赛跑

（考题）... but I did know I was good enough to win the race.

（考题）The application of science and technology to the development and production of weapons of mass destruction has created a real danger to the continued existence of the human race on this planet.

vi.（考题）Thirteen vehicles lined up last March to race across the Mojave Desert, seeking a million in prize money.

radar /ˈreɪdə/ *n*. 雷达

radiation /ˌreɪdɪˈeɪʃn/ *n*. 辐射；放射

（考题）A cave is also a protection from radiation.

radio /ˈreɪdɪəʊ/ *n*. 收音机；无线电

radioactivity /ˌreɪdɪəʊˈæktɪvɪtɪ/ *n*. 放射性

radium /ˈreɪdɪəm/ *n*. 镭

rail /reɪl/ *n*. 铁路；路轨；栏杆、扶手

railway /ˈreɪlweɪ/ *n*. 铁路

　railway station 火车站

rain /reɪn/ *n*. 雨；雨水 *vi*. 下雨

（考题）Deserts are found where there is little rainfall or where rain for a whole year falls in only a few weeks' time.

rainbow /ˈreɪnbəʊ/ *n*. 彩虹

raincoat /ˈreɪnkəʊt/ *n*. 雨衣

rainy /ˈreɪnɪ/ *adj*. 下雨的；多雨的

（考题）We are getting into the rainy season now.

raise /reɪz/ *vt*. 使升高；提出；筹集；喂养

（考题）Over time, people began to catch the animals and raise them.

（考题）... help raise employee's living standards.

　raise a question 提出一个问题

（考题）You were brave enough to raise objections at the

meeting.

raise money 筹款

（考题）They decided to set up a shop to sell some of these donations to raise money for that appeal.

n. 提升；加薪

（考题）After only six months he was due for a raise if this assessment was satisfactory.

random /ˈrændəm/ *n.* 偶然、随意的行动或过程

at random 随意地、随机地

（考题）On some services, prices went up and down at random.

range /reɪndʒ/ *n.* 山脉；范围

a wide range of ... 广泛的…

（考题）If there are gases coming out, they could provide energy for a whole range of bacteria.

in the range of ... 在…范围内

out of one's range 能力达不到

（考题）— Can you shoot that bird at the top of the tree? — No, it's out of range.

vi. （在某范围内）变动、变化

range from ... to ... 范围从…到…

（考题）In the botanic garden we can find a variety of plants that range from tall trees to small flowers.

rank /ræŋk/ *n.* 地位；等级；军衔　　*vt.* 把…分等级

rapid /ˈræpid/ *adj.* 快的；迅速的

rare /reə/ *adj.* 难得的；稀罕的

a rare opportunity 难得的机会

（考题）In such a period it is a rare comfort to find a cobbler who gets his greatest satisfaction from pride in a job well done.

rat /ræt/ *n.* 老鼠

rate /reɪt/ *n.* 率；速率；比率

（考题）Safe drinking water is a precondition for health and the fight against child death rate ...

at the rate of ... 以…的速率/速度

at any rate 无论如何

rather /ˈrɑːðə/ *adv.* 相当；颇为

（考题）The rent was rather reasonable.

or rather 更确切地说

rather than 而不是

（考题）Because you were fixing your attention on his message rather than on his way of speech-making.

would rather do sth. 宁愿做某事

（考题）I'd much rather read two 300-page books than one 600-page book.

would rather ...（从句中用虚拟语气）宁可、宁愿…

raw /rɔː/ *adj*. 生的；未加工的

raw materials 原料

ray /reɪ/ *n*. 射线；光线

reach /riːtʃ/ *vi*. 抵达、到达；*vi*. 延伸；伸手拿 *n*. 可及之处

（考题）Make sure you're in the right channel when you reach Passport Control.

reach (one's hand out) for sth. 伸手去拿…

（考题）There are all sorts of tricks at play each time we reach out for that particular brand of product on the shelf.

beyond/out of sb.'s reach 某人力不能及的

（考题）This new model of car is so expensive that it is beyond the reach of those with average income.

within sb.'s reach 某人力所能及的

react /rɪˈækt/ *vi*. 做出反应；回应

react to sth. 对…做出回应

（考题）How did the couple's parents react to the wedding?

reaction /rɪˈækʃən/ *n*. 反应

reaction to ... 对…的反应

（考题）I do not get lost in my own personal reaction to what people are saying.

read /riːd/（read, read）vi.，*vt*. 读、阅读

（考题）I read in order to get a point of view.

read sth. (from cover to cover)（从头至尾）读…

read of/about ... 读到有关…的内容

（考题）Then I read about a nationally famous jogger who died of a heart attack while jogging, and I had something else to worry about.

read between the lines 读出话外之音

read sb.'s mind/thoughts 看出某人的心思

read sth. through 从头至尾读…、通读…

reader /ˈriːdə/ *n.* 读者;读物

readily /ˈredɪlɪ/ *adv.* 乐意地;欣然地

reading /ˈriːdɪŋ/ *n.* 阅读

ready /ˈredɪ/ *adj.* 做好准备的;乐于做某事的

be/get ready for sth. /to do sth. 做好做某事的准备

(考题)Once she has fully studied her subjects, ready to dive into the book, she can spend twenty hours nonstop at her desk.

get sth. ready for/to do sth. 为…准备好某物

(考题)We have to carry it on, since we've got everything ready.

real /rɪəl, riːl/ *adj.* 真的;真正的

(考题)... man-made plants could replace real plants and grow more quickly.

(辨析:real 表示客观存在的,而非想象的;true 表示与事实相符,而非虚假、错误的;actual 指已经发生或存在的,而非可能发生的;genuine 则强调真的,不是冒充的。)

realistic /ˌrɪəˈlɪstɪk/ *adj.* 现实的;逼真的

(考题)Therefore, it is important for each person in our society to try to maintain a healthy and realistic self-image.

reality /rɪˈælɪtɪ/ *n.* 现实;真实

(考题)... people feel less happy if the gap between reality and desire is bigger.

realize /ˈrɪəlaɪz/ *vt.* 使视线;意识到

realize ... 实现…;意识到…

(考题)... in short, people look on work as a path to ever-increasing consumption rather than a way to realize their own abilities.

realize that ... 意识到、明白…

(考题)... we look back and realize that all those years waiting for Real Life to come along were in fact real life.

(见 recognize)

really /'rɪəlɪ/ *adv.* 确实;实在;真实地

rear /rɪə/ *n.* 后部

reason /'riːzən/ *n.* 理由;原因

for some reason 由于某种原因

(考题)For some strange reason, I had been waiting until my retirement to start doing watercolors again.

have reason for /to do sth. 有理由…

(考题)I believe the main reason why the modern hunter kills is that he thinks people will admire his courage in overpowering dangerous animals.

vi., *vt.* 推理;推断

reason with ... 与某人论理

reasonable /'riːzənəb(ə)l/ *adj.* 合理的;公道的

rebel /rɪ'bel/ *vi.* 反叛;造反

rebel against ... 反叛、反抗…

rebuild /ˌriː'bɪld/ *vt.* 重建

recall /rɪ'kɔːl/ *vt.* 回忆;回想

(考题)If the system fails to recognize your account, you can recall the Windows user name and password by using a hot-key combination.

receipt /rɪ'siːt/ *n.* 收到;发票;收据

receive /rɪ'siːv/ *vt.* 收到;接收

(考题)She must receive long-time training.

recent /'riːsənt/ *adj.* 新近的;近来的

reception /rɪ'sepʃən/ *n.* 收到;接收;招待会

(考题)The festival will end with an open reception at which other films will be shown.

reception desk 服务台

recitation /resɪ'teɪʃən/ *n.* 背诵;朗读

recite /rɪ'saɪt/ *vt.* 背诵

recognize /'rekəgnaɪz/ *vt.* 认出;识别;意识到、明白;承认

recognize ... (as ...) 认出…(是…)

(考题)Different groups often use clearly identifiable styles of clothes so that they can be easily recognized.

recognize sth. /that ... 意识到…

（考题）Make sure that everyone recognizes the importance of safety before doing the job.

（考题）Every year more people recognize that it is wrong to kill wildlife for "sport."

（辨析：在表示"意识到"时，可以和 realize 替换使用。）

recommend /rekə'mend/ *vt.* 推荐

recommend ... to sb.（for/as ...） 向某人推荐…（作为/以…）

（考题）The writer of this passage aims to recommend an approach to correcting children's bad behavior.

recommend doing sth. 建议做某事

recommend sb. to do sth. 建议某人做某事

recommend that ...（从句中用虚拟语气）

record /'rekɔːd/ *n.* 纪录；唱片

break/beat the record 打破纪录

keep a record/records of ... 保留…的纪录

（考题）You are encouraged to keep records of the important things you have done in case you forget them.

vt. /rɪ'kɔːd/ 纪录；录音

（考题）Photos record the beauties of nature.

recorder /rɪ'kɔːdə/ *n.* 录音机

recover /rɪ'kʌvə/ *vi.* 恢复；康复 *vt.* 恢复；找回

（考题）Once environmental damage is done, it takes many years for the ecosystem to recover.

recover from ... 从…中恢复过来

（考题）I was trying to recover from the loss of my father.

recover sth. 找回某物

recover oneself 恢复镇定

recreate /'riːkrɪ'eɪt/ *vt.* 再创造；再创作

recycle /riː'saɪk(ə)l/ *n.* *v.* 再循环；回收利用

red /red/ *adj.* 红色的 *n.* 红色

reduce /rɪ'djuːs/ *vt.* 减少；缩小

reduce ...（to ...） 把…减少（到…）

（考题）They could spread everywhere, replicate swiftly, and reduce the earth to dust in a matter of days.

reduce ... by ... 减掉…

（考题）The system aims to reduce deadly road accidents by 20%—40% that are caused by tiredness.

refer /rɪˈfɜː/ vi. 提到；查阅　vt. 提交；归结于

　refer to ... 提到…；查阅…；与…有关

　（考题）The underlined words "natural law" in the third paragraph refer to the fact that heat goes in the upward direction.

　refer to ... as ... 把…看成、说成是…

　refer sth. to sb. 把某事交由某人处理、决定

reference /ˈrefərəns/ n. 参考；提及；查阅

　（考题）The project aims to list every species on Earth in a single, easy-to-use reference guide.

　for sb.'s reference 供某人参考

　reference books 参考书

reflect /rɪˈflekt/ vt. 反射；反映

　（考题）For example, there's the obvious tendency to smile when smiled at and there are less obvious changes that reflect emotions of surprise, anger or sadness such as a change in our heart rate and blood pressure.

reform /rɪˈfɔːm/ n. 改革；革新

　（考题）The latest reform in testing is the computerized test.

　vt. vi. 改革；革新；改良

　（考题）The passage is mainly concerned with scientific ways to help criminals reform themselves in prison.

refresh /rɪˈfreʃ/ vt. 使振作；消除疲劳

　refresh oneself（with ...）（用…）使自己振作、恢复精神

　（考题）Ontario Parks offers visitors many choices to relax and refresh themselves.

　refresh one's memory 唤起记忆；回忆起

refrigerator /rɪˈfrɪdʒəreɪtə/ n. 冰箱

refugee /refjuːˈdʒiː/ n. 难民

refusal /rɪˈfjuːzəl/ n. 拒绝

refuse /rɪˈfjuːz/ vt. 拒绝；拒不

　refuse sb./sth. 拒绝…

　（考题）The second letter suggests that Mr Expert advises Joan on how to refuse people.

refuse to do sth. 拒绝做某事

（考题）That may explain one of life's great mysteries: why men refuse to ask for directions ... and women often need to!

refuse sb. sth. 拒绝给某人…

regard /rɪ'gɑːd/ *vt.* 看待；看待

regard ... as ... 把…看成…

（考题）Although not regarded as a separate species from the African elephant, the desert cousin differs in many ways.

as regards ... 关于，至于，就…而言

n. 尊重；(*pl.*) 问候；致意

give/send one's regards to sb. 向某人问候

（考题）Send my regards to your lovely wife when you write home.

in/with regard to ... 关于…

（考题）In the city, styles of dress are particularly important with regard to self-presentation.

regarding ... 关于、至于、就…而言

（考题）Obesity is a major public health concern, so why shouldn't we change the law regarding unhealthy food ads?

（同义词：**as regards, considering**）

regardless /rɪ'gɑːdlɪs/ *adj.* 不管、不顾

regardless of ... 不管…

（考题）They are going to explore that area regardless of their own safety.

region /'riːdʒən/ *n.* 地区；地带

register /'redʒɪstə/ *n.* 纪录；名单；注册 *vt.* 纪录；登记

regret /rɪ'gret/ *n.* 遗憾；后悔

（考题）Zoe has been working on the farm since October of last year and says she has no regrets.

to sb. 's regret 使某人感到遗憾、后悔的是

with/without regret 遗憾地/毫无遗憾地

vi., *vt.* **regret (doing) sth.** 后悔（做）某事

（考题）Richard, when I was 23, my dad persuaded me to go into law. And I've always regretted it.

regret that ... 后悔、遗憾…

（考题）We regret that we do not have enough space for visitor items larger than 17×26 inches into the Gallery.

regret to do sth. 很抱歉地做某事

（考题）I regret to inform you that your application is not accepted.

regular /ˈreɡjʊlə/ *adj.* 常规的；固定的

regulate /ˈreɡjʊleɪt/ *vt.* 控制、管理；校准、调节

regulation /ˌreɡjʊˈleɪʃən/ *n.* 控制、管理；校准、调节

reject /rɪˈdʒekt/ *vt.* 拒绝；抵制；退回

relate /rɪˈleɪt/ *vi. vt.* 叙述；使有关系、有关联

（考题）If you are using a map, turn it so it relates to the way you are facing.

relate ... to ... 将…与…联系起来

（考题）We may be able to relate it to changes in the social classes.

be related to ... 与…有关

（考题）Each year diseases related to inadequate water and sanitation kill millions of people in the developing world.

relation /rɪˈleɪʃən/ *n.* 关系；联系；亲戚

relationship /rɪˈleɪʃənʃɪp/ *n.* 关系；联系

（考题）Multitasking is even changing the relationship between family members.

relative /ˈrelətɪv/ *n.* 亲属；亲戚

relatively /ˈrelətɪvlɪ/ *adv.* 相对来说

（考题）Over thousands of years the function of the arts has remained relatively constant.

relax /rɪˈlæks/ *v.* (使)放松、松弛

（考题）I love slipping into a comfortable chair for a long read — as I relax into the chair, I also relax into the author's world, stories and ideas.

relaxation /ˌriːlækˈseɪʃən/ *n.* 放松；消遣

release /rɪˈliːz/ *v.* 释放；解除 *n.* 发行；发布；释放；解除

（考题）After the trainer was sure that the whale could look after itself, he released it into the sea.

release sb. from ... 免除某人的…

relevant /ˈreləvənt/ *adj.* 有关的；中肯的；恰当的

（考题）Come for the music and stay to check out some relevant books for the rest of the week!

be relevant to ... 与…有关的

（考题）We want to make science more relevant, interesting and attractive to high school students by showing them how classroom studies can relate to practical experience.

reliable /rɪˈlaɪəbl/ *adj.* 可靠的；可以依赖的

（考题）However, the NRES website proved to be a much more reliable source of information.

relief /rɪˈliːf/ *n.* 减轻；解除

to sb.'s relief 使某人感到宽慰的是

relieve /rɪˈliːv/ *vt.* 减轻；免除

（考题）In the passage, the author calls on us to act now so as to relieve the global food shortage.

relieve sb. of ... 减轻某人的…；免除、解除某人的…

（考题）The pain killer will relieve you of your headache.

be/feel relieved to do sth. 松了一口气…

（考题）She moved on to English, and was relieved to find that she didn't have any trouble with this subject.

religion /rɪˈlɪdʒən/ *n.* 宗教；信仰

religious /rɪˈlɪdʒəs/ *adj.* 宗教的；虔诚的

rely /rɪˈlaɪ/ *vi.* 依靠

rely on ... (to do sth.) 依靠某人做某事

（考题）... people still relied on advertisements to get most information about products.

remain /rɪˈmeɪn/ *vi.* 留下

（考题）The physical book is so elegant that it disappears into the background, and what remains is the author's world.

link. v. 依然是、保持

（考题）Often, there is the double pressure to enjoy life through food and yet remain ultra-slim.

remark /rɪˈmɑːk/ *n.* 评论；注意 *vt.* 评论；觉察

make a remark about/on ... 对…发表评论

（考题）This remark was made by a Shanghai student when speaking to his fellow students at the Nixon Library in California, U. S. A.

remark on/upon ... 对…发表意见、评论

remark that ... 评论说…

（考题）The black woman turned the course of American history in December 1955 when she refused to give up her seat on a bus to a white man. "By sitting down," remarked John Lewis, "she was standing up for all Americans."

remarkable /rɪˈmɑːkəbl/ 显著的；值得注意的；非凡的

（考题）In today's climate of wealth and remarkable consumption, 10-course meals are no longer reserved for significant occasions.

remember /rɪˈmembə/ *vt.* 记得；记住

remember (doing) sth. 记得（做过）某事

（考题）— Let me tell you something about the journalists. — Don't you remember telling me the story yesterday?

remember to do sth. 记得要去做某事

（考题）Remember to throw the empty bottle in the recycling bin after you drink the last drop of liquid in it.

remember that ... 记得…

（考题）Remember that everything can be settled by discussion.

remember me to sb. 代我向某人问好

remind /rɪˈmaɪnd/ *vt.* 使想起；提醒

remind sb. of/about sth. 提醒某人某事

（考题）The programme reminds me of many things from my own childhood.

remind sb. to do sth. 提醒某人做某事

（考题）I think it is a wonderful phrase, reminding us, in effect, to enjoy the moment, to value this very day.

remind sb. that ... 提醒某人…

（考题）For students, the school uniform reminds them that their task for the six or seven hours they are in school is to get an education.

reminder /rɪˈmaɪndə/ *n.* 起提醒作用的事物

remote /rɪˈməʊt/ *adj.* 遥远的

remote control 遥控

remove /rɪ'muːv/ *vt*. 拿开；去除；排除

（考题）Get someone to remove the trouble!

remove sth.（from/off ...） 将某物（从…）排除

（考题）Their thin fingers can easily remove the twin leaves and new shoots from the plant, which are the parts used for processing tea.

renew /rɪ'njuː/ *vt*. 更新；重新开始

rent /rent/ *n*. 租金　*vt*. 出租；租借

repair /rɪ'peə/ *n*. 修理

（考题）He should provide free repairs within three months.

under repair 在修理中

（考题）Look out! Don't get too close to the house whose roof is under repair.

in good repair 保养良好

beyond repair 无法修理的

（考题）— Why do you suggest we buy a new machine? — Because the old one has been damaged beyond repair.

vt. reapir sth. 修理…

repeat /rɪ'piːt/ *vt*. 重复；转述

repeated /rɪ'piːtɪd/ *adj*. 多次的；重复的

replace /rɪ'pleɪs/ *vt*. 取代、代替

（考题）... man-made plants could replace real plants and grow more quickly.

replace sb./sth. with ... 用…替换某人/某物

reply /rɪ'plaɪ/ *n*. 答复

（考题）Teens say they feel good about what they say online or taking the time to think about a reply.

make/give a reply to ... 对…做出答复

in reply to ... 作为响应、答复

vi. *vt*. **reply to sth./sb.** 对某事/某人做出答复

reply ... 回答说…

（注意）表示"对…做出回答"时，reply 名词或动词后都应使用介词 to。及物动词 reply 的宾语表示回答的内容。）

report /rɪ'pɔːt/ *n*. 报告；*vt*. 报告；汇报；告发

report sth. to sb. 向某人报告某事

it is reported that ... 据报道…

（考题）It was reported that Mr. Evans' healthy long life was to a certain extent due to his mild temper.

sb. is reported to be/be doing/have done sth. 据报道、据说某人是/正在/已经…

（考题）The accident is reported to have occurred on the first Sunday in February.

report to ... 向…报到

reporter /rɪˈpɔːtə/ *n.* 记者

represent /ˌreprɪˈzent/ *vt.* 代表

representative /ˌreprɪˈzentətɪv/ *n.* 代表；代理人

republic /rɪˈpʌblɪk/ *n.* 共和国

the People's Republic of China 中华人民共和国

reputation /ˌrepjuˈteɪʃən/ *n.* 名声；信誉

（考题）Not all hotels are equal, of course, and it's a good idea to consult a guidebook with a good reputation.

enjoy a good reputation 有好名声

earn a good reputation 赢得好名声

（考题）She devoted herself entirely to her research and it earned her a good reputation in her field.

request /rɪˈkwest/ *n.* 请求

at sb.'s request 应某人的要求

（考题）We will send you full program descriptions at your request.

make a request 请求

vt. **request sth. (of/from sb.)** （向某人）要求得到某物

request sb. to do sth. 要求某人做某事

（考题）When requested to fill in a middle name, they generally write the father's family name.

request that ... 要求、请求…（从句中使用虚拟语气）

（考题）Albert has requested that the customs office change their decisions on the fine.

require /rɪˈkwaɪə/ *vt.* 要求；需要；命令

require sth. 需要某物

（考题）It usually disappears quickly and does not require any special attention.

require sb. to do sth. 要求某人做某事

（考题）Those who enter the area and cause road damage may also be required to pay for repairs.

It is required that . . . /sb. requires that . . . 要求…（从句中使用虚拟语气）

（考题）It is required in the regulations that you should not tell other people the password of your e-mail account.

sth. require doing 某事需要…

（同义词：need, want 也可表示"需要"。而且，后面如使用动名词，以主动的形式表示被动的意思。）

（辨析：request 语气客气，侧重"请求"；require 则侧重"要求"，有客观需要、或权威的内涵。）

requirement /rɪˈkwaɪəmənt/ n. 要求；规定；标准

meet/satisfy/fulfil the requirements 符合要求

rescue /ˈreskjuː/ n. 救援、救助 vt. 救援、营救；救助

come/go to sb.'s rescue 赶去/来营救、救助某人

SAR = search and rescue 搜救

research /rɪˈsɜːtʃ/ n. 研究

resemble /rɪˈzemb(ə)l/ vt. 与…相似

reserve /rɪˈzɜːv/ vt. 保留；储备

（考题）It is for these people that I reserve the glowing hours, too good not to share.

residence /ˈrezɪdəns/ n. 居住；住处

resident /ˈrezɪdənt/ n. 居民

resign /rɪˈzaɪn/ vi. 辞职

resist /rɪˈzɪst/ vt. 抵抗；抵御 vi. 抵抗

resist (doing) sth. 抑制（做）某事

（考题）Malaria has five thousand genes, and its ability to change rapidly to defend itself and resist new drugs has made it nearly impossible to control.

resistant /rɪˈzɪstənt/ adj. 抵抗的，有抵抗力的

be resistant to . . . 对…有抵御能力

（考题）Unfortunately, in most parts of the world, malaria

parasites have become resistant to it.

resolution /ˌrezəˈluːʃn/ *n.* 决心；决议

　　adopt/pass a resolution 通过一项决议

resolve /rɪˈzɒlv/ *vi. vt.* 使分解；解决；决定

　　resolve sth. into ... 使某物分解成…

　　resolve sth. 解决某事

　　（考题）No other discipline systematically follows the ideals of wisdom, leadership, and capacity to resolve human conflict.

　　resolve (sb.) to do sth. （使某人）决心做某事

resource /rɪˈsɔːs/ *n.* 资源

　　natural resources 自然资源

respect /reˈspekt/ *n.* 尊重；方面

　　（考题）I have watched, very carefully and with great respect and admiration, the theory and practice of selling satisfaction and serving millions of people on a daily basis successfully. It is what Disney does best.

　　show/have respect for sb. 对某人表示尊重

　　（考题）Now I teach my players to have respect for other people and their possessions.

　　pay/give respect to sb. 对某人表示尊重、敬意

　　（考题）After her casket was placed at the Capitol, U. S. President Bush, members of Congress and ordinary Americans paid their respects.

　　in this/that respect 在这/那方面

　　with respect to ... 关于…；涉及…

　　vt. 尊重；尊敬

　　respect sb/sth. 尊敬某人/某事

　　（考题）I was old enough to move out on my own, so why can't I seem to ask my friends to respect my privacy?

respond /rɪˈspɒnd/ *vt.* 反应；回应

　　respond to ... 对…做出反应

　　（考题）Don't respond to any e-mails requesting information, no matter how official they look.

response /rɪˈspɒns/ *n.* 反应；回应

　　（考题）This new consumer response to the colors and shapes of

packages reminds producers and sellers that people buy to satisfy
both body and soul.

in response to ... 对…的回应

responsibility /rɪˌspɒnsəˈbɪlɪtɪ/ *n*. 责任

responsible /rɪˈspɒnsəbl/ *adj*. 负责的；负责任的

（考题）Young people should become responsible adults.

be responsible for sth. 负责…；对…承担责任

（考题）He knew very well the other party was responsible for
the accident.

be responsible to do sth. 负责做某事

rest /rest/ *n*. 休息；其余的部分

（考题）In our modern life，we have lost the rhythm between
action and rest.

at rest 静止；安宁

have/take a rest 休息一会儿

the rest 其余的部分

（考题）Campus crime mirrors the rest of the nation.

vi. 休息；保持某种状态

rest assured 放心

restaurant /ˈrestərɒnt，ˈrestərənt/ *n*. 餐馆；饭店

restore /rɪˈstɔː/ *vt*. （使）恢复；（使）回复

restrict /rɪˈstrɪkt/ *vt*. 限制；约束

（考题）The problem with the stereotypes is that they restrict
experience.

be restricted to ... 被限制在…（程度、范围等）

result /rɪˈzʌlt/ *n*. 结果

as a result 结果；因此

（考题）As a result，many seek their main satisfaction in
recreational activities.

as a result of ... 由于…的原因

（考题）For some reason as yet unseen，but perhaps as a result of
something in their environment，the new bees began to develop
extremely attacking personalities.

vi. 结果

result from ... 由…而产生

（考题）Every year, major health problems result from dangerous waste.

result in ... 导致了、产生了

（考题）His loneliness resulted in his interest in writing.

retire /rɪˈtaɪə/ *vi*. 退休；退下

return /rɪˈtɜːn/ *n*. 返回；送回；归还；

in return (for ...) （作为…的）交换；作为回报

（考题）In their skins they have tiny plants which act as "dustman", taking some of the waste products from the corals and giving in return oxygen which the animal needs to breathe.

a return ticket 往返票

vi. 返回　*vt*. 归还

return (to a place) 返回某地

（考题）If the hamburger is not what the customer expected, they may not return.

（注意：return 表示"返回"时，不要使用副词 back。）

return sth. to sb. 把某物归还给某人

（考题）— I'm afraid I can't return the book to you before Friday. — Take your time.

reunite /ˌriːjuːˈnaɪt/ *vi*. *vt*. （使）重新团聚；（使）重新统一

reunite with ... 与…重新团聚、结合

reveal /rɪˈviːl/ *vt*. 展现；揭示；暴露

（考题）The design of the "forever stamp" remains to be revealed.

revenge /rɪˈvendʒ/ *n*. 复仇；报仇

do sth. in/out of revenge (for sth.) 为复仇…而做某事

have/take revenge on sb. for sth. 因某事向某人复仇

vi. *vt*. 复仇；报仇

revenge sb. 为某人报仇

to revenge oneself on/upon sb. 向某人报仇

reverse /rɪˈvɜːz/ *vt*. 颠倒；翻转

（考题）Remember that in may Asian cultures, the order of first and last names is reversed.

review /rɪˈvjuː/ *n*. 复习　*vt*. 复习

revise /rɪˈvaɪz/ *vt*. 复习；修正

（考题）During the summer holidays there will be a revised schedule of services for the students.

revision /rɪˈvɪʒən/ *n*. 复习；修正

revolution /revəˈluːʃən/ *n*. 革命；变革

（考题）If you think that is a simple question，you have not been paying attention to the revolution that is taking place in bio-technology.

revolutionary /revəˈluːʃənərɪ/ *adj*. 革命的；

reward /rɪˈwɔːrd/ *n*. 报答；奖赏

（考题）Whenever we take honorable action we gain the deep internal rewards of goodness and a sense of nobility.

vt. 报答；奖励

reward sb. for (doing) sth. 因（做）某事而奖励某人

（考题）... you should encourage them to carry on until they feel calmer，and reward them for 'being brave'.

reward sb. with ... 用…奖励某人

（考题）In this case，a little bit of kindness was rewarded with a huge amount of benefits.

rhythm /ˈrɪðəm/ *n*. 节奏；韵律

rice /raɪs/ *n*. 稻；米；米饭

rich /rɪtʃ/ *adj*. 富有的；丰富的

be rich in ... 在…方面很富有

the rich 富人

rid /rɪd/ *n*. 摆脱

get rid of ... 摆脱…

（考题）We live in a society which wishes to get rid of risk.

vt.（ridded 或 rid，rid）**rid ... of sth.** 使…摆脱某事

（考题）... these men go out after dangerous animals like tigers，even if they say they only do it to rid the countryside of a threat.

ride /raɪd/ *n*. 骑（马等）；乘（车）

（考题）I've often wanted a ride in one；but of course policemen can't buy things like that.

go for a ride 骑马、乘车去兜风

（考题）The gunman had stopped a car for a ride，and then

pushed out the driver.

give sb. a ride 让某人搭乘

(考题)— Shall I give you a ride as you live so far away? — Thank you. It couldn't be better

vt. (rode, ridden) 骑;乘

(考题)He would ride home from work with Elvio every night and then ride back to the station alone.

rider /ˈraɪdə/ *n*. 骑马者

ridiculous /rɪˈdɪkjʊləs/ *adj*. 可笑的

rifle /ˈraɪfl/ *n*. 步枪

right /raɪt/ *n*. 右边;权利

(考题)But for a good many people in the world, in rich and poor countries, choice is a luxury, something wonderful but hard to get, not a right.

on the/sb.'s right 在(某人的)右边

to the right 向右

(考题)When 16-week-old and 22-week-old babies watched the toy train disappear behind the left side of the screen, they looked to the right, expecting it to reappear.

turn to the right 向右转

(同义词：**turn right, take the right trun**)

have a right to do sth. 有权做某事

adv. 右边;朝右地;就、正

right now/away 此刻;立即

(考题)The committee is discussing the problem right now. It will hopefully have been solved by the end of next week.

(考题)— Shall we go to the art exhibition right away? — It's all up to you.

adj. 右边的;正确的

all right (口)好的;对的;正确的;可以的

put/set sth. right 校正、纠正…

It's right to do sth. 做某事是正确的

(考题)Make sure you're in the right channel when you reach Passport Control.

ring /rɪŋ/ *n*. 环;戒指;电话

give sb. a ring 给某人打电话

   vi. *vt*.（rang, rung）铃响；按铃；打电话

ring sb.（up） 给某人打电话

ripe /raɪp/ *adj*. 成熟的

rise /raɪz/ *n*. 升起；上涨；增加

give rise to ... 促进、助长…

（考题）Why do more choices of goods give rise to anxiety?

   vi.（rose, risen）升起；升高；上涨；起立

（考题）The warmth of the land heats the air above, causing it to rise and tiny drops of water to fall as rain.

rise to one's feet 站立起来

risk /rɪsk/ *n*. 风险；冒险

take/run a risk/take risks 冒险

（考题）To be a good leader, you should think twice before taking risks.

take/run the risk of ... 冒…的危险

do sth. at the risk of ... 冒…的风险做某事

   vt. **risk（doing）sth.** 冒险（做某事）

（考题）These people are willing to risk being killed by floods or 100-kilometer-an-hour winds for the excitement of watching the storm close up.

river /'rɪvə/ *n*. 河流；江

road /rəʊd/ *n*. 路；道路

roar /rɔː/ *n*.（狮、虎等）吼声 *vi*. 吼叫；咆哮 *vt*. 大声说出

roast /rəʊst/ *vt*. 烤；烘；炙 *adj*. 烤过的

roast duck 烤鸭

rob /rɒb/ *vt*. 抢、夺；抢劫

rob sb. of sth. 抢夺某人的某物

（注意：rob 和 steal 除了意思上的差异外，在用法上也不同。steal sth. from sb.）

robber /'rɒbə/ *n*. 强盗

robbery /'rɒbərɪ/ *n*. 抢劫；抢劫案

robot /'rəʊbɒt/ *n*. 机器人

rock /rɒk/ *n*. 岩石；大石块；摇滚乐

rocket /'rɒkɪt/ *n*. 火箭

rod /rɒd/ *n*. 杆;针

    a fishing rod 钓鱼竿

role /rəʊl/ *n*. 角色;作用

    (考题)However，the role of genetic learning depends upon how similar the future environment is to the past.

    play a role in ... 在…中起作用/扮演角色

    (考题)But no matter how well the equipment works, operators of the equipment still play an important role.

roll /rəʊl/ *vi*. 滚动;转动 *vt*. 使滚动、转动 *n*. (一)卷

romantic /rəʊˈmæntɪk/ *adj*. 浪漫的;传奇的

roof /ruːf/ *n*. 屋顶

room /ruːm/ *n*. 房间;余地;空间

    (考题)There's more room for joy in her life — and it wasn't just writing.

    there's/have/leave room for ... 有…的余地

    (考题)What he said left no room for doubt.

    make room for ... 为…腾出空间

    (注意：room 表示"空间、余地"时是不可数名词。)

root /ruːt/ *n*. 根;根茎

rope /rəʊp/ *n*. 绳子;绳索

rose /rəʊz/ *n*. 玫瑰

rotten /ˈrɒtən/ *adj*. 腐烂的

rough /rʌf/ *adj*. 粗糙的;粗略的;风浪急的

    a rough idea 粗略的想法

    the rough sea 波涛汹涌的大海

round /raʊnd/ *adj*. 圆的;*adv*. 周围;附近 *prep*. 围绕

    round-the-clock 昼夜不停

route /ruːt/ *n*. 路线;航线

routine /ruːˈtiːn/ *n*. 例行公事;惯例 *adj*. 例行的;常规的

row /rəʊ/ *n*. 排;列 *vi*. 划(船)

    royal /ˈrɔɪəl/ *adj*. 王的;皇家的;王室的;庄严的;高贵的

rub /rʌb/ *v*. 摩擦;擦 *n*. 摩擦;擦

    rub against ... 与…摩擦

rubber /ˈrʌbə/ *n*. 橡胶;橡皮

rubbish /ˈrʌbɪʃ/ *n*. 垃圾;废物

rude /ruːd/ *adj.* 粗鲁的；粗糙的

ruin /ˈruːin/ *n.* 废墟；*vt.* 毁坏；毁灭；破坏

（考题）... if the weapons had actually been used, the result could have been the ruin of the human race, as well as of many kinds of animals.

rule /ruːl/ *n.* 规章；规定；管辖；*vt.* 统治；管辖；规定

（考题）In 1066 the Normans led by William defeated the Saxons and began their rule over England.

as a rule 通常

by rule 按照规定

make it a rule to do sth. 养成做某事的习惯

（考题）You should make it a rule to leave things where you can find them again

under the rule of/ruled by ... 在…的统治、管辖下

ruler /ˈruːlə/ *n.* 直尺

run /rʌn/ (run, run) *vi.* 奔跑；运行 *vt.* 经营、管理

（考题）John and his wife went to evening classes to learn how to run a DIY shop.

run down 用完；变得衰竭

run into 撞上；偶遇；陷入（某种境地）

（考题）Lost in thought, he almost ran into the car in front.

(sth.) run out ... 被用完

（考题）Traditional sources of energy like oil and gas may someday run out.

run out of sth. …用完

（考题）We will never run out of wave power. Besides, wave energy does not create the same pollution as other energy sources, such as oil or coal.

run over 车压过、撞伤

（考题）I find a coin in the road, go to get it and get run over. I'm in hospital and then I die.

n. 跑；路程；趋势

（考题）So his best chance was to make a run for it.

runner /ˈrʌnə/ *n.* 跑步的人

rural /ˈruərəl/ *adj.* 农村的；田园的；农业的

rush /rʌʃ/ *vi*. 冲、奔;仓促行动　　*vt*. 使冲、奔;催促

(考题)A special edition of a newspaper was rushed out and delivered all over the country.

rush through ... 匆忙做完

(考题)You can share other members' troubles and successes, give your children some attention, or just sit down for a moment instead of rushing through life aimlessly.

n. 冲;急速行动;繁忙时段

in a rush 匆匆忙忙

(考题)There, in the rush of his busy life, Jack had little time to think about the past and often no time to spend with his wife and son.

rush hours 交通高峰时段

Russian /'rʌʃən/ *adj*. 俄罗斯的;俄国人的　　*n*. 俄罗斯人;俄语

S

sack /sæk/ *n*. 麻袋;包

sacrifice /'sækrɪfaɪs/ *n*. 牺牲;祭献;祭品

　　make a sacrifice for ... 为⋯做出牺牲

　　(考题) He held her in his arms and felt a great sense of the sacrifice that his mother had made for him.

sad /sæd/ *adj*. 伤心的、悲哀的、难过的

sadden /'sædən/ *vt*. 使伤心、使悲哀

safe /seɪf/ *adj*. 安全的、平安的

　　be safe from ... 没有⋯危险的

　　be safe to ... 对⋯安全的

　　(考题)... but it is often difficult and expensive to get rid of these chemicals or to store them in a way safe to human life and the environment.

　　n. 保险柜

safety /'seɪftɪ/ *n*. 安全;平安

　　carry/take/bring sb. to safety 把某人带到安全的地方

　　safety belt 安全带

　　safety island 安全岛

　　safety lamp 安全灯

　　safety helmet 安全帽

　　for safety 为了安全

　　in safety 安全地

sail /seɪl/ *vi*. 航行　*vt*. 驾驶(船舶)　*n*. 帆;船

sailor /'seɪlə/ *n*. 水手;海员

sake /seɪk/ 缘故;利益

　　for. . . 's sake 为了⋯

salad /'sæləd/ *n*. 色拉;凉拌菜

salary /'sælərɪ/ *n*. 薪水

　　(辨析:salary 指文职人员按月领取的薪金;wage 常指体力劳动者按时或计件领取的工资,通常每周发放;pay 是最常用的词,指

对任何劳动所付的报酬。)

sale /seɪl/ *n*. 出售；销售

for sale 出售的

（考题）The two men worked together on developing the game and in 1948 it was offered for sale in the United States under its new name-"Scrabble".

on sale 出售的；廉价出售的

（考题）Nothing pleased me quite so much as to buy a bargain lot of them on sale for several pounds.

salesman /'seɪlzmən/ *n*. 推销员

salt /sɔːlt/ *n*. 盐

salty /'sɔːltɪ/ *adj*. 含盐的；咸的

same /seɪm/ *adj*. 同样的；同一的

all the same/just the same 仍然、还是、同样

the same (...) as ... 与…同样

（考题）It is time to realize that animals have the same right to life as we do and that there's nothing fair about a person with a gun shooting the harmless and beautiful creatures.

the same ... that ... 同样的；同一个

all the same to ... 对…来说一样、没有区别

（考题）— When shall we meet again? — Make it any day you like；it's all the same to me.

be the same with ... …也一样

（注意：形容词 same 前通常使用定冠词 the。但如果由 this，that 等指示代词时，则不再使用定冠词。）

sample /'sɑːmpl/ *n*. 样品；试样；事例

adj. 样品的；试样的

sand /sænd/ *n*. 沙

sandwich /'sænwɪdʒ/ *n*. 三明治

satellite /'sætəlaɪt/ *n*. 卫星

satisfaction /ˌsætɪs'fækʃən/ *n*. 满意

（考题）A lot of people take relatively little satisfaction in their jobs，because much of their work is ordinary and boring.

to the satisfaction of ... 使某人满意

satisfactory /ˌsætɪs'fæktərɪ/ *adj*. 令人满意的

far from (being) satisfactory 远不能令人满意

（考题）What he has done is far from satisfactory.

satisfy /'sætɪsfaɪ/ *vt.* 使满意；满足

satisfy the need/demand/requirement ... 满足需求/条件等

（考题）Each of these museums has tried to satisfy the public's growing interest in the field with new ideas.

be satisfied with ... 对…感到满意

（考题）If you are not satisfied with the watch after you get it, you may simply return it within 30 days.

Saturday /'sætədeɪ, 'sætɪdɪ/ *n.* 星期六

sauce /sɔːs/ *n.* 沙司；调味汁

saucer /'sɔːsə/ *n.* 茶碟；碟装物

the flying saucer 飞碟

save /seiv/ *v.* 救；挽救；拯救；节省；储蓄

（考题）Asian people tend to save more money.

save sb. from ... 从…中救了某人；使某人免除…

（考题）They had only basic ways of creating light, and yet they found a way of using this simple technology in isolated places to save ships from hitting rocks.

saving /'seiviŋ/ *n.* 救助；节省（*pl.*）积蓄；存款

say /sei/（said, said）*vt.* 说；说出；假定

say ... (to sb.) （对某人）说…

say that ... 说…

I dare say 我敢说，我想

n. 发言权；决定权

have the last say 有最终决定权

（辨析：say 一般作及物动词使用，后面要有宾语，表示说的内容；speak 和 talk 在表示"说话、谈论"时，常作为不及物动词，用法是：speak to sb. about sth. , talk to (with) sb. about sth. ；tell 的用法是 tell sb. sth. 或 tell sth. to sb. 。但在表示"向某人介绍…"时，可使用 tell sb. about sth. 的结构。）

saying /'seiiŋ/ *n.* 谚语；格言；俗话

scale /skeil/ *n.* 刻度；尺度；秤

scan /skæn/ *vt.* 快读；扫描

（考题）Tony is scanning the guidebook, looking for information

about Japan, where he will travel soon.

scarcely /ˈskeəslɪ/ *adv*. 几乎不;仅仅;简直不

（考题）I scarcely dare think of such things.

（见 hardly）

scare /skeə/ *vt*. 使惊恐;使害怕

scare sb. 吓唬某人

be scared of ... 害怕…

（考题）Almost every child is scared of something, from monsters in the cupboard to dogs in the park.

scarf /skɑːf/ *n*. 围巾;领巾

scene /siːn/ *n*. 景色;场景;现场;地点

on the scene 在现场（同义词：**on the spot**）

scenery /ˈsiːnərɪ/ *n*. 风景;景色

schedule /ˈʃedjuːl, ˈskedʒʊl/ *n*. 时间表;进度表;计划　*v*. 计划

a time schedule 时间进度表

as scheduled 按计划

on schedule 准时

scholar /ˈskɒlə/ *n*. 学者

scholarship /ˈskɒləʃɪp/ *n*. 奖学金

school /skuːl/ *n*. 学校;(大学)院、系;学派

go to school 上学;读书

at school 在学校

finish/leave school 毕业

after school 放学;毕业

science /ˈsaɪəns/ *n*. 科学;技能

（考题）It takes science to have the photo come out clearly and art to make a photo that has a good design and expresses feeling.

science and technology 科学技术

applied science 应用科学

natural science 自然科学

a Bachelor/Master/Doctor of Science 理学学士/硕士/博士

scientific /saɪənˈtɪfɪk/ *adj*. 科学的

scientist /ˈsaɪəntɪst/ *n*. 科学家

scissor /ˈsɪzə/ *n*. 剪刀

a pair of scissors 一把剪刀

scold /skəuld/ *vt.* 责备；训斥

scold sb. for (doing) sth. 因(做)某事责备某人

(考题)They often scold me for nothing.

score /skɔ:/ *n.* 得分；分数、成绩；二十个

(考题)In general the more question-asking the parents do, the higher the children's IQ scores.

a score of ... 二十个…

scores of ... 许多

(考题)Scores of people attended the special performance.

vt. 得(分) *vi.* 得分

score a goal/point 进了一球/获得一分

scratch /skrætʃ/ *vt.* 抓伤 *vi.* 抓；搔 *n.* 抓痕；抓、搔

scream /skri:m/ *vi.* (因恐惧、痛苦而)尖声叫喊 *n.* 尖叫声

screen /skri:n/ *n.* 屏幕；银屏

scrub /skrʌb/ *vt.* 用力擦洗；擦净

sea /si:/ *n.* 海；海洋

at sea 在海上；不知所措、茫然

(考题)The mountainous island was settled around the 5th century, supposedly by people who were lost at sea.

by sea 乘船；经海路

go to sea 出海；当海员

go to the sea 去海边(度假)

seabed 海底、海床

seafood 海鲜

seasick 晕船

seal /si:l/ *n.* 封条 *vt.* 加封

search /sɜ:tʃ/ *vt. vi.* 搜、搜查；搜寻

search (...) (for ...) 搜查(…)(找…)

(考题)The policemen are searching the building for the said bomb.

(注意：search 的宾语总是搜查的对象或是搜寻的地点，而想要找到的东西则跟在介词 for 后面。)

n. 搜查；搜寻

in search of/for ... 搜寻……

（考题）When women also moved to the cities in search of work，they found that it was increasingly separated by sex and that employment opportunities for women were limited to the lower-paid jobs.

seaside /ˈsiːsaɪd/ *n*. 海边

season /ˈsiːzən/ *n*. 季节；时节

　be in season 上市；当令时节

　（考题）Strawberries are not in season at this time of the year.

　be out of season 落市；时节不对；淡季

seat /siːt/ *n*. 座位

　take/have a seat 请坐

　vt. 使坐下

　（考题）He politely seated his lady in the knee-deep water and then sat down himself. All people around laughed and cheered.

　be seated 就坐

　（考题）Please remain seated；the winner of the prize will be announced soon.

second /ˈsekənd/ *num*. 第二

　second to 仅次于

　（考题）India is only second to China in population.

　second to none 胜过任何一个

　（考题）Fred is second to none in maths in our class，but believe it or not，he hardly passed the last exam.

　the second ... 刚…，就…（引导时间状语从句）

　（考题）The second Tom broke free，Jeb threw himself on the cougar，just as it jumped from the rock.

　（同义词：the minute ...，the moment ...，as soon as ...）

secondary /ˈsekəndərɪ/ *adj*. 第二的、次等的；另外的

secondhand /ˈsekəndhænd/ *adj*. 旧的；二手的；间接的

secret /ˈsiːkrɪt/ *n*. 秘密

　keep ... in secret 对…保密

　in secret 秘密地

　（考题）Discouraged photographers began following him in secret as though he were an easily-frightened giraffe.

secretary /ˈsekrətərɪ/ *n*. 秘书、书记员

section /sekʃən/ *n*. 部分

secure /sɪˈkjʊə/ *adj*. 安全可靠的；牢固的；确定的；有把握的

be secure from ... 不会受到…的影响、危害

（考题）Stay here and you will be secure from any danger.

be/feel secure about ... 对…感到放心

（考题）He felt a bit uneasy as he was not secure about the result of the exam.

be secure of ... 对…有信心

（考题）Don't worry. we're quite secure of his success.

vt. 使安全可靠；保险

secure onself against ... 为自己投保…险

security /sɪˈkjʊərɪtɪ/ *n*. 安全(感)；保护(物)；保证、保障

（考题）But security concerns come before profit.

in security 安全地

the UN Security Council 联合国安理会

see /siː/ (saw, seen) *vt*. *vi*. 看见；明白；确保

see sb. (do/doing sth.) 看见某人(做某事)

see that ... 明白…；确保…

（考题）You can see that birds have a language all their own.

see sb. off 为某人送行

（考题）Please remind me when he says he is going. I may be in time to see him off.

see ... as ... 把…看成…

（考题）We don't see it as a big problem. We just look forward to replacing it.

see to sth. 关心、注意…

（考题）It's something important and I hope you'll see to it yourself.

see (to it) that ... 关心、确保…

（考题）The people at Disney go out of their way to serve their "guests", as they prefer to call them, and to see that they enjoy themselves.

see through sb. /sth. 看穿某人/某事

（考题）False statements are easy to see through.

I see. 我明白了

（考题）— It's a top secret. — Yes，I see. I will keep the secret between you and me.

Let me see. 让我想想

seed /siːd/ *n.* 种子

seek /siːk/（sought，sought）*vt.* 寻求；探求

seek sth. 寻求、设法得到…

（考题）I seek friends whose qualities illuminate me and train me up for love.

seek after/for sth. 寻求、寻找…

seem /siːm/ *vi.* 好像、似乎

seem（to be）... 看起来…

（考题）She and I agree that，at certain times，we seem to be parts of the same mind.

It seems（to sb.）that ... （在某人）看来…

（考题）So it seems that this generation of parents is much more likely than parents of 30 years ago to treat their children as friends.

... seems to be/be doing/have done sth. ... 看来是/正在/已经…

（考题）The world seems to have become smaller to the author because life is disappointing.

seize /siz/ *vt.* 抓住；夺取

seize a chance 抓住机会

seldom /ˈseldəm/ *adv.* 难得；极少

（考题）Unlike the average art museum visitors, design museum visitors seldom feel frightened or puzzled.

（注意：这是一个表示否定意义的副词，更侧重于表示发生的频率。常可以和 scarcely、rarely 等替换使用。）

select /sɪˈlekt/ *vt.* 挑选、选择

（考题）Selecting a mobile phone for personal use is no easy task because technology is changing so rapidly.

select sth. from ... 从…中挑选…

selfish /ˈselfɪʃ/ *adj.* 自私的

sell /sel/（sold，sold）*v.* 卖、出售

（考题）The shopkeeper did not want to sell what he thought was not enough.

sell sth. to sb. 向某人出售某物

... sells well 销路很好

（考题）At first, it didn't sell very well.

semester /sɪ'mestə/ n. (美)学期

send /send/ (sent, sent) vt. 发送；派出；寄出 vi. 派人

send sb. sth. /send sth. to sb. 给某人送去…

（考题）We will send you full program descriptions at your request.

send ... to a place 将…派往/送往某地

（考题）There is a plan to send humans to Mars.

send sb. to do sth. 派某人去做某事

（考题）The National Park Service had to send water trucks to provide water for the visitors.

send for ... 派人去请/取…

（考题）As nobody here knows what is wrong with the machine, We must send for an engineer to handle the problem.

senior /'siːnɪə/ adj. 年长的；地位高的；(同名者中)老的

be senior to ... 比…年长/地位高

Bush Senior 老布什

n. 年长的人；地位高的人

（考题）He was my senior at college by two years.

sense /sens/ n. 感觉；意识、辨别力

sense of sight/hearing/smell/taste/touch 视/听/嗅/味/触觉

（考题）One might be poor, but that is no reason for losing one's sense of pride and self-dependence.

in a sense 从某种意义上说

（考题）In a sense, they are spending a significant amount of time in fruitless efforts as they multitask.

keep one's senses 保持清醒、理智

lose one's sense 失去理智

make sense 有意义；有道理

（考题）It is a speech that doesn't make sense.

make sense of ... 能理解…

There's no sense in doing sth. 没有理由做某事

（考题）There is no sense in making a child suffer like that.

the sixth sense 第六感觉、直觉

vt. 觉得；意识到、感觉到

（考题）Parapsychologists say that humans have a natural ability to sense when someone is looking at them.

sense sth. 意识到…

（考题）It has been discovered that a shark senses pressure using hair cells in its balance system.

sensible /'sensɪbl/ *adj.* 感觉得到的；明智的；合情理的

sensitive /'sensɪtɪve/ *adj.* 敏感的

be sensitive to/about ... 对…敏感

（考题）I'm afraid you were too sensitive about that. He meant no harm.

sentence /'sentəns/ *n.* 句子 *vt.* 宣判；判刑

sentence sb. to ... 宣判某人…

（考题）... then sentenced him to eighteen months in a special prison for criminal with mental disorders.

separate /'seprɪt/ *adj.* 分开的；单独的

（考题）... earlier generations of parents and children often appeared to move in separate orbits.

vt. /sepəreɪt/ 使分开

separate sth. (from ...) 把某物（与…）分开

（考题）Having been separated from other continents for millions of years，Australia has many plants and animals not found in any other country in the world.

September /səp'tembə/ *n.* 九月

series /'sɪəriːz，'sɪərɪz/（单复数相同） *n.* 系列；连续；套

a series of ... 一系列、一套…

（考题）By asking a series of questions in Para 5，the author mainly intends to indicate that found photographs allow people to think freely.

serious /'sɪəriəs/ *adj.* 严重的；严肃的

servant /'sɜːvənt/ *n.* 仆人；佣人；服务员

serve /sɜːv/ *vt.* 服务；起作用；招待；供应；上菜

serve ... 为…服务

（考题）According to the writer of the text，imagining the future will serve the interests of the present and future generations.

serve the/no purpose 起作用/不起作用

（考题）We changed our way of doing the job，but it didn't serve the purpose.

serve to do sth. 有助于…

（考题）The accident serves to show the serious consequence of being careless when driving.

serve as ... 起…的作用

（考题）The stone crosses in Ampthill were built to serve as a road sign in Ampthill Park.

service /ˈsɜːvɪs/ *n*. 服务；帮助

set /set/（set，set）*vt*. 放；设置；安置；调定

set about (doing) sth. 开始、着手做某事

（考题）It is time we set about our task.

set sth. aside 省出；搁置；摆到一边

（考题）Einstein likes Bose's paper so much that he set aside his own work and translated it into German.

set ... back 阻碍…；使受挫

set off 出发；引爆

（考题）However，what he didn't know was that the first sting had turned his body into a time bomb waiting for the next to set off an explosion.

set out 出发；陈列、安排

（考题）As we set out，I was shocked at how narrow the path was.

set out to do sth. 开始做某事

（考题）The writer has set out to write a book about the history of civilization of that country.

set sth. up 树立；建起

（考题）They decided to set up a shop to sell some of these donations to raise money for that appeal.

set ... ＋adj . 使…如何

（考题）So set your imagination free when you think about the future.

vi.（日、月等）落下

（考题）Look，how magnificent the setting sun is!

setting /'setɪŋ/ *n*. 安装；调节；布置；背景

settle /'setl/ *vt*. 安排；处理；使平静；使定居；结算

　settle sth. 解决…

　（考题）Remember that everything can be settled by discussion.

　vi. 停留；下陷、下沉；定居；沉淀

　settle down 定居

　（考题）They have settled down happily in their new home.

　settle down to sth. 专心做某事

　（考题）It's terrible — I can't settle down to anything today.

settler /'setlə/ *n*. 移居者；定居者

seven /'sevən/ *num*. 七

seventeen /'sevən'tiːn/ *num*. 十七

several /'sevrəl/ *adj*. 几个；若干

severe /sɪ'vɪə/ *adj*. 严重的；严厉的；严格的

　（考题）I'm afraid the wound he got is too severe.

sew /səʊ/（sewed，sewed 或 sewn）*v*. 缝

　a sewing machine 缝纫机

sex /seks/ *n*. 性；性别

shade /ʃeɪd/ *n*. 荫；阴凉处；色调；细微的差别

　（考题）As the sun rose higher，Arizona's famous heat seemed to roast us. There was no shade and our legs were aching.

shadow /'ʃædəʊ/ *n*. 影子；阴暗部分

　（考题）However，men quickly found more convenient and reliable ways of telling the time. They learned to use the shadows cast by the sun.

　vt. 投影于；遮蔽；盯梢、跟踪

　（辨析：shade 指光线不能直接照射到的阴凉处，或是挡住光线的物体，如百叶窗等；shadow 则强调某物体所投下的阴影。夏天躲避阳光只能去找 shade，而不是 shadow。）

shake /ʃeɪk/（shook，shaken）*vt* 摇动；晃动　*vi*. 摇晃；

　shake sth. 摇晃、晃动…

　（考题）Nothing seems to shake his attention.

　shake hands with sb. 与某人握手

　（考题）"Let's shake hands on it" sometimes means agreement

reached.

shall /ʃæl, ʃəl/ *v. aux.* 将要

（注意：表示将来时时，与第一人称主语连用；如果和第二、第三人称连用，则有命令、要求的含义。）

shallow /ˈʃæləʊ/ *adj.* 浅的

shame /ʃeɪm/ *n.* 羞愧、羞耻；遗憾

　it's a shame to do sth. /that ... 很遗憾/很不好意思…

shampoo /ʃæmˈpuː/ *n.* 洗发剂、香波

shape /ʃeɪp/ *n.* 形状

　（考题）Leaves are found on all kinds of trees, but they differ greatly in size and shape.

　in good shape 模样、状况很好

　（考题）I could never say the same for jogging, and I've found a lot of better ways to stay in shape.

　out of shape 变形、走样

　take shape 成形

share /ʃeə/ *vt.* 分享；共有

　share sth. with sb. 与某人分享…

　（考题）Certainly, most of the world's great religions order us to be open-hearted and share what we have with those less fortunate than ourselves.

sharp /ʃɑːp/ *adj.* 锋利的；尖锐的；敏锐的；急剧的

　sharp eyes/ears/mind 灵敏的目光 /耳朵/思维

　take a sharp turn 一个急转弯

　It's five o'clock sharp. 五点整

shave /ʃeɪv/ (shaved; shaved, shaven) *vt.* 刮胡子；修剪

sheep /siːp/ *n.* 羊；绵羊

sheet /ʃiːt/ *n.* 薄片；一张（纸、塑料布等）

shelf /ʃelf/ *n.* 架子；搁板

shell /ʃel/ *n.* 壳；贝壳

shift /ʃɪft/ *n.* 移动；转换；轮班

　（考题）Working hours from 5:00 pm on Mondays, Wednesdays & Fridays. Approximately five hours per shift.

　the day/night shift 日班/夜班

　vi. vt. 替换；转换；移动；晃动

（考题）The ship is not in position. It has to be shifted two meters ahead.

shine /ʃaɪn/ (shined,或 shone, shone) *vi*. 照耀；发光

ship /ʃɪp/ *n*. 船

shirt /ʃɜːt/ *n*. 衬衫

shock /ʃɒk/ *n*. 休克；震惊；震动

（考题）A person will often go through the various stages of sadness, shock, anger, and so on.

vt. *vi*. (使)震惊

（考题）Those photos shocked the public.

shoe /ʃuː/ *n*. 鞋

shoot /ʃuːt/ (shot, shot) *vt*. 射杀　*vi*. 射击、开枪；很快上升

shoot ... 射杀…

（考题）You must properly respect what you are after and shoot it cleanly and on the animal's own territory.

（考题）Her 1998 book about the death of her work shot to the top of the New York Times best-selling list as soon as it came out.

shoot at ... 朝…开枪

（考题）He shot at a bird, but missed it.

shop /ʃɒp/ *n*. 商店　*vi*. 购物

（考题）The nearby Quebec village of St. Pamphile is where they shop, eat and go to church.

go/do shopping 购物

（考题）And while they wait for their number, they can do a bit of shopping.

shopkeeper /ˈʃɒpkiːpə/ *n*. 店主

shopper /ˈʃɒpə/ *n*. 购物者；顾客

shore /ʃɔː/ *n*. 岸

go to shore 上岸

short /ʃɔːt/ *adj*. 短的；矮的；短缺的　*n*. 扼要、实质

In short 总而言之，实际上

（考题）... in short, people look on work as a path to ever-increasing consumption rather than a way to realize their own abilities.

be short of ... 缺乏…

（考题）What you are short of is self-confidence instead of ability.

shortage /'ʃɔːtɪdʒ/ *n*. 短缺；不足；匮乏

（考题）Energy shortage calls for buildings of new design.

shortcoming /'ʃɔːtkʌmɪŋ/ *n*. 缺点；不足之处

shortcut /'ʃɔːtkʌt/ *n*. 捷径

shorten /'ʃɔːtən/ *vt*. 使变短；缩短

（考题）Library Hours have been shortened to 7 hours a day (9:00 a.m.—4:00p.m.) from March 24 to March 30.

shortly /'ʃɔːtlɪ/ *adj*. 不久；立即

　　shortly after/before ... 在…之后/前不久

shortsighted /'ʃɔːtsaɪtɪd/ *adj*. 近视的；目光短浅的

shot /ʃɒt/ *n*. 射击；枪声

should /ʃʊd/ *v. aux*. 将要（shall 的过去式）；应该；万一

shoulder /'ʃəʊdə/ *n*. 肩膀 *v*. 肩负；承担

　　should to should 肩并肩

shout /ʃaʊt/ *vi*. 喊、叫； *vt*. 喊出、叫出

show /ʃəʊ/（showed，showed 或 shown）*vt*. 出示；展出；说明；表明 *vi*. 显现

　　show sth. to sb. 将某物出示给某人看

（考题）Through body language，humans give each other very subtle but clear signals that show emotions.

　　... show that ... 表明…

（考题）It has also given these architects a chance to show how they can make more out of less.

　　show sb. round/around/about (a place) 带某人游览（某地）

　　n. 展览；演出、节目

　　on show 展出

（考题）The touch-screen devices are on show at the Food Marketing Institute's exhibition here this week.

shower /'ʃaʊə/ *n*. 阵雨；淋浴

　　take/have a shower 洗淋浴

shrink /ʃrɪŋk/（shrank，shrunk 或 shrunk，shrunken） *vi*. 收缩；缩水；退缩

shut /ʃʌt/ (shut，shut) *vi*. 关上、闭上　*vt*. 关上

（考题）... people shut doors heavily in your face and politeness is disappearing.

shut down 关闭；停止运作

（考题）Fear causes the thinking brain to shut down，making the person unable to function at his or her best.

shut up 住口

shy /ʃaɪ/ *adj*. 害羞的；胆怯的

be shy of ... 对…感到害羞、胆怯；犹豫、不想做某事

sick /sɪk/ *adj*. 有病的

be sick of ... 对…感到厌烦

（考题）That cold January night，I was growing sick of my life in San Francisco.

sickness /ˈsɪknɪs/ *n*. 患病；疾病

side /saɪd/ *n*. 旁边、一侧；侧面

stand/be on sb.'s side 站在某人一边

（考题）On one side stand those who see clothes dryers as a waste of energy and a major polluter of the environment.

side by side 并排、并肩

（考题）Forty minutes north of Banff，side by side with the Banff National Park，sits world-famous Lake Louise.

on the other side of the coin 事情的另一面

side effect 副作用

（考题）They also found that unlike some standard cough treatments，theobromine caused no side effects such as sleepiness.

sidewalk /ˈsaɪdwɔːk/ *n*. 人行道

sight /saɪt/ *n*. 视力；看见；景象

at first sight 第一眼

at the sight of ... 看见…

（考题）The driver somehow panicked at the sight of me.

in/within sight 在视力范围之内、看见了

（考题）Anyone may drive too fast when he is in a hurry and no police cars in sight.

catch/have sight of ... 看见…

lose sight of ... 看不见…

（考题）However，because of the Bismarck's speed and the heavy fog，they lost sight of her.

out of sight 看不见

（考题）I watched until she was out of sight.

short-sighted 目光短浅的；近视的

（考题）However，most of our ideas about the future are really very short-sighted.

sightseeing /ˈsaɪtsiːɪŋ/ *n*. 观光、游览

go sightseeing 观光、游览

sign /saɪn/ *n*. 标记；招牌；手势；记号

（考题）Musicians often called him Pops，as a sign of respect for his influence on the world of music.

sign language 身势语

（考题）In a special school for the hearing-impaired，he learned sign language and got to mix with other disabled children.

vi. *vt*. 签名；打手势

（考题）— Must he come to sign this paper himself？ — Yes，he must.

（考题）The speaker signed to the audience to be quiet.

signal /ˈsɪɡnəl/ *n*. 信号

signal flag 信号旗

signal lamp 信号灯

vt. 发出信号；向某人发信号

（考题）The best time to signal the rescuers is during the day.

signature /ˈsɪɡnɪtʃə/ *n*. 签名

significance /sɪɡˈnɪfɪkəns/ *n*. 重要性；意义

significant /sɪɡˈnɪfɪkənt/ *adj*. 意义重大的

silence /ˈsaɪləns/ *n*. 沉默；寂静

silent /ˈsaɪlənt/ *adj*. 沉默的；寂静的

keep silent 保持安静

silk /sɪlk/ *n*. 丝；绸

silly /ˈsɪlɪ/ *adj* 愚蠢的；傻的

silver /ˈsɪlvə/ *n*. 银；银色

similar /ˈsɪmɪlə/ *adj*. 相似的、类似的

be similar to ... 与…相似

（考题）Many French words are similar to English ones.

simple /ˈsɪmpl/ *adj*. 简单的；简易的、朴素的

since /sɪns/ *prep*. *conj*. 从…起（到现在）；

　　since then 从那时起

　　ever since 从那时起

　　It is/has been ... (time) since ... 从…到现在已经…时间了

（考题）It's thirty years since we last met.

（辨析：since 的含义是"从那时到现在"，因此，常和动词的现在完成时连用；from then on，after that 也可表示"从那以后"，但不一定强调"到现在"，常和过去时连用。）

conj. 既然（引导原因状语从句）

（考题）It's not so common nowadays to treat food that way, since you hardly ever bake your own bread.

sincere /sɪnˈsɪə/ *adj*. 真诚的

sincerely /sɪnˈsɪəlɪ/ *adv*. 真诚地

　　yours sincerely 你的真诚的（信中落款前使用）

sing /sɪŋ/ （sang, sung）*vi*. *vt*. 唱；唱歌

singer /ˈsɪŋə/ *n*. 歌手；唱歌的人

single /ˈsɪŋɡəl/ *adj*. 单一的；单个的

sink /sɪŋk/ （sank, sunk）*vi*. 下沉；沉没；降低　*vt*. 使下沉、沉没；降低

（考题）They sank all ships in case the enemy would get them.

（考题）Her heart sank as the list ended without her name.

sir /sɜː/ *n*. 先生

sister /ˈsɪstə/ *n*. 姐姐；妹妹

sit /sɪt/ （sat, sat）*vi*. 坐

　　sit down 坐下

　　sitting room 起居室

site /saɪt/ *n*. 场所；地点

　　worksite 工地

situation /ˌsɪtjuˈeɪʃən/ *n*. 情况；局面；形式

six /sɪks/ *num*. 六

sixteen /ˈsɪksˈtiːn/ *num*. 十六

sixty /ˈsɪkstɪ/ *num*. 六十

size /saɪz/ *n*. 尺寸、大小

skate /skeɪt/ *vi*. 溜冰、滑冰

ski /skiː/ *vi*. 滑雪

skier /ˈskiːə/ *n*. 滑雪者

skill /skɪl/ *n*. 技能；技巧

（考题）Being able to multitask — doing several things at the same time — is considered a welcome skill by most people.

skillful /ˈskɪlfʊl/ *adj*. 有技能的；灵巧的

skim /skɪm/ *vt*. 浏览；略读

skim (through)... 粗略地阅读…

（考题）Give me a few minues to skim through the notes, please.

skin /skɪn/ *n*. 皮肤

skirt /skɜːt/ *n*. 裙子

sky /skaɪ/ *n*. 天空

slang /slæŋ/ *n*. 俚语

slave /sleɪv/ *n*. 奴隶

slavery /ˈsleɪvərɪ/ *n*. 奴隶制

sleep /sliːp/（slept，slept）*vi*. 睡觉

sleep late 睡懒觉

（辨析：sleep late 表示"睡懒觉"。"睡得晚、熬夜"是 go to bed late 或 sit/stay up late at night。）

n. 睡；睡眠

go/get to sleep 睡着

（辨析：go to sleep 表示"睡着"，"就寝"是 go to bed，如：I went to bed early, but couldn't go to sleep until midnight。）

sleepy /ˈsliːpɪ/ *adj*. 要睡的；困倦的

slice /slaɪs/ *n*. 薄片

slide /slaɪd/ *n*. 滑动；滑梯；幻灯片

slight /slaɪt/ *adj*. 细小的；细微的

slim /slɪm/ *adj*. 苗条的

slip /slɪp/ *vi*. 滑跤；打滑； *n*. 纸片；纸条

slippery /ˈslɪpərɪ/ *adj*. 滑的

slow /sləʊ/ *adj*. 缓慢的 *adv*. 缓慢地

vt. *vi*. （使）缓慢

（考题）We all have to do at least something to slow down the

process of global warming.

small /smɔːl/ *adj* . 小的

smart /smɑːt/ *adj* . 美丽的；时髦的；聪明的

smash /smæʃ/ *vi* . *vt* . 捣毁；捣碎；猛冲；碰撞　　*n* . 撞击；猛拍

smell /smel/ *n* . 气味

vt . (smelt，smelt) 闻…的气味；嗅出…

(考题)He could smell the rain coming.

smell of . . . 有…的气味

(考题)You must have smoked a lot. your clothes smell of tobacco smoke.

link v . **smell ＋ *adj* ./like/as if . . .** 闻起来…

(考题)The little white wooden house smells as if it hasn't been lived in for years.

smile /smaɪl/ *n* . 微笑　　*vi* . 微笑

smog /smɒg/ *n* . 烟雾

smoke /sməʊk/ *n* . 烟；*vi* . *vt* . 抽烟；

smoking /ˈsməʊkɪŋ/ *n* . 抽烟

smoky /ˈsməʊkɪ/ *adj* . 有烟的；烟雾弥漫的

smooth /smuːð/ *adj* . 平稳的；平静的

snack /snæk/ *n* . 小吃；快餐

snake /sneɪk/ *n* . 蛇

sneeze /sniːz/ *n* . 喷嚏　　*vi* . 打喷嚏

snow /snəʊ/ *n* . 雪　　*vi* .下雪

so /səʊ/ *adv* . 这么；如此；因此

so that . . . 为的是…；以至、结果…

(考题)Products also need to have a short lifespan so that the public can be persuaded to replace them within a short time.

so . . . that . . . 如此、非常…以至于…

(考题)There are so many problems that can get you down.

so as to . . . 为的是

(考题)All these gifts must be mailed immediately so as to be received in time for Christmas.

soap /səʊp/ *n* . 肥皂

soccer /ˈsɒkə/ *n* . (英式)足球

sociable /ˈsəʊʃəbəl/ *adj* . 交际的；社交的

social /ˈsəʊʃəl/ *adj.* 社会的

society /səˈsaɪətɪ/ *n.* 社会

sock /sɒk/ *n.* 短袜

sofa /ˈsəʊfə/ *n.* 沙发

soft /sɒft/ *adj.* 软的;轻的

software /ˈsɒftweə/ *n.* 软件

soil /sɔɪl/ *n.* 泥土;土壤

solar /ˈsəʊlə/ *adj.* 太阳的

soldier /ˈsəʊldʒə/ *n.* 士兵;军人

solid /ˈsɒlɪd/ *n.* 固体　*a.* 固体的;固态的;实心的

solution /səˈluːʃən/ *n.* 解决;解决方法;溶液

a solution to/of/for ... 解决…的方法

（考题）... philosophy is the only solution to all the problems in the world.

solve /sɒlv/ *vt.* 解决;解答

（考题）Not only governments but ordinary people as well must work together to solve the problem.

some /sʌm/ *adj.* 一些;几个　*pron.* 几个;若干个

somebody /ˈsʌmbɒdɪ/ *pron.* 某人

somehow /ˈsʌmhaʊ/ *adv.* 不知怎么地;以某种方式

someone /ˈsʌmwʌn/ *pron.* 某人

something /ˈsʌmθɪŋ/ *pron.* 某事

make something of oneself 取得成功

（考题）They don't see men succeeding in society so it doesn't occur to them that they could make something of themselves.

something like ... 诸如;就像

（考题）If you leave your bike in a strange place，put it near something like a big stone or a tree.

something like that 大致如此;诸如此类

have something to do with ... 与…有联系、有牵连

（考题）I'm told that quite a few women had something to do with the terrorist attack and the explosion.

sometime /ˈsʌmtaɪm/ *adv.* (过去或将来尚未明确的)某个时候

（考题）An evaluation of it will be made sometime this year.

sometimes /ˈsʌmtaɪmz/ *adv.* 有时

somewhere /ˈsʌmweə/ *adv*. 某处

son /sʌn/ *n*. 儿子

song /sɒŋ/ *n*. 歌;歌曲

　pop songs 流行歌曲

soon /suːn/ *adv*. 不久;很快

　soon afterward 不久以后、很快

　(考题)Soon afterward，I received a Christmas present from them.

　as soon as ... 刚…,就…

　(考题)As soon as you become a member，you'll immediately have the right to our money-saving plan!

　as soon as possible 尽可能…;越…越好

　sooner or later 早晚;总有一天

　(考题)There is no way to stop all flooding — sooner or later nature will produce something that will beat even the strongest defenses.

　no sooner ... than ... 一…就…

　(考题)He had no sooner got to the lab than he set out to do the experiment.

sore /sɔː/ *adj*. 痛的

sorrow /ˈsɒrəʊ/ *n*. 悲哀;悲痛

sorry /ˈsɒrɪ/ *adj*. 遗憾的;难过得;抱歉的

　be sorry for ... /to do sth. /that ... 为…而感到遗憾、难过

sort /sɔːt/ *n*. 种类

soul /səʊl/ *n*. 灵魂

　body and soul 身心

　(考题)... people buy to satisfy both body and soul.

sound /saʊnd/ *n*. 声音 *adj*. 健康的;合理的;有效的

　(考题)It provides sound methods for distinguishing good from bad reasoning.

　sound asleep 酣睡

　vt. 发出声音 link. *v*. 听起来…

　(考题)The ideas expressed in foreign words sound new.

　(考题)Although this may sound like a simple task，great care is needed.

soup /suːp/ *n*. 汤

source /sɔːs/ *n*. 来源；出处

   the source of ... …的源头、来源

south /saʊθ/ *n*. 南方；南面 *adj*. 南方的

southeast /ˌsaʊθ'iːst/ *adv*. 向东南方

southern /'sʌðən/ *adj*. 南方的

southwest /ˌsaʊθ'west/ *adv*. 向西南方向的

sow /səʊ/ *vt*. 播种

soybean /'sɔɪbiːn/ *n*. 黄豆；大豆

space /speɪs/ *n*. 空间；天空

   （考题）The biggest advantage of this new system is that it saves time and space.

   （考题）Once in space, it can perform for a few months or up to several years, communicating information that could help find the signs of earthquakes.

   （注意：在表示"太空"时，space 前面不使用定冠词。但在表示"空间、场地"时，可以有冠词。）

spacecraft /'speɪskrɑːft/ *n*. 宇宙飞船

spaceship /'speɪsʃɪp/ *n*. 宇宙飞船

spade /speɪd/ *n*. 铲子；锹

Spain /speɪn/ *n*. 西班牙

Spanish /'spænɪʃ/ *adj*. 西班牙的；西班牙人的；*n*. 西班牙人；西班牙语

spare /speə/ *adj*. 业余的；空闲的；备用的

   spare time 业余时间

   spare parts 备件

   vt. 留出；节省；宽恕

   spare sb. a few minutes 留给某人几分钟时间

   （考题）I intended to compare notes with a friend, but unfortunately they couldn't spare me even one minute.

   spare no efforts to do sth. 不遗余力地做某事

   （考题）Food safety is highly important, so the government spares no efforts to prevent food pollution.

speak /spiːk/ (spoke, spoken) *v*. 说话；演讲

   speak about sth. to sb. 和某人谈论某事

speak ... (a language) 说某种语言

speaker /'spi:kə/ *n*. 说话者；演讲者

special /'speʃəl/ *adj*. 特殊的；专门的

specialized /'speʃəlaızd/ *adj*. 特殊的；专门的；

（考题）After passing "Traditions I", the employees go on to more specialized training for their specific jobs.

be specialized in ... 有…方面知识、特长的

species /'spi:ʃi:z/ *n*. （单复数相同）种类

speficic /spe'sıfık/ *adj*. 明确的；特定的

spectator /'spekteıtə/ *n*. 观众；旁观者

speech /spi:tʃ/ *n*. 发言；演讲

make/deliver a speech 发表演说

speed /spi:d/ *n*. 速度

at high/low speed 高速/低速

at full/top speed 全速

at a speed of ... 以…的速度

（考题）But now they are on the move, heading northwards in countless millions towards Central and North America, and moving at the alarming speed of 200 miles a day.

vi. (speeded，或 sped, sped) **speed up** 加速

（考题）If you ask your brain to learn, it will learn. And it may even speed up while in the process.

spell /spel/ (spelled，或 spelt, spelt) *vt*. 拼写；

spend /spend/ (spent, spent) *vt*. 花费；度过

spend ... (time, money, etc) on ... 在…上花费时间、金钱

（考题）... the better you are at managing the time you devote to your studies, the more time you'll have to spend on your outside interests.

spend ... doing sth. 花费…做某事

（考题）I have a beautiful teenage daughter who spends an hour making up her face in front of the mirror every day.

（注意：spend 的主语是人，而不能是事，或先行 it。比较 take 的用法。）

spider /'spaıdə/ *n*. 蜘蛛

spin /spın/ (spun, spun) *vt*. 纺织；旋转

spirit /'spɪrɪt/ n. 精神

(考题)On the road of life，the help of strangers can lighten our roads and lift our spirits.

in high /great spirits 心情好

in low /poor spirits 心情不好

(考题) Blamed for the breakdown of the school computer network，Alice was in low spirits.

spit /spɪt/ vi. 吐痰；吐口水　　vt. 吐出；说出

spite /spaɪt/ n. 怨恨

in spite of ... 尽管；不顾

(考题)He reached his goals in spite of his disability.

(同义词：despite)·

splendid /'splendɪd/ adj. 极好的；辉煌的；壮丽的

split /splɪt/ (split, split) vt. 劈开；切开；使破裂　vi. 裂开；

spoil /spɔɪl/ (spoiled，或 spoilt，spoilt)　　vt. 糟蹋；毁坏；宠坏

(考题)What we are sure about is the need to prevent children from being spoiled.

spoken /'spəʊkən/ adj. 口头的

spoken English 英语口语

sponsor /'spɒnsə/ vt. 资助；主办　　n. 发起人，赞助人

spoon /spuːn/ n. 匙；调羹

sport /spɔːt/ n. 运动

individual sports 个人运动

team sports 团体运动

sportsman /'spɔːtsmən/ n. 运动员

sportsmanship /'spɔːtsmənʃɪp/ n. 运动员精神；运动员品格

spot /spɒt/ n. 点

on the spot 在现场

spread /spred/ (spread, spread) vi. 传播；散开　vt. 传播；撒开

(考题)I learned how people used stories to spread their culture.

(考题)Funfairs were huge things that spread for miles around you with noise and lights and exciting danger.

spring /sprɪŋ/ n. 春天；弹簧；泉　　v. 跳跃，弹出

spy /spaɪ/ n. 特工；间谍　　vi. 侦查；刺探

spy into ... 打探、刺探…

spy on sb. 暗中监视某人

square /skweə/ *n*. 广场;方形;平方 *adj*. 方形的

　square meter 平方米

squeeze /skwi:z/ *vt*. 榨;挤;榨取

stable /'steɪbl/ *adj*. 稳定的;安定的

stadium /'steɪdɪəm/ (*pl*. ~s 或 stadia) (露天)体育场

staff /stɑ:f/ *n*. (全体)工作人员

stage /steɪdʒ/ *n*. 舞台;阶段

　(考题)I can play upon the stage like a child and make the crowd laugh and laugh with them.

　at this stage 眼下;在这个阶段

　(考题)Need to change your journey at any stage?

　by stages 分阶段

　(考题)The plan will be carried out by stages.

　stage by stage 逐步地

stair /steə/ *n*. 楼梯

staircase /'steəkeɪs/ *n*. 楼梯

stall /stɔ:l/ 货摊;书亭

stamp /stæmp/ *n*. 邮票 *vt*. 盖印;盖章;贴邮票

stand /stænd/ (stood, stood) *vi*. 站;站立 *vt*. 容忍、忍受

　stand up 起立

　stand by 袖手旁观

　(考题)There are three reasons why we tend to stand by doing nothing.

　stand for ... 代表…

　(考题)These words, which I have just made up, have to stand for things and ideas that we simply can't think of.

　stand out 突出;占据显著位置

　stand (doing) sth. 忍受…

　(考题)Modern plastics can stand very high and very low temperatures.

standard /'stændəd/ *n* 标准;水平

　(考题)... a standard room with full board will cost less than $100 a night.

　up to the standard 达到、符合标准

below the standard 低于标准、不符合标准

meet/satisfy/fulfil the standard 达到标准

（考题）Special classes are necessary to keep the school standards.

star /stɑː/ *n.* 星星；明星

a pop star 流行歌手

stare /steə/ *vi.* 凝视；注视

stare at ... 凝视…

start /stɑːt/ *vi.* 开始；出发 *vt.* 开始；发动

start to do/doing sth. 开始（做）某事

start out 出发

start the engine 发动

starvation /stɑːˈveɪʃən/ *n.* 饥饿

starve /stɑːv/ *vi.* 挨饿；饿死 *vt.* 使挨饿

starve sb. to death 把某人饿死

starve for sth. 渴望得到某物

state /steɪt/ *n.* 状态；国家；(美)州

（考题）At the time I was astonished by what appeared to me to be his completely abnormal mental state.

vt. 陈述；声明

（考题）A recent report stated that the number of Spanish speakers in the U. S. would be higher than the number of English speakers by the year 2090.

statement /ˈsteɪtmənt/ *n.* 陈述；声明

（考题）A statement of opinion by one writer may be re-stated as fact by another, who may in turn be quoted by yet another.

station /ˈsteɪʃən/ *n.* 站；车站 *vi.* 驻扎

a railway station 火车站

stationery /ˈsteɪʃənərɪ/ *n.* 文具

statue /ˈstætjuː/ *n.* 雕像

stay /steɪ/ *vi.* 停留；暂住 *link. v.* 保持…

（考题）So we have the dating shows where winners either pair off or stay true to their partners outside the TV studio.

steady /ˈstedɪ/ *adj.* 稳的；稳定的；持续的

steak /steɪk/ *n.* 牛排

steal /sti:l/ (stole, stolen) *vt*. 偷、偷窃 *vi*. 偷偷溜去

steal sth. (from sb.) 偷(某人的)…

(考题) Ana Luz has been told she could end up behind bars unless she can control the desire to steal from shops.

steal into/out of/away... 偷偷溜进/溜出/离开等

(考题) She had to steal into Bieber's bedroom and to watch him secretly.

steam /sti:m/ *n*. 水蒸汽；水汽

steamship /'sti:mʃip/ *n*. 汽船

steel /sti:l/ *n*. 钢

steep /sti:p/ *adj*. 陡峭的；险峻的

steer /stiə/ *vt*. 驾驶

step /step/ *n*. 步子；台阶；步骤；措施 *vi*. 挪动脚步

in/out of step with... 与…步调一致/不一致

step by step 一步一步地

take steps to do sth. 采取措施做某事

stick /stik/ *n*. 棍；拐杖 *vi*. (stuck, stuck) 坚持 *vt*. 刺；粘贴

stick to... 坚持…

(考题) But he stuck to it and did a lot of extra work after school.

be stuck with... 遇到困难,不知如何进行

... but now I am stuck with this number and everything it means.

still /stil/ *adv*. 仍然、还 *adj*. 静止的；寂静的

stimulate /'stimjuleit/ *vt*. 刺激；激励

(考题) ASIBOs may even one day have games that can help stimulate older people's minds.

stimulate sb. to do sth. 激励某人做某事

(考题)... but which are actually designed to stimulate a desire to own a gun.

stir /stɜ:/ *vt*. 搅动；激动；扰乱

stock /stɒk/ *vt*. 备货；n. 储存；存货；股票

be stocked with... 存有…

in/out of stock 有存货/没有存货

(考题) Sorry, but what you want is out of stock now.

stock market 股票市场

stocking /ˈstɒkɪŋ/ *n*. 长筒袜

stomach /ˈstʌmək/ *n*. 胃

have no stomach for ... 对…没有兴趣

stone /stəʊn/ *n*. 石头；石块

a stone's throw 一石之遥

the stone age 石器时代

stop /stɒp/ *n*. 停止

come to a stop 停止

vi. *vt*. **stop (doing) sth.** 停止(做)某事

(考题)This is not to suggest that we should stop using SAT scores in our college admission process.

stop (sth.) to do sth. 停下(某事)去做某事

(考题)Have you ever stopped to realize how much less self-conscious you would be on such occasions if good table manners had become a habit for you?

stop sb. (from) doing sth. 阻止某人做某事

(考题)People believed nothing could stop the brain slowing down.

(见 prevent)

store /stɔː/ *vt*. 贮存、贮藏 *n*. 贮存

have/keep sth. in store 贮存某物

(考题)When she first arrived in China, she wondered what the future might have in store for her, but now all her worries are gone.

storekeeper /ˈstɔːkiːpə/ *n*. 零售商；店主

storey /ˈstɔːrɪ/ *n*. 楼层；层

a five-storeyed building 一幢五层楼房

storm /stɔːm/ *n*. 暴风雨；暴风雪

story /ˈstɔːrɪ/ *n*. 故事；小说；借口；理由

stove /stəʊv/ *n*. 炉子

straight /streɪt/ *adj*. 直的 *adv*. 直地；一直往前

go straight ahead 一直往前走

(考题)But there are a few people who will get into their cars and go straight for the center of the storm.

straight away 立即、马上

strand /strænd/ *vt*. 搁浅；使陷于困境

    be/get stranded in ... 被困于…

strange /streɪndʒ/ *adj*. 奇怪的；陌生的

stranger /ˈstreɪndʒə/ *n*. 陌生人

straw /strɔː/ *n*. 稻草

strawberry /ˈstrɔːberɪ/ *n*. 草莓

stream /striːm/ *n*. 河；溪

street /striːt/ *n*. 街道；路

strength /streŋθ/ *n*. 力量；强度

    （考题）We miss the guide telling us where to go, the food providing us with strength, the quiet giving us wisdom.

strengthen /ˈstreŋθən/ *vt*. 加强；强化

    （考题）I can respect reasons like these, but they are clearly different from the need to strengthen your high opinion of yourself.

stress /stress/ *n*. 应力；紧张

    （考题）We say this to one another as if our tireless efforts were a talent by nature and an ability to successfully deal with stress.

    lay/put stress on ... 强调…

    （考题）We should lay greatest stress on safety in doing everything.

stretch /stretʃ/ *n*. 伸展；一片（区域）；一段（时间）

    （考题）What came in sight is a vast stretch of the sunlit beach.

    vt. *vi*. 伸展；铺开

    （考题）The first rays of sunlight stretched across the sea.

strict /strɪkt/ *adj*. 严格的；严密的；严谨的

    （考题）It has strict rules about visiting hours.

    be strick in ... 在…方面很严格

    be strick on/with sb. 对某人要求很严格

    （考题）Strict with myself, I included only once a title I might have read several times.

strike /straɪk/（struck, struck 或 striken）*v*. 敲、击；触及；突然想到；感受到；罢工

    （考题）When sunlight strikes an object, some of the energy is

absorbed and some is reflected.

(考题)A good idea suddenly struck me.

Strike while the iron is hot. 趁热打铁

n. 罢工;打击

be/go on strike 罢工

(考题)The workers will go on strike if the demands they put forward are turned down.

string /strɪŋ/ *n*. 细绳

strip /strɪp/ *n*. 条;带状物

strive /straɪv/ (strived 或 strove, striven) *vi*. 奋斗;努力

　strive for ... 为…而努力;争取得到…

(考题)He has been striving for recognition as an artist.

　strive to do sth. 争取、努力做某事

(考题)We all will strive to complete the task.

strong /strɒŋ/ *adj*. 强壮的;强烈的;有力的

structure /ˈstrʌktʃə/ *n*. 结构;构造

struggle /ˈstrʌgl/ *n*. 斗争

(考题)To sum up, understanding reality is a necessary struggle for artists of all periods.

　vi. **struggle to do sth.** 努力、争取做某事

(考题)Through determination, she had learned to read and write and struggled to become part of the leadership

　struggle for sth. 为…而奋斗

(考题)People there are struggling for better working conditions.

　struggle against sth. 与…进行斗争;努力克制…

　struggle with ... 与…进行斗争

student /ˈstjuːdənt/ *n*. 学生

studio /ˈstjuːdɪəʊ/ *n*. (画家)工作室;制片厂;播音室

study /ˈstʌdɪ/ *vt*. *vi*. 学习;研究　*n*. 学习;研究

(考题)The study provides evidence for changes in the workings of the brain with mental training.

　(见 learn)

stuff /stʌf/ *n*. 原料;材料;素材

　vt. 塞满;填满;填充

stupid /ˈstjuːpɪd/ *adj*. 愚蠢的;迟钝的

（考题）Tell a child he is "stupid", and he may play the role of a foolish child.

style /staɪl/ *n*. 风格；式样；方式

（考题）The most successful start-ups have been those by celebrities with specific personal style.

in a formal/easy style 以正式/随意的文体、风格

in style 入时的

out of style 过时

hair style 发型

subconscious /sʌbˈkɒnʃəs/ *adj*. 潜意识的；意识不清的

subject /ˈsʌbdʒekt/ *n*. 学科；科目；主题；主语

（考题）Conversations on subjects such as sex and drugs would not have taken place a generation ago.

adj. **be subject to ...** 顺从于…

（考题）We should be subject to the local laws.

vt. /səbˈdʒekt/ 使…顺从、驯服；征服

（考题）They are subjected to advertisements of gun producers who describe shooting as good for their health and guncarrying as a way of putting redder blood in the veins.

substance /ˈsʌbstəns/ *n*. 物质；材料

（考题）With the help of high technology, more and more new substances have been discovered in the past years.

in substance 基本上；实质上

（考题）What he told you, in substance, is believable.

substitute /ˈsʌbstɪtjuːt/ *vt*. 替换；代替

substitute sth. for ... 用某物代替、替换…

（考题）The researcher substituted a ball for the train when it went behind the screen.

substitute ... with/by sth. 用某物替换、替换…

（考题）They don't like coffee. So we substitute it with tea.

n. 替换物；替补

suburb /ˈsʌbɜːb/ *n*. 郊区

（考题）He lived in an unattractive London suburb and he spent much of his life sitting on Southern Region trains.

（注意：总称"郊区"时，用复数形式。）

subway /ˈsʌbweɪ/ *n.* 地铁；地道

succeed /səkˈsiːd/ *vi.* 成功；胜利

succeed in (doing) sth. 做成功某事

（考题）He will also play on the opponents among his buyers and succeed in getting a high price by encouraging two business competitors to bid against each other.

success /səkˈses/ *n.* 成功

（考题）I didn't want to make a success in the magazine business.

（注意：表示成功失败总体概念时是不可数名词。但表示某一项具体的成功或成功的人或事时，可作为可数名词）

successful /səkˈsesful/ *adj.* 成功的

such /sʌtʃ/ *adj.* 这样的；如此

such as ... 例如；如…之类

（考题）Dark-coloured surfaces, such as dark soil or forest, absorb more energy and help warm the surrounding air.

such ... as ... 诸如…

（考题）... studies show that childhood events, besides genes, may well cause such midlife diseases as cancer, heart disease and mental illness.

such ... that ... 这样、如此…以致…

（考题）Pop music is such an important part of society that it has even influenced our language.

no such ... 没有这种…

（考题）It may help you to know that there is no such thing as a perfect speech.

suck /sʌk/ *vt. vi.* 吸；吮

sudden /ˈsʌdən/ *adj.* 突然的；意外的

all of a sudden 突然

（考题）All of a sudden I started to feel rather hopeless.

suddenly /ˈsʌdənlɪ/ *adv.* 突然；忽然

suffer /ˈsʌfə/ *vi.* 遭受痛苦　*vt.* 遭受（痛苦、损失等）

（考题）They suffered great losses in the disaster.

suffer from ... 遭受…的痛苦

（考题）What feeling will you likely experience should a loved one suffer from Alzheimer's disease?

（注意：表示疾病等给人带来长期痛苦时，常使用 suffer from；其他笼统意义的痛苦、损失直接跟在 suffer 后面。）

suffering /ˈsʌfərɪŋ/ *n.* 痛苦

（考题）Their families and friends will experience mental sufferings.

（注意：复数形式表示种种痛苦、苦难。）

sufficient /sʌˈfɪʃənt/ *adj.* 充足的；足够的

（考题）Drexler in his book predicts a future world with sufficient material.

sugar /ˈʃʊɡə/ *n.* 糖

suggest /sʌˈdʒest/ *vt.* 建议；表明；暗示

suggest (doing) sth. 建议（做）某事

（考题）Circles often suggest happiness and peacefulness, because these shapes are pleasing to both the eye and the heart.

suggest that ... 建议…；表明、暗示…

（考题）Health experts suggest that a child take 12,000 steps each day and watch no more than two hours of television.

（考题）Statistics suggested that a decreasing number of children showed interest in reading.

（注意：如果 suggest 表示"建议"时，宾语从句中使用虚拟语气。但表示"表明、暗示"时，则使用陈述语气。）

suggestion /sʌˈdʒestʃən/ *n.* 建议

（考题）What do you think of his suggestion that a meeting be held to further discuss the problem?

（注意：在表示建议时，与 suggestion 有关的表语从句、主语从句及同位语从句中使用虚拟语气。）

suit /sjuːt/ *vt.* 合适；匹配

（考题）It doesn't suit me to work night shift.

n. 一套衣服

（考题）His back aches, his red suit feels like a spacesuit, his cheeks have gone tight from smiling for 12 hours — and still the kids keep coming and coming, like ants at a picnic.

suitable /ˈsjuːtəbl/ *adj.* 合适的，匹配的

be suitable for/to ... 适合…

（考题）What might be the most suitable title for the text?

suitcase /ˈsjuːtkeɪs/ *n.* 手提箱

sum /sʌm/ *n*. 总数;金额

(考题)He wrote to the government about his plan and was given £2,500 to start with, a sum worth much more in those days than it is now.

vt. 计算总数;总结、概括

to sum up 总而言之

(考题)To sum up, understanding reality is a necessary struggle for artists of all periods.

summarize /'sʌməraɪz/ *vt*. 总结;概括

(考题)Which of the following statements best summarizes the main idea of the passage?

summary /'sʌmərɪ/ *n*. 摘要;概要

summer /'sʌmə/ *n*. 夏天、夏季

sun /sʌn/ *n*. 太阳

sunbathe /'sʌnbeɪð/ *vi*. 沐日光浴

sunlight /'sʌnlaɪt/ *n*. 阳光;日光

sunrise /'sʌnraɪz/ *n*. 日出

Sunday /'sʌndeɪ/ *n*. 星期天

sunset /'sʌnset/ *n*. 日落

super /'sjuːpə/ *adj*. 超级的;极好的

superior /sjuː'pɪərɪə/ *adj*. 优越的;上级的;占优势的

be superior to ... 优于…

supermarket /'sjuːpəmɑːkɪt/ *n*. 超级市场

supervise /'sjuːpəvaɪz/ *vt*. 监督;管理

(考题)The manager supervises the work of these departments.

supper /'sʌpə/ *n*. 晚饭

supply /sʌp'laɪ/ *n*. 供应;供给

supply and demand 供求

vt. 提供;供应

supply sth. to sb. 向某人提供…

(考题)I wonder if you can supply some more information to us?

supply sb. (with) sth. 向某人提供…

(考题)Nowadays supermarkets supply us with all kinds of daily necessaries.

(辨析:见 provide)

support /sʌˈpɔːt/ *vt.* 支持；供养

support sth. /sth. 支持某人/某事

（考题）Although he received some money left by his father, it was not enough to support his design.

support sb. in doing sth. 支持某人做某事

（考题）I have strong faith in him and will support him in doing everything.

support oneself/one's family 养活自己/一家人

（考题）She wanted to earn more money to support her family.

n. 支持

suppose /səˈpəʊz/ *vt.* 假定；猜想；vi. 猜想

suppose that ... 估计

（考题）I don't suppose anyone will volunteer, will they?

it is supposed that ... 据估计

（考题）It is supposed that more than a hundred people will attend the lecture.

sb. is supposed to be/be doing/have done 据估计某人…

（考题）The research group is supposed to have made a breakthrough in their experiments.

sure /ʃʊə/ *adj.* 确信；有把握；肯定

be sure of/about sth. 对某事有把握

（考题）If you are not sure of your duty free allowances, or if you have something to declare, go through the Red Channel.

be sure that ... 确信、肯定…

（考题）— I'm thinking of the test tomorrow. I'm afraid I can't pass this time. — Cheer up! I'm sure you'll make it.

be not sure whether/if /when/why ... 吃不准、没有把握…

（考题）I'm not sure whether he can manage it.

be sure to do sth. 一定会做某事

（考题）Quite many people used to believe that disaster was sure to strike if a mirror was broken.

（同义词：**sb. will surely do sth.**）

make sure that ... 核实、使有把握

（考题）Make sure you're in the right channel when you reach Passport Control.

for sure 肯定(同义词：**for certain**)

(考题)And if you don't know for sure, it's a very likely that you can find out.

Sure.(回答对方的请求等)当然、当然可以。

(考题)— Can you show me Mr. Jaffer's office, please? — Sure. But I don't know if he is in at the moment.

(注意：sure 的主语不能是先行 it。如不能说 It is sure that he will come,而应将 sure 改成 certain。)

surely /ˈʃʊəlɪ/ *adv*. 当然；确定；肯定

(考题)Sutton's attractive style will surely inspire everyone present.

surf /sɜːf/ *vi*. 作冲浪运动；在网上浏览

surface /ˈsɜːfɪs/ *n*. 表面

surgeon /ˈsɜːdʒən/ *n*. 外科医生

surname /ˈsɜːneɪm/ *n*. 姓

surprise /səˈpraɪz/ *vt*. 使惊讶、使大吃一惊

　surprise sb. 使某人感到惊讶

　be surprised at/about/to do . . . 对…感到惊讶、意外

(考题)We were surprised by just how positive today's young people seem to be about their families.

　n. 惊奇、惊讶；意外

(考题)I didn't tell it to him earlier. I just wanted to give him a surprise.

　to sb. 's surprise 是某人感到惊讶的是

(考题)To our surprise, he finished the job in such a short time.

　in surprise 惊讶地

(考题)"How did they come to know it?" he asked in surprise.

surround /səˈraʊnd/ *vt*. 包围；环绕

　be surrounded with/by . . . 被…所环绕

(考题)We are surrounded by the word "diet" everywhere we look and listen.

surrounding /səˈraʊndɪŋ/ *n*. (复数时)环境；周围事物

(考题)People walking in cities ignore the surroundings because there is too much information to take in.

survey /səˈveɪ/ *vt*. 勘查；调查；　*n*. 勘查；勘测

（考题）More American people take their troubles with them on holiday，according to a new survey.

make a survey 调查

survive /sə'vaɪv/ *vi*. *vt*. 幸免于、幸存；在…之后依然活着

（考题）According to the passage，people most probably fail to survive if they do not keep themselves warm.

（考题）It's really lucky we survived the disaster.

suspect /sʌ'spekt/ *vt*. 怀疑

suspect sth. /sb. (of . . ./to be . . .) 怀疑某事/某人（是…/做…）

（考题）Bill was suspected of being infected with HIV after he found something wrong with his tongue.

suspect that . . . 怀疑…

（考题）The doctor suspected that he had been infected with HIV，the virus that leads to AIDS.

（辨析：如果使用 doubt，则用 whether/if 引导。见 doubt。）

suspend /sə'spend/ *vt*. 吊、悬（于空中或水中）；暂停；暂缓

（考题）The payment will be suspended until further agreement.

suspension /sə'spenʃən/ *n*. 悬挂；暂停

a suspension bridge 悬索桥

swallow /'swɒləʊ/ *n*. 燕子 *vt*. 吞下、咽下

（考题）Unlike vitamin C，leadership skills can't be easily swallowed down. They must be carefully cultivated.

swear /sweə/ (swore, sworn) *vi*. *vt*. 诅咒；发誓

swear to do sth. 发誓要做某事

（考题）He swore to keep it a secret.

swear that . . . 发誓说、诅咒说…

swear at . . . 咒骂…

sweat /swet/ *n*. 汗 *vi*. (sweated，或 sweat, sweat) 出汗

sweater /'swetə/ *n*. 厚运动衣；羊毛衫

Swede /swiːd/ *n*. 瑞典人

Swedish /'swiːdɪʃ/ *adj*. 瑞典的；瑞典人的 *n*. 瑞典人；瑞典语

sweep /swiːp/ (swept, swept) *vt*. 扫、打扫；猛退、拉；冲击

（考题）Millions of pounds' worth of damage has been caused by a storm which swept across the north of England last night.

sweet /swiːt/ *adj*. 甜的 *n*. (复数)糖果

swift /swɪft/ *adj*. 快速的；敏捷的

swim /swɪm/ *vi*. 游泳　*n*. 游泳

swing /swɪŋ/（swung, swung）*v*. 挥动；旋转；摆动

（考题）The east wind, which had swung around from the southwest, came to her help and pushed the boat towards the mountains.

Swiss /swɪs/ *adj*. 瑞士的；瑞士人的 n. 瑞士人

switch /swɪtʃ/ *v*. 开关　*n*. 开关

　　switch (...) on/off 打开/关掉…

Switzerland /ˈswɪtsələnd/ *n*. 瑞士

symbol /ˈsɪmbəl/ *n*. 象征

symbolize /ˈsɪmbəlaɪz/ *vt*. 象征

sympathy /ˈsɪmpəθɪ/ *n*. 同情；赞同

　　have sympathy for/with ... 对…深表同情

（考题）We wrote to express our sympathy for the victims in the accident.

　　be in sympathy with ... 同情、赞同…

（考题）They are in complete sympathy with your proposal.

　　out of sympathy 出于同情

symphony /ˈsɪmfənɪ/ *n*. 交响曲

symptom /ˈsɪmptən/ *n*. 症状

synthetic /sɪnˈθetɪk/ *adj*. 人工的；合成的

system /ˈsɪstəm/ *n*. 系统；体系；制度

　　the solar system 太阳系

　　a railway systme 铁路网

　　a social system 社会制度

　　the metric system 公制、米制

　　with system 有条理地

T

table /ˈteɪbl/ *n*. 桌子；表格

  at table 在吃饭

  lay /set the table 摆桌子（准备吃饭）

tablet /ˈtæblɪt/ *n*. 药片

tag /tæg/ *n*. 标签

tail /teɪl/ *n*. 尾巴

tailor /ˈteɪlə/ *n*. 裁缝

take /teɪk/（took，taken）*vt*. 拿、取；带走；就座、就职；买下；服药；纪录；花费；理解；

  take after sb. 长得像某人

  take … away 把…拿走

  take sth. down 取下；纪录；拆毁

  take effect 生效

  take it easy 别紧张、请随意

  take off 起飞；匆匆离开；脱下

（考题）We called to each other excitedly as the plane took off and circled around the Canyon.

  take on 呈现；承担

  take sth. over（from sb.）（从某人处）接收…

（考题）He took over the business from his father.

  take … to …（a place） 把…带去…

（考题）Here is a letter for Jack. Take it to his home, will you?

  take sth. up 占据；拿起；开始从事

（考题）These brain differences also explain the fact that more men take up jobs that require good spatial skills, while more women speech skills.

  take … for … 错把…当成…

（考题）The party guests took Merlin for a fool, but actually he wasn't.

  take … for granted 认为是理所当然

（考题）But now they seem to take it for granted that they can show up any time they like.

take to sth. 喜欢；沉溺于

（考题）In March，the month when we usually took to the woods again after winter，two friends and I set out to go exploring.

it takes sb. ... (time) to do sth. /it takes ... (time) for sb. to do sth. 某人花…(时间)做某事

（考题）It shouldn't take long to clear up after the party if we all volunteer to help.

tale /teil/ *n.* 故事；传说

fairy tales 神话故事

talent /ˈteɪlənt/ *n.* 天资、天赋；才能、才干；人才

（考题）Young people haven't been able to equate romance and talent with music.

have a talent for ... 有…的天赋

（考题）You have no talent. You will never be a pianist.

talk /tɔːlk/ *n.* 谈话、交谈

have a talk to/with sb. about sth. 与某人谈论某事

vi. vt. **talk to/with sb. about/of sth.** 与某人谈论某事

（考题）Getting paid to talk about the World Cup is a great job.

talk of sth. 说到、谈及某事

（考题）Parents should talk to each of their children frequently.

talk sth. over (with sb.) (与某人)讨论某事

（考题）It's something important and we'll have to talk it over in no time.

talk sb. over to (doing) sth. 说服某人同意某事

（考题）He was against the plan at first. But we managed to talk him over to our side.

（见 bring）

talkative /ˈtɔːlkətɪv/ *adj.* 健谈的

tall /tɔːl/ *adj.* 高的

tame /teɪm/ *vt.* 驯服　*adj.* 驯服的；顺从的；已开垦的

tank /tæŋk/ *n.* 箱；舱；坦克

tap /tæp/ *v.* 轻拍　*n.* 轻拍、轻叩；水龙头

tape /teɪp/ *n.* 带状物；磁带

target /ˈtɑːɡɪt/ *n*. 目标；对象

hit the target 击中目标

miss the target 错失目标；未能实现计划

task /tɑːsk/ *n*. 任务

taste /teɪst/ *vt*. 品尝 *link*. *v*. 尝起来…

（考题）Taste it and tell me how does it taste.

（考题）The coffee is wonderful! It doesn't taste like anything I have ever had before.

n. 味道；口味

（考题）Fermentation develops the rich taste of black tea.

have a taste for ... 对…有兴趣

（考题）She has no taste for this kind of things，I'm afraid.

to sb.'s taste 合某人的口味

（考题）I don't go in for rock 'n' roll. It's much too noisy and is not to my taste.

tax /tæks/ *n*. 税 *vt*. 征税

tea /tiː/ *n*. 茶

black tea 红茶

green tea 绿茶

teach /tiːtʃ/ (taught，taught) *vi*. 教 *vt*. 教

teach sb. sth. /teach sth. to sb. 教某人…

（考题）... young people should be taught certain skills to improve their sense of direction.

teach sb. (how) to do sth. 教某人做某事

（考题）School children must be taught how to deal with dangerous situation.

teach sb. a lesson 给某人以教训

teacher /ˈtiːtʃə/ *n*. 教师

team /tiːm/ *n*. 队

tear¹ /tɪə/ *n*. 眼泪

（考题）Tears also enable us to understand our emotions better; sometimes we don't even know we're very sad until we cry.

be in tears 流泪

（考题）The old man was almost in tears as he begged to let him take the bus home.

burst/break into tears 突然大哭起来

（考题）She just gets mad or bursts into tears.

move sb. to tears 使某人感动得流泪

（考题）Moved to tears, he made up his mind to follow the good example.

tear² /teə/ （tore，torn） *vt*. 撕开、撕裂；vi. 撕、扯；被撕破

tear sth. into pieces/into two/in half 撕得粉碎/撕成两半

（考题）He torn the letter into pieces after reading it.

tear sth. away (from . . .) （从…）撕去某物

（考题）The place was so beautiful that we found it hard to tear ourselves away.

technical /ˈteknɪkəl/ *adj*. 技术的；工艺的

（考题）We have already solved the technical problems in building new cells.

technician /tekˈnɪʃən/ *n*. 技师；技术员

technique /tekˈniːk/ *n*. 技术；技能、技巧

（考题）The course includes an introduction to the process of illustration and its techniques，workshop exercise and group projects.

technology /tekˈnɒlədʒɪ/ *n*. 技术；技术水平

（考题）It is exciting to imagine that the advance in technology may be changing the most basic condition of human existence

（辨析：technique 指做某种具体事情的技能、技巧，如 the technique of playing the piano 等；technology 则是指推动社会、科学、工业等发展的技术水平，是个总体的概念）

teenager /ˈtiːneɪdʒə/ *n*. 十几岁的孩子

telegram /ˈtelɪɡræm/ *n*. 电报

telegraph /ˈtelɪɡrɑːf/ *n*. 电报机；电报（通讯方式）

by telegraph 使用电报

telephone /ˈtelɪfəʊn/ *n*. 电话；电话机

talk on/over the telephone 在电话里交谈

by phone 通过电话

（考题）It was called a "watch and dial" show because viewers vote by telephone to decide who should leave or stay.

vt. **telephone sb.** 给某人打电话

（考题）At some point，the television viewers are asked to telephone the program to vote or to apply to take part in the show.

televise /ˈtelɪvaɪz/ *vt*. 用电视播放

televise sth. live 电视直播

（考题）— How was the televised debate last night? — Super! Rarely did a debate attract so much media attention.

television /teliˈvɪʒən/ *n*. (TV) 电视；电视机

watch TV 看电视

tell /tel/ (told，told) *vt*. 告诉；讲述；区分 *vi*. 讲述

tell sb. sth. /tell sth. to sb. 告诉某人某事

tell sb. to do sth. 叫某人做某事

tell sb. how/what/when/where to do 告诉某人如何…做

（考题）No one has ever told me who to ask for help when necessary.

tell sb. that ... 告诉某人…

（考题）Please tell me how the accident came about. I am still in the dark.

tell about/of ... 讲述、介绍…

（考题）I planned to tell my friend about my trouble.

tell ... apart 把…区分开来

tell ... from ... /tell between ... 把…与…区分开来

（考题）Consumers generally cannot tell between a product and its package. Many products are packages and many packages are products.

tell the time 报时

（考题）It is believed that many years ago kings kept special slaves to tell the time.

temper /ˈtempə/ *n*. 脾气；心情

be in a (bad) temper 心情不好，发脾气

（考题）She's always in a temper. No wonder she can't get on well with others.

be in a good temper 心情好

（考题）The boss is in a very good temper today and he smiles to everyone.

fly/get into a temper 突然发脾气

（考题）He flew into a temper just because I was a few minutes late.

lose one's temper 发脾气

（考题）At her supervisor's criticism, Martha lost her temper.

temperate /'tempərət/ *adj*. 温带的；温和的

temperature /'temprɪtʃə/ *n*. 温度

（考题）These clouds protect the forest from the daytime heat and night-time cold of nearby deserts, keeping temperatures fit for plant growth.

take sb.'s temperature 为某人测量体温

temporary /'tempərərɪ/ *adj*. 临时的

（考题）While temporary and situational loneliness can be a normal, healthy part of life, chronic loneliness can be a very sad, and sometimes dangerous condition.

tempt /tempt/ *vt*. 引诱；吸引

tempt sb. to do/into doing sth. 引诱某人做某事

（考题）Nothing but vanity tempted him into stealing.

be tempted to do sth. 很容易、很想做某事

（考题）Someone who's never suffered anorexia and never known an anorexic might be tempted to think. "It's simple-jusi tell them to eat more!"

ten /ten/ *num*. 十

tenant /'tenənt/ *n*. 租户；房客

tend /tend/ *vt*. 照看；护理；易于；倾向于

tend to do sth. 倾向于做某事

（考题）Unfortunately, passive learning has a serious problem. It makes us tend to accept what we are told even when it is little more than hearsay and rumor.

tendency /'tendənsɪ/ *n*. 趋势；倾向

have a tendency to do sth. 有做某事的倾向

（考题）There's the obvious tendency to smile.

tender /'tendə/ *adj*. 嫩的；温柔的

tennls /'tenɪs/ *n*. 网球

tense /tens/ *adj*. 紧张的；绷紧的　*n*. 时态

tent /tent/ *n*. 帐篷

term /tɜːm/ *n*. 学期;期限;术语;条件

in the long/medium/short term 就长远/中期/短期而言

(考题)The useful skills developed through the study of philosophy have significant long-term benefits in career advancement.

in terms of ... 就…而言

(考题)Thus, children were valued in terms of their productivity, and they played the role of producer quite early.

terminal /ˈtɜːmɪnəl/ *n*. 末端;终点;终端

terrible /ˈterəbl/ *adj*. 可怕的;糟糕的

terribly /ˈterəblɪ/ *adv*. 恶劣地;糟糕地;非常、极其

terrific /təˈrɪfɪk/ *adj*. 极度的;非常的;严重的(口)极妙的、了不起的

(考题)The book is worth reading again. It's terrific!

(考题)A terrific earthquake took place last night.

territory /ˈterɪtərɪ/ *n*. 领土;领地;版图

(考题)Russia occupies the largest territory in the world.

terror /ˈterə/ *n*. 恐怖;恐惧

test /test/ *n*. 测试;测验;

a test on/of ... 对…进行的测试、考验

(考题)In this part somebody wants to send information in writing to somebody else. There is a test on timetable and a test on text messages.

vt. **test sth. /sb.** 测试某事/某人

(考题)Then there are those that test people's abilities for specific jobs like running a kitchen, becoming an interior designer or a top model.

test sb. on ... 对某人的…方面进行测试

text /tekst/ *n*. 课文;正文

textbook /ˈtekstbʊk/ *n*. 教科书

than /ðæn/ *conj*. 比

thank /θæŋk/ *vt*. 感激;感谢

thank sb. for (doing) sth. 因某事感谢某人

n. **give/express/say thanks to sb. for sth.** 因某事感谢某人

thanks to ... 由于…；多亏…

（考题）Thanks to the NTS website, however, you don't have to live in the nation's capital to visit it. Take a tour online.

that /ðæt/ *pron.* *adj.* 那，那个 *adv.* 那么、如此地

theater /ˈθɪətə/ *n.* 剧院

theft /θeft/ *n.* 偷窃

their /ðeə/ *pron.* 他（她、它）们的

theirs /ðeəz/ *pron.* 他（她、它）们的

themselves /ðəmˈselvz/ *pron.* 他（她、它）们自己

then /ðen/ *adv.* 那么；当时；然后

theory /ˈθɪərɪ/ *n.* 理论

therapy /ˈθerəpɪ/ *n.* 疗法

there /ðeə/ *adv.* 在那里

thereby /ˈðeəbaɪ/ *adv.* 因此

therefore /ˈðeəfɔː/ *adv.* 因此；所以

these /ðiːz/ *pron.* 这些

they /ðeɪ/ *pron.* 他（她、它）们

thick /θɪk/ *adj.* 厚的；浓的；粗的

thief /θiːf/ *n.* 小偷、窃贼

thin /θɪn/ *adj.* 薄的；稀的；细的

thing /θɪŋ/ *n.* 事情；东西（*pl.*）情况

（考题）How are things with you?

think /θɪŋk/ (thought, thought) *vi.* *vt.* 想；考虑、思考；认为

　　think about ... 考虑、思考…

（考题）— Do you have any problems if you are offered this job?
— Well, I'm thinking about the salary ...

　　think of ... 想到…

（考题）Most people think of racing when they see greyhounds and believe they need lots of exercise.

　　think of ... as ... ... 认为…是…

（考题）Considering all, we think of his suggestion as the best one we've got up to now.

　　think ... (to be) ... 认为…（是）…

（考题）He thinks money management the most important for children.

think sth. over 考虑某事

（考题）I can't give you my reply for the time being. I need more time to think it over.

think that ... 认为…

（考题）It is thought that strong blues will stimulate clear thought and lighter，soft colours will calm the mind and aid concentration.

What do you think of ...? 你认为…怎么样?

（考题）— What do you think of the performance today? — Great! None but a musical genius could perform so successfully.

（同义词：**How do you like ...? How is ...? What/How about ...?**）

think highly/well/much/little/nothing of ... 看重/重视/轻视…

（考题）We think much of what you have done for us.

think of/about doing sth. 考虑、打算做某事

（考题）I haven't heard from him for weeks. I'm thinking of calling him to find out what's the matter.

think to do sth. 考虑、打算做某事

（考题）What a surprise! I never thought to see you here.

（注意：think 的过去时后接动词不定式时，表示"想到要去做，可实际并没有做。"）

to think ... 想不到…、没想到竟然会…

third /θɜːd/ *num*. 第三

thirsty /'θɜːstɪ/ *adj*. 口渴的；渴望的

thirteen /'θɜː'tiːn/ *num*. 十三

thirty /'θɜːtɪ/ *num*. 三十

this /ðɪs/ *pron*. *adj*. 这；这个

thorough /'θʌrə/ *adj*. 完全的；彻底的

those /ðəuz/ *pron*. *adj*. 那些

though /ðəu/ *conj*. 尽管、虽然

（考题）And they must give their children a mental break, for children also need freedom, though young.

as though 好像、仿佛

（考题）You never tell me what you think. You just smile as though everything is fine.

even though 尽管

（考题）They told me that even though it would be a financial problem，I could go wherever I would be happiest.

adv. 可是；然而；不过

（考题）— How is everything going on with you in Europe? — Quite well. Not so smoothly as I hoped，though.

thought /θɔːt/ *n.* 思想；想法

at the thought of ... 一想到…

（考题）He couldn't help feeling excited at the thought of meeting his wife again.

have/with no thougt for ... 不为…着想，没有想到…

（考题）He did it with no thought for others.

give no thought to ... 没有想到…

thoughtful /ˈθɔːtfʊl/ *adj.* 考虑周到的

it's thoughtful of sb. to do sth. 多谢某人考虑周到做了…

thousand /ˈθaʊzənd/ *num.* *n.* 千

thousands of ... 数千…

thread /θred/ *n.* 线 *vt.* 穿（针、线）

thread a needle 穿针引线

threat /θret/ *n.* 威胁

threaten /ˈθretən/ *vt.* 威胁；有…的危险、可能

threaten sb. (with ...) （用…）威胁某人

（考题）If a stranger should enter your territory and threaten you，you might shout. Probably this would be enough to frighten him away.

threaten to do sth. 威胁说/有可能做某事

（考题）Her brother threatened to leave her in the dark room alone when she disobeyed his order.

throat /θrəʊt/ *n.* 喉咙

through /θruː/ *prep. adv.* 通过；从头至尾

（考题）Experience is better gained through practice.

be through (with) sth. 做完…

（考题）He was about halfway through his meal when a familiar voice came to his ears.

go through sth. 经历…；检查…；阅读…

（考题）— The woman biologist stayed in Africa studying wild animals for 13 years before she returned. — Oh, dear! She must have gone through a lot of difficulties!

see through sth. 看穿、看破…

（考题）False statements are easy to see through.

carry sth. through (to the end) 把某事进行到底

be wet through 浑身湿透

throughout /θruːˈaʊt/ *prep.* 遍及；贯穿

Throughout the year 一年到头、终年

throughout the world 世界各地

throw /θrəʊ/ (threw, thrown) *vt. vi.* 扔、掷

throw ... away 把…扔掉

（考题）I feel so sorry every time I have to throw any food away.

throw ... into ... 使…突然处于、陷入…

（考题）With that, he threw the car into reverse, stopping a few feet in back of our car.

throw ... open 突然打开…

（考题）The door was thrown open and in rushed two men.

throw ... to sb. /throw sb. sth. 把…扔给某人

（考题）The couple toasted each other, the waiter and the crowd. And the crowd replied by cheering and throwing flowers to them.

throw ... at ab. 用…去砸某人

（考题）The boy picked up a stone and threw it at the dog to scare it away.

thunder /ˈθʌndə/ *n.* 雷；雷声 *vi.* 打雷

thunderstorm /ˈθʌndəstɔːm/ *n.* 雷雨

Thursday /ˈθɜːzdeɪ/ *n.* 星期四

thus /ðʌs/ *adv.* 如此；这样、因而

（考题）The elevators at Seven World Trade Center use a system that groups people traveling to nearby floor into the same elevator, thus saving elevator stops.

ticket /ˈtɪkɪt/ *n.* 票、券

tide /taɪd/ *n.* 潮、潮汐；趋势、潮流

tidy /ˈtaɪdɪ/ *adj.* 整齐的；整洁的

tie /taɪ/ *n.* 领带；领结 *vt.* 拴、扎；系上

tiger /ˈtaɪɡə/ *n.* 老虎

tight /taɪt/ *adj.* 紧的；紧身的

（考题）Some stage schools give their children too much professional work at such a young age. But the law is very tight on the amount they can do.

till /tɪl/ *prep.*， *conj.* 直到；到…为止

time /taɪm/ *n.* 时间；次数

ahead of time 提前

（考题）They planned weeks ahead of time, asking each other what they wanted for Christmas.

all the time 总是；始终

（考题）Tree leaves are green all the time in the monsoon forest.

at one time 一度、曾经；同时

（考题）At one time, computers were expected largely to remove the need for paper copies of documents because they could be stored electronically.

at a time 每次；一次；在…的时候

（考题）Women prefer doing many things at a time.

at the same time 同时

（考题）I bicycle to work when the weather is good. I'm getting exercise, and I'm enjoying it at the same time.

at times 时常；有时、不时地

（考题）At times photojournalists tell their stories through a single picture.

by the time … （截至）到…时

（考题）By the time he reached the small boat, a thick white mist had spread over the surface of the water.

every time 每次

（考题）Every time you spend or don't spend money, you have a chance to share your values.

from time to time 不时地

（考题）You need to understand that in true friendship it's okay to put your own needs first from time to time.

have a good time 过得很开心

in no time 立即、马上

(考题)Excuse me, but I'll be back in no time.

in time 及时

(考题)This geographical and cultural distance also prevents the grown-up children from providing response in time for their aged parents living by themselves.

on time 准时

(考题)No matter where he is going to what he is doing, he is never on time.

it is (about/high) time for sb. to do sth. 到做某事的时候了

(考题)Perhaps it is time for Britain to do the same, and stop wasting resources on a subject which few pupils want or need.

it is time sb. did sth. （某人）早该做某事了

(考题)If you find that believing in yourself is a challenge, it is time you built a positive self-image and learned to love yourself.

timetable /ˈtaɪmteɪbl/ *n*. 时间表

timid /ˈtɪmɪd/ *adj*. 胆怯的；害羞的

tin /tɪn/ *n*. 罐头、听

tiny /ˈtaɪnɪ/ *adj*. 微小的

tip /tɪp/ *n*. 顶端、尖端；小费 *vt*. 给小费

tiptoe /ˈtɪptəʊ/ *n*. 脚尖

  walk on tiptoe 蹑手蹑脚、很轻地走路

tire /taɪə/ *vt*. 使疲劳 *vi*. 厌烦、厌倦

(考题)Still, I was close enough to overtake her if she tired, so I didn't give up hope completely.

  tire of ... 对…感到厌烦

(考题)She never tired of talking about her son.

tired /taɪəd/ *adj*. 劳累的；厌烦的

  be tired of ... 对…感到厌烦、厌倦

(考题)He was very tired of his work and wanted to have a good rest.

  be tired out 累得要死；非常疲倦

(考题)Mum was tired out having prepared food for the whole family.

tissue /ˈtɪsjuː/ *n*. 薄纸；绵纸；(生物)组织

title /ˈtaɪtl/ *n*. 题目;称号;头衔

to /tuː, tʊ/ *prep*. 朝、向;给…;对…来说;到…

toast /təʊst/ *n*. 祝酒、干杯;烤面包 *vt*. 向某人祝酒;烘烤

today /təˈdeɪ/ *n*. *adv*. 今天

toe /təʊ/ *n*. 脚趾;足尖

together /təˈɡeðə/ *adv*. 一起;共同

  put ... together 加起来

  together with ... 与…一起

toilet /ˈtɔɪlɪt/ *n*. 盥洗室;厕所

tomato /təˈmɑːtəʊ/ *n*. 西红柿、番茄

tomorrow /təˈmɒrəʊ/ *n*. *adv*. 明天

ton /tʌn/ *n*. 吨

tone /təʊn/ *n*. 语气;音调

  speak in a ... tone 以一种…口气说话

（考题）I didn't know why he told me the news in a very strange tone.

tongue /tʌŋ/ *n*. 舌头;语言

  mother tongue 母语、本国语

tonight /təˈnaɪt/ *n*. *adv*. 今夜

too /tuː/ *adv*. 也;太

  far too ... 太…;远过于…

（考题）How many people have I met who have told me about something they have been planning to do but have never yet found the time? Far too many.

  much too ... 太…

（考题）Allen had to call a taxi because the box was much too heavy to carry all the way home.

  rather too ... 有些太…

（考题）Sorry，but the problem is rather too difficult to me.

  only too ... 非常…

（考题）We're only too glad to have the chance working together with the great man.

  too ... to do sth. 太…以至于不能…

（考题）Sometimes the Chinese abroad reach out their hands too often to be polite.

tool /tuːl/ *n.* 工具

tooth /tuːθ/ *n.* (*pl.* teeth) 牙齿

toothbrush /'tuːθbrʌʃ/ *n.* 牙刷

toothpaste /'tuːθpeɪst/ *n.* 牙膏

top /tɒp/ *n.* 顶点；顶部 *adj.* 最高的；头等的

topic /'tɒpɪk/ *n.* 题目；话题

torch /tɔːtʃ/ *n.* 火把；火炬

tornado /tɔː'neɪdəʊ/ *n.* 龙卷风

total /'təʊtəl/ *adj.* 总的；总计的；完全的 *n.* 总数；总计

　in total 总计

　(考题)The losses reached millions of dollars in total.

touch /tʌtʃ/ *vt.* 碰；触摸；涉及；触动

　(考题)This exhibition shows how progress will touch our lives.

　be touched by ... 为…所打动、感动

　(考题)Learning her story, Barrett was as touched as I by this tiny woman's achievements.

　n. 碰；触摸；联系

　be in/out of touch with sb. 与某人有/没有联系

　(考题)I know nothing about him. I have been out of touch with him for years.

　get in touch with sb. 与某人建立联系

　(考题)Instead, you should encourage them to get in touch with the thing they fear, in a safe and supportive environment.

　keep/be in touch with sb. 与某人保持联系

　(考题)Danielle Steel considers her readers to be the most important resource and has kept in touch with them by e-mail.

　lose touch with sb. 与某人失去联系

　(考题)He lost touch with his family during the war. And it was years before they reunited.

　to the touch 摸起来

　(考题)The material is very soft to the touch.

tough /tʌf/ *adj.* 坚韧的；强硬的；难对付的

tour /tʊə/ *n. vi.* 旅游；观光；巡视

　on a tour 周游

　(考题)During the next two days Mr. Evans will be taken on a

whistle-stop tour of London to see the sights.

a tour of the world 周游世界

a performance tour 巡回演出

tourist /ˈtʊərɪst/ *adj*. 旅游的 *n*. 旅游者

towards /təˈwɔːdz/ *adv*. 朝、向

towel /taʊəl/ *n*. 毛巾

tower /taʊə/ *n*. 塔

town /taʊn/ *n*. 城镇；市区、商业中心

go to town 进城、到市中心区

townsman /ˈtaʊnzmən/ *n*. 城里人

toy /tɔɪ/ *n*. 玩具

trace /treɪs/ *vt*. 跟踪 *n*. 踪迹

trace (...) back to ... 追溯(···)到···

(考题)You are encouraged to keep records of the sources used by each person，which helps you trace back to the origin of the problems that may happen unexpectedly.

track /trɒk/ *n*. 跑道；车道；小道

be on the right/wrong track 路子对/不对头；正确/不正确

(考题)Associate Professor Gary Wittert，said parents needed help in doing their job and the Opposition Party's policy might be on the right track.

track and field events 田径项目

vt. 跟踪；追踪

(考题)Miss Smith fixed hi-tech sensors to sharks to record pressure and temperature，while also tracking them using GPS (Global Positioning System) technology.

tractor /ˈtræktə/ *n*. 拖拉机

trade /treɪd/ *n*. 贸易；交易

arms trade 军火交易

free trade zone 自由贸易区

vt. *vi*. 交易

trade with sb. 与某人做生意

(考题)China is trading with nearly all countries in the world.

trade ... for sth. 用···交易、交换某物

(考题)Instead of hitting the beach，fourteen high school

students traded swimming suits for lab coats last summer and turned their attention to scientific experiments.

trademark /ˈtreɪdmɑːk/ *n*. 商标

trader /ˈtreɪdə/ *n*. 商人

tradition /trəˈdɪʃən/ *n*. 传统

  by tradition 根据传统

  customs and traditions 风俗习惯

traditional /trəˈdɪʃənəl/ *adj*. 传统的

  （考题）In countries where naps are traditional，people often suffer less from problem such as heart disease.

traffic /ˈtræfɪk/ *n*. 交通

  traffic accident 交通事故

  traffic jam 交通拥堵

  traffic regulations/rules 交通规则

  traffic lights 交通信号灯

tragedy /ˈtrædʒɪdɪ/ *n*. 悲剧；灾难

train¹ /treɪn/ *n*. 火车

  by train 乘火车

train² /treɪn/ *vt*. *vi*. 训练

  train sb. to do sth. 训练某人做某事

  （考题）... but new studies show that people of any age can train their brains to work faster.

  train for ... 为…而训练

  （考题）I seek friends whose qualities illuminate me and train me up for love.

training /ˈtreɪnɪŋ/ *n*. 训练；锻炼

transfer /trænsˈfɜː/ *vi*. *vt*. 调动；转移；迁移

  transfer ... to ... 把…转移、迁移到…

  （考题）The company transferred its headquarters from Tokyo to Beijing.

translate /trænsˈleɪt/ *vt*. 翻译

  translate ... into ... 把…翻译成…

  （考题）What I do is to focus on the value of the stories that people can translate into their own daily world of affairs.

translation /trænsˈleɪʃən/ *n*. 翻译

transplant /træns'plɑːnt/ *vt.* 移植 *n.* 移植

（考题）The heart transplant was performed successfully.

transport /træns'pɔːt/ *vt.* 运输 *n.* 运输；交通

（考题）Horses contributed to the spread of culture by serving as a means of transport.

transportation /ˌtrænspɔː'teɪʃən/ *n.* 交通；运输

（考题）The new from of rapid transportation helped cultures spread around the world.

trap /træp/ *n.* 陷阱 *vt.* 使陷入困境

be trapped in ... 陷入···、被困在···

（考题）People wearing safety belts are usually protected to the point of having a clear head to free themselves from such dangerous situations, not to be trapped in them.

travel /'trævəl/ *n.* 旅行 *vi.* 旅行

traveler /'trævələ/ *n.* 旅行者

tray /treɪ/ *n.* 托盘

treasure /'treʒə/ *n.* 宝物 *vt.* 珍惜

（考题）Meeting my uncle after all these years was an unforgettable moment, one I will always treasure.

treat /triːt/ *vt.* 对待；治疗；招待

（考题）I just try to treat my passengers the way I would want my mother treated.

treat ... as ... 把···看作···

（考题）73% of new teachers say too many parents treat schools and teachers as enemies.

treat sb. to ... 用···招待某人

（考题）I learned that lesson when I decided to treat Doug, my husband of one month, to a special meal.

treatment /'triːtmənt/ *n.* 治疗；招待

tree /triː/ *n.* 树

tremble /'trembl/ *vi.* 抖动；摇晃

tremendous /trɪ'mendəs/ *adj.* 巨大的；可怕的

trend /trend/ *n.* 潮流；趋势

（考题）As prices and building costs keep rising, the "do-it-yourself" (DIY) trend in the U. S. continues to grow.

trick /trɪk/ *n*. 诡计;伎俩;戏法

(考题)Half-truths are not technically lies, but they are just as dishonest. Some politicians often use this trick.

play a trick/tricks on ... 捉弄…

(考题)He hates to be played tricks on.

vi. *vt*. 欺诈

trick sb. into doing sth. 用计诱使某人做某事

(考题)She was tricked into marrying a man like that.

trick sb. out of sth. 骗走某人的…

trip /trɪp/ *n*. 旅行;旅程

make/take a trip to ... 到…旅行

trolley /'trɒlɪ/ *n*. 手推车;电车

trolleybus /'trɒlɪbʌs/ *n*. 电车

troop /tru:p/ *n*. 军队

trouble /'trʌbl/ *n*. 麻烦;困难;疾病

be in trouble 陷入困境

(考题)When one is in trouble, people think it's his own fault.

get into trouble 陷入困境

(考题)In Portugal, two TV channels got into trouble because they showed too much of the personal lives of the people in the shows.

take trouble to do sth. 不嫌麻烦做某事

have trouble (in) doing sth. 做某事有困难

(考题)The overly willful and unbending child may have trouble obeying teachers or coaches.

have trouble with ... 与/在…有麻烦

(考题)In order to have no trouble with the police, he had a talk with some of the police officers.

cause sb. trouble/cause trouble to sb. 给某人带来麻烦

vt. **trouble sb. /sth.** 打扰、干扰、困扰…

(考题)What troubles industries most in dealing with the dangerous waste problem?

trouble sb. with sth. 用…打扰某人

(考题)I'm sorry to trouble you with such little things.

trouble sb. to do sth. 麻烦某人做某事

（考题）May I trouble you to post the letter on your way home?

troublesome /ˈtrʌblsʌm/ *adj*. 讨厌的；令人烦恼的

trousers /ˈtrauzəz/ *n*. (*pl*.) 长裤

truck /trʌk/ *n*. 卡车

true /truː/ *adj*. 真的；真实的

   come true 实现

   （考题）His dream of being someone has at last come true.

   be true of ... 是这样的，对…适用的

   （考题）Most of what has been said about the Simiths is true of the Johnsons.

   true to ... 忠实于…

   （考题）So we have the dating shows where winners either pair off or stay true to their partners outside the TV studio.

trunk /trʌŋk/ *n*. 树干；皮箱；(汽车)行李箱

trust /trʌst/ *n*. 信任；信托

   （考题）If one person steals, it destroys trust and hurts everyone.

   have/put trust in ... 信任…

   （考题）Go ahead with it! We all have trust in your ability.

   vt. 相信、信任

   （考题）Whether you're on a sports team, in an office or a member of a family, if you can't trust one another, there's going to be trouble.

truth /truːθ/ *n*. 真实；真理；真相

   tell the truth 说出事实、真相

try /traɪ/ *n*. 尝试；努力

   have a try 试一试

   v. **try sth. out** 尝试

   （考题）The purpose is to provide an opportunity to try out new ideas and to think through difficulties with fellow learners.

   try to do sth. 争取做某事

   （考题）Therefore, it is important for each person in our society to try to maintain a healthy and realistic self-image.

   try one's best to do sth. 尽最大努力做某事

   （考题）You should try your best to attend your dream school.

   （同义词：**do one's best to do sth. , make an effort to do sth. , spare**

no efforts/pains to do sth.）

try doing sth. 试着用这种方法做

（考题）So why bother even to try imagining life far in the future?

tube /tjuːb/ *n.* 管子

test tube 试管

Tuesday /'tjuːzdeɪ/ *n.* 星期二

tug /tʌg/ *v.* 用力拉；猛拉

tug boat 拖轮

tune /tjuːn/ *n.* 曲子；曲调

tunnel /'tʌnəl/ *n.* 隧道；地道

turn /tɜːn/ *vi.* 转动；变化；变得　*vt.* 使转动；使变化

turn + adj. 变得…

（考题）As evening turns deeper into the night, the burning lava quietly falls down the side of the volcano.

turn away from ... 避开

（考题）He will certainly turn away from this kind of things.

turn sth. down 拒绝；调低音量

（考题）He decided to say no more as his suggestion had been turned down.

turn (sth.) into ...（把…）变成…

（考题）... but if they keep on blowing, those ripples get bigger and bigger and turn into waves.

turn (sth.) on 打开电源

（考题）Turn on the radio and listen to the news now.

turn (sth.) off 关闭电源

（考题）Ceiling fans cool people, not rooms, so before you leave, turn off the ceiling fan.

turn to sb. for ... 向某人请求…

（考题）He felt rather hopeless as he could think of nobody to turn to for help.

It turns out that ... 结果，最后…

（考题）It turned out that none of the applicants got the position.

n. **by turns** 轮流；交替

（考题）If we had done the job by turns, you wouldn't be so tired now.

in turn 轮流;依次

(考题)A statement of opinion by one writer may be re-stated as fact by another, who may in turn be quoted by yet another

It's sb.'s turn to do sth. 轮到某人做某事

(考题)Oh, it's my turn to take care of the old man.

take turns 轮流

(考题)One following another, groups of musicians and dancers from all over the Sahara take their turns to show off their wonderful traditional culture.

tutor /ˈtjuːtə/ 辅导教师;家庭教师;(美)大学导师

twelfth /ˈtwelfθ/ *num.* 第十二

twelve /ˈtwelv/ *num.* 十二

twentieth /ˈtwentɪθ/ *num.* 第二十

twenty /ˈtwentɪ/ *num.* 二十

twice /twaɪs/ *adv.* 两次

type /taɪp/ *n.* 型;类型;种类 *vt.* 用打字机打 *vi.* 打字

typewriter /ˈtaɪpraɪtə/ *n.* 打字机

typhoon /taɪˈfuːn/ *n.* 台风

typical /ˈtɪpɪkəl/ *adj.* 典型的;模范的;象征的

(考题)The computers are a typical example, which are almost out-of-date the moment they are bought.

be typical of ... …的特征

(考题)These constructions are typical of the Ming Dynasty.

It is typical of ... to do sth. 做某事是…的特征

(考题)It is typical of a Japanese woman to bow.

typist /ˈtaɪpɪst/ *n.* 打字员

tyre /ˈtaɪə/ *n.* 轮胎

get a flat tyre 轮胎爆了

U

UFO, ufo /ˈjuːˈfəʊ/ 不明飞行物，飞碟(unientified flying object)

ugly /ˈʌɡlɪ/ *adj*. 难看的

umbrella /ʌmˈbrelə/ *n*. 伞

unable /ʌnˈeɪbl/ *adj*. 不能的，不会的

unbelievable /ʌnbɪˈliːvəbl/ *adj*. 难以置信的

uncle /ˈʌŋkl/ *n*. 叔叔，舅舅，伯父

unconscious /ʌnˈkɒnʃəs/ *adj*. 失去知觉的

　　be unconscious of ... 没有意识到…

under /ˈʌndə/ *prep*. 在…下面；不到；在过程中

　　（考题）Among the most vocal are youngsters who have suffered under competitive pressures from their parents or society.

　　under age 年龄不到

　　under ... conditions 在…情况、条件下

　　（考题）Then the leaves are spread out on floors and left to ferment under wet conditions.

　　bring/get/keep sth. under control（对…）加以控制

　　（考题）They want to keep wildlife under control.

　　under construction 在建造中

　　（考题）A new eight-kilometer road is under construction that links the port area with motorway system.

　　under the circumstances 在这种情况下

　　under way 在进行之中

undergo /ˌʌndəˈɡəʊ/（underwent，undergone）*vt*. 经受、经历、遭受

　　（考题）The new device is about to undergo testing and can go on sale within 12 months.

　　undergo great hardships/sufferings 遭巨大的苦难

undergound /ˈʌndəɡraʊnd/ *adj*. 地下的

　　the underground 地铁

　　underground railway 地铁

understand /ˌʌndəˈstænd/（understood，understood）v. 理解

understand (doing) sth. 理解做某事

（考题）Scientists hope that they can learn in advance how the rainforest will manage in the future by understanding how rainforests reacted to climate change in the past.

understand that ... 理解、明白…；听说…

（考题）You need to understand that in true friendship it's okay to put your own needs first from time to time.

understand how/what ... to do ... 知道、理解如何做…

（考题）By the end of class，she understood how to get them right.

make oneself understood 使别人理解自己的意思

（考题）Try to explain it in an easier way and make yourself better understood.

understanding /ˌʌndəˈstændɪŋ/ adj. 谅解的；通情达理的　n. 理解

（考题）People have similar understandings of politeness.

undertake /ˌʌndəˈteɪk/（undertood，undertaken）vt. 接受

undertake (to do) sth. 接受（答应做）…

（考题）No one here dared to undertake the difficult task.

（考题）The boss undertook to improve the working conditions.

undo /ʌnˈduː/（undid，undone）vt. 解开、打开；破坏、毁坏

unfortunate /ʌnˈfɔːtʃənɪt/ adj. 不幸的；令人遗憾的

unhappy /ʌnˈhæpɪ/ adj. 不愉快的

uniform /ˈjuːnɪfɔːm/ n. 制服；军服

union /ˈjuːnɪən/ n. 团结、和睦；协会、联盟

the students' union 学生会

the European Union 欧盟

unique /juːˈniːk/ adj. 独特的、惟一的

（考题）Here are the things you can think of：the desire to explore a foreign and unique environment，the excitement of being the first humans to open up a new world，the expectation of fame and glory.

unit /ˈjuːnɪt/ n. 单元；单位

unite /juˈnaɪt/ vt. 联合；结合

unite ... with ... 联合；统一；团结

（考题）After our company united with another one last October，two different computer networks were driving us crazy.

united /juˈnaɪtɪd/ *adj*. 联合的；统一的

the United States 美国

universal /ˌjuːnɪˈvɜːsəl/ *adj*. 普遍的；全世界的

universe /ˈjuːnɪvɜːs/ *n*. 宇宙；世界

university /ˌjuːnɪˈvɜːsɪtɪ/ *n*. （综合性）大学

unknown /ʌnˈnəʊn/ *adj*. 未知的 *n*. 未知的事物

be unknown to sb. 是某人所不知的

unless /ənˈles/ *conj*. 除非

（考题）We will never know our deep feelings unless we cry.

unlike /ʌnˈlaɪk/ *prep*. 不像、和…不同 *adj*. 不同的、不相似的

（考 题）They also found that unlike some standard cough treatments， theobromine caused no side effects such as sleepiness.

until /ənˈtɪl/ *prep*. *conj*. 直到…为止

（考题）Many poor people stayed in their houses until the last moment.

（考题）I didn't know how to teach until I met you.

（注意：在 until 引导时间状语时，表示非延续性动作的动词使用否定形式，表示延续性动作的动词使用肯定形式。）

unusual /ʌnˈjuːʒʊəl/ *adj*. 不寻常的

up /ʌp/ *adv*. 向上

be up and about（病愈后）起来走动

up to sb.（to do sth.） 由某人决定、负责（做某事）

（考题）I think it's up to you to tell him the news.

up to ... 达到…；直到…

（考题）Unlike other productive authors who write one book at a time，she can work on up to five.

up and down 上上下下；来来回回

（考题）On some services，prices went up and down at random.

upon /əˈpɒn/ *prep*. 在…上

upper /ˈʌpə/ *adj*. 上面的；上部的

upright /ˈʌpraɪt/ *adj*. 挺直的；竖立的、正直的

upset /ˈʌpset/（upset，upset）*vt*. 使心烦意乱；弄翻；打搅

（考题）The bad news did upset us.

adj. 心烦的；弄翻的

（考题）I'm feeling upset these days because the result of my last English exam was not as good as I had expected.

upstairs /ˈʌpˈsteəz/ *adv*. 在楼上；住楼上

up-to-date /ˈʌptəˈdeɪt/ *adj*. 现代的；最新的

（考题）Reporters from around the globe provide you with a comprehensive world view to keep you up-to-date on world affairs.

upward /ˈʌpwəd/ *adj*. 向上的　　*adv*. 向上

urban /ˈɜːbən/ *adj*. 城市的

urge /ɜːdʒ/ *vt*. 催促；鼓动

　　urge sb. to do sth. 催促某人做某事

（考题）The author wrote this article to urge people to stand out when in need.

　　urge that ... 敦促；呼吁（从句中使用虚拟语气）

（考题）They urged that the library be kept open during the vacation.

urgent /ˈɜːdʒənt/ *adj*. 紧迫的；紧要的

usage /ˈjuːsɪdʒ/　　*n*. 使用；用法；惯用法；习语

use /juːz/ *vt*. 使用

　　use sth. up 用尽

　　used to do sth. 过去常做某事；一度、曾经…

（考题）Mr. Smith used to smoke heavily, but no longer now.

（考题）He used to be in the army, wasn't he?

（注意：否定形式为 used not/usen't to do sth. 或 didn't use to do sth.；反意疑问句中根据 used to 后面的动词提问。）

n. /juːs/ 使用

　　come into use 开始被使用

　　out of use 停止使用

（考题）This kind of material has long been out of use.

　　in use 使用着

（考题）Turn off everything not in use：lights, TVs, computers.

　　make (full/good) use of ... （充分）利用…

（考题）In the next part, the author would most probably discuss with you how to make good use of time.

put sth. into use 开始使用

（考题）Put into use in April 2,000, the hotline was meant for residents reporting water and heating supply breakdowns.

used /juːst/ *adj.* 已适应、已习惯

be/get/become used to (doing) sth. 习惯于（做）某事

（考题）The way he did it was different from what we were used to.

useful /'juːsfʊl/ *adj.* 有用的；有益的

useless /'juːslɪs/ *adj.* 无用的

usual /'juːʒʊəl/ *adj.* 通常的

as usual 像以往一样

V

vacant /ˈveɪkənt/ *adj.* 空的；空白的；空缺的

vacation /vəˈkeɪʃən/ *n.* 休假；假期

    on vacation 在休假

vague /veɪg/ *adj.* 含糊的；不明确的

valley /ˈvælɪ/ *n.* 山谷低凹处

valuable /ˈvæljʊəbl/ *adj.* 有价值的；很有用的

    （考题）We thought of selling this old furniture，but we've decided to hold on to it. It might be valuable.

value /ˈvæljuː/ *n.* 价值

    be of great value 有很大价值

    （考题）The book is of great value. Nothing can be enjoyed unless you digest it.

    vt. 珍惜；重视

    （考题）It is obvious that if students value highly their test scores, then a great amount of their self-respect is put in the number.

van /væn/ *n.* 有蓬载重汽车；运货车

vapour /ˈveɪpə/ *n.* 蒸汽

variety /vəˈraɪətɪ/ *n.* 种类变化、多样化

    a variety of ... 各种各样的

    （考题）Attitudes are learned in a variety of ways.

various /ˈveərɪəs/ *adj.* 不同的、各种各样的

vary /ˈveərɪ/ *vt.* 使不同；改变；使多样化　*vi.* 呈差异；变化

    vary sth. 使变化

    （考题）Try not to start every sentence with "the". Vary the beginning of your sentences.

    vary (from ...) 不同（于…）

    （考题）The customs in this country vary greatly from those in other countries round it.

vase /vɑːz/ *n.* 花瓶

vast /vɑːst/ *adj.* 巨大的

vegetable /'vedʒɪtəbəl/ *n.* 蔬菜

vegetation /ˌvedʒɪ'teɪʃən/ *n.* （总称）植物

vehicle /'viːɪkl/ *n.* 车辆

venture /'ventʃə/ *n.* 冒险（企业）

verb /vɜːb/ *n.* ［语］动词

very /'verɪ/ *adv.* 很

　very much 非常

vest /vest/ *n.* 背心、马甲

vice versa /'vaɪsɪ'vɜːsə/ *n.* （拉）反过来也一样；反之亦然

victim /'vɪktɪm/ *n.* 受害者

victory /'vɪktərɪ/ *n.* 胜利

video /'vɪdɪəʊ/ *n. adj.* 电视（的）；录象（的）

videotape /'vɪdɪəʊteɪp/ *n.* 录象磁带

view /vjuː/ *n.* 视域；看法；风景

　（考题）A special treat is to go up the mountainside on the Banff Gondola for a surprising view of the valley below.

　in sb.'s view 在…看来

　（考题）In my view, London's not as expensive in price as Tokyo but Tokyo is more organized in traffic.

　in view of ... 鉴于、考虑到…

　（考题）Environmentalists say such worries are not necessary, and in view of global warming, that idea needs to change.

　point of view 观点

　（考题）I lacked a point of view when I read. Rather, I read in order to get a point of view.

　with a view of doing sth. (= in order to do sth.)打算做…

　a bird's eye view (of sth.) 鸟瞰；俯视

vigour /'vɪgə/ *n.* 精力，生机

　with 'vigour 充满生机的

village /'vɪlɪdʒ/ *n.* 村庄

violence /'vaɪələns/ *n.* 暴力

violent /'vaɪələnt/ *adj.* 剧烈的；使用暴力的

violin /ˌvaɪə'lɪn/ *n.* 小提琴

vilolinist /ˌvaɪə'lɪnɪst/ *n.* 小提琴手

virus /'vaɪərəs/ *n.* 病毒

visible /ˈvɪzɪbl/ *adj.* 看得见的、可见的

vision /ˈvɪʒən/ *n.* 视力；视觉；幻想；眼力；看法

visit /ˈvɪzɪt/ *n. v.* 访问；参观；游览

（考题）If it is quite convenient to you, I will visit you next Tuesday.

n. 参观；访问；拜访

（考题）Where can you go for a visit on Monday?

pay a visit to ... 访问；参观；游览

visitor /ˈvɪzɪtə/ *n.* 访问者；参观者

vital /ˈvaɪtəl/ *adj.* 充满生机的

vitamin /ˈvɪtəmɪn/ *n.* 维生素

vivid /ˈvɪvɪd/ *adj.* 生动的；逼真的

vocabulary /vəˈkæbjʊlərɪ/ *n.* 词汇

vocation /vəʊˈkeɪʃən/ *n.* 职业；工作

voice /vɔɪs/ *n.* 嗓音

at the top of one's voice 以最大的嗓音

（考题）But Ella Fant, who was filled with happiness, shouted at the top of her voice.

in a ... voice 用…样的嗓音

（考题）Greeting me with a nod, she said in a soft voice, "Hi, you must be Cori."

with one voice 异口同声地；一致地

（考题）All employees in the company asked for a rise in their pay with one voice.

volleyball /ˈvɒlɪbɔːl/ *n.* 排球

volume /ˈvɒljuːm/ *n.* 容积；卷；册

volunteer /ˌvɒlənˈtɪə/ *vt. vi.* 自愿（做）

volunteer（sth.）自愿提供

（考题）There are many ways in which people can volunteer, such as taking care of sick people, working for homeless children, and picking up garbage from beaches and parks.

volunteer to do sth. 自愿做某事

（考题）We volunteered to collect money to help the victims of the earthquake.

n. 志愿者　*adj.* 志愿的

（考题）The meaning of the word "volunteer" may be a little different in different countries, but it usually means "one who offers his or her services."

vote /vəut/ *n*. 投票；选举；选票　*vi*. 投票决定（或选举等）

　　vote for /against ... 投票支持/反对

voyage /'vɔiidʒ/ *n*. 航海；航行

　　go on a voyage 在水上航行

W

wage /weɪdʒ/ *n*. 工资

（见 salary）

waist /weɪst/ *n*. 腰部、腰；衣服的上身部分；背心

wait /weɪt/ *v*. 等候

wait for … 等候、等待…

wait for sb. to do sth. 等待某人做某事

（考题）Because the idea of risk also carries with it the possibility of failure, many of us usually wait for others to take charge.

can't wait to do sth. 迫不及待地做某事

（考题）— Are you going to have a holiday this year? — I'd love to. I can't wait to leave this place behind.

waiter /ˈweɪtə/ *n*. 侍者、服务员

waitress /ˈweɪtrɪs/ *n*. 女侍者、女服务员

wake /weɪk/（waked, 或 woke, woken）*vi*. 醒来　*vt*. 唤醒

wake (sb.) up 醒来；唤醒

（考题）At that time — about eight hours after you wake up — your body temperature goes down.

（考题）This prevents you from falling asleep or wakes you up during the night.

wake (sb.) to … （使某人）意识到…

（考题）You'd better wake him to the danger of driving too fast in fog.

waken /ˈweɪkən/ *vi*. 醒来　*vt*. 唤醒

（辨析：和 wake 同义。wake 使用更为普通。但被动语态中常使用 be wakened。）

wall /wɔːl/ *n*. 墙

walk /wɔːk/ *vi*., *n*. 步行；散步

walkman /ˈwɔːkmən/ *n*. 随身听

wallet /ˈwɒlɪt/ *n*. （放纸币，证件等的）皮夹子

waltz /wɔːlts/ *n*. 华尔兹舞（曲）；圆舞曲

· 384 ·

wander /'wɒndə/ *vi*. 徘徊

want /wænt/ *vt*. 要；想要；需要

　want sth. 想要…

　（考题）— Do you want tea or coffee? — Either. I really don't mind.

　want to do sth. 想做某事

　（考题）When asked what they needed most, the kids said they wanted to feel important and loved.

　want sb. to do sth. 想要某人做某事

　（考题）She wanted me to "make something" of myself, and decided I had better start young if I was to have any chance of keeping up with the competition.

　... want doing ... 需要…

　（考题）There trees want watering. Or they will die soon.

　（辨析：见 need。但表示需要时 want 后面一般不使用不定式。）

war /wɔː/ *n*. 战争

ward /wɔːd/ *n*. 病房

warm /wɔːm/ *adj*. 暖和的

　warm (...) up 加温、预热；热身；使兴奋

　（考题）Some rival coaches used to take their teams quickly away from the floor before Power warmed up so that their players would not see him any sooner than they had to.

warm-hearted /'wɔːm'hɑːtɪd/ *adj*. 热情的；富于同情心的

warmth /wɔːmθ/ *n*. 暖和

warn /wɔːn/ *vt*. 警告；告诫； *vi*. 发出警告

　warn sb. of sth. /that ... 就某事警告某人

　（考题）Right before leaving Kennedy Airport in New York, my grandma warned me of the behavior of the native mosquitoes around the foreigners like me.

　warn sb. not to do sth. 警告某人别做某事

　（考题）The patient was warned not to eat oily food after the operation.

　warn sb. against (doing) sth. 警告某人提防/别做某事

warship /'wɔːʃɪp/ *n*. 军舰、战船

wash /wɒʃ/ *v*. 洗、洗涤

wash up 洗(餐具);将某物冲到岸边

washing /ˈwɒʃən/ *n*. 洗涤

waste /weɪst/ *vt. vi.* 浪费

waste sth. on ... /(in) doing ... 浪费;滥用

(考题)I don't want to waster time talking to him. He won't listen.

waste no time (in) doing sth. 赶紧做某事

n. 浪费;废料   *adj*. 废弃的;毁坏的

(考题)On one side stand those who see clothes dryers as a waste of energy and a major polluter of the environment.

watch /wɒtʃ/ *v*. 观看、注视   *n*. 钟表

watch ... 观看、观察…

(考题)Watch him and then try to copy what he does.

watch sb. do/doing sth. 观看某人做某事

(考题)But we know that to wound an animal and watch it go through the agony of dying can make nobody happy.

watch out (for ...) 小心、留神(…)

(考题)Watch out when crossing the street! There are so many cars.

keep a close watch on ... 密切注意…

watchman /ˈwɒtʃmən/ *n*. 看守人

water /ˈwɔːtə/ *n*. 水   *vt*. 浇水

waterproof /ˈwɔːtəpruːf/ *adj*. 防水的

wave¹ /weɪv/ *vi*. 挥手示意 *vt*. 挥手向…示意;挥动

wave sth. 摇动…

(考题)He waved his head to us and said,"No."

wave to sb. 朝某人挥手

wave sb. ... 朝某人挥手表示…

(考题)At the railway station, the mother waved goodbye to her daughter until the train was out of sight.

wave² /weɪv/ *n*. 波浪;浪潮;波

radio waves 无线电波

sound waves 声波

way /weɪ/ *n*. 路、道路;方法、手段

all the way 一路上

（考题）They were talking and laughing all the way here.

by the way 顺便说

by way of 经由；作为

（考题）He told us about his own experience by way of example.

give way（to ...）（对…）让步

（考题）You should not give way to his unreasonable request.

have one's own way（to do sth.） 有自己的做事方法

（考题）Some plants have their own ways to keep animals away.

in a way/ in one way/ in some ways 在某种程度上

（考题）In a way, calling for bans on research into molecular manufacturing is like calling for a delay on faster-than-light travel because no one is doing it.

in the way 造成不便或挡路

（考题）Sorry，but I really didn't mean to be in the way.

on the/one's way to ... 在（某人）去…的途中；在进行中

（考题）... but many technical problems still must be cleared up on the way to this wonderful future.

weak /wiːk/ *adj*.（in）弱的；稀薄的

weaken /ˈwiːkən/ *vt*. 使变弱；减弱

wealthy /ˈwelθɪ/ *adj*. 富有的

weapon /ˈwepən/ *n*. 武器、兵器

wear /weə/（wore，worn）*vt*. 穿、戴；穿破、磨损 *vi*. 穿破、磨损；耐用

（考题）You can't wear a blue jacket over that shirt — it'll look terrible.

wear ... away 把…磨去；使逐渐消失

wear ... down 磨薄、磨小；使变弱

（考题）Sand begins as tiny pieces of rock that get smaller and smaller as wind and weather wear them down.

wear sb. /sth. out 使损坏或耗尽

（考题）After years of non-stop hard work，he might wear himself out and die an early death.

be worn out 筋疲力尽/磨损

（考题）The Park is not only old but worn out.

weather /ˈweðə/ *n*. 天气

weatherman /ˈweðəmən/ n. 天气预报员

weave /wiːv/ vt. 编织

web /web/ n. 蜘蛛网；网状物

website /ˈwebsaɪt/ n. 网站

wedding /ˈwedɪŋ/ n. 结婚；婚礼

Wednesday /ˈwenzdeɪ/ n. 星期三

week /wiːk/ n. 周、星期

weekday /ˈwiːkdeɪ/ n. 平常日、工作日

  on weekdays 在周末以外的日子

weekend /wiːkˈend/ n. 周末

  at/on weekends 在周末

weekly /ˈwiːkli/ adv. 每周的 adv. 每周地 n. 周报

weep /wiː/（wept，wept）vi. 哭泣；流泪

weigh /weɪ/ vt. 称…的重量；斟酌、考虑 vi. 重量为

（考题）I can't weigh it without a scale.

（考题）I have to weigh the problem carefully before I can give you my reply.

  weigh anchor 起锚

  weigh one's words 斟酌词句

weight /weɪt/ n. 体重；重量

  gain /put on weight 发胖

  lose/ take off weight 减肥

（考题）Don't be taken in by products promising to make you lose weight quickly.

  over/under weight 过重/轻

welcome /ˈwelkʌm/ vt. n. 欢迎 adj. 受欢迎的；不必感谢的

（考题）The publishing house believes that modern readers will welcome the shorter versions.

  adj. 受欢迎的

  be welcome to ...（a place） 欢迎到…

（考题）Hi, everybody！Welcome to our newly-opened Richards Cinema Bookstore！

  be welcome to do sth. 可随意做某事

（考题）You're welcome to stay, as long as you like.

  be welcome to sth. 可以使用某物

（考题）You're welcome to anything useful to you.

You are welcome. 不用客气

welfare /'welfeə/ *n.* 福利

well /wel/（better，best）*adv.* 好;完全地;很、相当　*adj.* 健康的;

（考题）However well prepared you are，you still need a lot of luck in mountain climbing.

as well 也

（考题）— There were already five people in the car but they managed to take me as well. — It couldn't have been a comfortable journey.

as well as 除…之外（也）

（考题）E-mail，as well as telephones，is playing an important part in daily communication.

well done! 干得好!

may well do sth. 很可能做某事

（考题）... studies show that childhood events，besides genes，may well cause such midlife diseases as cancer，heart disease and mental illness.

may/might（just）as well do sth. 不妨、最好做某事

（考题）Now that you've got a chance，you might as well make full use of it.

well-known /'welnəun/ *adj.* 有名的，众所周知的

（见 famous）

west /west/ *n.*，*adj.* 西、西方（的）

western /'westən/ *adj.* 西方的

westerner /'westənə/ *n.* 西方人

wet /wet/ *adj.* 湿的;多雨的　*vt.* 弄湿

whale /weɪl/ *n.* 鲸

what /wɒt/ *pron.*（疑问代词）什么，什么人（|事、物等）

what if ... 如果…又怎么样?

（考题）But what if our own planet is hit by a comet?

whatever /wɒt'evə/ *pron.* 无论是什么

wheat /wiːt/ *n.* 小麦

wheel /wiːl/ *n.* 车轮

when /wen/ *adv.* 什么时候、何时

（辨析：as，when，while 都表示"当…时"。when 是最普通的用词；as 侧重某一时刻，while 侧重延续的状况。如在 As he came in，we all stood up 中，不能用 while 替换 as。）

whenever /wen'evə/ *conj*. 无论何时

where /weə/ *adv*. 在(往)哪里

wherever /weər'evə/ *conj*. 无论在哪里

whether /'weðə/ *conj*. 是否；不论

（考题）— Dad，I've finished my assignment. — Good，and whether you play or watch TV，you mustn't disturb me.

（考题）It remains to be seen whether Jim'll be fit enough to play in the finals.

（注意：在宾语从句中，可以用 if 替换 whether，但不能再使用 or not；但在主语从句或表语从句中，不能使用 if。）

which /wɪtʃ/ *pron*. 哪(个)

whichever /wɪtʃ'evə/ *pron*. 无论哪个

while /waɪl/ *conj*. 当…的时候；虽然；然而

（考题）The computer system broke down suddenly while he was searching for information on the Internet.

（考题）My sister was against my suggestion while my brother was in favour of it.

n. 一会儿

after a while 过了一会儿；不久

（考题）But that feeling goes after a while and when the next war starts，you'll be there.

for a while 片刻

（考题）What's the sense of having a public open space where you can't eat，drink or even simply hang out for a while?

once in a while 偶尔

（考题）He was busy writing a story，only stopping once in a while to smoke a cigarette.

whip /wɪp/ *n*. 鞭子 *vt*. 鞭打、抽打

whisper /'wɪspə/ *vi*. *vt*. 低语；低声说出

（考题）Mum whispered to us，"Be quiet! Your little sister's sleeping."

n. 低语

in a whisper 低声说

whistle /ˈwɪsl/ *n*. 口哨 *vi*. 吹口哨

white /waɪt/ *adj*. 白色的 *n*. 白色

white-haired /ˈwaɪtˈheəd/ *adj*. 白发的

who /huː/ *pron*. 谁

whoever /huːˈeə/ *pron*. 无论谁

whole /həʊl/ *adj*. 整个的、完整的

as a whole 作为整体

（考题）Genetic learning is learning by a species — animals of the same kind — as a whole, and it is achieved by selection of those members of each generation that happen to act in the right way.

on the whole 总的说来

（考题）On the whole, he did a good job, though there was still room for improvement.

whom /huːm/ *pron*.（who 的宾格）谁

whose /huːz/ *pron*. 谁的

why /waɪ/ *adv*. 为什么

wide /waɪd/ *adj*. 阔；宽

widely /ˈwaɪdlɪ/ *adv*. 广泛

widespread /ˈwaɪdspred/ *adj*. 普遍的；广泛的

width /wɪdθ/ *n*. 宽度；宽阔

wife /waɪf/ *n*. 妻子

wild /waɪld/ *adj*. 野的；荒芜的；疯狂的

（考题）His movie won several awards at the film festival, which was beyond his wildest dream.

in the wild 在野外、在自然状态下

be wild with joy 欣喜若狂

wilderness /ˈwaɪldənɪss/ *n*. 荒野，荒漠

wildlife /ˈwaɪldlaɪf/ *n*. 野生动物

will /wɪl/ *v. aux*. 将；愿意 *n*. 意志

（考题）Where there is a will, there is a way.

against one's/sb. 's will 违背自己/某人的意愿

（考题）They did it against my will.

at will 随意地

of one's own (free) will 出于自愿

（考题）No one forced her. She made the decision of her own free will.

willing /ˈwɪlɪŋ/ *adj*. 愿意的

be willing to do sth. 乐意做某事

（考题）Eugene's never willing to alter any of his opinions. It's no use arguing with him.

win /wɪn/（won，won）*vi. vt*. 获胜、赢；赢得

（考题）Mary wrote an article on why the team had failed to win the game.

（考题）Her comeback comes 32 years after she won three golds at the Munich Olympics.

win sb. over 争取到某人，说服某人（见 bring）

（注意：win 的宾语只能是一场比赛，或是赢得的奖品等，而不能是对手。如果要表示赢了某人，可使用 beat。）

wind /wɪnd/ *n*. 风

window /ˈwɪndəu/ *n*. 窗

wine /waɪn/　*n*. 酒

wing /wɪŋ/ *n*. 翅膀、翼

winner /ˈwɪnə/ *n*. 获胜者、得奖者

winter /ˈwɪntə/ *n*. 冬天、冬季

wipe /waɪp/ *vt*. 擦、抹

wire /waɪə/ *n*. 电线

wisdom /ˈwɪzdəm/ *n*. 智慧、学问、才智

（考题）There is an old proverb, "Love me, love my dog." But there is more wisdom in this: "Love me, love my book."

wise /waɪz/ *adj*. 有智慧的、聪明的；英明的

It's wise of sb. to do sth. 某人做某事是很明智的

（考题）It is really wise of you to stand on his side at the critical moment.

wish /wɪʃ/ *vt. vi*. 希望；祝愿

wish for sth. 希望

wish sb. sth. 祝愿某人…

（考题）There is nothing more I can try to persuade you to stay, so I wish you good luck.

wish to do sth. 希望做某事

（考题）We live in a society which wishes to get rid of risk.

wish sb. to do sth. 希望某人做某事

（考题）Reality is not the way you wish things to be, nor the way they appear to be, but the way they actually are.

wish that ... 希望

（考题）I wish you'd do a bit less talking but some more work. Thus things will become better.

（辨析：wish 的宾语从句表示很难实现的愿望，因此从句中使用动词的过去时或过去完成时表示虚拟语气；另外，在向别人表达"祝你早日康复"等祝愿时，不能使用 wish 接从句的结构，而要使用动词 hope，或是 I wish you a quick recovery 这一双宾语结构。）

n. 希望；祝福、祝愿

a wish/wishes to sb. for sth. 祝福某人……

（考题）People everywhere are also giving you best wishes every day and we are among those who are keeping you close.

wit /wɪt/ *n.* 才智，智力

with /wɪð/ *prep.* 和…在一起；使用；由于；伴有

（考题）With the help of high technology, more and more new substances have been discovered in the past years.

（考题）Professor Smith, along with his assistants, is working on the project day and night to meet the deadline.

withdraw /wɪð'drɔː/ (withdrew, withdrawn) *vt. vi.* 取回；提取；退股；撤退；退出

（考题）You can spend or withdraw what you have in you account, or as much as your agreed overdraft limit.

within /wɪ'ðɪn/ *prep.* 在…内

（考题）Amazingly, within this world there is a universal but silly saying: "I am so busy."

（考题）Products also need to have a short lifespan so that the public can be persuaded to replace them within a short time.

within call 在叫得到的地方·

without /wɪ'ðaʊt/ *prep.* 无，没有；缺少

（考题）Water can absorb and give off a lot of heat without big changes in temperature, thus creating a stable environment.

without doing sth. 没有做某事

（考题）Almost without thinking, I bent and gave her a hug.

witness /ˈwɪtnɪs/ *vt*，*vi* 目睹；作证；见证

（考题）The book was written in 1946，since then the education system has witnessed great changes.

n．目击者、证人

（考题）The accident happened at night and there were no witnesses.

wolf /wʊlf/ *n*．狼

woman /ˈwʊmən/ *n*．（*pl*．women /ˈwɪmɪn/）妇女、女人

wonder /ˈwʌndə/ *vt*．想知道 *vi*．感到惊讶（或疑虑）

wonder at sth. 对某事感到惊奇、不解

（考题）Joachim Schmid wondered at the artistic nature of found photographs.

wonder what/how ... to do 不知该做什么/如何…

（考题）I'm wondering how to complete the difficult job on time.

wonder whether/if ... 不知…

（考题）— I wonder if I could possibly use your car for tonight?

— Sure，go ahead．I'm not using it anyhow.

n．奇迹，奇事；奇怪

do/work wonders 创造奇迹

（考题）The internet is working wonders in raising standards.

(It is) no wonder 难怪、不足为奇

（考题）— I have got a headache. — No wonder. You have been working in front of that computer too long.

wonderful /ˈwʌndəfʊl/ *adj*．极好的；精彩的

wood /wʊd/ *n*．木材；木头

wooden /ˈwʊdən/ *adj*．木（质）的

wool /wʊl/ *n*．羊毛

word /wɜːd/ *n*．词；消息；保证、承诺

Word comes that ... 消息传来…

（考题）Word came that another important discovery had been made in the experiment.

have a word with sb. 和某人说话

（考题）— Could I have a word with you, mum? — Oh dear, if

you must.

keep one's word 遵守诺言

（考题）Now that you have promised, you should keep your word.

give sb. one's word to do . . . /that . . . 向某人保证…

（考题）Don't worry. We've got his word to help when necessary.

in a word 一句话、总而言之

（考题）In a word, Rip was ready to attend to everybody's business but his own.

in other words 换句话说

（考题）In other words, people were able to eat in a diner at any time.

word for word 逐字地；原原本本地

（考题）Then the person whispers it, word for word, to another person.

work /wɜːk/ *vi*. 工作；劳动；起作用

（考题）What a pity my new computer doesn't work. There must be something wrong with it.

work at . . . 在…上下工夫；努力做

（考题）He's still working at the problem for a good solution.

work on . . . 从事与

（考题）It makes sense to work on the problem before it gets out of control.

work . . . out 解决；算出；制定出

（考题）So difficult did I find it to work out the problem that I decided to ask Tom for advice.

n. 工作；著作；(用作单或复)工厂

at work 在工作；在起作用

（考题）You can come home to a comfortable house without wasting energy and creating pollution all day while you are at work.

in/out of work 有/无工作

（考题）She was out of work and didn't know what to do then.

work of art 工艺品

worker /ˈwɜːkə/ *n*. 工人

workshop /'wɜːkʃɒp/ *n*. 车间;工场

world /wɜːld/ *n*. 世界

　　all over the world 全世界

　　around the world 全世界

　　the world over 全世界

　　throughout the world 全世界

　　in the world 在世界上;到底(用于加强疑问语气)

worldwide /'wɜːldwaɪd/ *adj*. 全世界的

worm /wɜːm/ *n*. 虫;蠕虫

worry /'wʌrɪ/ *vi. vt*. (使)担心;(使)发愁

　　be worried about 为…担心

　　(考题)People in the receiving countries seem to be worried about competition for their jobs.

　　worry about 为…担心

　　(考题)When such moments occur, don't worry about them. Just continue as if nothing happened.

　　worry sb. 使某人担心

　　(考题)The fact that she's working all night doesn't worry Margaret at all.

worse /wɜːs/ *adj*. 更坏的　*adv*. 较坏

　　go from bad to worse 每况愈下

　　(考题)Things are going from bad to worse.

　　change for the worse 每况愈下

　　(考题)The twentieth century saw greater changes than any century before: changes for the better, changes for the worse; changes that brought a lot of benefits to human beings, changes that put man in danger.

　　To make matters worse 更糟糕的是

　　What is worse 更糟糕的是

　　(考题)What is worse, keeping your child away from what they fear can turn that feeling into a phobia.

worst /wɜːst/ *adj*. 最坏的,最差的,最糟的

worth /wɜːθ/ *adj*. 值得…的;价值为…

　　... be worth doing 值得一做

　　(考题)Patience is an important quality of a happy and

rewarding life. After all, some things are worth waiting for.

(注意：在 worth 后面的动名词是主动的形式，被动的意思。见 need、want。但 worth 后面不能使用动词不定式。)

be worth ... 值···；值得···

(考题) Roses require a good deal of care, and if it weren't for the pleasure they give, it wouldn't be worth the work.

n. 价值

(考题) Millions of pounds' worth of damage has been caused by a storm which swept across the north of England last night.

worthless /ˈwɜːθlɪs/ *adj.* 无价值的；无用处的

worthwhile /ˌwɜːθˈwaɪl/ *adj.* 值得的

it is worthwhile to do sth. 值得做某事

(考题) I wonder if it is worthwhile to spend so much money on an old building.

a worthywhile job 值得做的工作

worthy /ˈwɜːði/ *adj.* 值得的；有价值的

(考题) He is a worthy son of his country.

be worthy of sth 值得的···

(考题) It's something important and is worthy of attention and care.

be worthy of being done ... 值得一做

(考题) Their suggestion is worthy of another discussion/being discussed again.

be worthy to do sth. 值得、配做某事

(考题) The problem is not worthy to be given so much attention to.

would /wʊd/ *v. aux* 愿、要

would like sth. 想要某物

(考题) I would like a job which pays more, but, on the other hand, I enjoy the work I'm doing at the moment.

would like/love to do sth. 想要做某事

(考题) Now she would like to read some stories by writers from other countries.

(考题) — Are you going to have a holiday this year? — I'd love to. I can't wait to leave this place behind.

would like sb. to do sth. 想要某人做某事

（考题）I don't want to go there alone; I would like you to go with me.

wound /wuːnd/ n. 创伤、伤 vt. 使受伤；伤害

wrap /ræp/ vt. 包；裹

　　wrap sb./sth.(up) in ... 用…来包裹

　　（考题）Alice laid her baby on the sofa tenderly and wrapped it with a blanket.

　　wrap up 穿得暖和；住口（=shut up）

　　be wrapped up in 埋头于；全神贯注于；被…迷住

wreck /rek/ vt. 造成（船舶等）失事

wrinkle /'rɪŋkl/ n. 皱纹

write /raɪt/ (wrote，weitten) v. 写；书写

　　write to sb. 给某人写信

　　（考题）How often do you write to your parents?

　　write about sth. 写有关…的文章

　　（考题）I decided I would write about something my classmates couldn't write about.

writer /raɪtə/ n. 作家、作者

wrong /rɒŋ/ adj. 错的

　　（考题）Whatever rank you may be in, it would be wrong to take the law into your own hands.

　　go wrong 走错了路；（计划等）失败

　　（考题）Scientific experiments can sometimes go wrong and when they do the results may range from the disastrous to the troubling.

　　there's something/nothing wrong with ... …有/没有故障

　　What's wrong with ... …怎么了？出什么事了？

　　（考题）As nobody here knows what is wrong with the machine, we must send for an engineer to handle the problem

　　do sb. wrong 亏待某人

　　（考题）In spite of repeated wrongs done to him. he looks friendly to people greeting him.

X

X-ray /ˈeksˈreɪ/ *adj*. X光的，X射线的，使用X射线的　*vt*. 用X
射线检查

Y

yard /jɑːd/ *n*. 码;院子,庭院

year /jɜː, jɪə/ *n*. 年

   of late years 近几年

   in the years to come 在未来的几年里

yearly /ˈjɜːlɪ/ *adj*. 每年的、一年一度的   *adv*. 每年、一年一次地

yellow /ˈjeləʊ/ *adj*. 黄色的   *n*. 黄色

yes /jes/ *adv*. 是、是的

yesterday /ˈjestədeɪ/ *n*. 昨天   *adv*. 昨天

yet /jet/ *adv*. *conj*. 还;仍然;/同比较级连用/还要

   not yet 尚未;还没

   (考题) I hope I will not be called on in class as I'm not yet adequately prepared.

   and/but yet 然而;可是

   (考题) They had only basic ways of creating light,and yet they found a way of using this simple technology in isolated places to save ships from hitting rocks.

yoghourt /ˈjɒgət/ *n*. 酸乳;酸奶

young /jʌŋ/ *adj*. 年轻的;幼小的

youngster /ˈjʌŋstə/ *n*. 少年;年轻人

your /jɔː, jʊə/ *pron*. 你的;你们的

yours /jɔːz/ *pron*. 你的;你们的

yourself /ˈjɔːself/ *pron*. 你自己

yourselves /ˈjɔːselvz/ *pron*. 你们自己

youth /juːθ/ *n*. 青(少)年时期,青春

Z

zero /'zɪərəʊ/ *n*. 零;零点;零度;含量为零

(考题)Every time we have a zero-calorie drink，we are telling ourselves without our awareness that we don't have to work to get results.

(考题) As the sun is hidden by clouds of dust，temperatures around the world fall to almost zero.

above/below zero degrees 零度以上/以下

zip /zɪp/ *n*. 拉链

zip /zɪp/ *n*. （美)邮政编码（zip code）

zone /zəʊn/ *n*. 地带、地区

the time zone 时区

zoo /zuː/ *n*. 动物园

图书在版编目(CIP)数据

全新高考英语词汇必备手册/李宗骥主编.—上海：文汇出版社,2009.1
ISBN 978 - 7 - 80741 - 453 - 7

Ⅰ.全… Ⅱ.李… Ⅲ.英语-词汇-高中-升学参考资料　Ⅳ.G634.413

中国版本图书馆 CIP 数据核字(2008)第 194025 号

全新高考英语词汇必备手册

高考英语命题研究组
主　　编／李宗骥

责任编辑／乐渭琦
封面装帧／张　晋

出版发行／文汇出版社
　　　　　上海市威海路 755 号
　　　　　(邮政编码 200041)
经　　销／全国新华书店
照　　排／南京展望文化发展有限公司
印刷装订／上海长阳印刷厂
版　　次／2009 年 1 月第 1 版
印　　次／2009 年 1 月第 1 次印刷
开　　本／850×1168　1/32
字　　数／250 千
印　　张／12.75

ISBN 978 - 7 - 80741 - 453 - 7
定　　价／22.00 元